# A dictionary of modern painting

# A DICTIONARY
## *of*
# MODERN PAINTING

---

*General Editors*

CARLTON LAKE
*and*
ROBERT MAILLARD

TUDOR PUBLISHING Co. NEW-YORK

Translated from the French
*Dictionnaire de la Peinture Moderne*

(FERNAND HAZAN ÉDITEUR, PARIS)

by LAWRENCE SAMUELSON, KATIE KAPLAN,
MARY HART and BARBARA MARCHUTZ.

First published in 1956

Reprinted 1956

# LIST OF CONTRIBUTORS

ALAN BIRD

RAYMOND COGNIAT

PIERRE COURTHION

BERNARD DORIVAL

FRANK ELGAR

FLORENT FELS

MAURICE GIEURE

MARINA GREY

JACQUES LASSAIGNE

ANDRÉ LEJARD

JEAN LEYMARIE

EDWIN LIVENGOOD

JEROME MELLQUIST

FRANK Mc EWEN

FRANZ MEYER

MICHAEL MIDDLETON

MATHILDE POMÈS

MAURICE RAYNAL

JOHN REWALD

HENRI-PIERRE ROCHÉ

CLAUDE ROGER-MARX

DENIS ROUART

G. DI SAN LAZZARO

MICHEL SEUPHOR

PHILIPPE SOUPAULT

CLAUDE SPAAK

# PREFACE

The aim of this book is to give a simple and reliable account of modern painting from the Impressionists up to our own time. It is the joint work of a number of art critics, mostly French; but though it comes from Paris, the vital centre of most modern movements in art, the editors have been at pains to maintain a broad outlook and describe painting activities outside France.

This is a dictionary in the sense that two hundred and fifty entries follow one another in alphabetical order; but they are not simply dry recitals of dates and facts. Each entry is a considered essay on its subject, a critical and sympathetic appraisal of the artist or movement in question. In this sense we believe the book to be unique, and we hope it will prove an illuminating guide to all interested in modern painting.

The editors were faced with the problem of where to start and where to end. The Impressionists were chosen as a convenient starting-point, but what was to be the closing date? It was finally decided that the only living painters to be included should be those who had made their mark before the outbreak of the Second World War.

In addition to the names of painters and art movements, the reader will find accounts of men of letters such as Apollinaire and André Breton who influenced the development of painting in their time. There are also descriptions of places such as the Slade School and the Bateau-Lavoir, where painters assembled and worked.

In this English version, which has been done by five translators in Paris working closely with the original publisher, a number of additional entries have been inserted in their appropriate places, and the number of illustrations has been increased.

# A

**ABSTRACT ART** Discussion of abstract, non-representational art has generally led to controversy rather than to any real clarification of the subject. Fanatical opponents and supporters reach a deadlock, because it is as useless to deny the legitimacy of abstract art as to try and impose its principles as absolute dogma. No artistic formula can be justified or condemned in itself; it must be judged by reference to the quality of the works that exemplify it. After half a century of vicissitudes, and despite its present widespread acceptance, abstract art still presents difficulties of an historical and aesthetic nature which no article on the subject, no matter how brief and objective, can ignore. Architecture and music are naturally admitted to be abstract arts, not required to 'represent' something, and subject to their own laws, whereas poetry, painting and sculpture are considered arts of representation. Ought this traditional distinction to be maintained or, aesthetics being universal, can all arts claim the same inherent autonomy as music and architecture? It does seem that abstract art was born from the very desire to emulate music and architecture, with a freedom and discipline of its own. Kandinsky, with his suggestions of music, and Mondrian, with his ideal of architecture, demonstrate the limitations and, at the same time, the achievement of abstract art. In the general process of abstraction that characterizes modern art, is there a line of demarcation between the domains of representational and non-representational art? And if so, where should it be drawn? Can one speak of relative and absolute abstraction, and where does absolute abstraction begin? Finally, is abstract art in its various manifestations a truly original creation of the twentieth century, the outcome of historical conditions, or is it a cyclic phase whose equivalent is to be found in the arts of the past?

The term 'abstract' itself is equivocal and invites discussion. For one could easily claim that all art is abstract, just as one might follow Picasso in declaring that there is no abstract art. Attempts to substitute other terms for it have failed. One interpreter of the movement, Michel Seuphor, has said: 'I call abstract art all art that does not recall or evoke reality, regardless of whether that reality be the point from which the artist started, or not'. Abstract art falls into two historically defined periods: an initial period (1910–1916) when abstraction was the result of an anti-naturalist process, and a second period that began in 1917 with the *De Stijl (\*)* movement and is still going on, in which abstraction for abstraction's sake is the absolute principle from which the artist starts. It might perhaps be clearer, as is becoming the accepted practice to do, to call the first 'abstract art' and the second 'non-representational art'.

Fauvism *(\*)* and Cubism *(\*)* certainly favoured the autonomous development of forms and colours, and every kind of artistic experiment was tried during the extraordinary outburst of activity that preceded the 1914–19.8 war. The first deliberately abstract water-colour by Kandinsky (spots of colour in dynamic juxtaposition without any representational purpose) dates from 1910, the same year that he wrote his fundamental work *Concerning the Spiritual in Art*, one of the basic books on abstract art. What shocked him into this new technique was a brilliantly coloured dress and the sight of one of his pictures standing on its side. But it was in referring to music that he discovered his aesthetic principle. Significantly, he called his sketches 'Improvisations' and his finished works 'Compositions'. The value of his abstract imagination rests on his genius as a colourist and the quality of his lyricism (*vide* Kandinsky). In 1912 the Czech Kupka also exhibited some abstract canvases directly inspired

1

KANDINSKY. FIRST ABSTRACT WORK. *Water-colour.* 1910.

Kandinsky inherited from Fauvism and Expressionism, crystallized the intellectual and geometrical tendencies derived from Cubism and transformed abstraction into non-representation. Before *De Stijl* Mondrian's method was to make successive abstractions of a given subject (a tree, or the façade of a cathedral), purging it bit by bit of all natural appearance until it became no more than a diagram. This experiment, conducted systematically with that austere and methodical application so characteristic of puritan Holland, reached the same impasse as did Malevitch's, although Mondrian's approach was from the opposite direction. With Neo-Plasticism *(\*)*, Mondrian started from abstraction, from absolute plastic relationships, in order to attain the purity and universality of mathematics. He has had an influence on modern contemporary architecture and, through the Bauhaus *(\*)*, has left his mark on the development of Kandinsky (*vide* Mondrian, Van Doesburg).

by music: *Fugue in Two Colours, Warm Chromatic,* etc (*vide* Kupka). He was the forerunner of the Musicalists, who, about 1920, formed a group with Blanc-Gatti and Valensi. Picabia, whose *Rubber* (1909) was non-representational, joined the movement, while Delaunay, the founder of Orphism *(\*)*, exalted to abstraction the lyricism of pure colour, which, he said, was both 'form and subject' (*vide* Picabia, Delaunay). But it was in Russia that experimentation in abstract art was carried to its extreme limits, beginning in 1913: the Rayonism *(\*)* of Larionov and Nathalie Gontcharova, the Constructivism of Tatlin (revived in 1920 by the Pevsner brothers and Gabo), the Nonobjectivism of Rodchenko, and the Suprematism *(\*)* of Malevitch, which gave us the celebrated black square on a white ground. Most of the pioneers of abstract art are of Russian origin and the real precursor of it was the Lithuanian Tchurlianis, in 1906–1907. The Slav sensibility is haunted by the fascination of non-existence, the anguished flight from reality (*vide* Larionov, Gontcharova, Malevitch).

Another country in which abstract art has thrived is Holland. There Mondrian and the *De Stijl* movement (Van Doesburg, Van der Leck), in opposition to the lyrical tendencies which

Between the two world wars, abstract art, opposed by Surrealism *(\*)*, went through a period of alternating eclipse and resurgence. Picabia and Delaunay went back to representational art. But new abstractionists kept appearing, among them (from 1920 on) the Germans Freundlich and Voremberge-Gildewart, the Hungarian Moholy-Nagy (*vide* this name), who taught at the Bauhaus, and the Dutchman Domela, who joined the *De Stijl* group. In 1930, some former Cubists, including Charchoune, Reth and Herbin, allied themselves with the movement and (in 1935) Magnelli (*vide* this name) and Hartung. The first international exhibition of abstract art was organized in Paris in 1930 by Seuphor and Torres-García (group and review called *Circle and Square*). From 1932 to 1936 the *Abstraction-Creation* group brought out an annual album, and counted some four hundred members.

From 1937 to 1945 the vogue of Expressionism in war conditions slowed down the growth of abstract art. With the spectacular return of Picabia, it sprang up again everywhere with even greater vigour than before. In 1946 the Salon des Réalités Nouvelles in Paris became its first official salon of world scope, exhibiting a thousand works. Many of them were merely intellectual or purely ornamental exercises, an academic vulgarization of abstraction; but some of them expressed the profound need to flee from a discredited reality to conquer a 'new

reality', a pure plastic realm ordered in accordance with the rhythm and structure of the cosmos. Despite its vitality, however, abstract art is continually threatened by formalism and decoration. 'The most important thing about form', Kandinsky warned, 'is to know whether or not it emerges from an inner necessity.'

The first American practitioners of abstract art were Stanton MacDonald Wright and Morgan Russell. Calling themselves 'synchromists', they made a stir in Paris and Munich in 1913. That same year they were represented in New York's Armory Show *(\*)*. Both, however, returned to a naturalistic style, MacDonald Wright about 1919, Russell in the early 'thirties. Russell died in 1953. Wright has just recently gone back to abstraction with a brilliantly lyrical style.

Miss Katherine Dreier was the first to introduce to America the work of the leading European abstract artists, in an exhibition held at the Brooklyn Museum in 1926. A little later A. E. Gallatin followed her lead, in setting up his Gallery of Living Art (now at the Philadelphia Museum), and Baroness Hilla Rebay founded the Museum of Nonobjective Painting (now the Solomon R. Guggenheim Museum). But these steps in themselves did not bring about a full-fledged abstract art movement in America. Such painters as Max Weber, Marin, Feininger, Stuart Davis and Marsden Hartley flirted with abstraction but never gave themselves over to it wholly. During that post-World War I period only Covert (*Brass Band*) and Miss Dreier herself (*Abstract Portrait of Marcel Duchamp*) produced works which are completely abstract. It was not until 1935 that American artists threw themselves wholeheartedly into abstraction. The pioneers were Harry Holtzman and Burgoyne Diller, who widened the scope of Mondrian's influence. They were followed by Fritz Glarner, Charmion von Wiegand, and others.

With the Association of American Abstract Artists, founded in 1936, abstract art entrenched itself in New York. Among the participants in the group's first annual exhibitions were: George L. K. Morris, Holtzman, Holty, Ferren, Albers, Cavallon, Gallatin, McNeil, Reinhardt, and Charles Shaw. After the Second World War many others joined the group, among them von Wicht, Bolotovsky, Sennhauser, Alcopley, Wolff, Xceron, Frelinghuysen, Slobodkina, Perle Fine; more recently still, Beate Hulbeck and Ado Fleischmann. But since 1950 the ranks of American abstract artists have swelled far beyond this group to cover the entire country. Pure abstraction, particularly in the manifestation termed Abstract Expressionism, which Jackson Pollock spearheaded, has its devotees in every state in the Union. In the 'official' exhibitions put on by the Metropolitan Museum, abstract works are as numerous as representational ones. One notes frequently an emphasis on calligraphy, in the Oriental sense of the word. This art of the sign goes from an extreme of finesse in the work of Mark Tobey to an extreme of power in that of Franz Kline, passing, meanwhile, through the tortured meanderings of Pollock. Another form of abstraction, built around the 'spot', and hence closer to Impressionism, is encountered in the work of such painters as Clifford Still and Mark Rothko. Arshile Gorky, who died in 1948, worked a very individual abstract vein stemming from Surrealism. Other abstract expressionists include Tworkow, Stamos, Donati, Hans Richter, Richard Poussette-Dart, Alfred Russell, Motherwell, Gottlieb, Congdon, Baziotes and Willem de Kooning. De Kooning, however, has veered away from abstraction in the past few years and gone over to a more pronounced expressionism. One of the stronger influences on the work of many of these painters has been Hans Hoffmann, whose school has helped to develop a number of remarkable artists.

In Great Britain pure abstraction, in the sense that Mondrian or Kandinsky, for example, gave it, has never had much of a vogue. Even Ben Nicholson, who, over the past twenty years, has been the standard-bearer of English abstract art, returns frequently to a figurative style of painting, and is even so unorthodox as occasionally to group within the bounds of one canvas a purely abstract motif and a recognizable landscape – and successfully.

The magazine *Axis*, founded by Myfanwy Evans in 1935, was the first British review to speak out on behalf of abstract art. It carried articles by Sir Herbert Read, Geoffrey Grigson, James Johnson Sweeney, George L. K. Morris, and Roland Penrose, and reproduced works by the leading Continental artists and, along with them, those of English abstractionists Ben Nicholson, Winifred Dacre, Ivon Hitchens, Arthur Jackson, Henry Moore, Edward Wadsworth and John Piper. Piper was at that period the great hope of the new English abstract art, but he later abandoned abstraction completely and returned to his personal landscape style.

About this time Paule Vezelay, an independent English artist, began painting abstract canvases. She has a very individual style, with crisply distinguished forms, sometimes close to Arp's, and a subtle palette. She has exhibited more often in Paris than in London. Toward the end of the 'twenties Miss Marlow Moss, working in Paris, was a fervent disciple of Mondrian.

In 1937 Ben Nicholson, Naum Gabo, and the architect J. L. Martin, brought out an important book, *Circle, An International Survey of Constructivist Art*, but it was not until 1951 that there was a real spurt of activity in the abstract domain. In that year a new convert, Victor Pasmore, had his first exhibition of purely abstract work – a combination of parallel curved lines, Celtic in origin, with constructions of rectilinear planes. Other young abstract painters followed his example and their activity was summarized in a book by Lawrence Alloway, *Nine Abstract Artists, their Work and Theory*, published in 1954. These nine include, along with Pasmore, Robert Adams, Terry Frost, Adrian Heath, Anthony Hill, Roger Hilton, Kenneth Martin, Mary Martin, and William Scott. In addition to these artists there are Stephen Gilbert, Vera Spencer, and William Gear, each of them pursuing a different path toward abstraction. The latter three are shown more frequently on the Continent than in England. But over all his countrymen the figure of Ben Nicholson looms, internationally, as by far the most important among British abstract painters.

**ACADÉMIE CARRIÈRE** About 1898, the French painter Eugène Carrière opened an Academy in Paris, where he used to come each week to correct the work done by his pupils, among them Matisse,

4

Derain, Puy and Laprade. Although he did not wholly approve of their efforts, Carrière always gave them friendly encouragement. The young *Fauves*, therefore, were all the more sincerely grateful to their teacher because they knew that he sponsored them more out of broadmindedness than any faith in what they were trying to do. In fact, the painter of the *Maternités* (all of them drowned in that hazy umber that made Degas remark: 'Someone's been smoking in the nursery again!') was always grumbling at the flaming colours that his pupils used. They drove him one day to ask: 'What would you do if you had to paint a parrot?'

The Académie Carrière was short lived. After only a few years of existence, it was obliged to close for lack of pupils. Carrière's teaching was always very liberal. He let his pupils work according to their individual gifts and inspiration, contenting himself, as Matisse has said, with merely curbing anything that he considered excessive.

**ACADÉMIE JULIAN** Founded in Paris in 1860 by Rudolph Julian, this was the first Academy to be formed in the shadow of the École Nationale des Beaux-Arts. It was never a rival institution but served from the beginning as a kind of preparatory studio for those waiting to enter the École Nationale. After some initial difficulties, involving several moves, from the Faubourg Montmartre to Montparnasse before eventually setting itself up in the Rue du Dragon, it finally became very successful when, about 1888, Bonnard, Vuillard, Denis, Ibels, Ranson, Roussel and Vallotton – later to become the Nabis *(\*)* – began to meet there. Some years later, in 1892, Matisse came also, to work mainly under the guidance of Bouguereau, an honest painter though devoid of originality, who once said to him: 'You rub out your charcoal with your finger, which shows that you are a slipshod person . . . You will never know how to draw.' Derain and Léger came to work at the Academy in 1904. Marcel Duchamp also found his way there and stayed just long enough to contract that profound aversion for the semi-official

CHIRICO. PROPHETIC PORTRAIT OF APOLLINAIRE. 1914. *Wood engraving by P. Roy*

conception of art represented by Bouguereau that prompted him to start his pre-Dada revolt.

**ACADÉMIE RANSON** In order to provide a centre of activity for the Nabi movement, founded under Gauguin's influence, Paul Ranson and his wife France, founded an Academy in Paris in 1908. They had been acquainted for some time with Gauguin's ideas through Sérusier, who had met Gauguin in Brittany in 1888 and been immediately carried away with enthusiasm for his art and perhaps even more for his theories. These Sérusier transmitted to Ranson as well as to his other friends at the Académie Julian *(\*)*: Bonnard, Denis, Roussel, Vuillard. These young artists, who called themselves the Nabis, propounded a new type of painting characterized by the simplification of line and colour with a view to achieving the decorative effect which was their main preoccupation. But they needed a headquarters where they could teach the results of their research. This they found at the Académie Ranson. Maurice Denis and Sérusier (who had La Fresnaye and Goerg among his pupils) taught there in 1908, as did Vuillard and Roussel. Later, such different artists as Vallotton and La Patellière, Kisling and Maillol, Christian Bérard and Gromaire frequented the school. Closed during the Second World War, the Academy reopened in 1951, and is now continuing its work, still faithful to the principles of independence and liberty.

MODIGLIANI. PORTRAIT OF APOLLINAIRE.

**ACADÉMIE SUISSE** In wretched premises on the Quai des Orfèvres, some time between 1825 and 1830, a former model by the name of Suisse (whom they used to call *le Père Suisse*) opened a free academy, provided with models if not with instructors. There one could meet, in 1842, Bonington, Delacroix and Courbet. The Académie Suisse was at its zenith in about 1860, when the future

Impressionists frequented it. It was there that Pissarro made the acquaintance of Monet and Guillaumin in 1859, and in April 1861 met Cézanne, who had just arrived from Aix-en-Provence. Cézanne was then twenty-two years old, Pissarro thirty-one. The friendship that immediately sprung up between the two artists was a particularly fertile one, for it was to his contact with Pissarro that Cézanne owed his initiation into the Impressionist technique during his stay at Auvers-sur-Oise in 1872–1874. Among the regular models of the Academy was a Negro by the name of Scipion, who figures in Cézanne's famous canvas now in the São Paulo Museum (*see* illustration, page 49). For a long time the Académie Suisse constituted the antechamber of the very official École Nationale des Beaux-Arts to which, as is well known, admission was not easily gained by *avant-garde* painters.

**APOLLINAIRE** Guillaume de Kostrowitsky (born in Rome 1880, died in Paris 1918). Born of a Polish mother and a Swiss-Italian father, Apollinaire used to like to pass himself off as the son of an Italian prelate. An extraordinary character and an inordinate hoaxer, but at the same time a poet of captivating charm and sincerity, Apollinaire played a most important role in the history of modern art. One of his claims to distinction – and by no means the least – stems from his having perpetuated the tradition started by the nineteenth-century French poets headed by Baudelaire of devoting some of their finest work to the exaltation of the plastic arts, particularly the new painting of their time. Apollinaire's poetic temperament, his constant preoccupation with creativity, his enlightened faithfulness to the art of the past, destined him for the role that he was to play as the standard-bearer of Cubism. This taste for the plastic arts, far from being gradually acquired, as it was with many poets and writers, was marked in Apollinaire from an early age, the product of a mind 'ardent in its search for beauty'. Apollinaire was passionately drawn to any work of art that tended to give Nature the aspect of something outside the bounds of reality. He was inordinately sensitive to all subjects or

R. DELAUNAY. WINDOWS. 1912.
*Collection of J. Cassou, Paris*

evolutions of the art of his day. Only after careful analysis – *méditations esthétiques*, to quote from the title of one of his books – did he permit himself to be drawn into the art movements of which he was a witness. He never, for example, concealed the fact that *Les Demoiselles d'Avignon* (*see* plate, page 64) had disconcerted him at first. He was always honest in his criticism, both of himself and of those he championed.

It was not until 1913 that he came out with a passionate defence of Cubism in his book on the Cubist painters, *Les Peintres Cubistes*. From then on he did not hesitate to recognize in the new aesthetic movement a revolution 'renewing the plastic arts' and 'restoring order and craftsmanship to their place of honour'.

He was considerably perturbed by the conflict in painting between the processes of the mind and those of the senses. But what he extolled in Cubism was the idea of creation, which formed its core. Cubism is 'not an imitative art but a conceptual art that aspires to creation', he wrote.

Apollinaire was to strengthen further the new bonds he had forged between painting and poetry when he coined the term 'Orphism' to describe the art of Robert Delaunay. The glittering enchantment of this artist's *Windows*, opening out on to a world of pure colour, actually had a far greater effect on Apollinaire's sensibility than the austere dialectics of the Cubist compositions ever had, although Apollinaire took over some daring examples of Cubist syntax which, transposed into the sphere of poetry, inspired him to a totally new way of writing (as evidenced in his ellipses, his omission of punctuation and his *calligrammes*). One of his finest poems, *Windows*, was written under the inspiration of Delaunay's picture.

Because of his insatiable curiosity, Apollinaire allowed himself to be charmed by the Futurist adventure, from 1912 on. The surmise is, however, that he was attracted more by its scintillating dynamism that tended to convert painting into a kind of cinematography than by its negation of all tradition and the advice given by the Futurists to set fire to all museums. Apollinaire soon gave up his collaboration with the Futurists. But it was with profound conviction that he upheld the metaphysical conceptions of Chirico,

objects that in any way transfigured our all too humdrum lives. Hence that love that he manifested for odd curios, for the arts of primitive peoples, of Negroes, for children's drawings; that enthusiasm for the unexpected, the esoteric and the rare.

When, in 1904, he first came in contact with Derain, Vlaminck and Matisse, he was completely staggered by the apparently anarchical riot of colour in the work of the future Fauvists and by their ambition to conjure up a reality more authentic than mere appearances. That was something that matched his penchant for the unknown and the bizarre. It did not take him long to discover that these painters' ideas also had something stirring and true in them. Soon, through his writing, he was giving his new friends every support in their efforts.

At this point Apollinaire met Picasso, whose blue period opened up new and somewhat conflicting vistas before him. Apollinaire emerged considerably shaken by the totally contradictory things he had seen. Confronted with Picasso's work, he could not have reacted otherwise. He never gave lightly his support to any of the in his opinion 'the most astonishing painter of his time'. The search for unsuspected relationships between objects, propounded by Chirico, led Apollinaire to stress the importance of dreams and to throw light on certain elements of the subconscious which were to be the basis of Surrealism (a name which he invented in 1917). We have been left an extremely disturbing testimony of the friendship between the two men at that time: the portrait of Apollinaire, dated 1914, in which Chirico gives a silhouette of the poet as a human target with a bullet-hole in his head. The portrait was indeed prophetic. Apollinaire died in 1918, an easy prey to the 'flu epidemic, after being wounded in the forehead by a German bullet in the war.

Apollinaire applied his initiative to the most decisive and daring art movements of his time. The close union between poets and painters which he promoted created a kind of poetic effervescence around the plastic arts which has gone far towards placing their creations on a radically new plane. It is to Apollinaire's courage, his convictions and, above all, to the confidence which his culture and genius inspired, that painting of the first half of this century owes the audacity and the daring of its concepts, if not the actual creation of its general aesthetic doctrine. Apollinaire's work has, in addition, the merit of having enabled artists to overcome, with surprising rapidity, the inevitable opposition and fatal incomprehension that this most sensational revolution in art history was bound to stir up.

**ARMORY SHOW** An international exhibition of modern art held in February 1913 in New York. Coming after the first exhibitions of Matisse (1908) and Picasso (1911), both arranged there by Alfred Stieglitz (*vide* this name) in his Gallery 291, it has remained famous in the annals of artistic life in the United States. On the initiative of an artistic *avant-garde* which had already got itself talked about, a number of artists such as Matisse, Picasso, Braque, Léger, Derain, Vlaminck, as well as Kandinsky, Brancusi and Marcel Duchamp, were invited to exhibit their works, under prudent

ARP. CONFIGURATION. 1928.
*Kunstmuseum, Basel*

cover of some paintings by Courbet, Ingres, Delacroix and several of the leading Impressionists. The works of a number of young American painters were also on exhibit, chaperoned, so to speak, by a few artists of long standing such as Whistler, Ryder and Twachtman. Thus, every trend was represented: Classicism, Romanticism, Realism, Impressionism, Fauvism, Cubism, Expressionism and Abstract Art. The exhibition showed a perfect unity, the canvases having been selected with care. There seemed to be every reason to hope that it would be a success. Eleven hundred works were assembled in the armory of the 69th Cavalry Regiment, hence the name 'Armory Show'. The experiment was received with scandalous demonstrations unprecedented in the United States. Amid howls of derision and laughter, the Cubist room and, in particular, Marcel Duchamp's *Nude Descending a Staircase*, were attacked by a frenzied mob that threatened to destroy the canvases it considered offensive to good taste. The Press, as was to be expected, endorsed the public's hostile attitude. Nevertheless, the exhibition was a great success, stirring up curiosity if nothing else. It moved to the Chicago Art Institute, where it was received with similar scenes. Boston showed the same disapproval, but with more restraint. Everywhere the exhibition provoked the same reaction. The Armory Show did, nevertheless, manage to find a few supporters and became the subject of somewhat penitent comment from its critics after it closed. But from then on modern art found a large audience in the United States.

**ARP** Jean (or Hans). French painter, sculptor, poet, born in Strasbourg in 1887. The part that Arp has played, and continues to play, in the sphere of the arts is considerable. Like his antithesis Mondrian, he has not set up a school but has followers of varying degree of skill. But the catalytic action of these two pioneers is such that they find themselves, often unwittingly, in the midst of every controversy and every advance in art today.

Very much attracted to painting, and considerably shaken by his first contacts with modern art in Paris in 1904, Arp managed to prevail on his parents to send him to Weimar to study at the Academy (1905–1907), and then to Paris, where he attended the Académie Julian in 1908. But

ARP. PAINTING ON CRUMPLED PAPER. 1942

this official instruction failed to appeal to him, and he retired to meditative isolation in Weggis, Switzerland. There he met Klee in 1909. In 1912 he paid a visit to Kandinsky in Munich, and took part in the famous *Blaue Reiter (\*)* exhibition. The following year he went to Berlin where, together with the leading Expressionists, he took part in the *Erste Herbstsalon* (First Autumn Salon) organized by Walden, who, in his magazine *Der Sturm*, had already published some curious drawings by Arp, human figures sketched in undulating lines. In 1914 he was back in Paris, where he met Max Jacob, Modigliani, Apollinaire and Delaunay. When war broke out, he returned to Switzerland, and in December 1915 he exhibited his first abstract works at the Tanner Gallery, Zurich, paintings in generally rectilinear forms. But he gave up ordered movement almost immediately, in order to give preference to objects 'arranged according to the law of chance, rudimentary, irrational, mutilated, broken', already heralding Dadaism *(\*)*, which he founded at the beginning of 1916, together with Tzara, Janco, Ball and Hülsenbeck. The movement held its noisy sessions at the Cabaret Voltaire *(\*)* in Zurich, and Arp remained one of its central figures, contributing to all its publications. In 1916 he illustrated Hülsenbeck's *Phantastische Gebete (Fantastic Prayers)* with a series of abstract woodcuts which he called studies in symmetry. In 1917 he brought out his first polychromatic reliefs and, the following year, his first woodcuts in the form of spots to illustrate Tzara's *Cinéma Calendrier du Cœur Abstrait*. Meanwhile he had made the acquaintance of Sophie Taeuber, who later became his wife, and he was for a while influenced by her more severe art. Together they created large *collages* of geometrical, rectilinear cutouts (1918).

In Cologne, in 1920, he collaborated with Baargeld and Max Ernst in new Dadaist enterprises. He met Schwitters in Hanover in 1923, and contributed to the *Merz (\*)* review, which published, among other things, a series of his lithographs entitled 7 *Arpaden*. In 1925 he published, together with El Lissitzky, *The Isms of Art*, a survey of all the movements then in existence. The following year he went to live at Meudon, near Paris, with his wife, Sophie Taeuber, and became a member of the Surrealist group (1926-1930). At the same time, in collaboration with Sophie Taeuber and Theo van Doesburg, he undertook the decoration of the *café dansant* 'L'Aubette', in Strasbourg, an important piece of work which has since been destroyed. Arp was a member of the *Circle and Square* group, and took part in its international exhibition in April 1930. The following year he became a member of the *Abstraction-Creation* group. This was the period of pictures made out of bits of twine and torn paper, and of the first sculptures in full relief, in which Arp accentuated more and more that supple and clear-cut style which has earned him universal renown. All this time he continued to write poetry, sometimes in German, sometimes in French. He is equally well versed in both cultures. In 1940, fleeing before the invading Germans, Arp and Sophie Taeuber took refuge in Grasse, without interrupting their poetic or plastic work. In the course of a clandestine journey to Switzerland his wife was killed in an accident in January 1943. After the Liberation several important exhibitions of his work were held in New York, where his monograph *On My Way* appeared in 1948. In 1949 and 1950 Arp himself went to the United States, where he enjoys a considerable reputation. A collection of his poems in French, *Le Siège de l'air*, was published in Paris in 1946. In 1952 Curt Valentin published his *Dreams and Projects* in New York. In 1953 two collections appeared in Germany: *Word Dreams and Black Stars* in Wiesbaden and *Hairy Hearts* in Frankfurt. In the same year Arp executed a large bronze for the university city of Caracas, which he entitled *Cloud Shepherd*.

Arp is a sensitive artist, but one who seeks clarity of line and original purity of form. He likes to compare art to a fruit that has to be born of man, in the same way that other fruits grow on trees. In fact, much of his work reflects the suppleness of the plant world without, however, any attempt at imitation or description. Arp's constant concern is to create as easily as he walks, to model as freely as he breathes. His ideal is natural simplicity linked with perfection of organic form. This very Greek love of perfection combined with lack of artifice explains the admirable unity of his work, which cannot be compared with any other of this century. In between the various currents of Dadaism, Surrealism and Abstract Art, Arp has created a kind of cross-roads that is his exclusively, and can be defined only by using his name. Whether it be poetry, *collage*, relief, sculpture, or torn bits of paper, Arp brings into modern life an element of simplicity and calm, always tinged with humour. His work is a kind of new Arcadia, a soothing haven in the midst of a frenzied, machine-age world.

**ATELIER GLEYRE** If the name of Gleyre, a painter of Swiss origin (1808–1874), is remembered at all, it is because he opened a studio to which Monet, Bazille, Sisley and Renoir used to come in 1862. According to Renoir, who considered him an admirable person, Gleyre used to give his pupils a certain freedom. All the same, he one day asked Renoir, 'Do you paint to amuse yourself?' To which Renoir replied, 'Not for any other reason'. The Atelier Gleyre was a complement to the École des Beaux-Arts, where the instruction was not yet as important as it was soon to become. The academic advice of the Swiss master had little influence on the Impressionists, who did not submit to it for long – in all, about one year, just long enough to save his name from oblivion.

# B

BALLA. MERCURY PASSING BEFORE THE SUN. 1916.
*Private Collection, Milan*

**BALLA** Giacomo. Italian painter, born in Turin in 1871. Balla is Futurism's *(\*)* most astonishing manifestation. He made himself known through academic paintings, which were thought highly of by the critics of the time. During a brief stay in Paris, he discovered Impressionism and Divisionism and developed a passion for problems of light and colour. On his return to Rome he made the acquaintance of Severini and Boccioni, and imparted the new creed to them. In 1901 he was converted to Futurism by Marinetti. Three years later his picture *Dog on a Leash*, now in the Museum of Modern Art, New York, was received with derision by a public still hostile to *avant-garde* tendencies. In this rather childish analysis of

movement he reproduced the mechanics of walking by depicting on the canvas the successive positions taken up by a woman's legs and a little dog's paws, in the manner of a film in slow motion.

Of the five signers of the Futurist manifesto, he was the only one who did not take part in the Paris exhibition. He never really understood the meaning of Futurism until he saw Severini's *Spherical Expansion in Space*. From 1913 to 1916 he painted a whole series of pictures, among them *Mercury Passing Before the Sun*, which are reckoned among the most abstract works that Futurism has given us, although they are inspired by Nature. Balla succeeded in giving an original and finished plastic form to the sensations, the movement, and the 'states of the soul' which Futurism, at first analytical, afterwards sought to synthesize in a single and unique expression, taking its example from Cubism. If we consider not the intention but the results, it must be recognized that Balla, unwittingly perhaps, went beyond the limits of Futurism to take his place alongside the leading masters of abstract art. Unfortunately, this period of authentic invention, which found no response in a world entirely preoccupied with war at the time, was of brief duration. His pioneering work remained almost unknown for a long time, and has only recently been brought to light, thanks to a number of exhibitions and some very just writing on the subject.

**BALLETS RUSSES** Serge de Diaghilev (1872-1929), that 'impresario of contemporary art in all its forms and expressions', applied his genius not only to the dance but also to music and painting. He converted the ballet, hitherto nothing more than a danced interlude confined within narrow, fixed rules,

PICASSO. DIAGHILEV AND SELISBURG. 1917

performances but an exhibition of Russian art at the Salon d'Automne in 1907, and a series of concerts in 1908 which included, notably, Chaliapin. In his youth Diaghilev was at first inclined towards music and painting. While studying Law at the University of St Petersburg he attached himself to a group of painters and became friendly with Benois. Under the editorship of Diaghilev and Benois the group started a publication called *The World of Art*, whose aim was to reform painting. The main plank in its platform was individualism, and through it Diaghilev attacked what he called sterile academism, and made a plea for the recognition of individuality, defining art as a 'free and disinterested act taking place in the soul of the artist', its only function being pleasure, and its only instrument beauty. Ballet struck him as an ideal medium for such reform, and one in which the quickest results could be obtained. One of the reasons for the founding of his ballet troupe was to give the new painting a platform. Thus it was Diaghilev's passion for music and painting that led him to ballet. In 1899 he had organized an exhibition of international art, where some important works by the French Impressionists were presented, and caused a considerable stir in Russia.

Having staged a dance performance in St Petersburg in 1907, with Fokine, Nijinsky and

into a spectacle in which everything was united to delight the eyes, ears and mind. Under his influence ballet became a synthesis of the arts of the theatre, in which music and painting were no longer embellishments but essential elements integrated into the performance and an indispensable part of it. With Diaghilev the word 'décor' lost its traditional meaning. It no longer signified that artificial setting, as false as a photographer's back-cloth, the aim of which was simply to limit the spectator's range of vision. Henceforth, form and colour were made to harmonize with the movement of the dancer, and become an integral part of it. The first artistic events arranged in Paris by Diaghilev were not ballet

LAURENCIN. CURTAIN FOR 'LES BICHES'. 1924

Pavlova, which encountered considerable opposition, Diaghilev decided to take his troupe to Paris. They gave their first performance at the Théâtre du Châtelet on the 19th of May, 1909, with a programme consisting of *Le Pavillon d'Armide*, *Prince Igor*, *Polovtsian Dances*, and *Festin*, with décors by Bakst, Benois, Korovine and Roerich respectively. This performance was one of the most extraordinary events of the early years of the twentieth century. The novelty of the spectacle, the lavishness and magnificence of the costumes and décors, and the quality of the dancers, aroused a feeling of utter bewilderment which soon changed to delirious enthusiasm. Nijinsky astounded the spectators with his prodigious leaps. The following year Diaghilev presented *Schéhérazade*, a fantasy of movement, colour and light. The richness of Bakst's décor, the like of which had not been seen before, filled the audience with wonder and amazement. It seemed as though all the barbarism of the Orient was tempestuously sweeping away a theatrical tradition which was to be, from then on, nothing but a futile survival. *Schéhérazade* was followed by the *Fire Bird* (décor by Golovine, costumes by Golovine and Bakst).

Until 1914 the *Ballets Russes* had a Paris season every year. Among the most celebrated works presented during that period were *The Spectre of the Rose* (décor and costumes by Bakst); *Petrouchka* (décor and costumes by Benois); *The Afternoon of a Faun* (décor and costumes by Bakst), one of the most outstanding ballets of the first period, which provoked a scandal, Nijinsky's performance having stressed the erotic aspect; *The Rite of Spring* (décor and costumes by Roerich). *Le Coq d'Or* (décor and costumes by Gontcharova) marks the end of this period. The novelty of these productions can be gauged if we bear in mind the fact that at that time an exaggerated, almost religious, feeling for *trompe-l'œil* was current in the theatre. In real life, as on the stage, half-tones and pale colours were the mode. Dim light, a mysterious melancholy – even dust – had become in some way indispensable to any theatrical production. The works produced for the *Ballets Russes* by the painters with whom Diaghilev surrounded himself played a decisive role. Although they used only a few colours, these

PICASSO. ACROBAT ('PARADE'). 1917.

were generally extremely vivid: orange, black, pink, blue, white, emerald or Veronese green. The painter had full say in all matters affecting not only the décors but also the costumes and other accessories. For *Jeux* (music by Debussy, 1913) Léon Bakst used only three colours: against a décor of blue and green, flashes of white provided by the dancers themselves, dressed as tennis-players. In *Petrouchka* Alexander Benois depicted white-shuttered windows in a blue wall, with painted flags and banners waving in the sky; in the background a merry-go-round with wooden horses in a blaze of colour, not far from a big, yellow wall with the outline of a staircase sketched on it. When the fantastic motley crowd invaded the stage the frame was there, ready to hold it and transform it into an ordered and harmonious whole.

The second period of the *Ballets Russes* began in 1917. It was marked by the creation of some forty ballets of extraordinary diversity. Until then Diaghilev had drawn primarily on Russian artists: musicians like Stravinsky and painters like Benois, Bakst, Larionov and Gontcharova. Now he began to turn to French and other

BRAQUE. DECOR FOR 'ZEPHYR ET FLORE'. 1926.

foreign artists for their collaboration. Among the musicians that he enlisted, apart from his compatriots Stravinsky and Prokofiev, were Sauguet, Satie, Milhaud, Poulenc, Manuel de Falla and Hindemith; among the painters were Picasso, Derain, Matisse, Braque, Marie Laurencin, Gris, Utrillo, Max Ernst, and Miró. The new trends in French painting were well suited to his purpose of providing something surprising, and he sensed so exactly the value of the enrichment that the painters brought to the theatre, that he made a point of reproducing their décors without any modification of his own, respecting even the tiniest details of the artist's model. He wanted from these non-specialists a new outlook that could not come from professional theatre designers, who were too tied to rules that had by then become habit.

The first ballets that marked the resumption of Diaghilev's activities in 1917 were *Contes Russes* (décor and costumes by Larionov), *Les Femmes de Bonne Humeur* (décor and costumes by Bakst), and Cocteau and Satie's *Parade* (décor and costumes by Picasso), which created another scandal. Satie's music was accompanied by the noise of sirens and typewriters. The audience was so incensed that it hissed not only at the music but also at the splendid costumes designed by Picasso. In 1919 came the *Boutique Fantasque* (décor and costumes by Derain) and the *Three-Cornered Hat* (décor and costumes by Picasso), followed in

1920 by *Pulcinella*, also designed by Picasso, and *Le Chant du Rossignol* (décor and costumes by Matisse). The year 1924 saw the creation of *Les Fâcheux* by Georges Auric, with décor and costumes by Braque – who also did those of *Zéphyr et Flore* in 1926 – *Les Biches* (décors and costumes by Marie Laurencin), and *La Tentation de la Bergère* (décor and costumes by Juan Gris).

Later, Diaghilev presented *Les Noces* by Stravinsky (décor and costumes by Gontcharova), *Le Train Bleu* by Darius Milhaud (décor by Laurencin, costumes by Chanel), Stravinsky's *Oedipus Rex* (there were neither décor nor costumes for this ballet, it was performed in ordinary street clothes), *Apollon Musagète* (décor and costumes by Bauchant), *Barabau* (décor and costumes by Utrillo), and *Le Fils Prodigue* (décor and costumes by Rouault). Two ballets testify to Diaghilev's constant search for novelty: *Roméo et Juliette* (1927), with décor and costumes by Max Ernst and Miró, and *Le Bal* (1929), with décor and costumes by Chirico. Both of them, the latter in particular, caused minor scandals. This list would be incomplete without mention of the constructivist ballets: *La Chatte* (costumes and constructions by Pevsner and Gabo), presented in 1927, *Pas d'Acier* (costumes and constructions by Jacoulov) and *Le Renard*, previously performed in 1922 with décor and costumes by Larionov, but this time (1929) with constructivist décors by the same artist. From this rich and impressive list one can see to what an extent the indefatigable impresario of the *Ballets Russes*, by giving painters a platform worthy of their talent, helped them to overcome the indifference, sarcasm and opprobrium that still threatened their art.

The death of Diaghilev, which resulted in the dispersal of the *Ballets Russes* company, marked the end of an exceptionally happy and fertile period in the history of the arts. But the fact remains that the brief sojourn of this impresario of genius in the world of the theatre turned upside down and inside out all the ideas then existing about production and the use of the stage. From then on the names of such painters as Matisse, Derain, Chagall, Bérard, Miró and Dufy began to figure on the posters of ballet companies, to look no farther than that. Then, too, Diaghilev started the tradition that painters be asked to supply not only a model of the décor and the costumes for any particular ballet, but also production ideas. The painter's role was now considered a key one. Throughout the life of the Diaghilev ballet the décor maintained an exceptionally high standard. Ballet after Diaghilev has had little to show in the way of discovery, and there has been a tendency to neglect décor (and music) and develop choreography. This is particularly true of England, where the choreographer is the leader of the creative team (and sometimes the whole of it) instead of being but one of the four partners that went to make a Diaghilev ballet. The result is that England's record in scenic design is not very impressive, whereas her record in choreography and dancing

PICASSO. STUDY. 1917.

is outstanding. Ballet in England, as in France, derives directly from Diaghilev, whose company included a number of English dancers. His company died with him, but through the dispersed members his inspiration was carried to all the leading countries of the world, where it dominates ballet to this day.

Ballet in the United States is also descended from the *Ballets Russes*, although Diaghilev was almost unknown there. A number of Russian dancers settled there as teachers, but were for a long time quite unable to implant the idea that ballet was an art form and not merely a technique. This changed only with the visits of Colonel de Basil and his troupe in 1933–1934. The seeds of a sound tradition that is today growing and developing were planted by George Balanchine, who founded the American School of Ballet in 1934, and whose work is often featured by the New York City Ballet.

PICASSO. PORTRAIT OF STRAVINSKY. 1917.

**BALLETS SUÉDOIS** The Swedish Ballet first appeared in 1920. It was founded by a wealthy patron named Rolf de Maré and Jean Borlin, dancer and choreographer. As Sweden offered too limited a field for their activities and was, moreover, poor in talent, they decided to emigrate to Paris. At first they attracted little notice, but they had the good fortune to win the help of Hébertot, who welcomed them to his theatre. Their first proper performance was given on October 25th, 1920, at the Comédie des Champs-Élysées. On the programme were Debussy's *Jeux* (décor by Bonnard), Albeniz's *Iberia* (décor by Steinlen), and *La Nuit de la Saint-Jean*, drawn from Swedish folklore. Although somewhat disconcerted by this new ballet form, which was primarily a mimed transcription of a pictorial motif, the public gave the troupe a warm reception. The dancers were, on the whole, rather mediocre, and Jean Borlin's choreography was unimaginative. He had the good fortune, however, to find some first-rate collaborators among the musicians, painters and poets of the day, the *Groupe des Six*, Cocteau, Cendrars, Pirandello, Jean Hugo, Chirico, Irene Lagut especially, and the painter Fernand Léger. Rolf de Maré and Jean Borlin created some fifty ballets, of which the most outstanding were *l'Homme et Son Désir* by Claudel, *Les Mariés de la Tour Eiffel* by Cocteau, *Skating Rink*, *Relâche* by Picabia, and particularly *La Création du Monde* by the poet Blaise Cendrars, music by Darius Milhaud, with a magnificent curtain and superb costumes by Léger.

**BATEAU-LAVOIR** In the early years of the century the poet Max Jacob gave this name to a strange conglomeration of artists' studios in Montmartre, at the top of the steps leading to No. 13 Rue Ravignan. They were situated in a modestly shaded square which later took the name of the singer Émile Goudeau. It was a gloomy heap of dark and dirty premises made of beams and planks that had all the appearance of scrap. On stormy days they swayed and creaked so dangerously on their uncertain foundations that they reminded one of the washing-boats on the Seine – hence the name. There are all sorts of conjectures as to the origins of the Bateau-Lavoir. It has even been suggested that it was once a factory. In any case,

the painter Maufra appears to have been its first artistic tenant, about 1890. When Van Dongen, and later Picasso, came to live there, that is to say between 1900 and 1904, the tenants included a costermonger, a washerwoman, and a restorer of old pictures, a solemn gentleman with a white beard who was introduced to the Douanier Rousseau as the Minister of Fine Arts, on the occasion of the famous banquet given for him by Picasso in 1908 in his studio. The Douanier presided over the banquet, while poems and speeches extolled him in uproarious though kindly vein. The Douanier sang some compositions of his own, and played the violin. That was the occasion when, a little intoxicated by so much unaccustomed attention, he confided to Picasso: 'Actually, you and I are the two greatest painters: I in the modern *genre*, you in the Egyptian'. The function ended with everyone drunk, but it was certainly the most wonderful day in the life of the pathetic Douanier.

Beginning in 1904, there was a change in the social status of the tenants of the place. Little by little, writers and artists began to take it over. Among those who came to live there, at one time or another, were Pierre MacOrlan, Juan Gris, André Salmon, Gargallo, Max Jacob and Pierre Reverdy. It became a kind of club that soon had its *habitués* – artists like Matisse, Braque, Derain, Dufy, Marie Laurencin, Modigliani, Laurens, Utrillo, Lipchitz, Maria Blanchard, Metzinger, Marcoussis; poets and writers like Apollinaire, Jarry, Cocteau, Coquiot, Cremnitz, Paul Fort, Warnod, Radiguet, Gertrude Stein; actors like Dullin, Harry Baur, Gaston Modot; and dealers like Vollard, Sagot, Kahnweiler and Berthe Weil; not to mention inquisitive strangers. It was with this outstanding group that Picasso first discussed Cubism *(\*)*. From 1908 on, daily discussions took place, either in the studios of Picasso or Juan Gris or in the neighbouring cafés, with a passion that never abated. The new aesthetic doctrine slowly took shape around Picasso in the course of discussions that went on night and day between Braque, Derain, Gris, Marcoussis and Metzinger, joined later by Apollinaire, Raynal and the mathematician Princet. It goes without saying that the relations between so many different kinds of temperament were not always idyllic, but the history of art certainly knew, then, some of its greatest moments.

When war broke out in 1914 painters left the Bateau-Lavoir and Montmartre for more comfortable lodgings.

BAUCHANT. FATHER TRUFFAUT. 1925.
*Private Collection, Paris*

**BAUCHANT** André. French painter born at Châteaurenault, Indre-et-Loire, in 1873. This inspired market-gardener was like a figure out of Genesis, a veritable patriarch. He started to paint at the age of forty-six. Immediately he proved himself a prodigious portrayer of Biblical, mythological and even historical scenes. He had a certain Franciscan grace about him, and it was as a lover of flowers that he composed his hymn to Nature. His father was a gardener, and as soon as the boy was old enough to do so he helped his father with his work. He married in 1900, and visited the Ex-

position Universelle in Paris on his honeymoon. After the First World War he left his flower-beds and devoted himself to art. In 1921 he exhibited nine paintings at the Salon d'Automne. He attracted the notice of Le Corbusier, Ozenfant, Lipchitz and Diaghilev, for whom he painted the décor for *Apollon Musagète*. His career as a painter had begun. After trying a number of salons, Bauchant confined himself to the Salon d'Automne and that of the Surindépendants from 1929 on. In the winter of 1949 he had a big retrospective exhibition at the Galerie Charpentier, with 215 of his pictures on view.

With Bauchant our eyes seem to be present at the creation of the world. Everything vibrates in his painting: everything has the glittering purity of the first days of the world. It is wonderful to see how the painter arranges his colours on the canvas: dahlias, magnolias, narcissus spring up, the sea teems with fish, and all the birds of the air are in flight. There is abundance everywhere. Apples, pears and grapes fill the dishes, crowned by flowers. In his best work the paint is applied smooth and shining and not too thick, covering the white of the canvas without any preparation. His colours are sharp, and at the same time delicately shaded. Bauchant is more than an illustrator. He is an illuminator of life and vision who paints as a warbler sings in the hawthorn. It is good, it is tonic for us, in the midst of disputes about the spirit of form and the psychology of colours, to pause before this elderly child of grace. Here is a world glorified by a brush that revels in profusion. The sky is full of birds, the sea full of fish, and the slopes thick with trees and houses. Everything is fertile in these compositions that burst with harmonious and exciting discoveries. Here is all the joy of Nature, disturbed only by the flames and battles of history and legend.

**BAUHAUS** In 1919 Walter Gropius, one of the leading contemporary German architects, founded in Weimar the *Staatliches Bauhaus* (State Building House), a grouping together of the schools of fine arts and crafts. The inaugural manifesto concluded with these words: 'We seek to form a new body of craftsmen who will no longer know that pride of class that erects a high wall between artisans and artists. We must desire, devise and work together to prepare the new edifice of the future, which will harmoniously unite architecture, sculpture and painting. This edifice will be raised by the hands of millions of workmen – a crystalline emblem of the new faith in the future.' Stemming from the historical and social conditions of defeated Germany, the Bauhaus showed a desire for positive, rational reorganization, as a reaction against expressionist individualism. Its conscious ambition was to revive the lost unity of all the arts, in relation to modern architecture on the one hand and the concrete needs of our industrial civilization on the other. The 'Bauhaus', according to its programme, 'wishes to re-establish the harmony between the different artistic activities, between craftsmanship and artistry, and bind them all together in a new conception of building.

KLEE. OVER AND UPWARDS! 1931.

Our final but still distant aim is one unified work of art – the *magnum opus* – where there will no longer be any distinction between monumental and decorative art.' It was at the same time a School of Fine Arts, and a School of Arts and Crafts, with a broader and more modern spirit than the old, backward-looking institutions of the same name. It was a self-contained centre of artistic instruction and culture, with tremendous breadth of scope.

The leading teachers, together with Gropius, were artists of the first rank: Lionel Feininger (from 1919 to 1933), Paul Klee (from 1920 to 1929), Oskar Schlemmer (1921 to 1929), Wassily Kandinsky (from 1922 to 1932), and Ladislaus Moholy-Nagy (from 1923 to 1928). Klee taught theory, then painting on glass and tapestry. He summed up the basic essentials of his method in his book *Pedagogical Sketchbook*, published in 1925. Kandinsky gave lessons in general theory, but concentrated more on abstract composition and monumental painting. The influence of these two great artists was tremendous at the Bauhaus but, despite their will to discipline, there was a certain contradiction between their romantic instincts and the clearly architectural and purist tendencies which dominated the group and which suited Feininger, Schlemmer and Moholy-Nagy better. In the spirit of the Bauhaus the latter two renewed the technique of working in metal and plastic materials, the arts of the theatre and the ballet, photography, typography, publicity, and so on. But it was undoubtedly Feininger, faithful to the Bauhaus from its first day to its last, who best exemplified the constructivist aesthetic doctrine in its flexibility and its purity (*vide* Feininger, Kandinsky, Klee, Moholy-Nagy, Schlemmer).

In 1929, under reactionary pressure, the Bauhaus moved to Dessau where, a victim of National Socialism, it had to close down in 1933.

Gropius, who gave up the management of the Bauhaus in 1928, and Feininger settled in the United States in 1937, where their work and influence continue. Moholy-Nagy joined them there, and tried to revive the tradition of the group, founding a New Bauhaus in Chicago. Two complete retrospective exhibitions have been held, one in New York in 1938, the other in Munich in 1950.

BAUMEISTER. GOUACHE. 1923.
*Private Collection*

**BAUMEISTER** Willi. Born in Stuttgart, 1889. He is the least German and, possibly, the most European of the German painters. At a time when all modern German painters are more or less strongly attached to Expressionism, which is a specifically German movement, Expressionism is almost nonexistent in Baumeister. Instead, one can notice Neo-Plasticism, Constructivism, Negro or Aztec art, speleology, prehistory and calligraphy; that is to say, universal rather than national influences. Baumeister is eminently a painter of today, and his art shows the major themes, the fleeting loves, as well as the nostalgia and secret desires of this highly complex era. The variety of his work, the sudden changes, his heaviness and his lightness, sometimes coupled together, could easily baffle the spectator; yet the work as a whole remains one of the most curious of our time by reason of its explorations in unexpected places, and one of the most moving by reason of its varied themes, each one revealing a new style, each one bringing something surprisingly novel into the plastic arts. The logical evolution of these themes is in

itself significant. After canvases offering nothing but horizontal and vertical lines, from 1920 on he began to paint his *Mauerbilder*, mural paintings, in which curved and sloping lines are again admitted. About 1928 he began the series entitled *Painter with His Palette*, in which undulating lines appear together with rectilinear planes, with vivid touches of colour in the palette. At the same time he developed the sports theme (*Tennis Players*, *Runner*) which, towards 1933, changed to a simple ideogram (*The Jumper*, *Homo Footballensis*).

During the war, prohibited from teaching by the Hitler regime, Baumeister began to devote himself to scientific research on colour, and became passionately absorbed in the study of prehistoric archaeology. In secret he executed a series of paintings of weird, organic forms, usually in an earth colour on a white ground, which he called *African Histories*. They are very much like the *Perforations* and *Paintings in Relief* of the same period, all of them strongly impregnated with the prehistoric and the archaic. After the war these forms were made more ordered and civilized (1946–1947), and became a kind of script – not yet deciphered, according to the painter himself. After some new detours, Baumeister then produced an astonishing series of paintings with large black surfaces, which he called *Montaru*. This was in 1953. Then, almost at once, he began a new series, in which black gave way to white, and these he named *Monturi*. Such is the bewildering – and, to some, exasperating – course of Baumeister's work. Affinities with Léger and Miró are discernible at certain points, but only in details. His work is never systematic, never hardened into any one method, and stays supple and inventive at every moment of its evolution.

**BAZILLE** Frédéric, French painter born at Montpellier 1841, died in action at Beaune-la-Rolande during the Franco-Prussian war, 1870. Bazille came of good Protestant, bourgeois stock. He was about the same age as Monet, Renoir and Sisley, whom he met shortly after his arrival in Paris, in 1862. He went there to study medicine and painting. He soon failed in medicine, which bored him, but applied himself with passion to his art studies. He enrolled as a pupil of the Swiss painter Gleyre (*vide* Atelier Gleyre) and met in his academy the three painters who were to become his friends. Very often they – Monet in particular – would appeal to his generosity, and as he was less impecunious than they, thanks to a modest allowance he received from home, he found it quite normal to come to their aid. With Monet and Renoir he often went to paint in the open. More than either of them Bazille liked to express himself in light colours and convey the limpidity of the atmosphere. Everyone recognized his merits. Thus Impressionism, which was to manifest itself some ten years later, was unconsciously being prepared. But Bazille, who had a share in its evolution and was one of its most enthusiastic and gifted exponents, and – according to his friends – one of its most devout supporters, was destined not to be there when the group made its first public appearance in 1874. War had come. Bazille had enlisted in the army and was killed. Impressionism had lost at the very outset one of its finest artists. Later on, Bazille was forgotten. But time gives things their proper perspective, and now his qualities are being rediscovered. Bazille's work provided a link between Courbet, whose work he admired at Montpellier, and that of the

Impressionists, whom he foreshadowed, and shows how the aesthetic revolutions of the nineteenth century formed a logical chain with classicism in a far more direct manner than was generally believed. If he had lived to become one of the great masters of the movement, perhaps the significance of his work would have seemed less exceptional. Dramatically limited to fewer than one hundred paintings, his work shows an astonishing mastery, and impresses one with its unity and firmness of style. His most significant canvas is *Family Reunion*, which seems like a summing-up of his work as a whole. All the seriousness and fervour of Bazille's character are expressed in it, and all his favourite themes are to be found there: flowers, placid portraits, landscapes with distant horizons, trees, and the peace and quiet of family intimacy. This untroubled, unaffected art is neither banal nor indifferent. It seeks to attain grandeur through tranquillity; and the immobility of his figures gives the composition an amazing density which never becomes overpowering. It is difficult to know what to prefer in this work: the brilliant colouring of the still life in the middle of the picture or the intensity of the portraits.

**BEAUDIN** André. French painter born at Mennecy, Seine-et-Oise, in 1895.

BAZILLE. FAMILY GATHERING. 1867.                    *Louvre*

From 1911 to 1915 Beaudin worked at the École des Arts Décoratifs. In 1921 he paid a visit to Italy. The most important factor in his formation was his meeting with Juan Gris, whose teachings he admired and understood undoubtedly better than anyone else. Like him, he considers that Cubism remains an excellent method of knowing and defining form, and organizing colour. Developing this idea to its logical conclusion, Juan Gris succeeded in humanizing to the utmost an art based on a rigid preliminary order. His followers, in their turn, resolved the problem of the apparent contradiction between construction and expression. Few solutions have the balance, elegance and solidity of that brought by Beaudin. His compositions, which were at first tormented and far too crowded with meaning, gradually grew quieter and more restrained. The canvas became the meeting-ground of opposing forces which harmonized and united. Beaudin is a painter of pure light as it appears emerging from the night. His art, in its clear limpidity, never escapes from honest reasoning. It is full of subtle poetry. Whether he takes as his model horses fighting, or a horse race, or the varied faces of Paris – its monuments, bridges and quays – or the flight of a bird before an open window, he liberates the universal quality, and at the same time adorns this image with the most subtle nuances of the passing moment. In a few simple lines, harmonizing with cold, vivid colours, he depicts the birth of day, or its various hours. Beaudin has illustrated the books of such poet friends of his as Paul Eluard and Francis Ponge. He has also done some important sculptural work, which, with its superimposed planes, is like a concrete representation of his painting. The dignity of this painter, his reserve, his classicism, have kept him clear of fashions and

BEAUDIN. SOLITARY WINDOWS. 1950. *Private Collection, Paris*

infatuations. His work has, consequently, all the more unity and lasting value. It seeks not to strike or astonish, but to convince, to satisfy the mind and the heart.

**BECKMANN** Max. German painter born in Leipzig in 1884, died in New York in 1950. From 1906 on Beckmann was part of the artistic life of Berlin. He remained attached to German Impressionism and also, though less openly, to the symbolism of Marées. Most of his work, however, the moving portrayal of human nature, was painted after his experiences on the battlefields from 1914 to 1918. In 1933 political persecution forced him to flee from Frankfurt, where he had been living for a long time, to Berlin and then to Amsterdam in 1936. In 1947 he left for the United States, where he died some three years later. The main subject of his work was the human figure in all the glory of its vital force, and the misery of its debasement. He was trying – to quote him – to enclose man, 'monster of such terrifying, convulsive vitality', in a structure of planes and lines. His vigorously constructed compositions of 1920 thus become nightmarish visions in which women, in all the crudity of their physique, cripples squatting on their maimed stumps, and bloated characters, jostle one another in horrible carnival

BECKMANN. THE TRAILER. 1940.

masquerades. During the following years, as his memories of the war grew fainter, other human realities came to the fore: landscapes and still lifes, portraits and nudes. These landscapes and objects also have a haunting vitality. The man in the portraits – it was his own face that Beckmann kept on scrutinizing endlessly – remains brutal and enigmatic; the woman is elemental, often brazen, sometimes tender. At this time, his increasing contact with French painters helped Beckmann to acquire a new breadth and greater simplicity of expression, without in any way changing the basic structure of his art. A more fastidious art with freer colours and deeper blacks began in 1932 and was developed during his years of exile. The principal works of this last period were seven immense triptychs, and paintings like *The Trailer*, which are stamped with a complex symbolism. In the triptychs, *Departure* (1932–1935), *Hide-and-Seek* (1945), and *The Argonauts* (1949–1950), the enigma of our existence is expressed in allegorical language which, at times, attain an intensity and a force that actually have a physical effect on the spectator.

**BERNARD** Émile (1868–1941). Born in Lille, died in Paris. The role played by Bernard was an unusual one – interesting but tragic. At the age of sixteen he already showed brilliant talent. He started work at the Cormon studio in Paris but was expelled for insubordination. He had met Toulouse-Lautrec there, and after making friends with Van Gogh and Gauguin in 1886 he decided to go and work with the latter at Pont-Aven. In collaboration with his friend Anquetin, Bernard had worked out the theory of Cloisonnism, a style which featured bold flat surfaces and vigorous colours, with black or blue contours separating the forms, like partitions (*cloisons*). In Brittany he used all his persuasive powers to advocate this theory, and succeeded to some extent in influencing Gauguin. Though this influence was later to become the cause of bitter antagonism between the two artists, Bernard's name will always be linked with this curious Pont-Aven school, which played an important part in the years around 1890. Bernard's early work was tremendously forceful. Competent and original as a painter, he also made woodcuts, sculpture, furniture and tapestries. He was also a poet and writer, with an alert mind charged with religious mysticism and predisposed to philosophical digression. Keen and unselfish in character, he was the first before 1890 to proclaim admiration for Cézanne and Redon, both of whom were partly indebted to him for their rise to fame. He was on intimate terms with Van Gogh, and here again, with utter disinterestedness, did all he could to force recognition of a genius he was practically alone in recognizing. In 1894 he visited Italy, then went to Egypt, where he stayed ten years, working out on his own a new art style inspired by the Venetian masters, for whom he had an unbounded admiration.

On his return to France in 1904 he paid a visit to Cézanne, whose pleasure at the younger painter's enthusiasm did not preclude a subsequent criticism of his work: 'He completely turns his back on all his theories; his drawing is old stuff based on a vision prompted not by a feeling for Nature but by what he has seen in museums, and even more by a philosophic turn of mind acquired through too vast a knowledge of the masters he admires'. Unfortunately, this tendency was only to increase with time.

Bernard was a tremendous worker, and found time, apart from his painting, to write articles, letters, memoirs and polemical pieces, and to give lectures and even to found and edit a review – *La Rénovation Esthétique*. Among other things, he published the extremely interesting letters he had received from Van Gogh, Gauguin, Redon and Cézanne – documents which are indispensable to an understanding of modern art.

Though his early works, full of both promise and achievement, are the only ones to attract any attention today, Bernard nevertheless holds an enviable place in art history, for he was one of the rare beings to whom the great painters of his time offered their friendship. He himself felt deeply embittered at being known only as the advocate of Cézanne, Van Gogh, Gauguin and Odilon Redon while his own later work remained permanently in the shade – from where it is unlikely ever to emerge.

**BISSIÈRE** Roger. French painter born at Villeréal in the Lot-et-Garonne in 1888. He came to Paris in 1910, and lived there for a long time in complete isolation, in so far as his art was concerned. Only in 1920 did he begin to exhibit, first at the Salon d'Automne, then at the Salon des Indépendants. He was a member of the *Esprit Nouveau* group (*) and published, in the review of that name, a series of studies on modern painting and the old masters, the result of long meditation on the problems of art. At

BERNARD. PONT-AVEN. 1889.     *Musée d'Art Moderne, Paris*

that time Bissière was one of the painters who were trying to humanize Cubism. His severe constructions were brightened by subtle nuances of colour. He became widely known through his many exhibitions. But far from seeking to exploit his success and develop the happy and balanced vein of his art, he broke completely with anything that threatened to become a formula. He preferred to abandon his conquests and devote himself to his still inconclusive researches into accidents of form and the secret chemistry of his materials. During a long period of inner conflict, during which he produced very little that he considered worth exhibiting, Bissière accumulated technical experience and psychological discoveries. He accepted a teaching post at the Académie Ranson (*), and there found himself in contact with the best of the new generation of painters. Because he put himself on the same plane of research as they, despite difference of age and experience, he soon achieved an extraordinary influence with these painters, attracting to him the most promising and widely varied talents.

However, Bissière was then an almost forgotten painter. In 1938 he decided to retire to the country, in the Lot, where he has been living since. During the war he stopped painting altogether. Serious eye trouble gave rise to fears for his sight. Nevertheless, helped by his wife, he worked at some curious mural canvases, for

BISSIÈRE. COMPOSITION. 1952.

which he made use of whatever he had at hand – old multicoloured materials, woollens and other fabrics – to replace the colours he did not have. These he assembled and arranged into grandiose, monumental compositions on profoundly religious themes. The result is striking, and gives an impression of extraordinary freedom. These glittering, barbaric works at once focused attention on the painter, who was renewing himself in this remarkable way. Since then his work has grown remarkably, gradually freeing itself from all representation while retaining a concrete savour all its own. Restless by nature, he is one of those conscientious people who would never seek to exert any influence or play any important role and yet, despite their self-effacement, are masters.

His art, which used to have a severe, hieratic character through his link with Cubism, has now emerged from its long retirement full of youth and wonderment.

**BLANCHARD** Maria. Born in Santander, Spain, 1881; died in Paris in 1932. Does she owe her troubled, complex art to the Spanish influence of her father and the part French, part Polish influence of her mother? These three nationalities might partly explain her painting, in which one finds the Spanish sense of tragedy and grandeur, a kind of coloured imagery reminiscent of popular Slav art, and finally a human presence, a restraint even in deliberate distortion, an emotional self-control which seem to come from the French side of her. To Cubism Maria Blanchard owed her method of composing a picture, of organizing the planes with a rhythm which accentuates the contour of forms. But this severity, no matter how geometrical it became, never ended in abstraction; nor did the emphasis on volume ever become mechanical: the surface is modelled with a freedom that is never brutal, the gestures of the people she depicts are full of tenderness and the impression of grandeur comes from the judicious use of plastic elements, as well as from the sentimental expression that shines from the subject. As a painter of children she seems to have bent over their faces with a real maternal solicitude. Despite a general impression of tranquillity and contentment, very few of her canvases are free from a deep melancholy which doubtless had its origins in the sad life of the artist herself. Her palette, limited to earth colours, muted blues, olive greens, dull whites and blacks – helps to heighten this feeling. Small and hump-backed, Maria Blanchard did not sink to despair in her art, despite her physical handicap. On the contrary, her misfortune gave her a keen sense of the grandeur and tragedy of everyday life which, had it not been for her, would have been almost totally absent from the art of her time.

**BLAST** 'Vorticism' was the only movement in Great Britain comparable in intention with Parisian Cubism *(\*)* and Italian Futurism *(\*)* before 1914. Wyndham Lewis *(\*)* was the creative pivot around which Vorticism revolved, and the publication *Blast*, which he edited, was the group's public platform. It was a period of polemic, of artistic turmoil, of group activity and noisy manifestos. '*Putsches*', Lewis has written, 'took place every month or so.' The Futurists held an uproarious exhibition at the

Sackville Gallery in March 1912, and it was during this year that Lewis made his first drawings (e.g. *The Centauress*), which are now recognized as Vorticist. (The word was actually coined by Ezra Pound the following year.) Vorticism was

BLANCHARD. BOY WITH ICE CREAM.
*Musée d'Art Moderne, Paris*

abstraction, often totally non-figurative, and characterized by flat, plan-like systems of arcs and angles organized radially from a particular focal point (the 'Vortex') which draws the spectator into a whirling recession. Like Cubism and Futurism, the movement was essentially anti-Impressionist; like the latter, it 'accepted the machine world . . . it sought out machine forms'. The 'political' purpose of the movement was to 'hustle the cultural Britannia' and *Blast* – or, to give it its full title, *Blast: Review of the Great*

*English Vortex* – was to blow the cobwebs from her eyes as though with a flame-thrower. There were, in fact, only two issues, published by John Lane, The Bodley Head. The first, in a puce cover, appeared on June 20th, 1914; the second, in a white cover, the following year. The main manifesto in No. 1 was signed by R. Aldington, Arbuthnot, L. Atkinson, Gaudier-Brzeska, J. Dismorr, C. Hamilton, E. Pound, W. Roberts, H. Sanders, E. Wadsworth, and Wyndham Lewis. Humour ('Quack ENGLISH drug for stupidity and sleepiness'), sport, and the years 1837–1900 ('curse Abysmal inexcusable middle class') were blasted; hairdressers, seafarers and ports, England were among the blessed. Reproduced were works by Gaudier-Brzeska, Epstein, Frederick Etchells, Spencer Gore, Cuthbert Hamilton, William Roberts and Wyndham Lewis. C. R. W. Nevinson and Edward Wadsworth were among the additional names in No. 2. Between these two issues, in June 1915 at the Doré Gallery, there took place the 'First' (and last) Vorticist Exhibition. Besides the artists from the Rebel Art Centre ('the Great London Vortex') founded by Miss Lechmere and Lewis in Great Ormond Street, some half a dozen sympathisers contributed. But, as Lewis wrote nearly a quarter of a century later, 'a bigger *Blast* than mine had rather taken the wind out of my sails'. The exhibition coincided with the deaths in France of the movement's philosopher, T. E. Hulme, and its most talented sculptor, Gaudier-Brzeska. Many of its other artists subsequently employed Vorticism's precise, clear-cut, sharp-edged, metallic handwriting to record aspects of the war upon which Europe was embarked, and incidentally to start the modern movement in England, but all subsequently retreated to a greater or lesser extent from Vorticism's extreme point of complete abstraction.

**BLAUE REITER** (Der). The name, derived from a small picture by Kandinsky, *The Blue Rider*, is used to designate the most fertile artistic movement that arose in Germany before 1914. At the beginning of the century Munich was one of the main centres of German artistic activity. When Kandinsky settled there in 1896, the *Jugendstil (\*)* was thriving. In 1902 he opened his own school of art, and became president of the 'Phalanx' group. In 1904 all the advanced groups of artists united, and exhibitions were arranged of works by Cézanne, Gauguin, Van Gogh and the Neo-Impressionists. In January 1909 Erbslöh, Jawlensky, Kandinsky, Kanoldt, Kubin, Gabriele Münter, Marianna von Werefkin, Schnabel and Wittenstein formed the New Artists' Federation of Munich, and held their first exhibition at the Tannhäuser Gallery from December 1909 to January 1910. Other artists joined the movement: Bechtejeff, Erma Bossi, Kogan, Sacharoff (1909), Girieud, Le Fauconnier (1910), Franz Marc, Otto Fischer (1911) and Mogilewsky (1912). In addition, Picasso, Derain, Rouault, Vlaminck, Braque and Van Dongen were invited to take part in the exhibitions.

BOCCIONI. ELASTICITY.                     *Private Collection, Milan*

This vast group, with no definite programme, had no aim other than to unite all the young artistic forces. To show its importance and its variety, Marc and Kandinsky took it upon themselves, in July 1911, to prepare a collective volume of aesthetic studies and numerous illustrations under the title of *Der Blaue Reiter*. But even before it appeared, in the course of the third combined exhibition (December 1911) differences of opinion arose over questions of jury, and Kandinsky, Kubin, Marc and Gabriele Münter left the Association. On the 18th of December, also at the Tannhäuser Gallery, the first exhibition of the new *Blaue Reiter* group was held, showing forty-three pictures by Henri Rousseau, Delaunay, Epstein, Kahler, Macke, Bloch, Schönberg, David and Wladimir Burljuk, Bloè-Niestlé, Gabriele Münter, Kandinsky, Marc and Campendonck. A second exhibition, confined to drawings and engravings (in black-and-white), took place at the Goltz Gallery three months later. The circle was enlarged by the inclusion of the *Brücke* group *(\*)* of Dresden, the New Secession of Berlin, the French artists Braque, Derain, Picasso, La Fresnaye, Vlaminck, Lotiron and Véra, and the Russians Nathalie Gontcharova, Larionov and Malevitch. In 1912 Paul Klee, moved by the works of Marc, Delaunay and Kandinsky, joined the group and exhibited his poetic water-colours.

The *Blaue Reiter* year book gives a fairly good picture of the scope of this movement, which embraced all the arts, and its revolutionary enthusiasm. 'Traditions', said Franz Marc, 'are a fine thing, but what is really fine is to *create* a tradition, and not just live off one.' Kandinsky, prime mover and fighting theoretician, contributed an article on the problem of form, a sequel and conclusion to his basic work, *Concerning the Spiritual in Art*, which had appeared a little while before. (An English translation of this work by Michael Sadleir, under the title of *The Art of Spiritual Harmony*, was published in 1914.) Marc wrote a study of the different tendencies in modern art in Germany; David Burljuk, of tendencies in Russia. Roger Allard introduced Cubism; Erwin von Busse wrote of Delaunay. Theodor van Hartmann, Sabanjeff and Arnold Schönberg dealt with modern music. There was no formulation of any aesthetic rule, unless perhaps an aversion to academic formulas, and a faith in what Kandinsky called the 'inner necessity'. This was the simple declaration that appeared on the title-page of the inaugural catalogue: 'We do not seek to propagate any precise or particular form: our aim is to show, through the variety of forms represented, how the inner desire of the artist expresses itself in different ways'. Expressionism *(\*)*, Cubism *(\*)*, Orphism *(\*)* and Abstract tendencies (*vide* Abstract Art) were to be seen there in a generous fraternity of romantic inspiration.

The war dispersed the efforts and energy of the *Blaue Reiter*. Macke was killed in 1914, Franz Marc in 1916. Klee and Kandinsky went back to the Bauhaus *(\*)* at Weimar and Dessau. A retrospective exhibition of the movement was arranged in Munich in 1949 (*vide* Jawlensky, Kandinsky, Klee, Macke, Malevitch, Marc).

**BOCCIONI** Umberto. Italian painter and sculptor born at Reggio in Calabria, 1882; died at Sorte, 1916. In Rome at the same time as Gino Severini, he learnt the basic rules of Divisionism (then the fashion in France) from the painter Giàcomo Balla, who had just returned from Paris. He made the acquaintance of Marinetti, after the publication of the first Futurist Manifesto in *Le Figaro*, and became the theoretician of the group (*vide* Futurism). His main preoccupation, both as painter and sculptor, was to give life to matter by translating it in terms of its movement. Above all, he struggled desperately to shake off previous influences, such as the 1900 style in particular, by which he felt poisoned. In his manifestos, and his book *Futurist Sculpture and Painting*, he stressed the necessity of universalizing the 'impressionist moment'. 'While the Impressionists create a picture in order to render a particular moment, and subordinate the life of the picture to this moment, we synthesize all moments (time, place, form, colour-tone) and so construct a picture.' The Futurist picture was required to express, in addition, sensations and states of mind, a far cry from the objectivity of Cubism. Banishing horizontal and vertical lines, which metaphysical painting, on the contrary, glorified, Boccioni invented 'line-force'; that is, the energy

with which every object reacts to light and shade, energy which creates form-force and colour-forces. His masterpiece is the canvas *Elasticity*, painted in 1912 after the Futurist exhibition in Paris. It is evident that if Boccioni had not seen the Cubists, he could not have painted this work, which is one of the most important of Futurist works. But *Elasticity*, the synthesis of a horse's movements in a race, nevertheless does express something more than a Cubist canvas of the same period. The same powerful lyricism is to be found in his sculptures: *Syntheses of Human Dynamism*, exhibited in 1913 with the famous *polimaterici* (sculptures composed of various elements such as iron, wood, glass, etc).

Umberto Boccioni was called up when war was declared, and died in 1916, at the age of thirty-four, as the result of a fall from a horse.

**BOMBOIS** Camille. French painter born at Venarey-les-Laumes, Côte-d'Or,

BOMBOIS. THE DANCER'S CURTAIN. 1926.

BONHOMME. SEATED NUDE. 1920.
*Collection of Harry Goldschmidt, Paris*

in 1883. His father owned a barge, and it was on canal waters that Bombois spent his childhood. He has always retained his love for rivers and stretches of calm, moving water, and landscapes framed by the arches of a bridge. After brief periods of schooling, the boy was sent, at the age of twelve, to Migennes, in the Yonne, as a farmhand. At sixteen he began to draw scenes from his life as a shepherd and worker in the fields. Strong and pugnacious, he loved to challenge his companions in the village square, and was soon regional champion in wrestling. He liked to pit himself against the athletes of travelling circuses. One day he left with them. The wrestlers, the female equestrians, and the country shows furnished him with new themes. Eager to see Paris, he set off on foot one day for the capital. He worked for a while as a road-mender, and then found employment as a digger in the excavations for the underground railway.

Through all these vicissitudes he never stopped dreaming about painting and drawing, and, in order to be able to devote the necessary time to it, he found himself night work in a printing plant. For seven years he worked like this, snatching only a few hours' sleep, and in his free time he succeeded in elaborating a technique, an art, an *œuvre*. Another four and a half years he spent in the trenches. Towards the end of 1922, having decided to show, at last, the results of so much labour, he put his best canvas on a chair in the street, and a few small ones on the ground around it. A passer-by, Noel Bureau, became enthusiastic and wrote the first article on him in a small review. Other buyers and admirers came forward, among them the German critic Wilhelm Uhde (*vide* this name), friend of Rousseau and Séraphine. Bombois was at last able to devote himself entirely to painting. Soon he established himself in his own house in a Paris suburb, in a studio which he filled with the landscapes of his own life. Camille Bombois's case is undoubtedly the most characteristic of the so-called naïve painters, the one that shows most clearly the path of a self-taught painter, guided from the beginning by an artistic instinct which will not be denied, which depends on no formal cultural background and is stronger than all the circumstances life puts in the way. From his youth painting has been one of the manifestations of a prodigious strength which asserts itself in every sphere. When Bombois paints people he gives them extra weight and greater girth. His distortions are not dictated by plastic reasons but by his contact with the shattering realities over which he has triumphed. By his physical force Bombois has won the right to be a painter, and he has succeeded in introducing this force into his painting, using it entirely for that end. That is why, in contrast to most naïve works, his figures have weight and volume, his landscapes shape and depth. He has rediscovered the skill and distant vistas of the primitives.

**BONHOMME** Léon. French painter born in Paris in 1870, died at Saint-Denis in 1924. During the bombardment of Paris in 1870 and the Commune, Bonhomme's mother reared her infant in a cellar, while Prussian shells rained on the city. The boy who was to become the outstanding depicter of prostitute life was brought up in a working class atmosphere. He lacked Lautrec's delicacy in portraying brothel scenes, but his painting has a pathos that no other painter of the underworld has succeeded in bringing out, for he knew how to create beings addicted to debauchery, and his female animals inspire both terror and pity. His women's faces gleam like black diamonds, streaked with blood that clots in the veins. He uses remarkable blues and reds to produce these faces. He is a painter of the night and its denizens, whose sombre poetry is reminiscent of Baudelaire. Under Gustave Moreau he was a fellow-pupil of Matisse and Georges Rouault (to whom he has often been inaccurately compared). The formidable blue, black and red souvenirs that Bonhomme brings back with him from the underworld are entirely original. He died without having known the success that his work, with its exceptional violence of tone and expression, so fully deserved.

**BONNARD** Pierre. French painter born at Fontenay-aux-Roses in 1867; died at Le Cannet, 1947. About 1891 Bonnard and his friends, who called themselves the Nabis *(\*)*, and whom the critics named the Symbolists or the Revue Blanche *(\*)* painters, exhibited their work for the first time at the Salon des Indépendants and in the small gallery of Le Barc de Boutteville. Maurice Denis was only twenty-three, Vuillard, Roussel and Bonnard were almost twenty-five, and Lautrec was three years their senior. Tall, thin, bony and withdrawn, Bonnard used to baffle people at first. He seemed to hold himself aloof from everyone and be perpetually on the defensive, even to a point of actual mistrust. Still uncertain of himself, he was first attracted by the applied arts: furniture, fans, screens, ceramics, theatre décors. In 1891 a coloured poster (*France-Champagne*) was the first to display in Paris the initials and energy of this painter, who readily accepted any kind of work that came his way. There was already a mixture of playfulness, humour and tenderness in his

BONNARD. BOULEVARD DES BATIGNOLLES.
*Private Collection, Paris*

pictures, his first lithographs, and his sculptures. With boldness and precision, yet with the eyes of a Romantic, he explored the unknown around him, transforming everything he looked at: gardens and flower-filled rooms, the sea, the breakfast table, the boulevards, women, children, dogs. Of an extremely retiring nature, he went to live at Le Cannet, a village above Cannes, in a little villa with bare, white wooden furniture. This tiny studio, like the place he bought at Vernon in the Eure, and called 'The Trailer', testified to his profound disinterest in material comfort. He never showed his pictures in a frame to enhance their value. Water-colours, sketches, all done on any piece of paper that happened to come to hand, were carelessly tied up with string, or lay about in the dust of his studio. Humble in his methods but uncompromising

BONNARD. NUDE AT THE FIREPLACE. 1917.
*Musée de l'Annonciade, Saint-Tropez*

strong, Bonnard should be reproached for his lack of construction and the sketchiness of his drawing. His critics did not realize that the strength and freedom of his artistic response allowed him to carry off even the most complicated of problems. He was not a theoretician, and it was by the most contradictory – often the most paradoxical – routes that this modest explorer succeeded in fulfilling the missions he set himself. The constant transposition of line as well as of colour, the gift of forgetting the local tone of objects as well as the usual way of treating them, the art of considering the picture a closed universe with its own private needs – that is what is so deeply moving and charming in these miracles of invention, where fantasy becomes more true than reality. The originality and courage of this painter, who was so frail and cautious in appearance, is shown by the sense of mystery he extracts from everyday scenes. Bonnard always reminds one of a sleeper startled

in character, incapable of any concession to vanity or to money, preserving to the last his original shyness and diffidence, his ardour and his animal vitality, he always started from his own version of truth, rebelling against fashions and theories. Superficially there might be a certain similarity between some of his landscapes and still lifes, and certain creations of the great Impressionists (particularly Claude Monet), arising out of the way he deliberately forgot realities when he began to paint. But Bonnard's method of procedure was actually quite different. Suffering, like his friends Vuillard and Roussel, from the inadequacies of a technique which they were obliged to reinvent, working simultaneously on a number of different pictures, he was eternally making changes in them, sometimes for years, before he was satisfied. He would even go to retouch his canvases in the museums, much to the astonishment of the guards.

It was natural that, between the two wars, when reaction against Impressionism was so

BONNARD. WOMAN WITH UMBRELLA. 1895.
*Lithograph*

out of his sleep, who no longer knows either the name or the weight of things, nor even the proportions of his own room. In Bonnard, however, this is never the effect of systematic or deliberate confusion. Delivered from the tyrannies of perspective and lighting, Nature becomes fairylike. Where we think we should encounter a solid, there is only transparency; where we expect shade, there is only light: every assumption is foiled by a great creative vision and an intuition which reconstructs the universe. With the marvellous simplicity of a poet, he amuses himself, and wonders, and is moved by everything and nothing. Referring to one of

BONNARD. BEACH AT LOW TIDE. 1932.
*Musée d'Art Moderne, Paris*

his *Bouquets*, he confided to a critic who was interviewing him: 'The presence of the object, the motif, is disturbing to a painter. An idea being the starting-point of a picture, there is danger that he will allow himself to be influenced by the immediate, direct view of its details, if the object is there while he works. Through the sway his original idea holds over him, the painter attains the universal. If this idea fades, there remains only the motif, the object, which overcomes the painter. From that moment he is no longer painting his own picture.' He also said: 'Defects are what give life to a picture'.

There is no abrupt break, no inconsistency in his work, from the first small panels inspired by Paris and its suburbs – washerwomen, children, errand boys and dogs, painted on pasteboard with a cold palette of velvety black and Watteau-like greys and whites – to the compositions of the latter part of his life: luminous bathers, fabulous animals and people, still lifes saturated in colour, landscapes in which skies are of an opaque black, shadows of translucent gold, and rose-coloured meadows. Sometimes we see a glossy interior, shimmering with colour, contrasting its clarity and transparency with the

resistant opaqueness of a landscape, an inert block framed by a window. There, nude bodies appear so integrated with the room that it is difficult to say whether they colour the surrounding space or take their existence from it. The pearly flesh of a thigh seems to be composed of the same substance as the furniture against which it stands out miraculously; but at the same time the back of this bathing woman, like an idol, seems part of the golden atmosphere of the room. Certain torsos, the focal point of so many reflections, seem to be marked with azure scars and pink stigmata. Some fruit baskets carry miraculous shadows. No one has ever made such a poetic fairy tale out of the most ordinary objects of our daily lives. At seventy-five, as at twenty, before woman – such a little girl in spite of the fullness of her body! – he shows the same trembling, the same love for that most mysterious of fruits, that incomprehensible and complementary being; and he feels the same sense of wonder before a dog, a child, or the sky.

Whether it be a picture, a print, a poster, an illustration, a statuette – and all these activities were complementary – Bonnard was never hampered by scene or action. He never lapsed into artificiality, sham antiquity or conventionalism if he tried to create a Greek atmosphere, and he avoided what might become outdated when he depicted the present. For he knew that the same events keep on repeating themselves under changing skies, that life will always have the same charm and the same limitations, that desire always follows the same course. No matter what he undertook, he questioned everything, re-invented the theme as well as the means of executing it, and right to the end of his life he devoted his seriousness and his experience to exploiting the most marvellous of his gifts – his youthfulness.

**BORÈS** Francisco. Spanish painter born in Madrid in 1898. He began to paint at the age of seventeen in a private academy and spent long periods copying pictures in the Prado Museum. In 1922 he joined the Ultraists, a literary and artistic *avant-garde* group. In 1925 he exhibited for the first time: twenty canvases at the Salon of Iberian Artists. A few months later he went to Paris, where he has lived ever

since. At first he was close to the young painters who made a cult of Juan Gris, and, following the latter's example, started from a plastic synthesis to find reality. But Borès by nature reacted against the rigidity of the Cubist conceptions; he refused to consider the object in itself; he feared the stagnation of forms. He broke with the geometrical spirit, and the idea of formal construction. Interested in expressing the dynamism of objects, he tried to place them in space again and evoke the surroundings that they seem to need – which led him to the practice of allusion and ellipses. Already at the time of his first exhibition at the Galerie Percier in June 1927, his work was a selection of symbols and a delicate and subtle balance of colours. From 1929 on Borès, who was interested by the Surrealist experiment, although he remained outside the movement, began to work nearer to Nature and found again a close affinity between plastic creation and the visual sensation it expressed. His scope widened. People, objects and back-grounds crowd the canvas to evoke a café terrace or a Sunday afternoon; they are some-times treated with humour, or burlesqued, but

BORÈS. THE PAINTER'S TABLE. 1937. *Private Collection, Paris*

BOUDIN. CRINOLINES ON THE BEACH AT TROUVILLE. 1869. *Private Collection, Paris*

always with the same economy of means, the same discreet detachment. They are based on reality, but they give evidence of unexpected syntheses, where imagination plays as big a role as memory. Various exhibitions in France, London and America mark this turbulent period. But very soon his work evolved towards a return to pure painting. More recently he has undertaken pictures which are more and more concentrated, based on the subtle play of inner relations and the skilful harmonies of minor tones. His themes are deliberately limited to simple and familiar objects, but his still lifes, in the successive stages of their chromatic variations, are strangely alive.

**BOUDIN** Eugène. French painter born in Honfleur in 1824; died in Deauville, 1898. Two-thirds of a picture taken up with sky, the other third with the sea and a tiny fringe of sand scintillating with the fresh colours of women in crinoline – that is what the name of Boudin conjures up. But this is an unjust definition of a body of work that derives its unity from the way in which the subjects are treated, rather than from the subjects themselves. In fact, whether it be on the shores of the Channel or in Brittany or Holland, or in Brussels, Bordeaux or Venice, Boudin always looks at Nature with the

tender solicitude of a lover of light. He did not paint landscapes or figures so much as the way in which they received this light, and lived on it. He did not represent volumes, but caught reflections. No more need be said to make it understood that he was one of the most obvious precursors of Impressionism (*vide* plate, page 125). Boudin, however, was not trying to do anything revolutionary when he painted those cloudy skies iridescent with an infinite variety of greys; he exhibited very properly at the official salon, where he won the Gold Medal in 1889, at the time of the Exposition Universelle, and the Legion of Honour in 1892. Success had come at last, to reward him for years of patient work; but, despite this official recognition that came to him so late, he thought that his young Impressionist friends (who actually owed much to him) were infinitely greater than he was. For he was as modest and quiet as his painting. However, Corot said to him 'You are the king of skies', and Courbet: 'You are a seraph; you alone know the sky'. This confirmed what Baudelaire said when he wrote that one can guess the season, the hour and the wind from Boudin's studies. This concern for exactness, which matters less to us today, was not unimportant in the eyes of artists at that time. Boudin never dreamed of denying the importance of the subject. 'Peasants', he wrote, 'hold an attraction for some painters . . . but, between ourselves, have not these bourgeois who stroll along the jetty towards the setting sun the right to be put on canvas, to be led towards the light?' But Eugène Boudin did not deceive himself as much as might appear from that confession of faith, for he wrote elsewhere, referring to the same people: 'One feels a certain shame in painting this complete idleness. Happily, the Creator has shed a little of his splendid and warming light everywhere, and we do not reproduce the world so much as the element which envelops it.' These two quotations are contradictory, but there is one word that figures in both – light. And that is what dominates all Boudin's work; that is how he understood the lesson of Jongkind, and proclaimed the necessity of painting in light colours and raised the curtain on Impressionism. Boudin also painted still lifes, landscapes and even a few portraits. But he constantly came back to the seaside beneath vast expanses of sky, less to satisfy a clientèle that admired him as a 'seascape painter' than to satisfy his own longings, and doubtless because he found there what we find when we look at every one of his canvases – a sense of relaxation and peaceful expansiveness, a sweet intoxication. For in his works Nature is alive but not troubled. The vision is clear but not static, and everything is said in it without anything being affirmed brutally.

BOUSSINGAULT. LITHOGRAPH
FOR L.-P. FARGUE'S 'D'APRÈS PARIS'.

**BOUSSINGAULT** Jean-Louis. French painter born in Paris in 1883; died there, 1943. He was the grandson of a famous scientist. He was a friend of Dunoyer de Segonzac, with whom he did military service in 1903, and whose studio he shared, and also of Luc-Albert Moreau at the Académie Julian. While still a young man, Boussingault, who first exhibited in 1909 at the Salon des Indépendants (*Nude Woman in a Tall Hat*), was commissioned by the couturier Paul Poiret to do a vast decoration crowded with Amazons, mannequins, swings and fabulous staircases. He was hailed as a new Constantin Guys. With a kind of suppressed humour and fundamental bluntness, this frequenter of race-courses and big bars, who had the bony features and colouring of an El Greco,

took hold of the fragile present. Few pictures are as characteristic as his of the rhythms and the pleasures peculiar to the period of the *Ballets Russes (\*)* and Poiret and the years that followed the 1914–1918 war, in which he was wounded. His faces, particularly in his lithographs and engravings, are essentially Parisian, like his landscapes (*The Champs-Élysées*), where intertwined couples and statues which seem to be made of flesh stand out clearly against the curtains of the night. Death came to the painter in the middle of his evolution. His palette, dark at first, grew richer from day to day without losing the style that characterizes all his work. The still lifes and portraits, and the decorations that he executed, particularly for the Théâtre de Chaillot in 1937, show the same sensitivity and subtlety as his drawings, his water-colours, and his illustrations for Baudelaire's *Le Spleen de Paris* and Léon-Paul Fargue's *D'Après Paris*. It is his etchings and lithographs that best demonstrate the brilliancy and sureness of his work, and make him one of the most original engravers of the twentieth century.

**BRAQUE** Georges. French painter born in Argenteuil in 1882. His father was a house-painting contractor and amateur artist. Braque was eight years old when the family left the Paris region to settle in Le Havre. He became a pupil at the École des Beaux-Arts there in 1899, and also worked in his father's business. He came to Paris in 1900 and settled in Montmartre in a small, uncomfortable room, where he drew and painted with fervour. In 1902 he spent a short while in Bonnat's studio at the École Nationale des Beaux-Arts, and then went to study at the Académie Humbert. He spent the summer of 1904 near Honfleur, returned to Paris, rented a studio – his first – and soon joined the Fauvist movement, as a result, no doubt, of his friendship with Othon Friesz, also from Havre. The two young artists travelled together to Antwerp in 1906, and to La Ciotat in 1907. He went three times to paint at l'Estaque near Marseilles, one of Cézanne's favourite spots. He was profoundly influenced by Cézanne in 1908. Soon moving on from Cézanne, he found himself at the head of the Cubist movement, alongside Picasso. It was in reference to Braque that Louis Vauxcelles, the art critic, made his jibe about painting in 'little cubes' in a review of the 1908 Salon d'Automne. Braque's first private exhibition took place in November of that year, sponsored by Apollinaire. In some of the canvases exhibited the artist introduced for the first time in contemporary painting the musical-instrument theme. Although his stay with the *Fauves* was only transitory – only thirty works are known –

he gave Fauvism an interesting side. Closer to Friesz, Derain and Vlaminck than to Matisse, he disapproved, nevertheless, of their careless workmanship, their orgy of colours, and the violence of their line. With his well-balanced temperament, he did not abuse the freedom that went to the heads of most of the *Fauves*. Although he used the most intense colours – reds, blues, greens and orange – and placed them in little squares or sticks, like Vlaminck or Derain, he

BRAQUE. THE HARBOUR.                 *Musée d'Art Moderne, Paris*

did it with more circumspection and elegance. He preferred to paint landscapes where outlines, contours and brush-strokes are used not so much to produce a brutal, decorative effect as a sense of balance and construction. He was a *Fauve* who thought, who worked with method, who guarded against excess; a *Fauve* who looked to Cézanne rather than to Van Gogh. In his Fauvism there was the impatience of the heretic. At this period he even executed several works in a single colour, which foreshadowed the monochromatic compositions of the years 1910–1911. His manner of painting soon betrayed intellectual needs foreign to his friends. At l'Estaque, in 1907,

BRAQUE. THE GUITARIST. 1914.

of the greatest artistic revolution since Paolo Uccello. The new aesthetic doctrine was born from the collaboration of these two opposite natures. One brought to it the intuition of the Spaniard, the concepts of the architect, the other the qualities of observation, analysis and *savoir-faire* of the French artisan.

In a manner peculiar to him in which deduction and flexible sensibility share equally, Braque has developed Cézanne's teachings with a calm coldness. He looks at Nature, dissects it and reorganizes it according to an order much less abstract than lyrical. His famous saying 'I like the rule which corrects the emotion' conveys his hostility toward excess, his innate sense of order and discipline, his taste, his prudence, his simplicity, without which Cubism might well have been a short-lived affair. Cubism made a clean sweep of all the former data of vision, and gave painting its old autonomy: a picture became a work of architecture, and an object, something more real than reality itself. In this courageous enterprise Braque played a predominant role. He, more than any other Cubist – and perhaps he alone – brought to it an indomitable sense of the concrete, a keen sense of analysis, rare tonal harmonies, and a particular elegance of line – straight or curved. If Picasso showed himself particularly interested in volume, Braque knew better than anyone else how to create a plastic space and give the illusion of a new depth. On the whole, his painting of that period is distinguished by its unity, its coherence, the sobriety and, at the same time, precious beauty of its tones: blacks, greys, beiges, greens, whites, which, despite their lack of brilliance, have a mysterious vibrancy. Under these colours, ordinarily considered the most dull and lustreless, it seems as though a fire burns discreetly, slowly, without ever consuming itself. He loves precision, harmony, modulation and the subtle play of values. He detests roughness, violent contrasts, the tyranny of a method or a system, and the random outpourings of lyricism. He prefers analysis to synthesis, deduction to intuition, the decomposition of forms to their reduction or schematization. That is why Braque dominated the first phase of the movement, and it is undoubtedly to him that Cubism is indebted

he painted landscapes strangely influenced by Cézanne, in which, along with the curves and intense colours, one can already see straight and angular lines, geometrical structures, a more subtle blending of his colours and a lighter touch. He was ushering in the Cubist movement at the time when Picasso, too, was taking a new road with his *Demoiselles d'Avignon*. Braque, however, did not disavow the conquests of Fauvism, which saved him from the austerity and dryness which Picasso has not always been able to avoid. To this influence he owes the captivating complexity and fragrant distinction of his work both then and since.

Thus we see Braque, together with Picasso, raising the insurgent flag of Cubism (*) in 1908, before a scandalized public – the heralds for its analytical character. At first he applied his research to the human figure, then to still life. He imagined a new space; he found new forms based on a more complete, almost stereoscopic, vision of the reality around us. The combination of lines and angles, the overlapping of multiple planes, the setting out of the various parts of the object and their simultaneous projection on the surface of the picture, constitute the essential means of a method which sacrificed all previous conventions for purely plastic values. Towards 1911 Braque's art relaxed its ties with the real and became more abstract, less subject to the variable, less constructed. The subject was eliminated. It was no longer necessary to represent the object in its totality through the complex play of lines and the superimposing of planes, but to consider it as a pure sign. The works of this hermetic period suggest nothing but strictly pictorial sensations, and the picture, no longer referring to a fragment of Nature, appears as an absolute creation, a reality conceived or imagined *a priori*, a reality which is sufficient in itself, and an end in itself. It was during that same year that Braque introduced, for the first time (in one of his compositions, *The Portuguese*), an inscription in typographical letters. From then on the letters of the alphabet became a plastic element for all the Cubists. This innovation answered a need in Braque. He had already begun to feel the dangers of an art entirely cut off from the

BRAQUE. ARIA OF BACH. 1914.
*Private Collection, Paris*

visible world, of a dialectic which might reduce painting to mere decoration. And so the letter came into his work as a reminder from the world of appearances. After the letter, the imitation wood, the imitation marble, the *trompe-l'œil* works (that Braque had seen painted as a child and had himself painted in his father's workroom) were incorporated in the picture: concrete elements opposed to the poetry of pure forms. In 1910 Braque had already painted, at the top of one of his pictures, a nail which looked like a real nail and from which the picture seemed to hang. The Press openly made fun of it, but the idea was soon taken up by the other Cubists. They no longer confined themselves to imitating a nail

BRAQUE. BOATS ON THE BEACH. 1926.     *Private Collection, Paris*

BRAQUE. STILL LIFE. 1929.         *Private Collection*

for bravery. Wounded in 1915, he spent long months convalescing. When he began to, paint again in 1917 he was disconcerted by the works of Picasso and his followers. From then on he was to follow the course of his own destiny. Though he still remained friendly with Picasso, he no longer worked with him. He began to turn to a relaxed and more tranquil art, closer to reality, and characterized by a less angular design and heightened colours. Though his *Guitarist* (1917) is still Cubist, his still lifes, his landscapes and his nudes are now done in another spirit, with a freer and more supple handling. Light, so long neglected by him, claimed his attention more and more every day. His craftsmanship gained in ease and grace, though he used his talents with even stricter economy. Between 1919 and 1930 Braque seemed to be well on the way to joining the painters of the French tradition. His classicism was more evident, his audacities tempered by the well-balanced judgement which has always made us forget his virtuosity. More respectful of the subject than before, he sought to translate the freshness of his inspiration into more stable forms, set out in a *new* space.

or the grain of wood or marble; in the middle of the composition they fixed on the canvas fragments of various materials, generally paper. Thus, the technique of *papier collés (*)* developed, initiated by Braque. The artist would fix these bits of figured or decorative paper on a sheet and then trace around them, or over them, lines in pencil or ink, with touches of gouache or oil. Mixed in this way with subjectively created elements, these different substances acquired a convincing plastic and human value, entirely unexpected. Cubism now entered its synthetic period (1912–1913). The lines became less complex, the planes broadened, and the small, delicate brush-strokes more flattened. The partitioning of the composition disappeared; even colour lost its austerity. Braque defined his intentions very clearly in his *papiers collés*: *Fruit Bowl* (1912), *Woman with Guitar* (1913), *Aria de Bach*. This form of art was carried a step farther when Braque started using, on his canvases, bits of cloth or wood, which at once lost their inert and prosaic reality, to live the same poetic life as the work of art.

Up to 1914 Braque and Picasso were inseparable. In 1911 they were seen together at Céret, in the Eastern Pyrenees, and at Sorgues, near Avignon, in 1912. When war was declared, Braque was sent to the front. He was commended

And then, towards 1930, his style changed again: line became dynamic, the arabesques more enveloping, the relief softer and (perhaps through the influence of Matisse) the palette brighter, while his drawing grew more expressive (through the influence of Picasso), notably in the 1931 *Beach* series. The four or five years that followed were probably the most fertile of his career; not the most prolific, but those in which he mustered all the resources and conquests of his genius into a supremely balanced whole. Never before or since has Braque attained such harmony between inspiration and technique, intellect and sensibility, richness of expression and inner humility. He made an inventory of his acquisitions, and knew exactly where he, personally, belonged. From his Cubist past he retained principally the simultaneity of vision, the development of objects on the same plane, the inversion of space. These he used with a freedom derived from experience, giving up geometrical figures, thin colours, static constructions, and artificial disintegrations. 'I saw', he said in 1935, 'that I had taken the reflections of the world in several mirrors for the world itself.' And he applied himself to grasping the real world in all its vibrancy and fullness. He transcribed objects in cross-section and elevation; he multiplied the angles of vision; he rounded forms, displaced their axis, and modified their contours in such a way as to give the impression that they were bending. They would have tottered were it not for the mastery of the artist, who consolidated them by combining their proportions. Likewise, it was through the combination of tones that he found the most exquisite harmonies. He used the most common, the hardest and least attractive colours; yet as soon as he laid them on the canvas, white ceased to be mute, sienna was no longer dreary, black became luminous, and violet transparent. Feline elegance of line, and precision of colour; fullness, and yet lightness, of composition; knowledge that hides itself modestly behind ease of manner; an iron will that veils itself with nonchalance; boldness full of cautiousness; cold lucidity, yet so much emotion – such are the complex ingredients that consciously go into the making of a work by this man, who seems to revel in doing things the hard way.

During this period of expansion Braque produced his most concentrated and vivid still lifes, his cliffs, his grounded boats, his two-faced figures. He also executed limestone sculptures, fish and horses in bronze or lead, coloured reliefs in plaster . . . a happy and fertile period in which all the artist's faculties were miraculously attuned, each contributing in equal measure to the elaboration of his work. But since 1940 he has not always been able to avoid certain pitfalls: sometimes gracefulness gives way to mannerism, delicacy to preciosity, and his sureness of hand to virtuosity. Even a tendency towards Realism has manifested itself in his latest work. Style seems to have more nuances, to be more flowing, more lazy, as if it had abandoned itself to a desire to charm rather than astonish. Nevertheless, Braque has never for a moment betrayed the lofty consciousness that he has of his mission, expressed with such persuasive force in his *Cahiers*, written from 1917 to 1952. And in his blameless life, as well as in his exemplary work, he has never at any time lost sight of the fact that, though an artist, he is also a man.

**BRETON** André. French poet born at Tinchebray, Orne, in 1896. 'To me a picture is a window that looks out on something; the question is – on what?' said Breton. Only an ardent, ascetic temperament like Breton's could organize and order a tendency capable of transcending art by denying it the power to give pleasure. Breton is primarily a poet, and once again (after Hugo, Baudelaire and Apollinaire),

BRAQUE. ENGRAVED PLASTER. 1948.

BRAQUE. IVY.

Miró of having collaborated with the *Ballets Russes (\*)*, or when he censured Salvador Dali for his 'deviationism' and made the famous anagram 'Avida Dollars' out of Dali's name. The severity with which (in his writings, from *Surrealism and Painting*, 1928, to *Birth and Prospects of Surrealism*, 1941) he demanded of artists that they hew to a 'straight line' both in their work and in their way of life, shows how highly he prizes the search for an expression that will be, above all, the reflection of the most secret aspirations of the subconscious in all its primitive creative force. Unlike Dada, Breton, in his unwearying search for the supernatural, did not disdain to resort to traditional data, as when he evoked the fabulous side of certain mythologies, or the monstrous divinities of antiquity or Negro art, making use of all their spells, miracles and enchantments. Then, painters like Giovanni di Paolo, Leonardo da Vinci, Hieronymus Bosch, Blake, Goya, Fuseli and – to come closer to our

with Surrealism. *(\*)*, the role of widening the field of knowledge has fallen to a poet. Breton began with Dada *(\*)*, that is to say, a cult of the irrational and an anarchical desire to destroy, and to undermine the conformism of logical, moral or artistic values. Out of Dada grew Surrealism. The Surrealists' desire to reach back to the very beginning of expression and know 'what is being contrived in the depths of man's mind, unknown to him' led them, under Breton's leadership, to study dreams and to seek in the drawings of children or the art of madmen the irrefutable evidence of that primordial spontaneity which they valued above all else. But Breton did not content himself with destroying; he reconstructed. The 'Pope of Surrealism', as he has been called, required of his followers a constant fight against artistic amorality, especially against attempts that could lead them to betray, to a greater or lesser degree, the supernatural faculties he recognized in them. This uncompromising attitude could be seen when he reproached Chirico for his abdication and renunciations; when he accused Max Ernst and

PICASSO. PORTRAIT OF ANDRÉ BRETON.

own time – Redon, Chagall, Picasso and others, are considered to be, in varying degrees, precursors of Irrationalism.

In exalting the role of the subconscious, Breton proposed to the painter the discovery of an element with unsuspected resources and shock power, an element which, wherever it is given free rein, is capable of abolishing space and time. For only by starting from this abolition can one perceive, simultaneously, such contradictory notions as life and death, the past and the future, the real and the imaginary; and that, he felt, was what counted the most.

BRIANCHON. THE LIBERATION.                                    1944.

**BRIANCHON** Maurice. French painter born at Fresnaye in the Sarthe in 1899. Brianchon's career has followed a straight, unswerving course without any inconsistencies: pupil at the École des Arts Décoratifs in 1915, winner of the Prix Blumenthal in 1924, teacher at the École Nationale des Beaux-Arts since 1937. There could hardly be place for daring adventures in such a life. Although he has not put forward any new theories, nor noisily associated himself with any of those elaborated in his youth, one cannot help feeling that he is complete master of himself and fully aware of what he wants to do. His work is not provocative, nor does it seek to surprise. Amidst the clamour and turbulence of the most vehement professions of faith, Brianchon plays soft music full of discreet harmonies, in which even discords lose their bite. Sometimes he carries this discretion to extremes, with a very reduced palette: a scene in grey and green only; a landscape in grey and white, with some red and yellow to give value to the complexity of the grey or green nuances. Sometimes he does not hesitate to offer more violent contrasts: resonant reds splashed against

large black surfaces. But even there he knows how to avoid extreme violence, through his refinement and astonishing sense of balance. Theatre scenes, still lifes, portraits, compositions, form an ensemble varied in subject but with a common technique: mat painting that does not seek easy effects through the materials used or through flashy brushwork that catches the eye here and there. However, the materials and the brushwork do play an important part in Brianchon's art. No surface is completely flat or inert, no colour smooth. Everything vibrates. This art, which gives one the feeling of intimacy when a picture is hung in a room, can also adapt itself to large areas. The tapestries made from his sketches have the majesty of the great seventeenth-century wall-hangings. There, again, Brianchon is free of the fashions of our times which, in the revival of the art of tapestry, offer him a new imagery with vivid colouring, reduced to a very simple design. There is no doubt that to understand Brianchon's art well, one must bear in mind that he worked on theatre décors in his youth. Is that where he learnt the merits of mat painting? Brianchon's art is calm, but it is also without constraint: that calm is not one of indifference; there is a human quality in even the slightest of his works.

**BRÜCKE** (Die) (The Bridge). A federation of artists founded in 1905 by Fritz Bleyl and a group of pupils of the Dresden Technical School – Ernst Ludwig Kirchner, Erich Heckel and Karl Schmidt-Rottluff. One of the aims of the *Brücke* was to attract to itself all the revolutionary elements of the period. Thus, in 1906, Emil Nolde and the Swiss Cuno Amiet (an old friend of Gauguin at Pont-Aven), who used to exhibit at the Arnold Gallery in Dresden, were invited to join the movement. Max Pechstein and the Finn Axel Gallén joined the same year. In 1908 Kees Van Dongen, who at the time enjoyed a prominent position in Paris, was approached, and expressed his sympathy with the cause. From 1905 on, regular exhibitions were held, and meetings took place in Kirchner's studio, a converted shop in the Berlinerstrasse, which he had adorned with frescoes, wood sculptures, and furniture made out of packing-cases, and where members worked together from the same models. The last painter to join was Otto Müller, who was admitted in 1910, a few months before the group moved to Berlin. But rifts had already begun to appear. Nolde left in 1907, Bleyl in 1909. Pechstein was expelled in 1912. The *Brücke* was officially dissolved in 1913 (*vide* Heckel, Kirchner, Nolde, Schmidt-Rottluff). This movement – from which one can date the beginning of modern art in Germany – represented, for that country, the more or less contemporary equivalent of French Fauvism, from which it drew its main inspiration (Van Dongen was the significant link), but with an expressionist and social emphasis characteristic of the Nordic anguish. All these artists were restless creatures, over-sensitive, haunted by religious, sexual, political or moral obsessions. Dramatic landscapes and nudes, mystical and visionary compositions, scenes of the countryside, the streets, the circus, the cafés-dansants and the demimonde were their principal themes. Their pure colours blaze in acid stridency, encompassed by rough, dry contours which show the influence of Negro art and primitive woodcuts. The first style of the *Brücke* group is characterized by a strong similarity of technique, made even stronger by their working together, that runs through all the different media: painting, sculpture and wood-engraving, posters, fabric-printing, and so on. After the transfer to Berlin of the already divided group, individual styles became more pronounced. In the nervous atmosphere of the big city, Heckel and Kirchner began to evolve in the direction of an expressionism intensified by sharp, broken forms and dissonant and darkened colours. On the eve of the First World War the group dispersed, each one setting out on his own artistic way.

# C

**CABARET VOLTAIRE** The Dada *(\*)* group, founded by the Alsatian Hans Arp, the Rumanian Tristan Tzara, and the Germans Hugo Ball and Richard Hülsenbeck, first came into the public eye when, on the 8th of February, 1916, it opened an arts club in Zurich, called the Cabaret Voltaire, with a theatre stage and an exhibition and lecture hall. On March 30th Dada inaugurated the series of entertainments that so shocked the public. In the words of the Surrealist poet Georges Hugnet: 'On the stage someone thumped keys and bottles to make music until the audience, nearly crazy, protested. Serner, instead of reciting poems, laid a bouquet at the foot of a dressmaker's dummy. A voice from beneath an enormous hat shaped like a sugar-loaf declaimed Arp's poems. Hülsenbeck bellowed his poems, while Tzara emphasized the rhythms and crescendos by banging on a bass drum.'

A slim volume entitled *Cabaret Voltaire*, to which Apollinaire, Cendrars, Marinetti, Tzara and others contributed, was published in June of that year. A performance, which degenerated into a brawl, was put on in the Kaufleute Halle in 1919, before an audience of 1,500. About that time the Dada movement developed in Berlin, Cologne, Hanover and, finally, Paris.

**CAFÉ GUERBOIS** Situated in Montmartre, at No. 9 Avenue de Clichy, the Café Guerbois (today the Brasserie Müller) was the meeting-place of an artistic circle which, as early as 1866 (but especially during 1868 and 1869), was frequented every Friday by Manet and the writers and art critics Zola, Duranty, Théodore Duret; the painters Bazille, Degas, Renoir, Pissarro, Monet, Sisley, Guys, Stevens; the sculptor Zacharie Astruc, the engraver Bracquemond, and the photographer Nadar. The first principles of the Impressionist movement were laid down there. Inspired by the lengthy discussions that took place there, Zola enthusiastically launched his crusade for the movement, which he was soon to disavow. After the Franco-Prussian war these gatherings were resumed. Manet was always the central figure. It was there that Clémenceau met Monet. They were to remain lifelong friends. About 1876 the group began holding its sessions at the Nouvelle Athènes *(\*)*, also in Montmartre.

**CAILLEBOTTE** Gustave (1848–1894). Originally a Realist painter, Caillebotte became a disciple of the Impressionists and one of their few patrons. He took part in the second (1876) Impressionist exhibition and in those of 1877, 1879, 1880 and 1882. Caillebotte's touch had a delicacy which brought him some success along with a certain amount of hostile criticism. One critic of the period accused him of having, in a picture called *Rainy Weather*, depicted anything but rain; likewise, in *Pont de l'Europe*, nothing stands out but a little dog trotting along, he claimed. Through his generosity Caillebotte made many friends. He acted as buffer between the Impressionists and those around them, and he was helpful in straightening out the difficulties raised by Degas at the time of the exhibitions. When Caillebotte died, Renoir was named executor under the terms of his will. On the recommendation of the Institut de France, the Government rejected Caillebotte's donation of his collection (65 works) to the Musée du Luxembourg. As a result of protests in the Press and of the intervention of Clemenceau, the museum advisory committee finally yielded. However, they remained adamant in refusing 28 of the 65 pictures: one Manet, three Cézannes, eight Monets, two Renoirs, three Sisleys and

43

eleven Pissarros. It is all the harder to understand this official opposition when one realizes that Caillebotte's donation included such master-pieces as *Le Moulin de la Galette* and *The Swing* by Renoir, Sisley's *Regatta Near London*, and Pissarro's *Red Roofs*. It was not until 1928 that these paintings were officially accepted by the Louvre.

**CAMOIN** Charles. French painter, born in Marseilles in 1879. His father, a decorator, encouraged him to paint and sent him to Paris in 1896. Camoin studied under Gustave Moreau at the École Nationale des Beaux-Arts, together with Marquet. The two of them spent a good deal of time in the Louvre, and sketched scenes from life in the streets and the music halls. From 1899 to 1902 he did military service in Arles, then Avignon, and finally Aix-en-Provence, where he visited Cézanne, with whom he kept up a correspond-ence from then onwards. After exhibiting at the Salon des Indépendants in 1903, he was a regular exhibitor at the Salon d'Automne until 1908. He took part in the Salon d'Automne of 1905, the year Fauvism was officially born. In 1912–1913 he went with Matisse and Marquet to Morocco. During the war, when he was serving in the camouflage section, he met Renoir, who made a deep impression on him. Renoir's in-fluence, together with that of Bonnard, is notice-able in his post-war work. Camoin can be con-sidered a *Fauve*, in so far as it became customary to include as *Fauves* (together with the great creators of the movement) a number of painters of the same generation who, in the early part of the century, evinced the same taste for striking colours. Their youthful enthusiasm prompted them to follow in the tracks of Matisse or Derain, but their quieter nature kept them within more restrained limits. Camoin is one of those painters for whom Fauvism was not a repudia-tion of Impression but its culmination; his sen-sibility places him in this tradition, rather than among the revolutionaries. Nevertheless, a certain predilection for light colours, and fre-quent visits to the South of France, explain his place in Fauvism *(\*)*. His nudes, interiors, and

CAMOIN. SEATED WOMAN. 1910.
*Museum of Modern Art, New York*

Mediterranean landscapes – his favourite themes – show his even temperament, which, through-out the countless distractions of contemporary art, has managed to preserve a note of poetic freshness and a pleasing tranquillity.

**CAMPIGLI** Massimo. Italian painter, born in Florence in 1895. Campigli began to paint in Paris, working according to the plastic laws set out in Ozenfant and Jeanneret's review, *L'Esprit Nouveau (\*)*. 'In the manner of a bee,' writes Jean Paulhan, 'Campigli begins by enclosing his characters in their cells.' Certainly like a bee, also like the Cubists, although his work is more reminiscent of Etruscan and Roman painting than of Braque and Picasso. He is not insensitive, either, to metaphysical painting, and his figures have 'faces of a magical truth, as exact as anthropometric record cards, as impersonal as death masks'. His busts shaped like money-boxes, and his women shaped like amphoras, have a universal quality, as old as the earth. They are entirely different from Chirico's mannequins, whose oval skulls are full of tragic humanity, whereas Campigli's heads are empty. His women, however, have the same pleasing grace as Seurat's promenaders; their waists are extremely slender, and their arms stand out from their sides like the handles of a vase. He borrowed the anatomy of his figures from the world of childhood. At a time when the painters of his generation are constantly in search of youth, or the illusion of it, Campigli stays faithful to himself, to the poetic, painted world of his dreams.

**CARRÀ** Carlo. Italian painter, born at Quargnento in 1881. Carrà was one of the signers of the Futurist Manifesto (*vide* Futurism). He borrowed from Cubism its structure and monochromes, and tried, at the same time, to insert into its austere construction the crowd movements so dear to Futurist dynamism. He introduced whole words into his compositions. (The Cubists were content with a few letters.) The words do not merely have a lyrical quality; they exercise a sort of plastic magic. When, in 1916, Carrà made the acquaintance of Giorgio de Chirico, the originator of Metaphysical Painting

CAMPIGLI. ON THE BALCONY. 1953

(*), he believed he had at last found his true vocation: to rediscover the magic of painting by means of the representation of the most simple objects. He wrote: 'It is the most ordinary objects that fill the soul with grace. The artist who scorns them inevitably becomes absurd. On the artistic plane, as well as on the intellectual, his work is of no account. Ordinary things have that simplicity which is the very secret of the most sumptuous art.' When reproached for ceasing to paint that feverish life that he had exalted in his Futurist days, he replied: 'I don't see why mannequins, copper fishes, or maps, should be less worthy of study than the apples, bottles and pipes to which Cézanne owes his fame'. But for Carrà, as for Chirico, it was not just a matter of substituting

CARRA. MANNEQUIN. 1917

CARRÀ. HERMAPHRODITE IDOL. 1917.
*Private Collection, Milan*

density of tones, and the preciousness of colour, all too neglected during the Futurist experiment. He, in his turn, set Chirico an example with his enchanted interiors and his enigmatic irony. Between 1921 and 1925 Carrà painted seascapes full of that magical feeling which, without repudiating the play of colour and light, without disregarding the problems of form and space, tries to reconcile the past and the present, the powerful art of Giotto and the living art of Cézanne.

**CARRIÈRE** Eugène. French painter, born at Gournay in 1849, died in Paris in 1906. Although his outspoken nature, his love of freedom and, above all, his respect for the freedom of others, made Carrière take part in the most daring enterprises and, consequently, very often associate with the most modern artists, his own art is very far from their aesthetic theories and their technical processes. His deep-rooted sense of humanity saved him from dry academism, but he was not a revolutionary by nature, nor had he any desire to shock. That is what kept him out of the various schools of painting that followed one another in quick succession at the end of the nineteenth century. One might better define him, or at least get some insight into the nature of his art, by speaking not of the painters that he knew but of the writers who were his friends: Verlaine, Alphonse Daudet, Mallarmé, Anatole France, Edmond de Goncourt. Eugène Carrière did not believe in 'art for art's sake', he did not paint just for the pleasure of painting, but to express a sentiment, not an aesthetic sensation. Thus, what characterizes him is an intense feeling of humanity. Two themes dominate all his work, the two themes in which he could most completely show the imprint of the human soul: his pictures of motherhood and his portraits. The former show forth all the gestures of tenderness, the attitudes of hope and anxiety, the moving embraces. He did the same picture over and over again, but it was always new, because the emotion with which he contemplated his models was never exhausted. In his portraits each detail was a reflection of the artist's thought. Emerging out of the penumbra,

dressmaker's dummies for Cézanne's apples. What they set out to find again was the magic that emanates from old paintings, and which the open-air painting of the Impressionists had dispelled. This magic was one of the effects of perspective, and the relationship between full and empty spaces in the composition of a picture. It is therefore through perspective that Chirico and Carrà wanted to renew the miracle of the Renaissance artists. Carrà's paintings of this period, less known abroad than Chirico's, are often more elaborate than those of his friend, to whom he obviously owes his first ideas. Carrà rejected everything that Chirico took from the French and the Germans. He took his inspiration from Giotto, but not without a certain heaviness; from this point of view he is much more German than Chirico. Despite his heaviness, Carrà rediscovered the beauty of paint, the

the faces are blurred, softly receiving the light which models their features in grey monochrome. But Carrière was less interested in representing the actual features than in describing the sentiments they aroused. His drawing is as supple and sensitive as writing, and his painting has all the delicacy of a poem. He always honestly admitted that his painting had literary affinities. Perhaps that is why he had little difficulty in getting accepted, and admired. Perhaps, too, the apparent moderation of his increasingly monochromatic art served to inspire confidence. There was no reason to fear that he might spring a revolt or some other unpleasant surprise. However, on closer examination, it can be seen that Carrière had a broad manner, even very free and somewhat spirited. That was his discreet way of showing his passion. To get a real idea of its extent, one must bear in mind his last words, at the close of an exemplary life: 'Love one another with frenzy'. Carrière gave us one of today's rare examples of art put to the service of an idea, a cause. He made a point of depicting humanity in its moments of family intimacy. His

dreamlike painting is, after all, the reflection of a realistic conception of life, of which his picture, though sometimes disturbed, is always profoundly true (*vide* Académie Carrière).

**CASSATT** Mary. Born in Pittsburg, Pennsylvania, in 1845; died in France in 1927. Predisposed in favour of French culture by her family background, Mary Cassatt spent the first few years of her childhood in Paris, then went to America. A short while before the Franco-Prussian war of 1870 she came back to Paris, no doubt in the hope of learning to paint under conditions more interesting than those then existing at the Pennsylvania Academy of the Fine Arts. Not content with studying at the Atelier Chaplin, she went to look for inspiration in the museums in Italy (where she made a study of Correggio), in Spain, and in Antwerp (where she developed an admiration for Rubens). It was in Antwerp, a few years later, that she met Degas, who suggested that she should exhibit with the Impressionists, and also gave her guidance and advice. It is wrong to conclude from this that Mary Cassatt was either a pupil or an emulator of Degas. Although Degas, confirmed woman-hater that he was, relented a little towards her, and although she admired him greatly, and a certain kinship to Degas is discernible in the style and composition of her early work, Mary Cassatt mostly maintained a complete independence of technique and inspiration. A more obvious influence is that of the Japanese artists, particularly in her drawings and drypoints. Her precise, simplified drawing has all the skill and the impressive quality of the work of the Japanese masters. Mary Cassatt had an admirable understanding of their technique and the effects that could be obtained with it. The works she created under this influence were not pastiches but creations carefully thought out according to a definite technique. However, her art never froze into system, and she managed to escape all formulas. It is dominated far more by feeling than by technique, and the majority of her works are motherhood scenes of the most tender affection. She gave this hackneyed mother-and-child theme a new freshness by stripping it

CARRIÈRE. PORTRAIT OF VERLAINE.
*Lithograph*

of all artifice and literature. Just as the great Impressionists show us landscapes in their every-day lighting, Mary Cassatt shows us mother and child in all their simplicity, when their gestures are not made for the purpose of being seen and reproduced. By participating in this rehabilitation of the acts of everyday life, which was a characteristic of the Impressionist move-ment in which she felt so much at home, Mary Cassatt made a very personal and important con-tribution to the body of Impressionist creation.

CASSATT. MOTHER AND CHILD.
1905. *Pastel. Louvre*

**CÉZANNE** Paul. French painter, born in Aix-en-Provence in 1839; died there in 1906. Cézanne came of a long line of artisans and small tradesmen of Piedmontese origin. He went to a primary school, then to a religious school, and was later sent to college by his father, who, by that time, had left his hatter's shop to become manager of a bank. Cézanne left college in 1858, with a sound educa-tion, his religious faith intact, and a close friend-ship with his fellow-student Émile Zola. Having done well at his studies, he entered a law school, in compliance with his father's wishes. This did not prevent him from carrying on with his

drawing classes, which he had been attending since 1856. Hard-working, conscientious, but sensitive and exuberant, he was not a very gifted pupil. He was short, thick-set, very dark, with an unprepossessing face, obstinate forehead, an aquiline nose, a keen glance and quick gestures. He enjoyed swimming, hunting, and long rambles through the countryside. He was fond of music, and played the cornet in the students' orchestra, in which Zola was a flautist. In 1859 his father acquired a seventeenth-century country house, the Jas de Bouffan, on the outskirts of Aix, and spent the summers there with his wife, his son and his two daughters. There Cézanne set up his first studio. He had already made up his mind about his future: despite his father, he was going to be a painter. His father, who intended that Paul should succeed him as head of the bank, admonished him in the following words: 'Think about your future, my boy. With genius you die; it is only with money that you live.' – a 'bourgeois' conception of life that irritated Paul considerably, but in which he nevertheless acquiesced. He went on painting secretly, giving his legal studies only moderate attention. Émile Zola, who had settled in Paris, urged him to come and join him there. Cézanne's father opposed the idea. But in April 1861, realizing his son's unfit-ness for business, and under pressure from his wife and eldest daughter, Marie, he finally gave his reluctant consent. And so Paul Cézanne went to Paris. He took lodgings in the Rue des Feuillantines, studied at the Académie Suisse *(*)*, became friends with Pissarro and, later, Guillau-min, and resumed his former intimacy with Zola *(*)*. He was just about able to exist on the 125 francs which his father sent him each month. The tumult of Paris was not at all to his taste, and he was far from satisfied with the first works he produced. Eventually he was refused admis-sion to the École Nationale des Beaux-Arts, on the ground that he had 'the temperament of a colourist' and painted 'with excess'. Discouraged, he went back to Aix, to the great delight of his father, who offered him a position in the bank. But Paul, far from sacrificing the brush to finance, went on sketching and painting with ardour. He painted four large panels, *The Four Seasons*, on the walls of the Jas de Bouffan (today in the

Petit Palais Museum in Paris), parodies that he irreverently signed 'Ingres' just for the fun of it. He painted a portrait of himself and one of his father. In November 1862 he went back to Paris. He associated with the Impressionists without, however, being carried away by them. He made the acquaintance of Monet, Degas and Renoir, but the works he admired most were those of Delacroix and Courbet. Cézanne's own work at that period was very romantic. It pleased him no more than it did anyone else. In fact, nothing pleased him, and he was ill at ease everywhere, breaking off a budding friendship, avoiding a famous artist whose work he liked, changing his lodgings constantly, leaving Paris in disgust and going back to it out of curiosity, retiring to Aix and then leaving it soon after. When his work was rejected by the Salon in 1866, he left for Aix, disgusted. He was back in Paris in the winter of 1867–68, in new lodgings, naturally. He put in brief appearances at the Café Guerbois *(\*)*, where he met Renoir, Manet, Stevens, Zola, Cladel, Duranty. . . . He never felt comfortable there. His *Grog au Vin* or *Afternoon in Naples* was rejected by the Salon in 1867. That same year he met Marie-Hortense Fiquet, a young model, whom he took with him to l'Estaque when he went there to hide in 1870, to escape the draft. After the war, he settled in Paris. He was thirty-two years old. Until then he had indulged in a violent, sombre, and theatrical kind of painting, in which his sexual obsessions and distraught dreams figured. He painted landscapes, still lifes and portraits – of Zola, Achille Emperaire, and Valabrègue – but also death scenes and orgies, weird, fantastic scenes with a thick impasto brutally applied, where sickly blues and livid whites slash the gloomy backgrounds. Tintoretto, Magnasco, Crespi, Goya, Daumier, all the great baroque painters, seem to preside over these lyrical effusions, these convulsed forms, these trite colours, over all the works that gave satisfaction to his turbulent nature. *The Abduction*, and *The Temptation of Saint Anthony*, *The Negro Scipio*, *The Magdalene, or Grief* and *The Modern Olympia* (the latter two in the Louvre) – these were the works that Manet condemned when he said to the Impressionist Guillemet: 'How can you like messy painting?'

In 1872 Hortense Fiquet bore him a son, to whom he gave his own name, Paul. He settled at Auvers-sur-Oise, where he lived for two years in the company of Pissarro and Guillaumin, who gave him advice and influenced his work. He abandoned his wild, lusty manner, his palette became lighter, his strokes gained in precision, and he employed simpler methods. *The House of the Hanged Man* (Louvre) and *Doctor Gachet's House* (Kunstmuseum, Basel) mark this renewal,

CÉZANNE. THE NEGRO SCIPIO. 1866–1868.
*São Paulo Museum*

brought about as much by a prolonged contact with Impressionism as by a personal need of order. Cézanne made the acquaintance of Van Gogh. Doctor Gachet *(\*)* gave his encouragement, and some astute connoisseurs bought a few of his canvases. On his return to Paris he found the Impressionists once more, at the Nouvelle Athènes *(\*)*. He exhibited with them, although not very welcome, at the first Impressionist Salon at Nadar's in 1874, which was greeted with sarcasm and jibes. Cézanne naturally came in for his share, even more than his share. On the other hand, Count Doria bought

CÉZANNE. THE HOUSE OF THE HANGED MAN.
1873. *Louvre*

annual rejection of his canvases by the Salon, the raillery of the students at the École des Beaux-Arts, and the persistent incomprehension of the public, intensified his hypochondria. He sent sixteen canvases to the 1877 Impressionist exhibition. The reception was as hostile as in 1874. His father, who had never approved of his artistic career, nor of his liaison with Hortense Fiquet, reduced the already meagre allowance that he made him. That made Cézanne tend to isolate himself even more, to withdraw into himself. He exasperated his mistress with his unreasonableness, his

his *House of the Hanged Man*, and a Government official, Victor Chocquet *(\*)* became his admirer, his confidant, and, on several occasions, his model. From 1874 to 1877, in a studio that he rented at 120 Rue de Vaugirard in Paris, he enjoyed a period of tranquillity and productivity. The *Pool at the Jas de Bouffan* still belongs to his Impressionist style, but his *The Sea at l'Estaque*, painted during the summer of 1876, is constructed according to the principles of a new classicism, an evolution confirmed by the opulent still lifes which followed, the various portraits of Madame Cézanne, and a series of *Bathers*. He gave up small brush-strokes and the division of tones, and painted in masses. He accentuated volumes, and sought unity of composition. His work gained in thought, firmness, and plastic intensity. But he was growing bitter, and found it increasingly difficult to tolerate the company of men and worldly vanities. Truly generous and kind by nature, everything – no matter how trifling – irritated him, and he suffered very much when his ingenuous pride came up against an obstacle. That is why the

friends with his caprices. Nevertheless, many of them remained devoted, among them the painter Guillemet, who succeeded in having one of Cézanne's pictures exhibited at the Salon of 1882. From then on he lived in Provence, leaving it only for essential trips to Paris, or when he was invited to La Roche-Guyon by Renoir in 1883, or to Hattenville in 1886 by Victor Chocquet.

In 1883 he made the acquaintance of Monticelli. The two artists wandered through Provence on foot, haversacks on their backs, painting side by side, preferably in Gardanne, a little village in the South of France quite close to Aix-en-Provence. In 1884, in the presence of his parents, he married Hortense Fiquet, although he no longer had any feeling for her. Two years later his father died, at the age of almost ninety, leaving him two million francs, a considerable fortune in those days. Feeling only repugnance for human society, Cézanne devoted himself exclusively to painting. He had broken with Zola. His wife and his sister kept house for him and supervised his son's education. In 1888 he went to live in Paris for a year. He frequently met Van Gogh, Gauguin and Émile Bernard, although he did not care for them very much. He retired finally to Aix, leaving it only for brief trips to Fontainebleau, Giverny, Vichy or Paris. His irascibility increased with the first onset of diabetes. Without any serious reason, he quarrelled with several of his friends, particularly Claude Monet. He painted feverishly, but continued to have doubts about his work. Yet there never was so well-balanced and serene a period in his career as the ten years between 1885 and 1895. That was when he painted *The Commode* (Munich), *The Blue Vase* (Louvre) and *Mardi Gras* (Moscow), the *Portrait of Gustave Geffroy*, the three versions of the *Boy in the Red Vest*, and the series of portraits of Madame Cézanne. He also painted five versions of the *Cardplayers*, the last of which is in the Louvre, and more than ten versions of *Bathers*, which he treated in the manner of a geometrical problem, striving to determine the laws that governed the composition of the picture. In landscapes his favourite themes at that time were the family property, Jas de Bouffan (he painted its avenue of chestnut trees several times), the village of Gardanne, the Gulf of Marseilles, as seen from l'Estaque (one version in the Louvre) and *Mount Sainte-Victoire*, notably the one with the big pine tree: in all, more than 250 canvases. His perseverance, if not his stubbornness, was beginning to bear fruit. This was not yet fame, but he was acquiring a reputation. One of his works was shown at the Exposition Universelle in 1889, thanks to the intervention of the faithful Chocquet. When the Théodore Duret collection was put on sale, Claude Monet bought Cézanne's *Village Street* for eight hundred francs, while the dealer Ambroise Vollard *(\*)* exhibited 150 of his works in his gallery in the Rue Laffitte. The Press was outraged and the public incensed. The academicians turned up to voice indignant protest, but Cézanne's reputation emerged from this experience considerably enhanced. A number of independent painters and new connoisseurs voiced their appreciation. Although he was isolated within the walls of his own mistrust, and overcome with grief at the death of his mother, his lyricism increased and his art glided towards the

baroque. He decided never to go back to the Jas de Bouffan, and to sell it. He went to work at the Château Noir instead. He went to Paris for the last time in 1899, then returned to Aix, where he spent his last years, looked after by a devoted housekeeper, Madame Brémond. In 1902 he had a studio built in the Chemin des Lauves. Age, and the suffering his illness gave rise to, made him even more suspicious and irritable. In 1905 he completed his *Grandes Baigneuses* (now in the Philadelphia Museum), which he had begun seven years before. On the 15th of October, 1906, overtaken by a storm while out painting, he caught a chill and collapsed. He was brought home in a cart, and Madame Brémond hastily summoned his wife and son. They arrived too late. Cézanne died on the 22nd of October.

Despite the hostility of the public and of academic circles, Cézanne's fame had continued to grow. After Victor Chocquet's death, seven of Cézanne's canvases were sold for 17.600 francs. One of his landscapes was acquired for the Berlin Museum. He took part in the Exposition de la Libre Esthétique in Brussels in 1901, and in the

CÉZANNE. SELF-PORTRAIT. 1880.
*Kunstmuseum, Bern*

Salon des Indépendants in 1899, 1901 and 1902. An entire room was reserved for him in the Salon d'Automne of 1904. He also exhibited in that Salon in 1905 and 1906. He had triumphed at last. He was accepted by the public, admired by the younger generation, and surrounded with sympathy and veneration. Painters, writers, poets came to Aix to pay homage. Nevertheless, Cézanne continued to live simply in morose and hard-working isolation, revolutionary artist and

get him the Legion of Honour, but in vain. Cézanne's reserve in matters of love was proverbial. His one sentimental venture was disappointing and abortive. In fact, women frightened him. Timidity, clumsiness and shyness formed impassable barriers to his passionate temperament, as both his correspondence and his early works bear testimony. Violent and timid, churlish and kind-hearted, reserved and generous, passionate and level-headed, faint-

CÉZANNE. MOUNT SAINTE-VICTOIRE. 1885–1887.
*Courtauld Collection, London*

reactionary citizen; for the boldest precursor of modern art was, at the same time, the most conservative of French bourgeois. He used to go to Mass every Sunday, and scrupulously observe all the conventions of the bourgeois, conservative society to which he belonged. He had an unexpected respect for people with official standing and for State institutions. One of his lifelong desires was to be admitted to the very official Salon, already looked down upon by good painters, which kept its doors obstinately closed against him. He longed to be decorated, and the novelist Octave Mirbeau tried hard to

hearted and proud, brimming over with affection yet distrustful of it in others, eager for honours yet indifferent to fame, small in his life yet sublime in his art, gnawed at by doubts about his work yet convinced of his superiority – such was Cézanne, the most balanced of painters and the most torn by contradictions; for, having repressed his instinct, he could feel it stirring tumultuously within him. There was a continuous struggle between the will to organize and the impulse to improvise, between the exigencies of a classical conscience and the pressure of a baroque temperament. Up to 1873 his southern impetuosity and erotic imagination, a fever of subversion and the naïveté of the self-taught, produced a pictorial licentiousness, the dangers of which Cézanne soon perceived. For a while, under the influence of the Impressionists, hoping to get rid of the waywardness of his youth, he tied himself down to a discipline, and subjected his imagination to the laws of Nature. Then began his classical period. The secret of style was no longer to be found in the delicate play of light or the banal imitation of appearances, but in the severe ordering of forms and the right distribution of colours. In his still lifes, his portraits, his *Cardplayers*, and his views of l'Estaque or Gardanne, he resorted to an aesthetic system whose principles and appropriate means he discovered for himself; principles and means that issued from his need for perfection, his painful, groping search for an absolute. We have now to examine Cézanne's contribution to the art of painting, a contribution so rich and weighty that it has influenced the whole of modern painting, nourished all the movements that seek renewal, and inspired all the talent and genius of our century.

To understand properly the prodigious upheaval wrought by Cézanne (since, after him, a radical change occurred in the manner of seeing and in the manner of painting), he has to be seen in relation to the painting of his time. Although he is indebted to Pissarro for freeing him from the excessive romanticism of his youth, developing his gift of observation and his colour sense, nothing was more opposed to his ambition than the empiricist ideal of the Impressionists. He was a Realist as much as they were – even more so, for he wanted to go beyond the 'simple sensation' and the immediate data of the senses. 'To make of Impressionism something as solid and durable as the paintings in the museums', he once said. By sheer will-power and meditation he rediscovered the innate freshness and vigour of sensation, the fundamental sensation that he wanted to make strong and permanent. He built a world whose form, construction and colour ensure permanence and universality. Although he was an ardent admirer of Poussin, Daumier, and Courbet, he wanted none of that form drowned in chiaroscuro and modelling. On the contrary,

he disengaged it, encircled it, put it in evidence and accentuated its internal structure. He gave consistency even to air, mist, vapour, to the most volatile and least palpable things in the universe. The sky and sea in his landscapes have as much breadth and solidity as the trees, rocks and houses. 'Nature must be treated through the cylinder, the sphere, the cone', he said, as the Cubists were to repeat later. But reality has three dimensions. How can it be represented on a

CÉZANNE. MAN WITH PIPE. 1890–1892.
*Courtauld Collection, London*

flat surface? This is where the organizer comes in. With a firm and careful hand, he ordered and combined in the space of the picture the cubes of his houses, the architectures of his trees, the concrete blocks which are his people, the spheres that are his fruits. Verticals and horizontals intersect at right angles to give an effect of magnitude, balance and serenity. Realizing that Nature is 'more depth than surface', he suggested the third dimension by arranging planes in an unexpected manner, by displacing the visual angles, by raising the horizon line (as in *The Sea at l'Estaque* in the Louvre), without bothering

CÉZANNE. THE SEA AT L'ESTAQUE. 1883–1885.
*Louvre*

volume and drawing. Since form is created gradually by the brush as the artist works, it follows that drawing and painting cannot be distinct from each other. 'When colour has its richness, form has its plenitude', is his famous saying. From that time on the Impressionist division of tone began to give way to the juxta-position of two opposite tones, the proximity of warm and cool. Each spot of paint becomes a coloured plane, a small, dense, rough-grained mass, placed there by a hand guided by reason, yet full of sensuality and flavour. Cézanne wanted

about the rules of perspective as taught in the academies. But this tireless and exacting genius wanted to render Nature in its totality. How was he to express, at one and the same time, things and the air that envelops them, form and atmosphere, without resorting to the chiaroscuro of the classical painters, or the soft variegations and the shimmering glints of the Impressionists? Rejecting current conventions, Cézanne made a discovery which was to have a far-reaching effect on Western art: light and shadow no longer exist. From now on they are expressed with the aid of colours. Tone takes the place of modelling of form; the relationship of colours takes the place of chiaroscuro. He respects local tone. He substitutes pure tone, and contrasts of pure tone, for the mixture, gradations and modulations of colour. 'Model by the colours', said Antonello da Messina. This suggestion, taken up by the Venetians, has become a definite acquisition, thanks to Cézanne, who invented a pictorial light as different from natural light as a picture is from Nature itself. The difficulty lay in finding exact tones, and the exact interrelation of tones. This difficulty Cézanne triumphantly surmounted. In doing so, he arrived at a new interpretation of

to be a painter to the exclusion of everything else. Nothing counted in his eyes except painting. 'Be a painter', he wrote to Émile Bernard, 'and not a writer or a philosopher.' Disdaining literary subjects, *genre* scenes and allegorical compositions, he preferred to paint common objects, familiar landscapes, and portraits of humble folk. He did not create his *Bathers* to glorify the splendours of the flesh, or to follow a fashion, but in order to seek new forms and new plastic rhythms. Passionately a painter, he made the picture a concrete and complete world, a reality which is an end in itself. From this it is easy to understand the profound influence he has exercised over the generation that followed him. He brought them a method, a perfect creation, the 'picture': that is to say, an architecture of tones and forms which is not an analysis of the passing moment, does not represent an anecdote or a chance incident, but is a coherent reality, indestructible and eternal. Cézanne never wanted to betray Nature. He found in himself the heritage of the old masters, which he took and enriched with his own discoveries, and exalted to the extreme limits to which his indomitable courage and genius could bring it. 'To do Poussin over again from nature. . . . To make of Impressionism something solid and durable like the art in the museums' – that, in short, was his credo. His work is a lesson in energy. It gives us a profound sense of comfort, religious feeling, joy mingled with sadness. For beyond this robust and balanced art his suppressed instincts rumble, and the man groans, torn between the classicism he has so patiently sought and his latent baroque tendencies. Hence the rickety tables, the crooked vases, the tottering chairs, the stiff limbs, the squint-eyed faces, the sloping postures, the forms that crumble when the vertical and horizontal break, the seeming awkwardness, the distortions that have for so long given Cézanne's hostile critics food for condemnation.

CÉZANNE. STILL LIFE WITH ONIONS. 1895–1900.
*Louvre*

In the last ten years of his life the baroque invades his work without ever overstepping the limits laid down by a lifetime of conscientiousness and effort. He paints still lifes swaying on slippery supports, views of Mount Sainte-Victoire shaken by internal fires, trees which seem struck by lightning, *Château Noir*'s flaming beneath stormy skies. Fauvism is already there, just as Expressionism was in the *Temptation of St Anthony* (1867), and Cubism in the *Cardplayers*. Who of the masters of modern art has not turned to him when in doubt and drawn comfort and inspiration from his example? Matisse, Derain, Vlaminck, and many others have. 'We all start from Cézanne', Braque, Léger and Jacques Villon declared in 1953. On the other hand, the neo-classicists claim him as their model in so far as he remained faithful to the naturalist tradition. Precursor of pure painting, but also promoter of an intellectual adventure that still continues today, Cézanne is a valid source for the non-

realists as well as the realists. There is not a painter today who is not indebted to him. Destiny chose this torn creature with the anguished heart and confident mind to weave the threads of a new tradition. 'I am the primitive of the way I have discovered', he wrote one day, in the full consciousness of his originality. There have undoubtedly been other innovators who have had something to give the painters of today, but they are only predecessors. He is the ancestor, the father of modern painting.

**CHAGALL** Marc. Born in Vitebsk, Russia, in 1887. Marc Chagall's father, a simple, kindly soul, was employed in a herring depot. His mother, a small, lively woman, was hard put to keep her large family of eight girls and two boys, and opened a small grocery shop. In his book *My Life* Chagall writes about his home, describing the vivacity of his sisters and the eccentricity of his uncles – Neuch, who carried cattle in a jolting trap and played the violin, and Zussy, who was a hairdresser and curled his whiskers. He also tells of his grand-

CHAGALL. BIRTH. 1911

father's house, where animal hides hung like linen. All these were themes that inspired his first drawings and, after a number of transpositions, nourished his paintings. Chagall was apprenticed to a painter named Pen, an honest portraitist of the notables of the town, who showed an interest in Chagall's early works. These were on everyday, familiar subjects: water-carriers, little houses, proccessions over the hills. Chagall went to St Petersburg, where he went through particularly difficult times. Having failed the entrance examination to the School of Arts and Crafts, he was admitted to the Society for the Protection of the Arts, where he even obtained a grant of ten roubles a month. But the teaching there was nonexistent, and the atmosphere depressing and dreary. But the new school run by Bakst, the theatrical designer, had a growing reputation, increased by its contacts with France and modern art. Chagall, admitted to this studio, received a profound shock. Although the decorative research being conducted there was new to him, he found justification for his previous rebuffs and his instinctive

boldness. He arbitrarily renewed his palette, discovered the expressive value of colour as such, and the distortion of line. This is to be seen in his *Red Nude*, 1908. When Chagall returned to Vitebsk, he had a style of his own, still sombre and heavy but with flashes of light. He used it in scenes that are outside and beyond direct observation, and represent the beginnings of an effort towards synthesis; these are the great themes of life: birth, marriage, death. Chagall made several versions of each, always trying to attain a more complete representation. By his side he now had an extraordinarily intuitive girl, Bella, who fired his imagination and encouraged him in his efforts. Chagall painted her in the *Portrait with Black Gloves*. When he returned to St Petersburg, with work that was quite distinct from contemporary Russian painting, he gained the patronage and friendship of a Deputy of the Douma, Winawer, who offered him a small grant to enable him to go to Paris.

When he arrived in Paris in 1910 he took up lodgings at La Ruche, and became intimate with the poets Blaise Cendrars, Max Jacob and Apollinaire, and the painters La Fresnaye, Delaunay and Modigliani. This was a highly productive period for Chagall, during which he put all the energy that was bubbling up inside him at the service of a vision which integrated the forms of the modern world with the disciplines that stemmed from Fauvism and Cubism. It was in Paris – to use his own expression – that he washed his eyes. His ideas, his instinct for geometrical composition in the construction of a picture were confirmed by the experiments he saw going on all about him. But whereas the Cubists sought to interpret objects, such as a pipe or a guitar, in their essences, Chagall applied this methodical organization to describe the elements of reality seen through his imagination or memory. Since, for him, reality always has projections into the past and the future, his work unfolds on several planes. The laws of gravity do not apply to his people and objects. Every detail keeps its full liberty and all its chances of beauty and grace. Within the solid framework created by the artist, concrete elements, becoming memories, move freely at all angles, in all dimensions. Chagall's great canvases of this period

*(The Village and I, To Donkeys and Others, The Soldier Drinks, The Drunk, Portrait with Seven Fingers)* reveal a pure vision of an absolutely unique inner world, which the artist succeeds in transmitting without spoiling or weakening, giving it an eternal existence, outside time. Almost all his canvases of this period, under (sometimes odd) names supplied by Blaise Cendrars, were selected by Apollinaire for the Chagall exhibition arranged in Berlin in 1914. This exhibition, at the Der Sturm Gallery, created a sensation and had a marked impact on the Expressionist movement after the 1914–1918 war.

Chagall had just arrived in Russia when the war broke out. Drafted into a camouflage unit, he remained in St Petersburg, and in 1915 married Bella. During this period he acquired a heightened awareness of the tragic reality of his inner world. Thus, in the *Green Rabbi* cold, strident colours and broken lines clarify his interpretation. The village, which is an extension of his own individuality, forces itself on him,

no longer through the magic of memory but in naked and searing purity. It is as if the infinitely fragile and threatened world of childhood were being offered to him again. Hitherto, he had expressed its sadness, its horror and its poetry with vehemence, in intense lines and colours. Now he perceived it differently. He painted it in delicate pinks, acid greens and transparent blues. He saved only what was essential. In this unreal atmosphere only the painter and his beloved could move, growing with their love, becoming one single, fabulous being, floating through space, above life.

When the Revolution came, Chagall was appointed Commissar for the Fine Arts in the District of Vitebsk by Lunacharsky, whom he knew when the latter was in exile in Paris in 1912. The new regime encouraged the most advanced forms of modern art. Chagall founded an academy, which he opened to all art movements, but a conflict arose between him and Malevitch, who was not so liberal, and Chagall resigned. In Moscow he joined Granowsky, director of the Yiddish Theatre, who commissioned him to paint murals for the auditorium and foyer of the theatre. When he was also asked to do the décors and costumes, he gave the actors themselves a new dimension. He transformed them into a gallery of representative types, so complete in their portrayal of the feelings they were supposed to represent, that action became almost redundant. These décors and characters were depicted in enormous compositions on the auditorium walls, so that the audience was completely overwhelmed by a psychic world that enveloped it entirely.

In 1922 Chagall decided to return to France. It was then that Vollard *(\*)*, having noticed one of his paintings, suggested that he do some illustrating. Selecting Gogol's *Dead Souls*, he made eighty-five etchings, which were not published until 1948. In 1927 he illustrated the Fables of La Fontaine with one hundred etchings,

CHAGALL. THE GREEN EYE. 1944

CHAGALL. CLOCK WITH BLUE WING. 1949

in his work. He completed the great composition entitled *Around Her*, which he had begun in 1937, and which became a synthesis of all his favourite themes, grouped around the evocation of Bella. In 1945 Chagall undertook the vast backdrop, curtains and costumes foy Stravinsky's ballet *The Fire Bird*. He finally returned to France in 1947, and settled down at Vence on the Côte d'Azur in 1949. Using some old sketches, he began a series of new paintings in which Parisian landscapes are peopled with fantastic evocations.

Chagall's importance in contemporary art increases daily. In 1941 André Breton *(\*)*, in search of the precursors of Surrealism *(\*)*, stressed the fact that already in 1911 Chagall's work had broken down the barriers of the elements and the laws of physics. Chagall's unique and individual artistic achievement is reflected in many of the new developments of modern painting, for, with a sure instinct, he has applied himself to the problems of our times and given them an answer.

published in 1952. At that time, after the severity of Cubism and the explosion of Expressionism, painting felt the need for a period of contemplation. It wanted to please, and tried numerous experiments to that end. Chagall discovered the beauty of flowers and vegetation in the South of France. He painted his first landscapes and lyrically described a new language of flowers. With unerring taste, he avoided insipidity. In 1931, invited to the opening of the Tel Aviv Museum, he went to Palestine and Syria to see the scenes of the Bible which, at Vollard's request, he later illustrated.

Beginning in 1935, profoundly affected by the atmosphere of persecution and war spreading over the world, Chagall introduced dramatic, social and religious elements into his pictures. He painted numerous Crucifixions.

In 1941 he decided to go to the United States, at the invitation of the Museum of Modern Art in New York. Tragically alert to all that was happening in Europe, Chagall found powerful and renewed inspiration in the misfortunes of his race and the threats to human liberty. In 1944 Bella Chagall died. Moving evocations of the past and the beyond began to appear

CHAGALL. THE BOY. 1952.

**CHIRICO** Giorgio de. Italian painter born at Volos, Greece in 1888. His father, a Sicilian from Palermo, came to Greece as an engineer. Several years later, his family having settled in Athens, Chirico studied at a polytechnic school where both painting and engineering were taught. He devoted himself to painting and did landscapes and seascapes. In 1906 he went to Munich, attracted by the prestige of the German romantic painters (and Arnold Boecklin in particular). On completion of his studies, in 1909, he went to Italy. Turin amazed him with its rectilinear architecture, adorned with statues placed at man's height, which seemed to rise from the crowds of passers-by. In 1910 Chirico moved to Florence, where he painted his first characteristic works: *Enigma of the Oracle* and *Enigma of an Autumn Evening,* in which two people part at the foot of a white statue while, behind a wall, a sail rises on the horizon. In July 1911 he arrived in Paris with his canvases *Sabaudian Enigmas,* which he exhibited at the Salon d'Automne. At the Salon des Indépendants he also showed the first works inspired by the Gare Montparnasse in Paris. These were noticed by Picasso and Apollinaire. Apollinaire became his friend and proclaimed him the most astonishing painter of his time. Chirico made a prophetic portrait of the poet, depicting him with a bullethole in his skull (*see* illustration, page 5). In the works of this period Chirico strove to discover new relationships between objects, to reveal the secret connections that can exist between them. His unusual associations of images and ideas arouse in the spectator a feeling of subdued but profound anxiety. Flying lines cut the immobility of space, absent people throw shadows. Silence vibrates, waiting for the cry or whistle that will rend it. Around these cold, pure architectures the air is charged with mystery and invention. A spatial magic is created. Chirico's objects,

CHIRICO. ENIGMA OF ARRIVAL. 1912.
*Private Collection, Paris*

plaster statues or heads, vegetables or fruit, and (later) dressmaker's dummies, rubber gloves and dry biscuits, are all represented with absolute indifference. They are so impersonal that they lose all their natural meaning. Their grouping – which owes nothing to chance but is the result of systematic experimentation – creates limitless possibilities of elusiveness and mystery. According to his friends, Chirico had at this time prophetic and visionary powers, powers consciously created, the product of a method which he later repudiated. Back in Italy at the outbreak of war Chirico was conscripted in 1915, at Ferrara, where he met Carlo Carrà. The architecture of this town, with its vast white, deserted perspectives, was particularly favourable to hallucination. What is termed Metaphysical Painting *(\*)* arose from the combination of the world he had already created and this new setting. The metaphysical aspect of landscapes, objects or beings is the meaning they acquire when seen suddenly in unusual isolation or in unexpected relationships, or when seized in their nakedness, with their magical power intact. The painter made an obvious effort to define and characterize his art, and then to develop it in that metaphysical sense. That is why it soon betrayed an excess of intentions, not always clear or coherent. That probably is the origin of the crisis that destroyed the artist and his work. The composition was complicated with numerous and divergent perspectives; the dissonances between the different parts of the picture were emphasized. The picture was soon crowded with fragments of reality painted in *trompe l'œil*.

Chirico had an enormous success at the *L'Epoca* exhibition in Rome in 1918. He was one of the leaders of the *Valori Plastici* group in 1919. While in Rome he plunged into technical researches which are, perhaps, at the root of the radical change that occurred in his work. He experimented with various old processes of painting in tempera, and, haunted by the transparent colours of the masters, tried to solve the mystery of great painting by copying Raphael, Michelangelo and Botticelli. Chirico's metaphysical universe is close to the universe of dreams, where the extraordinary precision of the details results in a new reality, secret and unpredictable. Perspective is no longer the search for the ideal line of sight, but a steep short cut leading straight into the inexplicable. The strangely grouped objects give the same bizarre sensation as the clear images of a dream. When there is a human figure, it is in the form of a clothed or plaster statue, or an articulated dressmaker's dummy. Chirico never let himself be guided by the contingencies of psychic automatism, or the dictates of his feelings: his creatures are rigorously sexless. His evolution was so rapid that when he returned to France in 1924 he was already far from the Surrealists who welcomed him as a master and made him join in their first exhibition. He executed décors for the *Ballets Suédois* and the Monte Carlo Ballet. He presented new themes (horses and gladiators) in a new kind of painting in which he seemed to have retained only the semblance of his former gifts. His works founder in literature and academism, and only his novel in the form of a dream, *Hebdomeros*, published in 1929, reflects the grandiose visions of the Chirico of old. After 1930 he broke brutally and violently with his past, disowned his friends and former works, and immersed himself in a feverish and frenzied exploration of empty techniques.

**CHOCQUET** Victor. This enthusiastic and keen collector ('good old Chocquet', as he was called in his time) was born in Lille about 1840. A minor Customs official, he devoted a substantial portion of his meagre income to buying Impressionist works. His first acquisitions were a small Delacroix and Manet's *Peonies*, now in the Louvre. In the little shop run by Père Tanguy *(\*)*, a dealer in art supplies and paintings, he discovered the then unknown Impressionist painters, to whom he gave at once his unqualified admiration. In 1875, at the Hôtel Drouot, the Paris auction rooms, he met Renoir at the famous sale organized there by Renoir, Monet, Sisley and Berthe Morisot. The sale was not a success, and they were not even able to pay all the expenses. In 1876 Renoir painted Chocquet's gentle, pensive face, and then made a portrait of his wife. Renoir introduced him to Cézanne, who also painted him several times: first in 1877 and again in the summer of 1886 when he was staying at Chocquet's place at

CHIRICO. (false attribution) COMPOSITION. *Musée d'Art Moderne, Paris*

Hattenville, in Normandy. It is indeed amazing that when he died the collection of this minor civil servant comprised, among others, 32 Cézannes, 11 Monets, 11 Renoirs and 5 Manets, as well as some drawings and water-colours. This collection was sold by Madame Chocquet on the 3rd and 4th of July, 1899, at a considerable profit. The famous *Mardi Gras* by Cézanne fetched 4,400 francs, a record price for the time.

MONET. FISHERMEN. 1880
*Fogg Art Museum, Cambridge, Mass.*

**CLEMENCEAU** Georges (1841– 1929). It was probably psychological fatalism which led Clemenceau to take up the cudgels for those who were making the Impressionist revolution. Naturally enough it was Monet, another rugged individualist, who particularly took his fancy. Years later, at the end of a turbulent political life, he could still take time to write about Monet in *The Water Lilies* (1928). He was a fervent admirer, too, of Rodin, but Rodin confided that Clemenceau made him start over again no fewer than fourteen times when he sat for his bust, apparently convinced that no material, however plastic, could adequately suggest the volcanic mobility of his feelings. There is no doubt, though, that Monet's intensity of feeling harmonized with Clemenceau's. The Tiger's enthusiasm was strong for the series of *Haystacks*, *Cathedrals* and *Water Lilies* – those works in which Monet pushed to its extreme consequences his single-minded passion for colour. Clemenceau took sides with most of the young talent of his day and was one of the first to demonstrate that the future is always to the *avant garde*. It was by his order, as Premier, in 1907, that Manet's *Olympia*, which had been offered to the Government in 1890, following its purchase by public subscription, was finally allowed to enter the Louvre, in spite of rabid opposition from members of the Insti-

tut de France. It is thanks to Clemenceau, too, that the *Water Lilies* are now on view at the Orangerie. Monet agreed to give this famous series to the State after Clemenceau promised that it would be exhibited under the same conditions as those in which he had always seen it in the artist's studio at Giverny.

**CLOISONNISM** See Pont-Aven (School of) and Nabis.

**CONCRETE ART** A term invented by Theo Van Doesburg in 1930 to replace the term Abstract Art. A review bearing that name, which appeared only once, was started by Van Doesburg in April 1930, less than a year before his death. Since then Concrete Art has been used in preference to Abstract Art in the writings of certain artists such as Arp and Max Bill. It has had a certain vogue in *avant-garde* circles in Switzerland and the Argentine. The term is interchangeable with Abstract Art, but it should not be forgotten that from 1910 to 1930 the masters of this art (Kandinsky, Malevitch, Mondrian and Van Doesburg himself) never used any term other than *Art Abstrait*, or Abstract Art.

**CONSTRUCTIVISM** See Abstract Art, Suprematism, Lissitzky.

**CORINTH** Lovis. German painter born in Tapiau in Eastern Prussia in 1858; died in Zandvoort, Holland, in 1925. Corinth studied painting in Koenigsberg, Munich, Antwerp, and Paris. After ten years in Munich, he settled in Berlin, about 1900. From 1918 until his death he spent the summers at Urech in Bavaria, near the Walchensee, whose intense blue sings in the landscapes of his latter years. With Liebermann, Corinth belonged to what is sometimes called German Impressionism. But his heavy, sensual early work is more Naturalist than Impressionist, and the spontaneity of style to which it owes its brilliancy is inspired more by Frans Hals than by the French Impressionists. The pictures of this period were voluptuous and vivid, or else heroic allegorical scenes. This gushing creation was interrupted in 1911, when the artist had an apoplectic stroke. His painting then underwent a profound transformation: his spontaneous style lost its externally sensuous character and, instead of naïvely presenting a three-dimensional world, Corinth tried to merge the planes in a single, strong, nervous movement of colour. The vitality of his painting no longer depended on its subject: it was fully contained in the flow and intoxication of paint. Flowers and landscapes – first of the Côte d'Azur, later of the Walchensee – painted in strong, thick, luminous colours, seem born of an intimate participation in the deep and powerful song of Nature.

Before he took ill, Corinth painted some vigorous portraits, but those that came afterwards, such as that of Meier-Graefe, painted in 1917 (Museum of Modern Art, Paris), and the self-portraits of his latter years, have a superior emotional power. When this giant, worn down by illness and hard work, painted himself, all the strength and weakness, the reality and unreality of man, appear in this pathetic testimony. These same contrasts are to be found in his religious pictures, of which the most important is the magnificent *Ecce Homo* of 1925, now in the Basel Museum. Kirchner said of Corinth: 'In the beginning, he was only of average stature; at the end, he was truly great'.

CORINTH. WALCHENSEE.                              *Dresden Museum*

**CROSS** Henri-Edmond (1856–1910). Cross's real name was Delacroix. He was born at Douai and died at Saint-Clair in the department of Le Var. In 1884 he was one of the founders of the *Société des Artistes Indépendants*, along with Seurat, Signac and others, and in that year he began to abandon his more or less Impressionist and rather academic style in favour of Divisionism (*see* Neo-Impressionism). The reasons he later gave were that 'in the act of creating, will as well as instinct plays a large part; and will can only be based on exactitude. I am engrossed in this question of exactitude, seeking it in the laws of contrasting colours. Reasoning doesn't come easily to me – in fact, it is perhaps the thing I lack most; and if a painter is endowed with artistic sensibility, studying a method is not likely to hinder him in expressing what he has felt.' In fact, as he freely admitted, 'because of my temperamental make-up, my sensations are in need of grammar, rhetoric and logic'. And this was just what he found in Seurat's method disciplined by the

CROSS. THE HARBOUR AT TOULON.                    *Private Collection, Paris*

laws of optics: simultaneous contrast, the use of pure colours, and optical blending. However, he never became a slave to these theories, and if they enabled him to become the artist he was, they always remained a means rather than an end, and he even admitted that he would gladly abandon them if he were to find more fruitful ideas elsewhere. But the discipline of his friend's system suited his character well, helping him on what Signac called 'the road towards the logic of colour and synthesis of form'.

In Cross we find both a methodical, dispassionate thinker and a strangely troubled dreamer. His dream, quite contrary to that of Seurat, was to follow the call of his imagination more freely. He wrote to a friend: 'Can the goal of art be nothing more than to set fragments of Nature in a rectangle, with what taste the artist has at his disposal? As the starting-point, I come back to the idea of chromatic harmonies invented outside Nature, so to speak.' Of all the Neo-Impressionist group, Cross used the brightest scale of colouring, and his Pointillist technique was of almost abstract quality.

By his will to achieve a certain independence of Nature, linked with a pronounced decorative

sense and a strong feeling for colour, Cross can be considered a precursor of Fauvism. In 1904 Matisse went to work with him and Signac in the South of France, fascinated by the richness of their palette, their animated way of painting, their free interpretation of what they saw. The characteristics of Fauvism – bright colouring, contrasts perhaps startling but never gaudy, synthesis of forms, a preference for flat surfaces – are all partly based on the liberties Cross took with Nature, particularly striking in his big water-colours. Less preoccupied than Signac with bringing a method to perfection, Cross made his way, in an adventurous spirit all his own, along the path opened up by Seurat; and it is just this blending of spontaneous emotional expression controlled by logic which constitutes the distinctive beauty of his work.

**CUBISM** is the name given to the aesthetic and technical revolution brought about by Picasso, Braque, Juan Gris and Léger between 1907 and 1914. Matisse and Derain also contributed to the formation of this movement, which influenced the majority of the *avant-garde*

PICASSO. LES DEMOISELLES D'AVIGNON. 1907.
*Museum of Modern Art, New York*

artists during the years that preceded the 1914–1918 war. Like Impressionism, Cubism at first encountered nothing but general hostility, or incomprehension, and was given its name in derision. In his account of the first Braque exhibition at the Kahnweiler Gallery, the critic Louis Vauxcelles picked up one of Matisse's sallies and spoke of 'cubes' (*Gil Blas*, November 14th, 1908). The following spring, in the same paper, and again on the subject of Braque, he spoke of 'Cubist bizarreries'. The creators of Cubism accepted the term with reserve, and constantly denied they were theorists. Picasso declared: 'When we painted as we did, we had no intention of creating Cubism, but only of expressing what was inside us'. Braque said: 'For me, Cubism – or rather, *my* Cubism – is a means I created for my own use, with the aim of putting painting within range of my talents'. The vitality and fecundity of Cubism comes from the coupling of these two exceptional temperaments, who worked enthusiastically together, without surrendering their own personalities. Later, they were joined by Gris and Léger. The history of the development of Cubism falls into three phases: a Cézanne phase (1907–1909), an analytical phase (1910–1912), and a synthetic phase (1913–1914).

A favourable climate for it had been prepared by the vogue of Negro sculpture and primitive art, the Seurat retrospective exhibition in the Salon des Indépendants of 1905 and, particularly, the Cézanne retrospective in the Salon d'Automne of 1907. Matisse and Derain had already disciplined Fauvism and tried to organize, methodically, the painted surface of the picture. In the spring of 1907 Picasso completed *Les Demoiselles d'Avignon*, 'hacked out with an axe', of which the right-hand section, violently simplified and constructed by drawing alone, without the use of chiaroscuro, marks the beginning of Cubism. He met Braque, whose natural evolution he speeded up. That autumn, Kahnweiler *(\*)* opened, in the Rue Vignon, the gallery that was to become the home of Cubism. The famous Bateau-Lavoir *(\*)* group was formed in 1908 at No. 13 Rue Ravignan, Montmartre, where Picasso, Max Jacob and Juan Gris went to live. It also included Apollinaire, Salmon, Raynal, Gertrude and Leo Stein, and others. The new aesthetic movement, intuitive with Picasso and deductive with Braque, can be clearly seen in the landscapes painted by Picasso at La Rue-des-Bois in the Oise in 1908, and at Horta de Ebro in Spain in 1909 (the latter exhibited by Vollard), as well as in the landscapes painted by Braque at l'Estaque in 1908 (exhibited at Kahnweiler's; catalogue preface by Apollinaire), and at La Roche-Guyon in 1909. Braque, fresh from Impressionism and Fauvism, controlled his colour by an austere sense of form; Picasso, the instinctive draughtsman, tried to introduce colour into his work. Each on his own was striving to find the same solutions by developing whatever quality he lacked. They made a study of the fundamental problem of painting: the representation of coloured volume on a flat surface. The history of Cubism is that of the successive solutions discovered to resolve this difficulty. The result was a new plastic language, lyrical and conceptual at the same time, which put an end to that respect for appearances which had been observed since the Renaissance. In their reaction against Impressionism and its visual spontaneity, Braque and Picasso discarded from their world all fortuitous appearances and atmospheric accidents. They tried to define the permanent properties of objects and their stability in a closed space, without perspective or light, through a geometrical crystallization inspired by Cézanne; hence the significant and very restrained choice of themes, which were limited to very simple things: trees, houses, fruit-bowls, bottles and glasses – later, small tables and musical instruments – that could be reduced to geometric forms and easily identified by the spectator. They were less interested in making an inventory of the world than in creating, with a few characteristic 'signs', a language which would renew its significance. But in this initial, groping phase, in spite of their efforts, the antinomy of object and colour, local tone and volume, was overcome only by painting in monochrome, or an imitation of sculpture (*vide* Picasso, Braque).

In 1910 Braque gave up landscapes for figures and still lifes. In his own words, he passed from visual space to tactile and manual space. Picasso left the Bateau-Lavoir for the Boulevard de Clichy, also in Montmartre, where he painted a series of heads and portraits. The second phase of Cubism, described as analytical by Juan Gris, because of the increasing breakdown of form, is characterized by the use of simultaneity. Several aspects of the same object are put together on a single canvas, rather as a child sees an object, as it exists in itself and in our minds. Thus, the object appears as if broken, spread out and open from the inside. This concern for complete realism differentiates Cubism from all the other abstract movements derived from it, and separates it from the decorative tendencies of Fauvism. The problem of simultaneity has always preoccupied artists who, in the imitative, visual phase of painting, from Van Eyck to Manet, have been unable to find any better means than a mirrorlike reflection. For, spatial simultaneity through successive juxtapositions, used by the

painters of the Trecento or the Quattrocento, cannot be compared with the unitary, structural principles of Cubism, obtained by the flattening and superimposing of planes, and the polyhedric fragmentation of volumes. This period of extreme analysis and systematic experimentation was not without a certain danger of 'hermetism' which Braque and Picasso proposed to remedy by the use of *papiers collés (\*)* and real materials, such as sand, glass, newspaper and cloth, inserted

BRAQUE. HOMAGE TO J.-S. BACH. 1912.
*Collection of H.-P. Roché, Paris*

in the canvas to stimulate perception. During this period Cubism was widely publicized, thanks to the publication of the doctrinal work of Gleizes and Metzinger, *Du Cubisme*, in 1912. It also saw its division into many tendencies, of which the principal two were Orphism *(\*)* and the Section d'Or *(\*)*, which preceded the later derivations of Abstraction (*vide* Abstract Art) and Purism *(\*)*.

In the following year, 1913, Apollinaire published *Les Peintres Cubistes*, in which he spoke already of conceptual painting (*vide* Apollinaire). This term was premature, because it can be applied only to the last, or synthetic, phase of Cubism, which began in 1913, with the very active participation of Gris and Léger (*vide* these names). Although Léger's interest in Cubism dates back to 1910, he did not go through the analytical period, being restrained by his sense of the monumental and his taste for the massive. In 1911 Juan Gris had begun to break down the object methodically in his painting, but reversed his procedure in the summer of 1913, during his stay at Céret with Braque and Picasso. He defined the change in attitude in these words: 'From a cylinder I make a bottle'. The multiple figuration of the same object on a canvas had made it difficult to understand and distorted its rhythm, even though it remained figurative. In synthetic Cubism the break with the naturalist and traditional representation practised since the Renaissance is complete. The new method discarded completely all imitative processes, and used freely invented plastic 'signs' comparable to the metaphors of poets. These signs created a reality through lyrical allusion, rather than representative illusion. Gone was the initial austerity of their palettes. The planes grew broader and more supple, the colours of the spectrum began to appear, form and local colour could at last be harmoniously united without breaking the basic architecture of the picture. Cubism ceased to be an aspect, an empirical technique, and became a conceptual aesthetic philosophy, an objective ordering of the world represented in its essence, and not its appearance. The realist cult of the 'object' (the importance of which has been revealed by psychology and sociology) played, at the beginning of the twentieth century, the same role as the passion for 'subject' did during the Romantic period. In line with the evolution of science and contemporary thought, a new plastic language has been created, whose rigour fosters, without fettering, the *élan* of the individual. The 1914 war dispersed the creators of Cubism, each to follow the course of his own artistic destiny. But the collective exaltation of those heroic years from 1907 to 1914 will never be lost.

GRIS. POEMS IN PROSE. 1915.  *Private Collection*

# D

**DADA** The Dada Movement developed between 1915 and 1922, between the dispersal of Cubism *(\*)* – from which it borrowed, and generalized for its own ends, the technique of *papiers collés (\*)* – and the advent of Surrealism *(\*)*, which succeeded i⁺ and for which it constituted a preparatory though negative phase. Dada made its first appearance almost simultaneously in Zurich, New York and Paris, before reaching Germany and then concentrating in Paris. Switzerland's neutrality during the war had made it a refuge for all kinds of political exiles and agitators. Lenin was there, rubbing shoulders with dissident elements and anarchists from almost every country. Among the latter were the Rumanian poet Tristan Tzara, the German writers Hugo Ball and Richard Hülsenbeck, and the Alsatian painter and sculptor Hans Arp. In February 1916 they founded the Cabaret Voltaire *(\*)*, a literary club, exhibition gallery, and theatre hall all in one; the name is a clear indication of its sarcastic and critical intentions. A dictionary, opened at random (this appeal to chance was to become systematic) furnished the name of the movement: Dada. Learned lectures on Klee, or Lao-tse, alternated with scandalizing or mystifying entertainments, designed to undermine by every possible means the traditional bases of culture and social order. Works by Arp, Chirico, Max Ernst, Feininger, Kandinsky, Klee, Kokoschka, Marc, Modigliani and Picasso were exhibited in a very eclectic manner at the Dada gallery in 1917. The typical artist of the movement was Arp, illustrator of Hülsenbeck and Tzara, who, with his coloured papers, his woodcuts and his sculptures, organized the so-called *'formes libres'* (free forms), born of fantasy and the unconscious (*vide* Arp).

The real precursor of the Dada spirit in its destructive sense was the painter Marcel Duchamp, a man of implacable logic and exceptional gifts, who sacrificed his career as an artist to the principles of inversion, negation and anti-aestheticism. He settled in New York in 1915, where his famous 'ready-mades' (mass-produced objects arbitrarily raised to the level of works of art) created a sensation, and became the central figure of the Stieglitz group and the review '291' (Man Ray, Picabia, de Zayas, Arensberg), an anti-artistic movement parallel to the Dada movement of Zurich. Picabia, a painter of Spanish origin, had visited New York in 1915. He went to Barcelona and founded the '391' review there in January 1917. He turned up in Switzerland in 1918 and contacted the Dada group. Two numbers of *Dada*, the review edited by Tzara, were published in 1917. *Dada III*, in which Picabia collaborated, appeared in December 1918, and contained the *Dada Manifesto*, in which the meaning and destructive force of the movement were confirmed. The *Dada Anthology* (number 4–5 of the review) appeared in April 1919 (*vide* Duchamp, Picabia). Tristan Tzara then settled in Paris, and was enthusiastically received by the group of the review *Littérature* (March 1919), run by the poets Breton, Aragon, Soupault, Eluard, Ribemont-Dessaignes and Péret. A Dada salon opened at the Montaigne Gallery on June 6th, 1922, but the Parisian movement was more literary and, after a summer demonstration in the Tyrol, it dissolved in internal disputes in the autumn of 1922 (*vide* also Breton, Tzara).

In Germany, because of the 1918 defeat and the social crises of the time, Dada found fertile soil for expansion. With the more direct participation of artists, the movement took on a more political character. The Berlin group, created by Hülsenbeck in 1917, broke up in 1920, after a large-scale exhibition which was a triumph for Georg Grosz, ferocious caricaturist of the German feudal bourgeoisie and militarism. The

Cologne group showed itself still more violent on the social plane, by the publication of the *Electric Fan* (a Communist and Dadaist periodical confiscated by the British occupation authorities). On the artistic plane it was, perhaps, the most interesting group, as a result of the activities of Max Ernst who, joined by Hans Arp, began to make his *collages*, of which the most famous series is entitled *Fatagaga* (short for *'fabrication de tableaux garantis gazométriques'*). The exhibition of April 1920, held at the Winter Café and closed by order of the police, reached a level of scandal and provocation which has never been surpassed. The departure of Max Ernst for Paris in 1922 marked the end of Cologne Dadaism. Mention should also be made of the movement in Hanover, founded by the poet and painter Kurt Schwitters, whose *collages* entitled *Merz (\*)* were formed of unusual materials and all sorts of litter (*vide* Ernst, Grosz, Schwitters).

Dada was less an artistic movement than an intellectual revolt, born of the convulsions of the 1914–1918 war, and too directly bound to its anguish to be anything other than a cry of negation, which inevitably carried within itself the seeds of its own destruction. But it was necessary for the coming of Surrealism, which was to build on its ruins.

Dada had little appeal in England, and, in the U.S.A., existed only briefly in New York. The living members of the original Dada groups, such as Hülsenbeck and Tzara, still pursue old feuds and keep alive controversies which no longer arouse public interest. Hülsenbeck lives in New York and practises as a Jungian psychiatrist under the name of Charles R. Hulbeck. Grosz also lives in America. His current work, though sometimes more spectacular than the old, is considerably less effective. Dada's main contribution to this century was its satirical character, and that, at least, is not quite dead.

**DALI** Salvador. Spanish painter born in Figueras, Catalonia, in 1904. His father was a notary, a native of the village of Cadaqués. It is the scenery of this village that is Dali's true spiritual home. After a stormy passage through the various schools in Figueras, during which he was given lessons by a drawing teacher named Núñez, Dali went to Madrid, where he entered the School of Fine Arts. With ease and conviction – for, despite his originality, he is methodical and conscientious – he absorbed the academic recipes of the old historical painter Moreno Carbonero, who had been teaching there even in Picasso's time. But, above all, he fed himself on Freud and books on philosophy which, he claimed, were the only ones that could move him, even to tears. Through art reviews he became keenly interested in Cubism, Futurism and, particularly, Metaphysical Painting, which seemed to him the prime ideal. A close friendship bound him to Federico García Lorca, and they spent long hours comparing notes on their respective problems. Lorca drew and painted with an ethereal fantasy; Dali countered its suggestiveness with concrete plastic forms. In his respect for an exact realism, he resorted to *trompe l'œil* and photography, the extraordinary possibilities of which he was to emphasize much later in such films as *Le Chien Andalou* and *L'Âge d'Or*. The paintings which he showed at Dalmau's in Barcelona in 1925, and in Madrid in

1926, at the first exhibition of the Iberian Artists, alongside Ferrant, Palencia, Cossio and Borés, were already founded on strangeness and contrast. After a brief period of Cubist influence, in which he tried to reconcile the teachings of Gris, Chirico and Carrà with the best technique of the past, his own universe revealed itself in all its distinctiveness: distant views of seascapes, clear and luminous, seen through deep windows framed in black, with silhouettes of bending women in the foreground. But this poise, so inconsistent with his excitable nature, could not satisfy him. He made a trip to Paris by taxi in order to get acquainted with Picasso, Versailles, and the Grévin Museum (the French Madame Tussaud's). He made contact with Surrealism, painted *Blood is Sweeter than Honey*, published (in Barcelona in 1928) the insulting Groc Manifesto, brought the members of the Parisian Surrealist group to Cadaqués, organized a triumphant exhibition at the Galerie Goemans, and married Gala, the wife of the poet Paul Eluard. A newcomer to the group, Dali was full of fight, fanaticism, and conviction. Using a rich philosophical terminology, he elaborated a new method of creation, which he defined as 'paranoiac-critical activity'. By intensifying the excitability of the mind, he wanted to create a lasting, frenzied pattern by the juxtaposition of chance objects. He knew very well how to use visionary experiences, interpretations of memory, and all the mental distortions that he came across in his systematic, conscious study of psychological derangement and pathological accidents. By absorbing oneself in the contemplation of something, he maintained, it is possible to enter another plane. The artist, placed before an external object, is led to describe the ascendancy that this object has over him. By painting it, he liberates – at one and the same time – his subconscious from this hold, and the object from its

conventional meaning (*vide* also Surrealism). Dali shows his desire to drain reality, and go beyond it, in one single operation. He may take as the basis of his work elements produced in the most mechanical fashion, such as a snapshot of an expressive face, or the reproduction of a very conventional painting, such as Millet's *Angelus*. Then he lets the image deteriorate by a sort of decomposition, expressed by the softening or the elongation of its substance, or, simpler still, by painting in a few flies or some other real and visible sign of putrefaction. Thus the object is taken far from its original meaning towards a new representation. In his Surrealist work, however, Dali has remained faithful to his initial mythology, pushing to the extreme only the

DALI. PERSISTENCE OF MEMORY. 1931.
*Museum of Modern Art, New York*

pathological and morbid distortions to which he subjects his materials. When he began to undergo the influence of the Italian Renaissance, in 1937–1938, and to prepare for the return to Classicism which has marked his recent work, he was on much less sure ground. He was disowned by his friends, and the Surrealist leader, the poet André Breton, denounced his technique as ultra-reactionary and academic. However, he has had considerable success with a certain set in the United States, where he went to live in 1940. He has influenced both fashion and advertising.

He now gives his models so-called 'atomic' interpretation, and tackles religious themes. When he returned to Spain he found nourishment for his basic pictorial realism, and also the elements of a baroque tradition which seems better suited to his temperament than the austerity of a classicism drawn from Raphael. Dali the man is even more of an enigma than Dali the painter. Although he has been very lavish with his secrets in his writings (*The Secret Life of Salvador Dali, Fifty Secrets of the Art of Magic*), in which the parts containing personal revelations are far more extensive than his essays with philosophical pretensions, Dali has assumed so many masks and poses, that it is hard to uncover his true personality. One can, nevertheless, discern elements of authenticity and continuity in his temperament. This applies particularly to the physical presence (which he never denied) of the landscapes of his childhood: the hills of Ampurdan, stretches of sand, and the shores of Cadaqués, bleached white by the sun. This landscape, which Dali, with unaffected pride, considers the most beautiful in the world, is in his subconscious mind. It is the common

DEGAS. DANCER ADJUSTING HER SHOE.

denominator of all his external adventures. In spite of the variety of themes that have been superimposed on it, nothing affects this persistence of memory. The survival of such aspects of his childhood helps to explain and, to a certain degree, gives a human quality to many of Dali's irritating caprices.

DEGAS. STUDY FOR A PORTRAIT OF MANET.
*Circa* 1864. *Metropolitan Museum, New York*

**DEGAS** Edgar. French painter born in Paris in 1834; died there 1917. He was the son of a banker, Auguste de Gas, and, like Manet, belonged to the upper middle class by birth. His taste for classicism, the correctness with which he conducted himself, seem to be in keeping with his origins, but his exceedingly strong personality and independence of mind threw him into the camp of the revolutionaries. He learned to paint at the École Nationale des Beaux-Arts, under Louis Lamothe, a pupil of Ingres, for whom Degas always had a profound admiration. Whatever the evolution of his genius, he was never critical of his early training. No doubt it was his great respect for human creation that was at the bottom of the misanthropy of which he is often accused, and behind which one can sense a deep tenderness. The evolution of his art explains the very special position that Degas occupied in relation to Impressionism. In his earliest paintings, such as *Spartan Girls and Boys Exercising* (1860), *Semiramis Building a City* (1861), and the *Misfortunes of the City of Orléans*, for which he made numerous studies, or even (a little later) the *Cotton Market in New Orleans* (1873), which he painted during his stay in the United States, we are indisputably looking at an extremely classical art, with meticulous draughtsmanship. Little by little, without weakening the rigour of his drawing, he allowed colour to become more and more important. Colour was, however, always subordinated to a realism which would have been dry and narrow had not the genius of Degas brought it a breadth of vision and an originality in composition which saved him from academism, and gave his work a significance far in excess of the place he is given in the Impressionist movement.

Degas certainly belongs to Impressionism because of his desire to capture the fleeting moment, and his concern for presenting exact reality. His division of colour, however, never went so far as the dispersal stressed by the landscapists. Whereas with the Impressionists, form tended to dissolve in the atmosphere, with Degas it kept its density. In fact, unlike them, Degas wanted to sum up the living world within strictly determined limits: he had no taste for suggesting the rustle of leaves, the shimmer of water, or the changing effects of the sky. When landscape does intrude into his composition – in his race-course scenes in particular – it never gives the impression of a work executed on the spot; nor does one feel, with him, that Nature was necessary to his inspiration. The picture-dealer Ambroise Vollard records this significant remark made by Degas: 'The air which one breathes in a picture is not the same as the air one breathes outside'. He did not seek chance beauty improvised by Nature, he preferred that created by man. He preferred the artificial light of the theatre to sunlight. He was interested in the human presence, and never treated the silhouettes of his figures in the casual manner of the other Impressionists. In that way his art was not a repudiation of the Classicism glorified by Ingres, but actually an extension of that formula enriched by new experiences. All these points, on which he differed with his friends, are not, in fact, sufficient to exclude him from the Impressionist movement – in the first place, because Degas himself decided otherwise (in fact, he participated, from the beginning, in a number of their exhibitions, at a time when this participation meant taking a stand, a declaration of war); but, above all, it should be understood that

DEGAS. STUDY FOR 'MISFORTUNES OF THE CITY OF ORLÉANS'. 1865. *Louvre*

although he had his differences of opinion with Monet, Sisley and Pissarro, he did not oppose the new school but, with Cézanne, completed it. Cézanne, it will be remembered, wanted to make of Impressionism a solid painting like that of the museums. One might say that Degas dreamed of creating a museum painting as living and modern as that of the Impressionists.

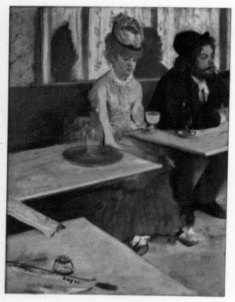

DEGAS. ABSINTHE. 1876–1877.
*Louvre*

Whereas Monet, Sisley and Pissarro sought the maximum possibilities of colour, and Cézanne did the same with respect to volume, Degas cherished an equally tenacious passion for drawing. 'I am a colourist with line', he said. He drew, and colour came only to complete, by its material and fixative quality, what the drawing had caught of the dynamic reality. Drawing was, for him, the result of swift observation. It was necessary to see quickly, and the mind must be able to select; painting was the result of a series of verifications, and did not require the same inventive qualities. Slowly, however, he began to discover the wider limits of colour. He began to seek in it something more than local tone,

and the means of characterizing a volume. From then on colour brightened the body surfaces, caught the light on the filmy *tutus* of the dancing girls, and produced some of the most glamorous and fairylike scenes of the close of the nineteenth century. These dancers, these women at their toilet, are certainly neither intelligent nor beautiful. They are commonplace, often vulgar in their physique and in their poses, but Degas strips them of matter, picking out only the essential rhythms of their movements, making beauty itself spring from the banality or vulgarity of their gestures. He does it so naturally, so completely, that he never gives the impression of resorting to artifice in order to transfigure reality. His was a more complex, intellectual creation than those achieved by most of the other Impressionists.

One thing is certain: if Degas, starting from Classicism, felt isolated in the midst of those who claimed to have broken with the past, he was still more opposed to those who wished to preserve it with a dismal and narrow fidelity. The deep hostility and spirit of revolt that made Degas reject all the trite academic formulas transmitted by the École des Beaux-Arts, can never be sufficiently stressed. This stubborn search for the new, the hitherto unattempted, was with Degas more a means than an end. He wanted to cast off all that was conventional, trite or commonplace, in order to transcribe reality without having anything impede or distort his vision. Degas is really the first artist in whom indifference to all that was not real was carried to its extreme. His attitude is similar to that of the zoologist, or the physiologist. He outlines a human attitude as a doctor describes a clinical case. It is therefore Naturalism that transformed this traditional artist (as he was at first) into one of the most daring innovators in the transcription of the scenes of modern life. But this search, however persistent, was never provocative. Breaking with the accepted conventions, his *Portrait of the Bellelli Family*, which he painted when he was only twenty-six, contains a real stage setting, which must have surprised his contemporaries somewhat. Degas portrayed M. Bellelli with his back turned, seated in an armchair, an arrangement which was hardly in conformity with custom. In his pictures of this period, no matter how traditional they might be, he seemed to be already avoiding static forms, seeking instead the effect of photographic instantaneity, which was to become characteristic of all his work. His *Cotton Market in New Orleans* (1873) is a synthesis of his art over a period of years: audacity in the placing of the subject, very important foreground, scrupulously exact draughtsmanship, and a very solid, though somewhat conventional perspective. Without a doubt this very need to represent life led him to paint his characters at work, such as laundresses, milliners (1880–1884), surprising them in characteristic attitudes. For several years before then dancers had revealed to him the resources of the human body, and shown him what an artist who cared about draughtsmanship could find in the acts of everyday life. It is only natural that the name of Degas should conjure up, for the less informed, dancers in *tutus*, practising their points, tying their shoe ribbons, or revolving about the stage from strange perspectives with oddly foreshortened bodies. For these dancers represent Degas's decisive contribution to the Impressionist movement. They represent the very movement of perpetually changing reality surprised, immobilized – that obsession of the artists of the period. However, the reality seen by Degas is his own: anxious to express the maximum of life, he selected aspects of reality that had never been observed before, and were thus more striking in their truth. His nudes – women at their toilet – reveal attitudes that do not appear very natural, the limbs being contracted in awkward gestures. For the same reason he tried to get from light effects which were contrary to natural lighting; he tried to capture the light of the footlights, which rises from the floor, inverts shadows, transforms faces, and brings gestures out in unusual relief. Degas went beyond this stage in the expression of movement and took up sculpture: his statuettes of horses and dancers became a real arabesque in space, and the analogy of gesture between dancer and horse, the same way of nervously extending the leg, reveals his keen and exacting observation.

If Degas belongs to Impressionism, it is by his mental disposition rather than his technique,

by his clear refusal to accept a conventional world. Study gave him a technique; the spectacle of reality gave him a sense of life. Degas appeared to divine the potentialities of the modern world to a far greater extent than his friends did. It is no mere accident to find in his work a forecast of new ways of disposing figures on the canvas, and unexpected angles of vision which, many

DEGAS. CARLO PELLEGRINI. 1876–1877.
*Tate Gallery, London*

years later, photography and the cinema were to use. His views seen from above, his method of depicting the main figure in a portrait off centre, of giving the foreground unexpected importance in relation to the subject as a whole, of putting the emphasis on an inert and accessory detail in order to accentuate, by contrast, the expression of life in a face – all these innovations correspond exactly to what the camera gives us today. In *Le Secret Professionnel* Jean Cocteau writes: 'I have seen photographs that Degas enlarged himself, on which he worked directly in pastel, amazed by the arrangement, the foreshortenings and the distortion of the foreground'. But that is reducing too much to chance the part played by the artist, without taking into account the sharpness of his magnificent drawing, which goes far beyond instantaneous photography, no matter how exceptional that may be. These new possibilities interested him only in so far as they enabled him to emphasize the everyday action. Degas always refused to paint from Nature. Although, in his work, he gives an impression of spontaneity, of having captured a gesture or pose at a dress rehearsal in the theatre, or on the racecourse, his pictures are all studio productions, the results of long hours of hard work under conditions where, unlike the artist who works from Nature, he is not limited by time. His painstaking drawings were made from memory, or from 'notes'. At a time when some painters were proclaiming their desire to depict their passing impressions, Degas's profound and patient observation produced masterpieces full of the feeling of life.

He brought the same research approach to the problems of technique, and there, too, his classical sense, far from limiting him, impelled him to seek that mastery of his craft which the painters of the past had had. Though he used the most varied mediums, he found pastel the one that suited him best. Sometimes he used different mediums in the same picture, or else he would superimpose coats of pastel in order to obtain, as in oil-painting, a play of transparencies between the strokes. Towards the end of his life, his sight failing, he developed a preference for working in charcoal, multiplying the sharp, nervous strokes, often enhancing them with pastel. Degas is as indispensable to the history of Impressionism as Renoir, Monet, Cézanne. Even if his work has had less influence than that of Cézanne, it contains enough mystery to enable it to be rediscovered one day for reasons which we do not suspect, and which will, perhaps, be far from those for which we admire him today.

**DELAUNAY** Robert. French painter, born in Paris in 1885; died at Montpellier in 1941. As painting was the only thing he really cared for, he gave up his studies early, and entered a school of theatrical design. From 1904 on he devoted himself exclusively to art. His work soon got away from traditional techniques. After a holiday spent in Brittany in 1904, he began to paint in large touches of pure colours similar to those of the *Fauves*. His self-portraits, with dominant reds and greens, are his first results in this direction. In 1906, when Delaunay was

DEGAS. AT THE RACES. 1869–1872.
*Louvre*

DEGAS. FIGURE STUDY FOR THE PICTURE IN THE LOUVRE, 'BALLET REHEARSAL ON STAGE'. 1874.
*Private Collection*

Nature, as well as a small panel with a grey atmosphere in which the first of his Eiffel Towers appears, date from 1908. It would seem as though before undertaking his great chromatic adventure Delaunay was gathering (while reducing them to the extreme) the essential elements of his inspiration. In 1909 he painted the Saint-Séverin series: in it light is broken down into the colours of the spectrum, while the architecture is simplified and tends to give the impression of forms turning in space. These fascinating works foreshadowed *The Windows* of 1912.

In 1910 Delaunay married Sonia Terk, whom he had known since 1907, and who worked side by side with him. With his two compositions called *The City*, Delaunay entered Cubism. This time he no longer had recourse to chromatic scales but to the search for values. Working in dominant greys and greens, his touch became finer and more precise. On the other hand, the three large compositions entitled *Eiffel Tower* (1910), now in the Basel Museum, the Guggenheim Museum in New York, and a private collection in Germany, represent a remarkable attempt to increase the height and depth of the canvas in a most audacious fashion, solely through construction and colour. Divergent planes are superimposed, the perspectives multiply and swell as in an accordion, space acquires a new thickness and consistency. In the large composition *The City of Paris* (Musée d'Art Moderne, Paris), painted in three weeks for the Salon des Indépendants of 1912, three large figures of nude women are developed according to the same principle of superimposition. In this major work Delaunay again takes up his prismatic method of composition, though in a more systematic manner, one part of the picture being dominated by a red and yellow light, the other by blue and violet shadow. Writing of it, Apollinaire said: 'It is the most important picture in the Salon'.

This work marks the beginning of what is called Delaunay's constructive period, as opposed to the preceding, so-called destructive period. Setting out to find something which would not be torn, jagged or dramatic, Delaunay composed his *Windows*. From then on he gave up all images drawn from reality, he abolished objects 'that come to break and corrupt the coloured work'

under the influence of Seurat, this technique evolved logically towards the breakdown of colour, not by Pointillist methods but by laying it on in large flat patches. In the composition of *Le Fiacre* he translated the movement by means of a kind of elongated mosaic, but in his *Manège de Cochons* (1906), a theme which he took up again in 1913 and 1922, he affirmed for the first time his preoccupation with circular rhythms. He began to study the theories of Chevreul, and became interested in Cézanne's conception of space. Cubism was just being born. Delaunay scrutinized the works of Braque and Picasso, Negro statues, and the works of art of Egypt and Mesopotamia in the Louvre. He became a great friend of the Douanier Rousseau, from whom, at his request, his mother commissioned *The Snake Charmer*, now in the Louvre. His large studies of foliage and vegetation, painted from

R. DELAUNAY. RUNNERS. 1926.
*Collection of S.D., Paris*

*(vide* illustration, page 7). Apollinaire fully appreciated the import of this transition from the representational to the non-representational: he invented the word Orphism *(\*)* to designate all those colourful manifestations which brought a ray of hope into the rigid and cold monotony of Cubism. Delaunay has been accused of having returned to Impressionism and become a decorative painter. In reality, a new art was created, which set forth the formal representation of space and movement.

After *Simultaneous Prismatic Windows,* Delaunay freed himself altogether, and reached pure painting in *The Discs* and *Cosmic Circular Forms,* all dated 1912. Modestly, he did not consider his research – so important for the birth of abstract art – as culmination but, rather, as a necessary transition. 'We are at the ABC of the new painting', he used to say. However, in *Homage to Blériot* (1914), even though his abstract research is predominant, Delaunay found again a certain meaning in representation. The theoretical importance of his discoveries, the shock power of his coloured universe, brought him considerable

prestige. His influence extended far beyond Paris. A great friendship sprang up between him and the two young German artists Franz Marc and August Macke. Kandinsky invited him to the two *Blaue Reiter (\*)* exhibitions. Klee translated one of his articles. Apollinaire's lecture at the Delaunay exhibition in Berlin, at the Der Sturm Gallery in 1913, made a tremendous impression.

During the 1914–1918 war Delaunay spent a long time in Spain and Portugal. In his Portuguese still lifes there is some return to the use of subjects, and a predominance of rounded forms. After the war he went back to his old themes: riding schools, runners. The Eiffel Tower continued to arouse his amazement. In 1925 ne painted his large *City of Paris* for the Mallet-Stevens Pavilion at the Exhibition of Decorative Arts in Paris. Returning to his *Discs* of 1914, he amplified them in his *Unending Rhythms* and *Coloured Rhythms.* He discovered new cadences and expressed them with an ever-renewed joy and youthfulness. The Paris International Exhibition in 1937 gave him the opportunity of realizing his greatest ambition. After two years of intensive preparation, he executed, in a month and a half, ten enormous bas-reliefs in colour for the Hall of Railroads and a gigantic *Rhythm* about a thousand square yards in size for the Hall of the Air, works which, with their enormous dimensions, represent one of the most imposing efforts in modern decoration. Colour had become the subject, and Delaunay achieved abstraction in the fullest sense of the term. In 1938, gravely ill, he painted his last *Rhythms,* and finished writing about his research. These writings are still unpublished. In 1940, fleeing from the German invasion, he took refuge in Auvergne, then in Mougins. He died in Montpellier on October 25th, 1941.

**DELAUNAY** Sonia Terk. French painter, born in the Ukraine, 1886. She was brought up in her uncle's house in St Petersburg. She was attracted by mathematics but chose painting. On the insistence of her drawing teacher (who was also an ethnographer), she obtained her parents' permission to go to study in Germany, where she stayed for two years, at Karlsruhe. Then she went to Paris and enrolled at the Académie de la Palette, which was frequented by Ozenfant, and by Segonzac and his friends. Under the influence of the work of Gauguin and Van Gogh, she sought a means of liberation and expression in the intensification of colour (*Philomena, the Seamstress*, and the portraits of little girls she painted in Finland). She made the acquaintance of Wilhelm Uhde, who was on the side of the Fauvist painters (then in their Cézannian period), and exhibited in his gallery. Cubism was soon to begin. She met Robert Delaunay, whose taste for poetry and pictorial ideas she shared, and married him in 1910. Swept along by his dynamism, Sonia elaborated a personal mode of expression, which summarizes her experience with Cubism and Orphism, and used it in designing bookbindings, cushions, rugs and *collages* made of violently coloured paper and cloth. She covered her walls with abstract compositions, and made herself dresses of 'simultaneous colours'. On the same principle she created pictures which are orchestrations of colours with no representational purpose, which suggest movement and emotion merely by their combinations. In 1913, at the Herbstsalon in Berlin, together with Robert Delaunay, she exhibited some twenty objects and pictures, and the first 'simultaneous book', created to illustrate Blaise Cendrars's poem, *La Prose du Trans-Sibérien et de la petite Jehanne de France*. In 1915 the vivid light of Spain awoke in

Sonia Delaunay coloured memories of her native village. In Portugal the beauty of the country and of the national costumes inspired some brilliant compositions (*Market at Minho*) and encouraged her to widen her field of decorative activities. In Madrid, inspired by the Spanish dances, she painted some abstract water-colours in which she studied the relationship of colours in their reciprocal action. She met Diaghilev, who commissioned her to design costumes for the ballet *Cléopâtre*. Robert Delaunay painted the décor. On her return to France in 1920 she decided to apply her ideas to fashion. She revolutionized the art of fabric design, replacing traditional patterns by geometrical motifs, combinations of coloured planes, and scales of tones with exciting contrasts of rhythmic variations. Her fabrics were reproduced and adopted by the leading couturiers, and exerted a great influence over many aspects of our life (the theatre, the cinema). This occupied so much of her time and energy, that Sonia was obliged, in the end, to give up her commercial obligations in order to be able to devote herself to painting. The practical application of her ideas shows their importance and, particularly, their architectural value. Sonia Delaunay's discoveries were shown at their best in the vast compositions in the Hall of the Air and the Hall of Railroads at the Paris International Exhibition in 1937. After their flight before the invading Germans in 1940, and the illness and death of Robert Delaunay in 1941, a

S. DELAUNAY. COMPOSITION. 1952

new period opened for Sonia, a period of meditation and research. In 1942, in Grasse, in the south of France, where she met Sophie Taeuber-Arp and Magnelli, she painted a series of harmonious and subtle gouaches. After the war she helped to found the Salon des Réalités Nouvelles (an idea put forward by Robert Delaunay in 1930), where, for the first time, abstract paintings from all over the world could be seen together. In 1953 an important retrospective exhibition of her work, held at the Bing Gallery, showed the evolution of an art which, for all its ascetism, has never sacrificed richness or intensity.

**DELVAUX** Paul. Belgian painter born in Antheit, Belgium, in 1897. This painter was a long time finding his way. He was alternately a Neo-Impressionist and an Expressionist until about the year 1935. Then, the combined influence of Giorgio de Chirico and René Magritte drew him into the Surrealist movement. His aim, from then on, was no longer to interpret faithfully the exterior world, but to explore the intimate and secret domain of his inner life. Objective reality ceased to interest him, except as a frame for his dreams. In his depiction of these dreams, one encounters strange combinations of people and places. From their contrasts and affinities, a disquieting poetry is born. Temples, moonlit towns, streets and public squares, empty rooms: these are settings for the same type of woman, young and beautiful, sometimes nude, sometimes dressed in lace, in foliage or in long robes with heavy folds. The painter is obsessed by this person. All his work, except for a few compositions with skeletons, reflects his need to come closer to an ideal being who, as the result of a paradoxical reversal of situations, seems to pursue him, instead of being joined by him. Surrealism *(\*)*, as a movement, envisaged the freeing of man through an appeal to his instincts and his subconscious. Each of its painters used different means of expression and different techniques. Delvaux's style, much more realistic than that of Max Ernst or Joan Miró, is closer to that of Chirico. But whereas Chirico's manner is dry, ascetically bare, deliberately barren, Delvaux is a lyrical artist who has inherited from his Flemish ancestors a taste for harmonious forms. He paints meticulously, but the excess of detail, the literary content of the overworked backgrounds, sometimes divide the attention instead of concentrating it on the principal subject of the picture. Delvaux's palette, sombre at the beginning, has grown progressively brighter until it is now brilliant. Several journeys to Italy have strengthened his taste for bright colours. Some handsome watercolours round off his work, which can be described as classical in method and Surrealist in spirit.

**DENIS** Maurice. French painter born in Granville in 1870, died in Saint-Germain-en-Laye in 1943. Maurice Denis was the

DELVAUX. HANDS. 1941.
*Private Collection*

originator of the famous definition used when-ever anyone wants to explain contemporary art: 'Remember that a picture – before being a horse, a nude, or some sort of anecdote – is essentially a flat surface covered with colours assembled in a certain order'. That text dates from 1890. Maurice Denis was then not yet twenty, but he showed already an unusual lucidity in such matters. Through Sérusier, who came back from Brittany in 1888, he had just been introduced to the message of Gauguin, whose ideas on Symbolism, and its offshoot Synthesism, were taking shape. In fact, it was the group at the Académie Julian (*), in which, around Sérusier and Maurice Denis, were to be found Bonnard, Vuillard, K.-X. Roussel, René Piot and Ranson, that began the reaction against Impressionism, which these young artists nevertheless admired. All the philosophical theories, all the ideological for-mulations, led to a new aesthetic doctrine (*vide* Nabis) which rejected the technique of the older generation. As against the improvisation of Monet and Sisley, and the dispersal of form, Gauguin put forward an art into which went a good deal of thinking, a choice, harmonies in which what the painter wanted counted more than the observation of Nature. Gauguin wanted the reconstruction of form by colour applied over large areas, and also strong, precise draw-ing, sometimes even going to the extent of a thick outline around the figures or subjects. Before adopting this formula, Maurice Denis had tried to paint the vibration of light by the use of small touches and the division of colour in accordance with the principles of Seurat. But, whatever the importance he attached to technical problems, his keenness for ideas inevitably led him to treat, in his pictures, subjects with a much more complex significance than simple land-scapes or still lifes. If, then, Symbolism was an intellectual and poetic concept which demanded that a picture should not be merely the material representation of the external world but should also express and suggest certain thoughts or states of mind, then the birth of Synthesism was inevitable. The desire to spiritualize painting sprang from a need for synthesis, a very con-trolled art, the opposite of Impressionist spon-taneity, which is analytic. The introduction of

DENIS. THE MUSES. 1893.
*Musée d'Art Moderne, Paris*

philosophical and poetic elements into painting was bound to satisfy Maurice Denis, who remains one of the most important theorists of the time, through his two basic works, *Theories* and *New Theories*. His work as a painter is an exact reflection of the state of mind which, little by little, led him to devote himself almost exclusively to religious art. He is – with Georges Desvallières – one of its most able renovators.

Nevertheless, there is a strange contradiction between Maurice Denis's work and his ideas. After having been one of the first to stress the idea that a work of art ought to find its justifica-tion in itself, the subject being only of secondary importance, Maurice Denis is also the man who has given the subject back its primary importance; for, in religious art, the representation of the Nativity or of the Crucifixion is the picture's main *raison d'être*.

Maurice Denis travelled widely in Belgium, Spain, Germany, Switzerland, Algeria, the United States and Canada. Greece and Palestine impressed him strongly. But it was Italy that influenced his work most decisively: Rome gave him classicism; Siena his harmony of colours;

Florence his simplicity of design; and Assisi the purity of his landscapes. For his art, like his faith, was nourished by his love for the loftiest embodiments of the mind and of beauty. He executed numerous mural decorations, especially for churches, and his predilection for static forms and almost immobile figures is particularly suited to this type of work. Through his calm drawing, his range of light colours, his delicate harmonies of blue and rose, he gives the impression of a serenity which is rather exceptional in the painting of his time. And that might, perhaps, be his main fault. At times one would like to sense more unrest in his work, a humanity less satisfied in its beatitude, a calm less manifest and less complete. In his writings one gets the distinct feeling that this calm is actually tremendous self-control, and that Maurice Denis the man, with his restlessness and his doubts, deliberately imposed on himself the solution of life to which Maurice Denis the artist bowed.

**DE PISIS** Filippo. Pseudonym of Luigi Tibertelli, an Italian painter born in Ferrara in 1896. A critic confronted with his work might get the superficial impression that he has never had any problems or submitted to any discipline. He lived in Paris from 1925 to 1939, but without arousing much interest, his preoccupations having nothing in common with those of the other artists of his age. He seemed to be living in reverse, anxious, as he was to revert to the Venetian origins of Impressionism, to throw a bridge across from Paris to Venice and thus hide the poverty of Italian painting of the previous century. In an epoch of serious and laborious researches, his apparent facility is disconcerting.

And yet, just as certain pictures by Picasso would not have been disowned by Ingres or Raphael, a snowy landscape by De Pisis would not have displeased Pissarro, Marquet, or Utrillo. As Delacroix wanted to, he really paints a man as he falls from a window and before his body crashes to the pavement. That is why the execution may appear sketchy, almost stenographic. He is clearly not a creator of forms but a painter of sensations, of unexpected encounters. Chance plays a great part in his work, which comprises some thousands of canvases. It is uneven: every painting by De Pisis is an adventure, but not every adventure is felicitous. Nevertheless, there are many successful pictures among them, which justify the popularity he enjoys among Italian collectors. Writer and poet, De Pisis is also one of the most original personalities in contemporary Italy. He is considered the greatest Italian landscapist of the century, but his love of Nature is hardly ever founded on direct sensation. He might, perhaps, have been indifferent to Nature, had it not inspired so many masterpieces. Reminiscence stimulates his imagination, and his most beautiful landscapes, like *Notre-Dame de Paris*, *Trafalgar Square* or *Saint Mark's*, are those which, for centuries, have inspired the most mediocre but also the greatest artists.

DE PISIS. SNOW IN BRUGHERIO. 1950.          *Private Collection*

**DERAIN** André. French painter born in Chatou in 1880; died in Paris in 1954. Intelligent and studious, he had a fine academic record. Then he suddenly decided to devote himself to painting. He became friendly with Vlaminck *(\*)* and shared a studio with him at Chatou. He painted with Matisse at Collioure, frequented the Bateau-Lavoir *(\*)* in the Rue Ravignan in Paris at the same time as Braque and Picasso. About the same time he made the acquaintance of Guillaume Apollinaire. Therefore none of the new ideas and new currents of sensibility that traversed the early years of the century were foreign to him. Derain was one of the first to discover Negro art, to feel the zest of popular imagery and the richness of folklore, to admire the beauty of the Sienese primitives and the painters of the École d'Avignon. But, first of all, he was an exponent of Fauvism *(\*)*. Like his friend Vlaminck, he employed the segmented touch, the swift curve, and garish colours. But his touch was less brutal, his curves more sustained, his colours more harmonious. The dominant tones in his palette were green, blue, and the whole range of violets from pink through purple. In his canvases there is none of that harsh, careless workmanship which indicates violence of instinct, but harmonies of propor-

DERAIN. STUDY. 1942

VLAMINCK. PORTRAIT OF DERAIN

tions and tones, a sign of careful thought and reflection and, even then, of virtuosity for virtuosity's sake. He knew all the glamour of colour, and yet continued to pay careful attention to form and construction. That is why he executed some of the best Fauvist paintings: *Westminster Bridge* (see illustration, page 101), *A Corner of Hyde Park*, his landscapes of Collioure and of L'Estaque, and *Woman in Deck Chair*. More eager than exacting, he wanted to include in a picture all the gains of modern painting, the discoveries of Impressionism, of Gauguin, of Van Gogh, and the influences of his friends Matisse and Vlaminck. It was this ambition that led him to paint *The Bathers* (1907), a work that seems to be a summary of the achievements of a quarter of a century. But, driven by an insatiable curiosity and, possibly, by lack of confidence in himself, he began to examine the masters of the past and delve into problems of technique. In fact, Derain was always concerned with problems of *métier*, and it began to assume a preponderant importance in his work. Setting

DERAIN. COLLIOURE. 1905.  *Private Collection, U.S.A.*

own mind. At a time when form was being dissolved in the shimmering light of the Impressionists, or broken down under the analytic efforts of the Cubists, Derain wanted to grasp it by the simplest and most direct means. Nature then became his inspiration, and the Old Masters of the museums his models. His landscapes, his still lifes and his portraits were composed with clear, precise draughtsmanship and rather dull, muffled colours. It is difficult to sort out in them the numerous influences to which he voluntarily submitted – those of Caravaggio, the Caracci, Corot, Cézanne and Renoir – for he amalga-

aside the dictates of the mind in order to triumph over some technical obstacle, the artist accomplished many a *tour de force* without, however, calming his restlessness. He went to the Louvre to copy the great Italians. Then, having been won over to Cézanne, he participated in the elaboration of Cubism, but refused to adhere to the movement. He was a man who lived with History, although he seemed to live with his time. He proceeded to study the secrets of the Old Masters, drawing from tradition the nourishment that his proud will demanded. Towards 1911 he became interested in the French and Italian primitives, who knew how to combine intellectual tension with grace of feeling. He admired the Gothic painters, but also the Douanier Rousseau, the Ferrara painters, and the old French folk-artists. From 1920 on he applied himself to the schools of the Quattrocento, Piero della Francesca, Raphael, the Bolognese painters and, still later, the art of Pompeii. From then on he became a Realist and (to his credit, let it be said), a sincere and convinced Realist. Although he had been a *Fauve*, he had the originality to treat the problem of colour as secondary, and concentrate primarily on structure, in order to satisfy the demands of his

mated them with infinite skill. Surrounded by colleagues who were all for mobility, intensity and sensory excitement, Derain advocated order, sobriety and reason. Methodical, if not dogmatic, curious but versatile, at times more concerned with surprising than persuading – he revived in French painting the old classical spirit, and with indisputable authority. His work may look like a product of the brain, like a technical exercise. He has crammed too many recollections into it, accumulated too many thoughts. Furthermore, the emotional quality of his work runs the risk of being smothered under the weight of intellectual constraints, although moments of softness and abandon come to remedy the essentially cerebral dryness of his style. But when his hand lets itself go there is such fantasy, such easy grace! Certain critics, thinking of his early promise, of what he might have been and wanted to be, have accused him of lack of faith, of apostasy. Others have regarded him as 'the greatest living French painter'. A return to the use of a subject, to chiaroscuro, to modelling; a return to academic ideas of resemblance, imitation and finish; a return to the human, not through the quivering thickness of flesh but through the severe discipline of museums;

discoveries instead of inventions; cautiousness rather than wisdom; an extreme virtuosity, yet restless and morose – such appears to be Derain's art. All the same, Derain is not a dry, academic painter. And he is more than just a talented painter. This is what Apollinaire said of him in 1916: 'Derain has passionately studied the masters. The copies he has made show how anxious he was to get to know them. At the same time, with unparalleled courage, ignoring all the audacities of contemporary art, he found in freshness and simplicity the principles and the rules of art.' Will posterity confirm this opinion? One way or the other, the fact remains that he has no influence today on the young French painters. But even if one rejects his later paintings, it would be unjust to forget the good canvases he painted at Vers, Martigues and Albano, his still lifes of 1912 and 1913, his astonishing illustrations for Rabelais's *Pantagruel*, as well as the décors and costumes that he designed for the *Ballets Russes (*)*. No other painter has shown, at one and the same time, so much doubt and so much mastery. No other painter has so conveyed the feeling of wanting to dominate his century and, at the same time, reject it.

DERAIN. COSTUME FOR 'FASTES'. 1933

DERAIN. THE WINDOW. 1913. *Kunstmuseum, Basel*

**DESNOYER** François. French painter born in Montauban in 1894. Cubism and Fauvism had already begun when Desnoyer was old enough to interest himself in painting. It was no longer tempting to adopt one or the other. Besides, a lucid and independent mind like his could not choose one trend to the exclusion of the other. Recognizing the importance of the contributions made by the new schools, Desnoyer took from each what best suited his temperament. He took over the rigid construction and geometrical framework of Cubism, and the intensity of colour of Fauvism. From this duality Desnoyer built up a stable and solid art. Everything in him lends itself to a double interpretation: he is a mild giant, and a placid southerner; his art has the freshness of spontaneous impressions, and the sureness of well-thought-out work. Desnoyer's originality lies in his having found unity in these apparent

DESNOYER. THE PORT OF MARSEILLES. 1940.
*Musée d'Art Moderne, Paris*

in addition to Marcel Duchamp, the painters Jacques Villon and Suzanne Duchamp, and the sculptor Raymond Duchamp-Villon. Marcel Duchamp was first a librarian at the Sainte-Geneviève library in Paris, a post which hardly interfered with his liberty at all. 'Comfortably seated, he let his thoughts dwell on anything he liked, and was pleased to give information or advice to anyone who came and asked for it politely.' About 1908–1910 he had painted a few canvases in the style of the great Impressionists, 'just to find out for himself how they did it'. In 1911 his own genius asserted itself in his *A Propos de Petite Sœur*. His breakdown of forms grew more marked until, in 1912, he finished up by producing a number of decisive works, including the famous *Nude Descending a Staircase*. When this canvas was shown at the Armory Show *(\*)* in New York in 1913, it made Duchamp famous over-

contradictions, of having created a healthy language for himself, in which everything is in place, without affectation. His personality is so much in evidence that it always dominates the subject. A landscape of Venice, Albi or Sète, a nude or a still life, is first and foremost a picture by Desnoyer, with his particular harmonies and structure; that is to say, a combination of vividly coloured planes, sonorous contrasts, clean-cut drawing with a rhythm provided by the play of straight lines; a work in which one feels the will but not the effort, a balance between reason and instinct, leaving no room for misunderstandings, just as there is no room for shadows in these compositions in which everything has the right resonance.

**DUCHAMP** Marcel. French painter and theorist, born in Blainville, near Rouen, in 1887. His father was a notary, and had six children, of whom four are well-known artists:

night. The conservatives thought the picture an abomination, a nameless horror, while those who were looking for something new called it the 'light at the end of the tunnel'. One critic described the canvas as 'an explosion in a shingle factory'. It was a series of five schematized human forms, overlapping one another, descending a winding staircase, with a marvellous rhythm and precision. Duchamp was offered several commissions at the time, but he replied: 'No, thanks. I prefer my liberty.' He earned his bread and beer by giving French lessons to New York artists (and anyone else who felt so inclined) at two dollars an hour (the current price). He became acquainted with Francis Picabia, and they were for a time inseparable. The friendship was a great source of pleasure to both of them. They were two of the people responsible for the Dada movement and the Dada spirit. Between 1915 and 1923, taking it very easy, he executed his major work, more than three yards high; the first picture to be made on a sheet of transparent glass, with fragments of cut-out and painted tin fixed to the glass with a permanent varnish. 'Canvases', he said, 'have dusty behinds.' This work was *The Bride Stripped Bare by Her Bachelors*. This is a mystical-mechanical epic of Desire. The bride-fiancée hangs from the sky, with her antennae, and communicates with the massed group of her bachelors: nine of them, red, erect in their uniforms or liveries – the priest, the cuirassier the gendarme, the police-

DUCHAMP. STUDY FOR 'BRIDE STRIPPED BARE BY HER BACHELORS'. 1915
*Collection of H.-P. Roché, Paris*

man, the bar boy, the department-store delivery man, the undertaker, the valet and the station-master. They receive the bride's essence and set in motion a dramatic-mechanical and interstellar ballet on 'human love seen by one from another planet, who can't make head or tail of it,' as André Breton, the Surrealist poet, said, not without humour. Little by little, the hermetic quality, precision and splendour of this singular work brought Duchamp world-wide acclaim, which left him quite unmoved. All he wanted was to play chess. He did not want to paint, anyhow.

His maxim was never to repeat himself. He alone among the great painters succeeded in carrying it out – by the simple expedient of just ceasing to paint, all of a sudden. His twenty canvases and glass panels, sold to intimate friends of his (now dead), were bequeathed by them, in accordance with his wish, to a single museum, that of Philadelphia, where nearly all his works are concentrated. He is the father of the 'ready-mades': mass-produced objects ready for use which, with a little inspired alteration, can be transformed into works of art. The most famous among those are: the big bottle-drier, the fountain urinal which he signed 'Mutt' and exhibited in New York in 1916, and the reproduction of the Mona Lisa, 'L.H.O.O.Q.' (1919), which he decorated with a becoming moustache. He was

intimately bound up with Surrealism (*). He invented the ceiling made of coal-sacks for the International Surrealist Exhibition in Paris in 1938 as well as the Rain Hall and the pink breast in foam rubber, labelled 'Please Touch', which adorned the cover of the de luxe catalogue of the 1947 exhibition. He made a kind of portable museum (three hundred of them) for his friends. It was a valise containing reproductions of all his principal works, and a little phial with fifty cubic centimetres of Paris air, a souvenir for an exile. One phial broke, and Duchamp had another specially sent to New York, containing genuine Paris air. Preferring a young and growing civilization to those that are too ripe or too cocksure, he has been living in New York for years now. His example of art for oneself, and of disinterestedness, has slowly had its effect. He has become a world legend. His name evokes independence, boldness, and total success in his own domain.

**DUFRESNE** Charles. French painter born at Millemont, in the Seine-et-Oise, in 1876; died at La Seyne, in the Var, in 1938. At a very early age he was sent to work for an industrial engraver, and attended evening classes in drawing. Despite the opposition of his family, he succeeded in gaining admission to the

École Nationale des Beaux-Arts, in the medal-engraving section. His first important canvases date from 1908, after a long stay in Italy. In 1910 he won the Prix de l'Afrique du Nord, and spent two years at the Villa Abd el Tif in Algiers. This contact with an Oriental civilization, even though a declining one, had a decisive influence on the evolution of his art. Dufresne had a gifted imagination. Like Delacroix, for whom he had the greatest admiration, he found his purity of form and violence of colour beneath Mediterranean skies. Later, in his studio crammed with curios brought back from his travels, he reconstructed an exotic and fabulous world of vivid intensity. He was not interested in historical reconstructions. On the contrary, he wanted to give back to the modern world the colour of life, and integrate this colour in large, sweeping rhythms, thus reacting in his own way against the fragmentation of themes and the exaltation of the object. He also had the courage to attempt religious themes and, among the painters of his generation, seems to have been the one most capable of giving the subject its full value. That is why he was able to exercise such great influence over the young painters whom he taught for several years at the Scandinavian Academy. Together with a few friends, he founded the Salon des Tuileries in 1923; in 1924 he decorated with tapestries a collection of furniture by the decorators Sue and Mare, which was one of the attractions of the Exposition des Arts Décoratifs of 1925. He executed décors for the Paris Opera (*Antar*), and sketches for tapestries

(*La Plage ou Plaisirs de l'Eté*). Finally, in 1937, he painted two panels (Le Théâtre de Molière) for the Chaillot Theatre in Paris, and some vast murals for the great amphitheatre of the École de Pharmacie, which he completed only a few days before his death. In these he showed his taste for broad swaths of colour, sweeping movements of figures, a measured lyricism full of passion, and an understanding of texture, which is to be found even in the smallest of his rough sketches.

**DUFY** Raoul. French painter born in Havre in 1877; died at Forcalquier in 1953. At fourteen Dufy worked as a clerk in a coffee-importing firm in his native town. Beginning in 1892, he attended evening classes at the municipal art school after work. In 1900 he went to study in Paris, in Léon Bonnat's class at the École Nationale des Beaux-Arts. Dufy seldom went to the Louvre, maintaining that the great Masters frightened him (although he loved the works of Claude Lorrain). What really interested him was the work of Van Gogh and the Impressionists, which he saw at the Galleries of Vollard and Durand-Ruel. He exhibited in Berthe Weil's gallery. In 1905 Dufy chanced to see a canvas by Matisse, *Luxe, Calme et Volupté*. It was a revelation to him. 'When I saw this picture', he said, 'I understood at once the new *raison d'être* of painting'. Dufy then decided to change his style: no more beaches in the manner of Boudin or Sisley, but streets bedecked with flags and very colourful open-air dances, like the paintings of the *Fauves*, who made the Salon d'Automne of that year so memorable. For a living, Dufy then turned to engraving and fabric design. After a short trip to Munich with Friesz (1909), he began a series of canvases showing the influence of Cézanne. He met Paul Poiret, the couturier, who assured his economic independence by giving

DUFRESNE. LION HUNT. 1932.　　*Collection of Lew Fox, Chicago*

DUFY. CONSOLE WITH YELLOW VIOLIN.
*Private Collection*

attacks of arthritis, which was later to cause him much suffering. When the war began in 1939 he finished the panel of the Monkey House at the Paris Zoo and that of the Seine, which decorates the smoking-room of the Palais de Chaillot. In 1949 he left Perpignan, where he had lived since 1940, returned to Paris, and then (1951) went to Boston to consult American doctors about his ailment. In America this charming and cheerful man was welcomed wherever he went. The American scene captured his fancy (he had been there previously, in 1937), and he gave the Americans some interesting and curious observations on their country and their culture, both verbally and in paint. He painted race-tracks, views of the Charles River (Boston), and the crowds and skyscrapers of Times Square, which enthralled him. In Arizona he drew rodeos and dramatic sunsets. 'The trouble with the American artist,' he said, 'is that he does not see what is around him until he sees it in a picture.' He advised them to throw away their cameras and then paint. On his return to France he settled down in his country house at Forcalquier, where he died on March 23rd, 1953.

Dufy was a painter of joy – the joy of seeing, imagining and creating, without ever repudiating the reality of the world around us. He did not mind admitting that there was representation in

him work as a dyer and painter on fabrics. He also worked for Bianchini-Ferrier, the silk manufacturer. In 1920 he stayed at Vence in the South of France, where he painted many land-scapes. Then he went on a journey to Sicily and Morocco, and brought back with him a collection of paintings and water-colours. Fame be-gan to come his way, and the first monographs on him were published. At the Georges Bernheim Gallery he exhibited deco-rated ceramics for indoor gardens. He executed an enormous decorative work (about 11 yards high and 65 yards long) for the Palais de l'Electricité at the Paris International Exhibition in 1937. About this time Dufy was be-ginning to feel the first

DUFY. THE THICKET. 1930.
*Musée d'Art Moderne, Paris*

his painting. 'My clients buy my subjects from me', he said jokingly. 'The rest is just thrown in.' From the visible world Dufy chose a few themes which pleased him, and he made successive variations of them up to the time of his death: streets gaily hung with bunting, the beaches of Normandy, regattas, homages to Mozart and Claude Lorrain, the Bois de Boulogne, race-tracks,

DUFY. THE PADDOCK.                    *Private Collection*

garden parties, the farms and forests of Normandy and the South, brass bands and orchestras, fields of corn, work in the fields. The painter would pick out and accentuate a few precise details, such as a palm tree, a balustrade, the hull of a ship, the curve of a shell, a violin bow. Such elements as these became his trade-mark. Dufy summed up all these themes on the cottons he decorated for Poiret, and used them on tiles decorating the walls of his indoor gardens. He spread them over his panel *Electricity*, and his other masterpiece, *Itinerary from Paris to Saint-Adresse and to the Sea*, in the home of Doctor Viard. There, in the limited space of the picture, Dufy, cleverly immobilizing everything that changes, succeeds in giving us the illusion of passing time. Far from weakening one another, Dufy's variations give one another value. They are the 'states of soul' of a particularly receptive painter, who started seeking afresh in every

picture. There is no repetition in his stages of progress. He said: 'When you have succeeded in something or other, quickly turn your back on it, and enter on a new adventure'.

Another of Dufy's points of originality, the most outstanding perhaps, is his prodigious draughtsmanship, the importance of which has not always been recognized. Dufy put infinite imagination and cunning into his drawings, using the whites of his paper with unequalled skill and knowledge. In fact, in his sketches of race-tracks one is astonished to find that what pleases so much is what has been left out. A few chairs, a few spots for the spectators watching the jockeys parade, suffice to suggest a crowd. Dufy's calligraphy, in graphite, India ink, oil or water-colour, with its precise, rapid, staccato signs, has often been compared to shorthand. But shorthand signs are fixed, stereo-typed. There is nothing like that about Dufy's 'handwriting', which, although it does show a few more or less fixed signs in the manner of the Japanese artists, has nevertheless been perpetually enriched and modified by constant observation of the visible world. There is nothing more amazing than a drawing by Dufy. The painter has succeeded in tracing in it the very dynamism of his intimate self. Through this multiplicity of squares, rectangles, triangles, ovals, ideograms of every sort, the charm of a vision is composed and presented. Everything, even the formless, has a contour, a rhythm. Everything is art, nothing is really Nature. By the direct use of line and colour, the painter transmits to us his state of mind, his feeling – with the result that the objects he depicts speak only through the man who created them, with a pleasure the like of which cannot be found in any painter since Renoir.

And now, his colours. These have, especially

in his water-colours, the resonance of primordial freshness. How can one describe Dufy's blue, his subtle red, the serene glow of his greens? Every painter has his dominant colour. Dufy's is blue, the only colour that keeps its individuality through all its nuances. Nobody knew its innumerable variations better than Dufy: vibrant blue, the blue of the sky broken by drifting white clouds, the fascinating blue of a creek at midday, the blue of the sea, ultramarine, the cerulean blue of a fair girl's eyes.

Later, he tried to restrain his palette. He began a series of yellow consoles, red violins, black cargo-boats, where the fundamental colour, skilfully modulated, is broken only by a few tones. 'What tempts me now', said Dufy (and this only a short time before his death), 'is to take up the problem of colour again outside the law of complementaries. I would like to try to contrast or combine colours which do not go together; that is to say, which our usual attitude to colour harmony makes us reject.' All that, coming after such considerable achievements, does not fit in with the 'petit maître', elegant and charming, that some people thought Dufy to be – he who was a difficult painter on the whole. Dufy could do well only what he did happily, without reworking. But how much reflection 'between the acts' before he took up his brush again! He would forget what he knew, and awake each morning like a child before the great secret of life and the universe.

Toning down a once proverbial desire to please, his illness intensified his vision and made him concentrate his entire being on his creative work. He lived only through and for his art, but without becoming a slave to it. For him painting was one of the superior activities, a means of communicating with others, of bringing them sustenance. Dufy knew how to do everything, and do it artistically. He liked to stress how important technique could be in the work of a painter. But, at the same time, he would state that the artist should get beyond technique, in the sense that he should cease to be preoccupied with it. In that, and only that, he belonged to the Renaissance. He did not work according to classical perspective. He rejected the laws of chiaroscuro, as well as everything based on the physical lighting of the object. He organized and illumined his canvas according to his own conception of light. He had conceived a theory of white shadows (neutrals) and coloured lights.

DUFY. YACHTS AT DEAUVILLE.     *Collection of Doctor Roudinesco, Paris*

Dufy was never satisfied with what he knew. Up to the last he could be seen throwing himself with extraordinary youthfulness into the quest for new ways of expression. For instance, he tried to convey, by using black, the effect of being dazzled by looking straight into the sun.

Dufy did not give a thought to fame, but at the end of his life he was overwhelmed by the indications of his triumph that came to him from practically all over the world. He lived to see the great retrospective exhibition of his works held in Geneva. That was a year before his death. The posthumous Paris exhibition, in the summer

DUFY. ORCHESTRA. 1936

of 1954, showed the importance and fecundity of his painting.

## DUNOYER DE SEGONZAC André. French

painter; born at Boussy-Saint-Antoine, Seine-et-Oise, in 1884. Dunoyer de Segonzac seems to have been untouched by the intellectual, technical and emotional restlessness of his time. Refusing to yield to any external pressure, hostile to fashion and theories at the risk of appearing out of date, he thought only of serving those talents that he had already revealed in 1907, in his drawings of nudes and his landscapes. A friend of La Fresnaye, Boussingault, Jean Marchand, and Luc-Albert Moreau, he reacted with them against the disintegration brought about by Impressionism and the excesses of the *Fauves*, by limiting himself to an austere palette dominated by ochres, earth colour, cadmiums and ultramarines. But the painter soon learnt that to use too many successive coats, meant risking the loss of one of the most powerful attractions of oil-painting: transparency. From 1919 on, his landscapes, his nudes and his still lifes are more relaxed. The lesson of Corot began to be added to that of

Courbet. Making long stays at Saint-Tropez and in the Île-de-France, Segonzac, whose cult of the great forces of Nature goes back to his childhood, fled from all dissonance and all that might disperse and compromise the over-all stability of a picture. He holds that all good painting needs, over and above the state of grace in which the artist ought to be, the quality of certain harmonies, and not contrasts and violence. One is struck by the unity of his work, whether it be his drawings, water-colours, oils or engravings: the same conception binds the masterpieces of his youth, such as *The Drinkers* (1910) or *Le Déjeuner sur l'Herbe* (1913), to the etchings illustrating the *Georgics* (1947). Is it a belittling of Dunoyer de Segonzac to say that he is primarily a great draughtsman? Just as he identifies himself with his characters when he depicts boxing matches (*Boxing*), a nude, soldiers at the front (*Wooden Crosses*), Grock or Isadora Duncan, he *is* that pear tree resisting the wind, that poplar pulsating in all its leaves. He is that field of tenacious vines, clinging to the slopes, that sun armed with rays, those ripples through which the sky and the water show their density. In his water-colours, as in his engravings, the more line dominates colour the more resonance colour has. Drama without emphasis, a quiet, deep vehemence, sometimes big scars, evoke the conflicts and varying moods of Nature. Drawing which keeps guard like a conscience forbids any slackness of form, any overflowing of colour. On his return from the 1914–1918 war Segonzac, after a brief initiation by his friend Laboureur, began to draw as freely on copperplate as on a sheet of paper. Far from losing the joyous quality of his work in his engravings, the artist instinctively discovered his methods and the means of condensing his inspiration on a small surface, and even intensifying its powers. A catalogue of his engravings would today list over two thousand works. Several of them are in series, such as *Le Morin* (1923), *Beaches* (1935), *From Joinville to Bougival* (1936), and, together with his illustrations, constitute the most brilliant work on copperplate that has come from any painter since Pissarro.

**DURAND-RUEL** Paul (1831–1922). The influence of the great picture dealers on the development of painting in the nineteenth and twentieth centuries has been considerable, probably owing to the fact that at the beginning they acted, more often than not, out of disinterested enthusiasm. Durand-Ruel was first a friend of Corot, Millet, Théodore Rousseau and Boudin, and gave them both moral and material support, sharing their enthusiasms and their disappointments, and disposing of their

DUNOYER DE SEGONZAC. LA QUEUE-EN-BRIE.
*1931. Musée d'Art Moderne, Paris*

canvases for them, often with reluctance. He was most heroic in his backing of the Impressionists in 1870. In 1871 he fled to London, and there made the acquaintance of Monet and Pissarro. On his return to Paris in 1872 he bought twenty-three canvases from Manet for 35,000 francs. For more than ten years Durand-Ruel did his utmost to popularize the Impressionist works, which no one wanted and everyone condemned. That is how Manet, Renoir, Monet, Sisley, Cézanne, Degas and Pissarro became his friends, and the correspondence that he carried on with each of them contains many pathetic letters. He was really a philanthropist, and narrowly escaped bankruptcy before he succeeded in interesting America in the new school in 1886. In the history of Impressionism his name is linked particularly with the second exhibition of the group, which he arranged in his premises at No. 11 Rue Le Peletier in 1876, as a protest against the pigheadedness of the official Salon, which refused to accept the adherents of the new school. It was because of this exhibition (which came up against the most violent hostility) that Duranty *(\*)* wrote his famous book in support of *The New Painting*. The stubborn refusal of French collectors to accept the Impressionists made Durand-Ruel decide to open galleries in London, Brussels, Vienna, and finally in New York in 1887.

In spite of all this, when Fénéon congratulated him on his eventual success, Durand-Ruel replied: 'It is the collectors that we have to thank for that'.

**DURANTY** Louis-Émile (1833–1880). This little-known novelist of the French realist school was one of the most ardent supporters of Impressionism right from the start. In his impassioned articles in the *Gazette des Beaux-Arts* he traced the relationship between the Impressionists and the Venetians and Constable. In 1876 he published his book *The New Painting: Concerning a group of artists exhibiting at the Durand-Ruel Gallery*, in which he developed some very accurate views in a lively polemical style. Taking to task the very official École Nationale des Beaux-Arts for inspiring in its young pupils 'a strange system of painting bounded in the South by Algeria, in the East by mythology, in the West by history, and the North by archaeology', he hailed the works of the Impressionists, all of them inspired (so he wrote) by things of their time. After paying tribute to Courbet, Corot, Boudin, and, in particular, Manet, whom he regarded as the initiators of the new painting, he extolled the great work begun by Monet, Degas, Pissarro, Sisley and Berthe Morisot. He expressed the hope that the wall separating the studio from everyday life had at last been broken down, and that the picture would be a window opened out onto Nature and modern life, seized in their dynamism and the inexhaustible diversity of their character. He was the friend of many painters and writers, and was included by Fantin-Latour in his painting *Homage to Delacroix*, together with Manet and Baudelaire. There is a well-known portrait of him painted in tempera by Degas.

**DURET** Théodore (1838–1927). French writer and art critic, a contemporary of the Impressionists and one of their first supporters.

However, in his *The French Painters*, published in 1867, Duret, not being sufficiently informed, strongly criticized Manet, who had already painted *The Fifer* and *Le Déjeuner sur l'Herbe*. The matter was evidently soon straightened out, as Manet painted his portrait (now in the Petit Palais, Paris) the following year. After having generously assisted Renoir, Duret became his friend and one of his most ardent supporters. Meanwhile, in 1873, he went to Japan and came back full of enthusiasm for Japanese art. 'The Japanese', he wrote, 'were the first and most perfect Impressionists.' In 1878 he published his *Impressionist Painters*, this time praising them unreservedly. The book included monographs on Monet, Sisley, Pissarro, Renoir and Berthe Morisot. Manet was presented as the initiator of the movement. In a revised edition which appeared in 1906 the author added studies of Cézanne and Guillaumin. His catalogue *Manet and His Work* was not published until 1912. In 1894 Duret was obliged to sell his collection, comprising six Manets, six Monets, four Pissarros, three Renoirs, three Sisleys, three Cézannes and eight Degas.

# E

**ELEMENTARISM** An offshoot of Neo-Plasticism *(\*)* started by Theo Van Doesburg. In 1924 Van Doesburg, while still advocating the right angle, gave up the horizontal-vertical position of this angle and so came into conflict with the conception of Neo-Plasticism formulated by Mondrian. In 1926, in his review *De Stijl (\*)*, Van Doesburg wrote an article in the form of a manifesto, in the course of which he said: 'Elementarism is partly a reaction against the too dogmatic application of Neo-Plasticism, and partly a consequence of Neo-Plasticism itself. What it seeks, above all, is a strict rectification of the Neo-Plastic ideas.' He then went on to explain what he meant by 'rectification'. As against the homogeneous construction of Mondrian's Neo-Plasticism, he proposed a heterogeneous form of expression, deliberately unstable, with inclined planes. He tried, in this way, to increase the dynamic effect, and renew the element of surprise. The painters Cesar Domela and Vordemberge-Gildewart,

previously disciples of Mondrian, followed Van Doesburg.

**ENSOR** James. Belgian painter of English and Flemish parentage, born in Ostend, 1860; died there, 1949. Except for a stay in Brussels, Ensor never left his native town, thus showing his indifference to the schools, aesthetic doctrines, and artists of his day. All the same, his early works show certain influences, such as Degas, Manet, Renoir, the Symbolists, and particularly Turner. To his father, who was of British origin, he possibly owed his fidelity to the real, even in the realm of the imagination, and that truculent vitality which seem derived from his more northern ancestry. In any event, it is this combination that characterizes Ensor's expressionism and clearly differentiates it from the popular and rustic tendencies of a Van den Berghe, a Gustave de Smet, or a Permeke. *Lamps* (1880), *The Rower* (1883), are of clearly Flemish

ENSOR. THE INTRIGUE. 1890.                    *Museum of Fine Arts, Antwerp*

93

inspiration; *The Living Room* (1881) would not have been disowned by the Parisian *intimistes*. *Carnival on the Beach* (1887) has the characteristic Ensor flavour, his ardour, his predilection for the fantastic, his lyricism, his creamy medium which diffuses a pallid light crossed by glittering flashes of clear yellows and vermilions. In 1888 he painted his most important and best-known canvas, *Entrance of Christ into Brussels*, about three yards by four, a work which is at the same time burlesque and grandiose, a sara-band of baroque forms and strident colours, a disordered, tumultuous, vulgar but thoroughly alive composition. In a flaming riot of reds, blues and yellows (these yellows are now dull), one can see yelling crowds, processions of masqueraders, surges of hilarious faces, streamers flapping in the wind, and brass bands parading. The work teems with grimacing faces, monstrous legions, exagge-rated gestures, and rattling bones, confirming his lineal descent from Breughel and Hieronymus Bosch. He had a taste for farce, for extravagance and caricature, and to this he sacrificed cohesion, construction, purity of form and accurate tonal harmonies. However, Ensor is a true painter. No matter how dissonant his colours may be, they have a density, a brilliance, a distinctiveness, which the other Belgian painters certainly lack. When he wanted to, he could show that he was an informed and original draughtsman, particularly in some of his admirable etchings and dry-points: *The Cathedral, Fan-tastic Ball, Kermesse at the Mill, Death Pursuing the Humans.* The best of his work was accomplished between 1888 and 1892. For this artist, who lived to the age of eighty-nine, had said everything he had to say in five years, at the end of the last century. De-cline set in immediately. Old age left him still clownish, but without any creative strength. He expended his imagination on his eccentric subjects and themes rather than on the search for a personal art.

**ERNST** Max. A painter of the *École de Paris*, born in Brühl, near Cologne, in 1891. He studied philosophy at the University of Bonn from 1909 to 1911. He became interested in the latest works of Picasso and Chirico, also in those of August Macke, and in the Expressionist trend among the young German painters. Dadaism, however, had a much more determining influ-ence on him. In 1914 he made the acquaintance of Hans Arp, who, three years later, became one of the founders of the first Dada group in Zurich. After the war Ernst, together with Baargeld, founded the Dadaist group of Cologne. In 1921 he came at last to Paris, and became one of the active figures of the Surrealist group, joining up with the poets André Breton, Paul Eluard, Louis Aragon, Philippe Soupault, Robert Desnos, and René Crevel, all of whom are represented in one of his canvases, in the company of Raphael and Dostoevski. Owing to certain techniques which he discovered or revived, Ernst became the Surrealist painter who fitted in best with the activities of his poet and writer friends. He found a pictorial equivalent for automatic writing (so much in vogue for the creation of a poem) in the process of '*frottage*': black lead was rubbed onto paper held against an object, producing the effect of the weave of a piece of cloth, the grain-ing of wood, or the veining of a leaf. These

ERNST. THE MASSACRE OF THE INNOCENTS. 1921. *Private Collection*

impressions, skilfully done and exploited, formed mysterious works suggesting strange landscapes and animals, and vast expanses of imaginary country. Ernst also used the process of 'collage', which the Cubists had used to integrate elements of purely plastic value into their work (*vide Papiers collés*). But Ernst looked for disparate elements of an anecdotal and descriptive nature, in the illustrations of such varied forms of writing as tales of adventure, love stories, technical treatises. Their juxtaposition in the same work increased (often humorously) their powers of evocation. A meaning which is always fantastic and sometimes horrible, sentimental, and pathetic, reveals itself behind his most innocent compositions. Yet these *divertissements* are characterized by a juxtaposition that is a little too mechanical. Each of his works has been produced with a precise aim in view: to induce a kind of confusion in the spectator in order to make him sensitive to the appeal of the bizarre and the fortuitous. Purely plastic preoccupations became secondary, if they were not sacrificed altogether. Later, particularly after his long stay in America, his works freed themselves more and more from this tendency. The artist created a world which was quite his own, without diminishing its poetic power. He remembered his '*frottages*' and created a strange chaos of forms which seem like an abbreviation of the cosmic evolution: madrepores and strange minerals, plants that change into insects, human eyes and animal muzzles on the surface of petrified silhouettes. All the kingdoms – animal, vegetable and mineral – meet in confusion on a planet in effervescence. These forms are freely created by the painter, in accordance with the requirements of his picture. Their perfect plastic coherence makes them seem intensely alive. They constitute one of Surrealism's *(\*)* greatest successes in its exploration of unknown worlds born of dreams and imagination.

**ESPRIT NOUVEAU, L'** The title of a review founded in 1920 by Ozenfant and Jeanneret (Le Corbusier), which for twenty years reflected the new trends in intellectual activity in the period following the First World War. The collaborators of the *Esprit Nouveau* felt that a great epoch had just begun, and that all forms of human activity were at last going to be governed by one single principle. The aim of their efforts was the triumph of the spirit of construction and synthesis, which they considered was as necessary in the sphere of art and letters as in that of philosophy and the applied sciences. 'The constructive spirit', they said, 'is as necessary for the creation of a picture or a poem as it is for the building of a bridge.' The review, which had many distinguished contributors in all fields of creative activity, had a significant influence on modern thought.

**EXPRESSIONISM** Impressionism, Fauvism, Cubism, Futurism, Surrealism – titles adopted by the artists themselves or given them by their opponents – apply to contemporary and clearly defined groups or movements. Expressionism, on the other hand, denotes a permanent tendency in art, characteristic of the

VAN GOGH. THE POSTMAN. 1888
*Los Angeles County Museum*

Nordic countries, which becomes accentuated in times of social stress or spiritual disturbance. Expressionism has found particularly fertile soil for expansion in our turbulent age. Although the idea always existed, the term for it is a recent invention of German aesthetics, popularized by Herwarth Walden, publisher of the *avant-garde* review *Der Sturm*, in Berlin, who classified under the heading of Expressionism – as opposed to Impressionism – all the revolutionary manifestations between 1910 and 1920, including Cubism and the abstract trends. This broad definition, as confused as it is exaggerated, is to be found in the writings of nearly all those who concerned themselves with Expressionism, prior to Sheldon Cheney, who takes it to signify modern art as a whole and at its best. As against that, a large number of critics, fascinated by the *École de Paris* and its technical advances, deny, or fail to recognize, the emotional value of Expressionism. There are two conflicting viewpoints – the one putting the accent on plastic *form* and its autonomy, the other on psychological *force* and

MUNCH. THE CRY. 1895. *Lithograph*

its impetus – bringing up again the traditional duality of Classicism and Romanticism, of being and becoming, of the Latin and German temperaments. Expressionism constitutes the present phase of Romanticism, in a tragic mode, bound to the anguish of our times, and to the resurgence of the Slavic and Nordic spirit. Unlike the painters of the *École de Paris*, who wanted to create an international language, Expressionism favoured individual and ethnic distinctions. Although every case in Expressionism is a particular one and cannot be covered by any overall formula, it is, nevertheless, possible to indicate briefly the successive phases it has passed through and its areas of expansion.

As a reaction against Impressionism *(\*)* and the objective tendency of Cézanne and Seurat, which Cubism *(\*)* continued, the first Expressionist movement, with Symbolist and Modernstyle influences, came into being in 1885 and lasted until 1900. The leading figures in it were Van Gogh, Toulouse-Lautrec, Ensor, Munch and Hodler. Their subjectivism expressed itself in obsessional and dramatic themes, and not only through their intensity of colour but also through the monumentality of their forms and the violence and sharpness of their drawing, which explains the return to the expressive line and simplified engraving and illustration techniques. Van Gogh, setting an example with his way of life as well as his work, was the founder and hero of modern Expressionism. Often in his letters, notably on the subject of his portraits, he explains what he is trying to do, afraid all the time lest his deliberate exaggeration be taken for caricature. Caricature is, in fact, a popular and spontaneous form of Expressionism, but with Van Gogh it acquires a very special value, attaining religious grandeur through its style. His essentially Nordic message, in the humanist train of Rembrandt, has hardly been heeded in France. Lautrec created the modern poster, and realized the synthesis of the contrary elements of illustration and decoration. Hodler, Munch and Ensor figured in the second wave of Expressionism, which arose (about 1905) in Germany with the creation of the *Brücke (\*)*, and in France with the decisive contribution of Rouault, of Picasso of the blue and Negro periods and, in

KIRCHNER. AMERICAN DANCERS. 1908

the arts), and in a general way permeated the various currents in Germany on the eve of the war up to the *Blaue Reiter (\*)* of Munich. The creative fever became dramatically intensified, but without being able to assimilate the constructive lesson of Cubism. There are some outstanding names in the movement: Nolde and Kirchner, specifically Germanic temperaments openly at war with the art of Paris; Kokoschka in Vienna, who, at the very moment when Freud, in the same city, was elaborating psychoanalysis, executed a striking series of portraits which resemble flights into the subconscious. Suddenly the Jewish

some respects, of Matisse and Fauvism (Derain and Vlaminck). The Belgian Ensor vacillated between Impressionism and an expressive symbolism which he resuscitated from Bosch. The Swiss Hodler often indulged in an allegorical and irritatingly exaggerated realism. Munch, a compatriot of Ibsen, touched by the morbid side of Kierkegaard's philosophy, was the central figure of Nordic Expressionism, and left his mark on it both in Germany and Scandinavia. His influence in those countries is eminently comparable, though in an opposite direction, with that of Cézanne in France. His first exhibition in Berlin in 1892 caused a scandal, but shook Germany out of its academic and non-realist torpor, so out of keeping with its temperament. He brought that country back to its true tradition, that of Grünewald and Gothic Expressionism. The Secession movement reached Munich, Vienna, Berlin (*vide* Van Gogh, Toulouse-Lautrec, Rouault, Ensor, Hodler, Munch).

Expressionism in its dual aspect – social and physical – took firm root in the *Brücke* group, nurtured by Munch, Van Gogh and Negro sculpture (the most Expressionist of all

and Slav soul, dormant for centuries, manifested itself in painting, its expressionist tendency bringing a new ferment into art. From far away in distance and in time came men like Soutine, Pascin, Chagall, full of nostalgia and anguish, brimming over with tenderness. They settled in Paris before 1914. Expressionism penetrated to the United States about 1908 through Max Weber, also of Russian origin (*vide* Nolde, Kirchner, Kokoschka, Soutine, Pascin, Chagall).

After the extraordinary outbreak at the beginning of the century, the interim period between the two wars stabilized itself in a sort of

KOKOSCHKA. PEN-AND-INK SKETCH. 1919

97

neo-classicism, interrupted by only one revolutionary movement, Surrealism *(\*)*. But the great masters of Expressionism, Munch, Ensor, Rouault, Nolde, Soutine, Kokoschka and Max Weber, continued on their own, each perfecting his own work, while national forms of Expressionism developed in other countries, notably in Belgium, with the School of Laethem-Saint-Martin (Permeke, de Smet, Van den Berghe), solidly bound to the Flemish soil; in Latin America, fertilized by the spirit of the old Indian races – Brazil (Segall, Portinari) and, particularly, Mexico (Rivera, Orozco, Siqueiros, Tamayo) in the monumental and popular form of the fresco. Defeated Germany tried desperately to react against its instinctive Romanticism, but the so-called New Objectivism group (*Die Neue Sachlichkeit*), graced with the presence of artists like Dix, Grosz and Beckmann, dominated the last phase of Expressionism with its trenchant realism and social violence. Expressionism was expelled by the Nazis. Beckmann took refuge in Holland, where Expressionism evolved in a parallel manner (Sluyters, Charley, Toorop). Expressionism gave us Gromaire in France, Auberjonois in Switzerland, Solana in Spain, Rossi in Italy, and, after the 1929 crisis, gained many recruits in the United States, notably Rattner and Knaths. The Civil War in Spain, and the Second World War, moved Picasso to a

KIRCHNER. WANNSEE STATION. 1914.
*Pen-and-ink Drawing*

new Expressionist style of hitherto unheard of violence, of which the masterpiece is *Guernica*. This brought in its wake a general revival of Expressionism, in Europe (1935–1950), in Latin America, and especially in the United States, as a result of the direct influence of Beckmann and the Germanic tendencies (*vide* Laethem-Saint-Martin, Permeke, Smet, Beckmann, Gromaire, Solana, Picasso).

KOKOSCHKA. PORTRAIT OF WALDEN

# F

**FANTIN-LATOUR** Theodore. French painter born in Grenoble in 1836; died at Buré in the Orne in 1904. Although he was a friend of the Impressionists, being about the same age as Manet (born 1832), Degas (born 1834) and Monet (born 1840), his work is not Impressionist, either in spirit or in form. He was more like a late Romantic, inclined to serve his imagination rather than to depict reality, even a poetic reality such as Monet's. The exact representation of ordinary landscapes and their changing lights did not interest him. He painted fairies gambolling in clouds, or in rivers, or – when music, which he loved passionately, invoked them – in airy farandoles. He also painted flowers in great quantities, because those were the paintings that his clientèle bought. Between 1864 and 1896 he painted flowers almost exclusively. His gift of transfiguration was so natural that he invested each canvas with that secret life, that sweetness, which makes his work as a whole so ineffably appealing. Can he be described as a Realist because he painted some fine portraits and knew how to catch a likeness? We are, in fact, indebted to him for some group portraits of his friends: leading musicians, writers and painters of his time, among them Baudelaire, Rimbaud, Zola, Manet, Monet, Renoir and Whistler. These are photographic documents (not unlike the early paintings of guild groups) which will hold infinite interest for later generations, and testify to Fantin-Latour's sentiments and good taste. But there again, what he sought, even in those portraits with their striking likenesses, was to gratify his own sympathies rather than to preserve any one particular moment, or any one particular aspect of these people. Fantin-Latour did not adhere to any of the revolutionary theories and techniques of his friends and of his time. This was not due to cautiousness on his part. He was by nature

FANTIN-LATOUR. FLOWERS.
*Louvre*

discreet and peaceful, and he wanted his art to be the same. Unattached to any school, Fantin-Latour propounded nothing and invented even less. He created a world of his own and gave it material form without seeking originality and without acknowledging any dominant influence – unless, perhaps, that of Delacroix, adapted to his own more modest capabilities.

**FAUVISM** Fauvism, based on the exaltation of pure colour, was the first art revolution of the twentieth century. It was not a school, complete with programme and theory, but the result of the temporary conjunction of a number of painters, actuated by the same motives

99

and brought together through the kind of chance meetings that so often create highly productive movements. In the famous Salon d'Automne of 1905 twelve colourists, grouped around Matisse and conscious of the similarity of their views, exhibited together. The explosive forces of their work provoked a scandal. They came together again for the Salon des Indépendants of 1906. Louis Vauxcelles, the art critic, noticing a small bronze in the Florentine manner by the sculptor Marque in the middle of the hall full of the riotous colours of those who were still called the 'Incoherents' or 'Invertebrates', exclaimed: '*Donatello parmi les Fauves!*' (Donatello among the wild beasts). The name *Fauves* caught on, and by the time of the Salon d'Automne of the same year it was in general use. The history of Fauvism is a brief one, beginning in 1905 and reaching its full development in 1907. It may be useful to go over briefly the succession of exchanges and contacts that assisted in its creation and crystallized around the dominant personality of Matisse, the oldest in experience and undisputed leader of the movement. Three main groups of different origin (joined by Van Dongen, an independent) came under his sway, and rallied to his principles during those heroic years: the group of the Atelier Gustave Moreau and the Académie Carrière (Marquet, Manguin, Camoin, Puy), the Chatou group (Derain, Vlaminck) and, lastly, the Havre group (Friesz, Dufy, Braque).

Matisse entered the École Nationale des Beaux-Arts in 1892 as a pupil of Gustave Moreau. Rouault was already there. Marquet joined them in 1894, and Camoin in 1897. Moreau's enthusiastic and liberal teaching permitted the strong temperaments of the *Fauves*-to-be, who had become close friends, to develop without restraint. 'I am the bridge', he told them, 'over which some of you will pass.' When he died, his pupils dispersed. Matisse, who already had considerable authority over his comrades, spent a year in Toulouse and in Corsica, and brought back from these two places, in 1899, a series of small landscapes violently sketched in pure tones with a Pointillist technique. On his return to Paris he rented a studio at No. 9 Quai Saint-Michel, in the same building as his close friend Marquet, and stayed there until 1907 – that is to say, for the whole period of Fauvism. He painted figures in pure blue, still lifes radiant with scarlet and orange, with the same audacious treatment as his Southern landscapes. In his researches he was closely followed by Marquet and, though more warily, by Manguin and Camoin. In 1899, at the Académie Carrière, he met Jean Puy, Laprade, Chabaud and Derain. Over all of them, and Derain in particular, he exercised a strong influence. He exhibited at the Salon des Indépendants in 1901, together with Marquet. 'We were the only two painters to express ourselves in pure tones', Marquet later said, adding: 'Already in 1898 Matisse and I were working

MATISSE. NOTRE-DAME. 1902. *Private Collection*

in what was to be called the *Fauve* manner.' Derain and the self-taught Vlaminck, who shared a studio at Chatou, outside Paris, tried similar experiments, in an even more violent manner. It was at the first Salon des Indépendants, in 1901, in the midst of the famous Van Gogh retrospective, that Derain introduced his friend Vlaminck to Matisse. The years 1899–1901 marked, therefore, the first *Fauve* 'push', one part of it led by Matisse and Marquet, under the structural influence of Cézanne, the other by Vlaminck and Derain, under the Expressionist

DERAIN. WESTMINSTER BRIDGE. 1906.          *Private Collection, Paris*

influence of Van Gogh. This period was different from the period of happy, free expansion, between 1905 and 1907 dominated by the decorative influence of Gauguin.

In 1902–1903 Matisse and Marquet painted interiors and views of Paris, going back to the sombre workmanship of the early Manets. Derain went on military service, and Vlaminck, on his own, surrendered himself to his passion for colour. A small gallery run by Berthe Weil (*) gave some preliminary exhibitions of the works of the future *Fauves* from 1902 to 1904: Matisse, Marquet, Manguin, Flandrin, Camoin; then the childhood friends from Havre, Friesz and Dufy; and, later, Van Dongen, a Montmartre bohemian of Dutch origin. They exhibited again as a group at the Salon des Indépendants of 1903 (Matisse, Marquet, Puy, Manguin, Camoin, Friesz and Dufy), still without attracting public attention. Matisse had his first one-man show in the shop of the art dealer Ambroise Vollard, in June 1904, and spent the rest of the summer at Saint-Tropez, on the Riviera, painting in the company of Signac and, particularly, Cross, whose Pointillist technique he adopted, intensifying its force and luminosity. At the Salon

d'Automne he showed thirteen pictures done in this manner, which were a revelation to Friesz. In the Salon des Indépendants of 1905, where Matisse exhibited his *Luxe, Calme et Volupté*, it was Dufy's turn to experience a decisive shock when he saw 'this miracle of the imagination at play in drawing and in colour'. He and Friesz abandoned Impressionism, the tradition in which they were trained, to follow the 'pictorial mechanics' of Matisse. Derain came back from military service, and there were some very active exchanges between Matisse and the reconstituted Chatou group, who manipulated colours like 'sticks of dynamite'. During the summer Derain joined Matisse at Collioure, and from the stimulating contact between these two lucid and lively natures there, beneath the brilliant southern skies, the first real Fauvist canvases were born. They were to create a sensation at the historic Salon d'Automne of 1905, together with those of Marquet, Manguin, Puy, Valtat, Vlaminck, Friesz and Rouault, the latter exhibiting with his friends but remaining on the fringe of the movement with his sombre colours and moral passion. The year 1905 also saw the formation of a parallel movement in Germany,

VLAMINCK. RED TREES. 1906. *Musée d'Art Moderne, Paris*

the *Brücke (\*)*, which, however, soon turned to Expressionism.

The Salon des Indépendants of 1906, in which Braque (the last of the three men from Havre to be won over) participated, and the Salon d'Automne of the same year (the Gauguin retrospective), when Van Dongen came to complete the group, mark the peak of Fauvism. Its principles can be summed up in a few words: uniformity of light, space-construction by colour, illumination of the flat surface without illusionist modelling or chiaroscuro, purity and simplification of means, absolute correspondence between expression (emotive suggestion) and decoration (internal organization) by composition. 'Composition', said Matisse, 'is the art of arranging in a decorative manner the diverse elements through which the painter expresses his feelings.' Form and content coincide, and are modified by mutual reaction, for 'expression comes from the coloured surface which the observer takes in as a whole'. In short, it is dynamic sensualism ('the shock to the senses of what the eye beholds') disciplined by synthesis ('condensation of sensations'), and subject to the economy of the picture ('whatever is useless is consequently harmful').

This unity of transposition distinguishes the *Fauves* from their immediate successors, who superimposed colour on a conventional framework, and from the Expressionists with their illustrative tendency. No doubt such a balance between order and passion, fire and restraint, could not be maintained at such a high level for long. At the end of 1907 the collective paroxysm of Fauvism had already given way to incipient Cubism, which Matisse and Derain, as well as Braque, helped to create. Each went his own way; some, misunderstanding the message of Cézanne, went back to a sort of neo-classicism, while Matisse alone (perhaps Dufy too, though in a different mood) kept to the end the eternal youth of Fauvism. But for all of them this heroic exaltation remained, to quote Derain, the 'trial by fire' which has purified painting, and revealed the best in themselves to a number of highly gifted temperaments.

**FEININGER** Lyonel. American painter born in New York in 1871. His parents, German immigrants, were both musicians. Having shown early a marked talent for music, he went to Germany to study, but in 1887 decided to devote himself to art instead. Towards 1912 the influence of Cubism helped him to find his own manner. Feininger was one of the first artists to be invited by Gropius, founder of the Bauhaus *(\*)* in 1919, to teach with him in Weimar. Although he did not teach for long, he stayed on at the Bauhaus until it was disbanded by the Nazis in 1933, and his art, as well as his personality, contributed largely to the formation of its spiritual climate. Feininger left Germany in 1937, for political reasons, and settled in New York. From Cubism he learnt the transposition of forms and volumes into simple planes limited by straight lines, very rarely by curves. These planes were segmented. The structure of his pictures, after 1912, is akin to that of the Cubism of the *Section d'Or* in Paris, but subsequently became more and more complex and crystalline, until it attained an almost non-representational autonomy, between 1915 and 1919. After 1919, influenced by the architectural spirit of the Bauhaus, the ordering of his planes became clearer: they are joined in an order without heaviness, and are organized into architectural visions in which the aspect of the medieval streets of the towns and villages around Weimar is marvellously transposed. But Feininger does not think and construct in terms of architecture, as Walter Gropius has justly said. In fact, the constituent elements of his pictures are, in the transparent fluidity of their colours, rays of light which, by their interpenetrations, create that atmosphere of purity and unreality which is so characteristic of Feininger's art. A romantic nostalgia, his German heritage, thus finds definite form in precise constructions of a delicate sensibility. Like the American painter John Marin (to whom he is akin), Feininger has, since childhood, had a passion for boats and the sea. As with Marin, water-colours occupy an important place in his work, particularly since his return to the United States. His language has become even more precise, more musical, and his colour denser. His work is always the slow and methodical ripening of a theme – architecture in Manhattan, or a view of the ocean – which the painter never relinquishes until it has been fully realized in the full expanse of the picture.

**FÉNÉON** Félix (1861–1944). French writer and art critic. He was a friend of Seurat and Signac, and became the spokesman of Neo-Impressionism *(\*)* setting out its basic principles in a kind of pamphlet under the title of *The Impressionists in 1866*, which was a great success. Using the scientific theories of Chevreul, Sutter, Charles Henry and Edouard Rood, Fénéon explained the Neo-Impressionist methods, and did so with a warmth and conviction that earned him considerable support. Although he railed against Gauguin, and criticized (though not without respect) Monet, Degas and Renoir for not having systematically applied the principle of division of colour, he adopted a milder attitude toward Pissarro, who had allowed himself to be for a while attracted by Divisionism, and championed Seurat, Signac, Cross and their friends unreservedly. In his eagerness to support the new school, Fénéon went so far as to organize, in 1900, an important Seurat retrospective (which has remained famous in the annals of painting) in the premises of the *Revue Blanche (\*)*, of which he was, at the time, one of the secretaries. Furthermore, faithful to his friend's memory, he took it upon himself, after Seurat's death, to compile a thorough and precise catalogue of his works.

Although he loved order and logic, he was never at any time insensitive to the painting of

FEININGER. SCHOONER AT SEA.
*Collection Dætsch-Benziger, Basel*

young artists, such as Vuillard or Bonnard, whom he got to know in 1891, and with great perspicacity he supported the Nabi *(\*)* movement from its inception. He was an ardent admirer of Toulouse-Lautrec, who depicted his curious silhouette in *The Dance of La Goulue and the Almehs*, which he executed in 1895 for the dancer's booth at the Foire du Trône. There are numerous portraits of Fénéon, but the most symbolical is the one Signac left, with a title that must have enchanted Fénéon himself, *Sur l'émail, d'un fond rythmique de mesures et d'angles, de tons et de teintes, portrait de M. Félix Fénéon en 1890.* (On enamel, with a rhythmic background of measurements and angles, tones and tints, portrait of Mr Félix Fénéon in 1890.)

**FRIESZ** Othon. French painter born in Havre in 1879; died in Paris, 1949. As a student at the school of fine arts in his home town he was guided in his early efforts by Charles Lhuillier, an obscure artist with a passion for the masters of French painting: Poussin, Chardin, Corot. The future *Fauve* never forgot what he had learnt from his kindly old teacher. In the latter part of his life, after having weathered the storms of the new century, Friesz returned to the spirit of this teaching, and began to listen to the voice of reason, rather than that of instinct. But what a strong and impetuous instinct that was! In 1899 Friesz went to Paris, to the École Nationale des Beaux-Arts. He was not at ease there. He soon left, in rebellion against the official instruction. He joined up with some good friends of his, to fight against prejudice and raise the banner of a living art. He exhibited at the Salon des Indépendants in 1903, and at the Salon d'Automne in 1904. One of the most enthusiastic and brawny of the *Fauves* (*vide* Fauvism), intoxicated with colour, a devotee of the arabesque, hostile by nature to affectation and preciosity, Friesz painted (up to 1907) his series of Flanders, La Ciotat, and *Bathers*, and his admirable *Portrait of the Poet Fernand Fleuret*. Then he went back to Normandy – and tradition. In 1908 the *Fauves* had already dispersed. Alone with himself, Friesz rediscovered the virtues of logical composition, simple tones, and thick volumes. Trips to Por-

tugal, Italy and Bavaria helped to accentuate his reconversion to Humanism and tradition. But the vigour, the robustness, the sensuality, which had given such emphasis to the work of his youth, still showed in his landscapes, in his still lifes, in the female figures which he grouped round a fountain, or on the banks of a river, beneath the shade of big gnarled trees. In 1912 he opened a studio and taught until 1914. On the outbreak of the First World War he was mobilized, returning to live in Paris in 1919. After that he rarely left, except for brief stays in Toulon or in the Jura. From then on, far from the revolutionary movements agitating modern art, Friesz went on producing rather than creating, resorting to the cheap devices, easy effects and outworn rules of his craft. The one-time *Fauve* had given up adventure. The son of a sea captain had cast anchor in the pool of stale ideas. And when, in January 1949, he died, he left a body of work in which the most brilliant promise was followed by skilful evasions. He boasted of having been one of the first to kill Fauvism. He did not realize at the time that it was his own art that he had destroyed.

**FRY** Roger Eliot (1866–1934). Eminent English art critic, little known as a painter; born and died in London. Fry studied Natural Sciences (taking a first-class degree) at King's College, Cambridge, but gave up this field for art. He went to Rome in 1891, where he was profoundly influenced by Raphael and Michelangelo, and then to the Académie Julian, Paris, in 1892. He again visited Italy in 1894, and wrote essays on Bellini and Giotto. In 1905 he published a critical edition of Sir Joshua Reynolds's *Discourses*. Unable to find a suitable position in England, he accepted that of Director of the Metropolitan Museum of Art in New York in 1905. (He returned to London five years later.) He wrote a study of Cézanne, published in 1906, and became interested in the work of Gauguin, Matisse, Van Gogh and Maillol. It was Roger Fry (together with Clive Bell) who aroused an interest among the English-speaking peoples in what he aptly named 'post-Impressionism', with his two Grafton Gallery Shows in 1910 and 1912,

FRIESZ. PORTRAIT OF FERNAND FLEURET. 1907.
*Musée d'Art Moderne, Paris*

the equivalent of the American Armory Show of 1913. In 1933 he was appointed Slade Professor of Fine Art at Cambridge, and died the following year.

Fry had a vast enthusiasm for, and an intellectual understanding of art, but little creative ability. As a painter he was soon forgotten. In his views on art he was elastic and always open to new ideas. His many short studies and articles on the subject of art and artists are of great interest. His honesty and lack of conservatism won him lasting respect as a sensitive, perceptive and helpful critic.

**FUTURISM**  Futurism burst on Paris in February 1909, when the Italian poet, novelist and essayist Filippo Tommaso Marinetti published in *Le Figaro* the manifesto of Futurist poetry, extolling the beauty of speed and aggressive movement, vowing to destroy museums, libraries and academies of every kind. Born in Egypt in 1876, Marinetti studied literature at the Sorbonne in Paris. In 1909 his play in French, *King Bombance*, was performed at the

Théâtre de l'Œuvre. In the early part of 1910 three Italian painters, Carlo Carrà, Umberto Boccioni and Luigi Russolo, met Marinetti in Milan and, after lengthy discussions on the state of Italian art at the time, decided to issue a call to the young artists in the form of a manifesto. Carlo Carrà, in his *Memoirs*, writes that 'when distributed a few days later in thousands of copies, this appeal to fearless and open rebellion . . . had the effect of an electric charge'. The manifesto also bore the signatures of Giacomo Balla, who was living in Rome, and Gino Severini, who had been living in Paris for several years. A second manifesto was launched in April of the same year. Like the text published in *Le Figaro*, the new manifesto extolled the dynamism of modern life, to which even the French *avant-garde* painters remained completely indifferent. The young signers of this programme then believed blindly in the neo-Impressionist technique which Balla had taught Severini and Boccioni. A short trip to Paris gave them an opportunity of seeing the paintings of Picasso and Braque. They had really gone there with the intention of holding a first exhibition, but Severini succeeded in convincing them of the necessity for further work before venturing to face the Paris critics. When the exhibition actually took place, in February 1912, Futurism appeared to be an attempt to introduce into Cubist composition (*vide* Cubism) the dynamic element. While Severini brought to Futurism the pure colours of Seurat, Carrà, on the other hand, adopted the grey tonalities of the Cubists. Boccioni, the theoretician of the movement, never lost sight of the 'realism' of Picasso, visible even in his Cubist compositions. Russolo, by sheer poetic intuition, was already foreshadowing the advent of Surrealism.

From the first exhibition Severini emerged triumphant. In the following year, 1913, Giacomo Balla painted a series of masterpieces, suggested to him, it is true, by three of Severini's canvases entitled *Spherical Expansion in Space*. While the technical means of his companions was still uncertain, Balla was the only painter of the group to succeed in giving plastic expression to the desire for power proclaimed by Futurism. Boccioni, in his picture *Elasticity* and his sculptures, achieved results which were no less miraculous (*vide* Balla, Boccioni, Carrà, Severini).

It is clear that Futurism was more than just an impetuous rush towards the spirit of modernism, more than just a doctrine. In linking art with life, and conceiving of life as force, the Futurists posed the problem of art in a way which was quite new at the time: philosophically, as well as scientifically. Among their happier intuitions are the ideas of 'simultaneity' and 'space'. While the simultaneity of which the French poet and critic Apollinaire *(*)* spoke in 1913 concerned only vision and the laws of optics according to the latest scientific discoveries, the simultaneity postulated by the Futurists is essentially psychic, and is concerned with memories, associations, and all the diverse emotions which assail an artist at the moment of creating. On the subject of space, Boccioni ventured to speak of a fourth dimension, but that was neither a sufficient nor a particularly Futurist definition. The Futurists touched on the real problem when they announced that 'henceforth the spectator will be placed in the heart of the picture', which implies an absolutely original conception of space. Italian Futurism (to which Apollinaire lent his support for a short while) had numerous faithful supporters and emulators. Apollinaire went so far as to propose that all *avant-garde* tendencies be labelled 'Futurist', but Marinetti turned the suggestion down. The 1914–1918 war marked the end of the really interesting period of Futurism (which had been joined by such other artists as Soffici, Ottone Rossi and Mario Sironi), but Marinetti never gave up his movement. By 1930 there were no longer five or six Futurist painters, but five hundred. A name that deserves to be mentioned here is that of Enrico Prampolini, a painter and theatrical designer of indisputable merit.

# G

**GACHET** Dr Paul (1828–1909). Born in Lille; died in Auvers. His innate taste for painting and abiding friendship for painters, rather than the collector's urge, prompted Dr Gachet to gather around him at his home in Auvers-sur-Oise the greatest painters of his time. Not only Cézanne and Van Gogh but Pissarro, Renoir, Monet and Guillaumin were frequent visitors at the doctor's home. He became fond of them all, and their friendship went far beyond the usual relations between artist and collector. In fact, Cézanne stayed in Auvers for two years, from 1872 to 1874; moreover – and this is of capital importance in his life – it was at Auvers that he abandoned his romantic style and turned towards the new vision of reality that was to characterize his work and revolutionize modern painting. It was during his conversations with the doctor, and in the company of Pissarro, that Cézanne made in a few hours the disordered version of his *Modern Olympia*, at the same time that he was painting, in quite another vein, the celebrated *House of the Hanged Man* (*see* picture, page 50).

The relations between Doctor Gachet and Van Gogh were particularly close. After leaving the asylum at Saint-Rémy, Vincent, on the advice of Pissarro, went to stay at Auvers on May 20th, 1890, and saw much of the doctor, who was the artists' physician as well as their benefactor. Their friendship was to be short and tragic, for it ended, on the 27th of July with Van Gogh's suicide. Dr Gachet had tried, with the utmost skill and discretion, to persuade Vincent that he was not so ill as he thought. He gave him a measure of confidence in his abilities, and patiently endured his rebuffs and violence. In his calmer moments Vincent showed a tender affection for the doctor and his wife. In June he painted a picture of *Mademoiselle Gachet at the Piano* and the celebrated

portrait of the doctor wearing his famous white cap. When Van Gogh shot himself near the heart on the evening of July 27th, Doctor Gachet tended him for two days in a desperate effort to save him. Gachet has left us two moving mementoes of Van Gogh on his death-bed – a charcoal drawing and an etching.

Dr Gachet was himself a competent artist with a strong predilection for engraving. There is a drawing in existence by Cézanne in which the artist is shown being given a lesson in engraving by the doctor. At his death his collection of Impressionist pictures was kept intact. The most important paintings such as Renoir's *Portrait of a Model*, Monet's *Chrysanthemums*, Cézanne's *Modern Olympia*, Sisley's *Saint Martin's Canal*, and Van Gogh's two pictures *The Doctor's Portrait* and *Auvers Church* were left by Dr Gachet's son Paul to the Louvre in 1952.

DR GACHET. VAN GOGH.
ON HIS DEATH-BED. 1890.

GAUGUIN. THE YELLOW CHRIST. 1889.
*Albright Art Gallery, Buffalo*

**GAUGUIN** Paul. French painter born in Paris in 1848; died in Fatu-Iwa, one of the Marquesas Islands, in 1903. A knowledge of the circumstances of his birth, marriage and belated career as a painter is indispensable to a proper understanding of Gauguin and his work. Paul Gauguin was born in the Rue Notre-Dame-de-Lorette in Paris, the son of Clovis Gauguin, a republican journalist from Orléans, and Aline Chazal, daughter of the painter and lithographer André Chazal, and Flora Tristan Moscoso, an eccentric writer and militant socialist. Through his maternal grandmother Flora Tristan, Paul was related to the Borgias of Aragon, who had given several viceroys to Peru. It was therefore quite natural for Clovis Gauguin to think of Peru as a refuge when Louis Napoleon's *coup d'état* forced him to leave France in 1851. He died on the journey. The family continued on its way and went to live in Lima. Aline Gauguin was a loving mother, simple and sweet. (In 1892 Gauguin painted a portrait of her from a photograph and his recollections of her.) After four years in Peru she decided to return to France

with her children. Paul was then seven years old. Aline was made welcome in Orléans by Isidore Gauguin, her brother-in-law. Little Paul was sent to a religious school in the town. At the age of seventeen he joined the Navy, and visited Rio de Janeiro, Bahia, Sweden and Denmark. After the death of his mother, he gave up the sea and went to work for a Paris Exchange broker. He remained there for twelve years. An intelligent, punctual and methodical clerk, he soon attained an enviable position in the firm. He made money, spent it wisely, and lived in comfort. Eventually he married a young, beautiful Danish girl, Mette Sophie Gad. Evidently Mette, a healthy, practical, steady and not unintelligent woman, thought she was marrying a distinguished man with a brilliant future, capable of bringing her happiness and security. What she wanted, above all, was the

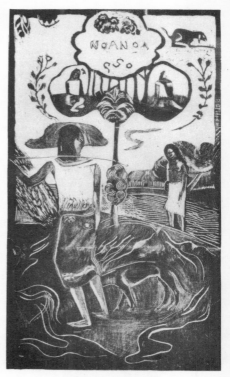

GAUGUIN. NOA-NOA.
*Woodcut*

peace and pleasure she derived from running her home and supervising the upbringing of her five children. It was not to work out that way. Gauguin struck up a friendship with Schuffenecker, also in the brokerage business, who painted in his leisure time. It was he who introduced Gauguin to painting. He soon recognized that Gauguin had exceptional gifts which he himself lacked. Answering the irresistible call of his vocation, Gauguin gave up his work in 1883 in order to devote himself entirely to painting. Mette was thunderstruck and frightened. From then on, incapable of understanding her husband, or really loving him, she never ceased to give vent to her resentment and deep humiliation, and heap endless acrimonious reproaches, grievances and complaints on his head. Paul Gauguin was free to paint, but he was to suffer till the end of his life. His first efforts were encouraging, but his financial resources ran out. Sick of her husband's 'foolishness', feeling insecure and fearful for the future, Mette decided to take the children and go to live with her parents in Copenhagen. Gauguin went with them. He felt as much a stranger among the Danes as he was to feel at home, later on, among the Polynesians. He took his favourite son, Clovis, and went back to Paris, promising to send for the others as soon as he could. Then began one of the most unhappy periods of his life. Without money, without any hope of making any, he could not even provide for his son. But his passion for painting sustained and stimulated him. He was convinced of his power, his mission, and his genius.

In 1886 he went to live in Pont-Aven, a charming village in Brittany, but stayed for only a few months. Brittany did not give him the stimulus he had hoped for. Old visions, long dormant, re-awakened in him. A year later he embarked for Panama with his friend Charles Laval. A typhus epidemic drove them away. They left for Martinique, where the revelation that Gauguin had so long awaited came to him: lush vegetation, ever-clear skies, lavish Nature, and a simple, happy existence. For lack of funds he had to drag himself away from this tropical paradise and return to France.

Gauguin was then a man of forty, vigorous, domineering, with a noble and haughty bearing. His features are well known, thanks to his numerous self-portraits: the narrow, prominent forehead, the blue, deep-set eyes, the hooked nose and determined chin, the thick neck that suggests heaviness and arrogant power. However difficult his character, however uncompromising his opinions, he could be extremely charming and friendly when he was not contradicted

GAUGUIN. WOMEN ON THE BEACH. 1891.                     *Louvre*

or when those he talked with inspired his confidence.

His was a strong personality, irritating and engaging, in which the rustic was mixed with the aristocratic, at heart generous and good, despite the legend to the contrary, built up and maintained by the spiteful letters his wife wrote to friends she had left in France. For this husband

GAUGUIN. VAHINI WITH GARDENIA. 1891.
*Glyptotek, Copenhagen*

Gauguin broke with Impressionism, which had hitherto influenced his painting (1887). On his return to France he expressed his disapproval of Monet's and Pissarro's naturalist fiction. He formulated and preached 'Synthesism'. It may well be that the aesthetic principles designated under this name were inspired by Émile Bernard, as Bernard claimed. But that does not matter, for it was Gauguin who first enunciated this new theory and practised it with supreme mastery. Massive, simplified forms, flat colours, cloisonnism *(*)*, shadowless drawing, abstraction of design and colour, free treatment of Nature – such were the principal articles of the credo that Gauguin formulated in 1888 during his stay at Pont-Aven, and completed in the same year at Arles (where Van Gogh *(*)* revealed Japanese art to him), and at Pont-Aven and Le Pouldu (from April 1889 to November 1890). It was at this time that he painted *The Yellow Christ*, *The Swineherd* and the *Young Breton Girls*. He also tried mural painting, sculpture, engraving and ceramics.

His ancestry, his childhood memories, the impressions he brought back from Martinique, his three stays in Brittany – all these gave him the incentive to renew an art that had been corrupted by the Impressionists. Eight painters grouped themselves around him, and constituted the School of Pont-Aven. Led by Sérusier, the Nabis *(*)* came and joined them. Fêted in Paris by the independent critics, by writers such as Stéphane Mallarmé the poet and Octave Mirbeau the novelist, Gauguin might well have been content with such a strong position. But in the midst of his court he began to feel more and more alone. Brittany had nothing more to offer him, and France was too small for him and his dream. On the 23rd of February, 1891, he put thirty of his paintings up at auction, and with the proceeds embarked for Tahiti on the 4th of April.

At Papeete he found Europe again, with its vices, its stupidity and its frivolity. He went to live in Mataiéa, in a straw hut, among the peaceful, ingenuous population. He joined in all their rites and games, determined to destroy whatever trace of 'civilization' still remained in him. When his money ran out, and his debtors in Paris ignored

whom she angrily accused of 'monstrous egotism', this 'unnatural father', never ceased to love his wife and to suffer because he was separated from his children. To get some idea of his real feelings, his humility, tenderness and shyness, one must read his letters. But he was an artist, a man apart, resolved to pursue his destined course regardless of what it might cost him. His social duty counted for nothing in the face of his artistic duty. And, as a result, he made himself suffer as cruelly as those he loved.

Why these various stays in Britanny, Panama and Martinique? As his friend Daniel de Monfreid put it: 'He went to find, in what he believed to be a country of ancient customs, an environment, an atmosphere different from our over-civilized one'. In the Antilles he found the answer to his quest: a paradise setting with clear-cut lines and hard, strong colour contrasts.

his requests for payment, he was left without food, without clothes, and completely debilitated by a year of fierce, feverish work. He decided to return to France. *Women on the Beach, Vahini with Gardenia, Otahi, I raro te oviri* (Minneapolis), *When will you marry?, Arearea,* are a few of the many canvases he painted during this period. When he returned to France, sick, and at the end of his resources, he found a small legacy awaiting him, left by his uncle,

GAUGUIN. OTAHI. 1893.

*Private Collection, Paris*

Isidore Gauguin. He had several months of happiness. Dividing his time between Pont-Aven, Le Pouldu and Paris, he soon disposed of all his money. In his studio in the Rue Vercingétorix he gave a number of noisy parties, presided over by Annah, the Javanese girl, a monkey and a parrot. The free-spending, easy-going days soon came to an end. An exhibition of his Tahitian works at the Durand-Ruel Gallery on the 4th of

GAUGUIN. WOMAN OF TAHITI. 1892.
*The Art Institute, Chicago*

November, 1893, was a fiasco from the financial point of view. But his new painting, mysterious and barbaric, aroused the enthusiasm of Bonnard, Vuillard and all the Nabis. After a series of misfortunes (including a last, painful interview with his wife in Copenhagen, and the flight of Annah, who ransacked his studio), Gauguin decided to return to the South Seas. A second auction to finance him was a complete failure. He set out nevertheless, for Tahiti, and arrived there in July, 1896. He settled in the north of the island, and set to work immediately. And that is how the legend began, so common today, so unusual then: the legend of the European casting off civilization, alone and naked before the splendour of Nature. In October Gauguin began to have severe physical suffering. Whenever it abated, he applied himself to his work with renewed ardour and frenzy. The year 1897 was one of great sorrow for him: his beloved daughter Aline died; his correspondence with Mette came to an end; he was in hospital for a time. But it was also the year of his masterpieces *Whence Come We? What Are We? Whither Do We Go?* (Museum of Fine Arts, Boston), *Nevermore* (Tate Gallery, London). His manuscript *Noa Noa* appeared in the *Revue Blanche (\*)*. The following year, after an attempt to commit suicide, he went to work as clerk and draughtsman in the

GAUGUIN. RIDERS ON THE BEACH. 1902. *Folkwang Museum, Essen*

Department of Public Works. Sick at heart, suffering from the effects of syphilis, he nevertheless had the courage to paint, draw, sculpt, engrave and write. He got himself into trouble defending natives from rough handling by the whites. He was even sentenced to three months' imprisonment and a fine of a thousand francs. Finally, worn out by privations, almost unable to move, he died on the 6th of May, 1903, after executing some of his finest canvases: *Barbaric Tales*, *Horsemen on the Beach* and *The Gold of their Bodies* (Louvre). The last thing he painted was a Brittany snow scene.

What Gauguin went to find in the South Seas was original purity, innocence, a way of forgetting oneself, natural man saved from the artificialities of civilization, and the universality and permanence of art. In his desire to reach the source of inspiration he reached the very sources of communication. He attained the solemn grandeur of ancient and primitive art through the immobility of his figures, the impassivity of their features, the serene gravity of their

attitudes. That is why he is as close to Cretan and Egyptian art as he is to that of his contemporaries.

A creator who wanted to dominate his aesthetic adventure by the intellect, he succeeded in finding the appropriate means for realizing his conceptions. It was in order to give his compositions a monumental and, consequently, decorative character that he deliberately rejected modelling, form values, linear perspective, recession of planes, and secondary details, and neglected movement, relief, and the sensuality of expression. His South Sea canvases inspire a feeling of awe toward life, bitter regret for lost love and liberty, and a fear of the unknown, through the quiet cadence of their lines, their broad, flat areas of colour, and their grave, transfixed sumptuousness. Gauguin excelled in the art of composition. More than that, he invented a composition as different from that of the classical masters as theirs was from the composition characteristic of the Middle Ages. It is true that other precursors have, like him, felt the need to go back to the beginnings of the world, and find again purity of style. But no one was more courageously resolved to do it than Gauguin. 'Barbarism', he said, 'is for me a rejuvenation.' In his search he renewed pictorial art, and gave modern painting a meaning. His companions at Pont-Aven and the Nabis submitted to his leadership, and the *Fauves* were his direct heirs. Gauguin was also the one who inspired the present interest in ancient civilizations. His sculptures prepared the ground for the acceptance of Negro and Melanesian fetishes. It was he who made possible many of the gains and discoveries of contemporary art. Of all the great innovators of the nineteenth century, it is Gauguin whom many non-representational artists of today regard as their precursor.

Like Cézanne, Gauguin lived a spiritual adventure; but, like Van Gogh, he lived a searingly temporal one too.

**GLEIZES** Albert (1881–1953). Born in Paris, died in Avignon; descended from a family that was half southern French and half Flemish, Gleizes was both painter and writer; his life was inextricably linked with the evolution of Cubism, and he was the exponent of its theory. He began to paint in 1901, in the Impressionist style. In 1906, however, he began to seek 'a simplification of colour, in accordance with his desire to simplify form', and thus turned naturally toward Cubism. In 1910 he exhibited at the Salon des Indépendants (*The Tree*) and at the Salon d'Automne, and in 1911 he was one of the exhibitors in the famous Cubist Room at the Salon des Indépendants. At the Salon d'Automne in the same year his *Portrait of Nayral* had a *succès de scandale*. In 1912 Gleizes published, together with Metzinger, the book *On Cubism*. This was the most important work up to then on the theory of the new movement (*see* Cubism). He exhibited in Moscow and Barcelona, at the Armory Show *(*)* in New York in 1913, and at the first Autumn Salon in Berlin. After being called up in 1914, he painted several pictures on military themes. When he was discharged he went to America, and during his stay there, in 1917, he had a religious revelation. Upon his return to France he continued his experiments in technique, and in 1923 set them down in a book, *Painting and Its Laws*, which was a study of the objective laws of art based on the religious experience of the Middle Ages. He proclaimed the impending return of the Christian era, and endeavoured to develop an objective technique that would be easily transmissible, so that painters should have the means of praising God. To this end he worked out a scientific discipline ordered by a whole philosophical framework. In the logical course of his research he came across Romanesque art, about which he wrote works full of insight, and he endeavoured to put artistic creation at the service of the highest ambitions of Catholicism. In 1932 he published *L'Homocentrisme ou Retour à l'Homme Chrétien* (*Homocentricity, or Return to Christian Man*) and *Form and History*, a vast work in which he set himself the task of showing the superiority of an art based on religious thought and expressing movement and life by means of symbolic rhythms. While remaining faithful to the spirit of Cubism, Gleizes applied himself to defining

GLEIZES. WOMAN WITH GLOVE. 1920.
*Private Collection, Paris*

quasi-impersonal modes of expression which constituted the language of a new type of mural painting. He returned to his former themes, transposing them in this spirit, and he was not afraid to present a modern version of the compositions dear to the Middle Ages – a majestic Christ or Virgin, popes and emperors. From 1939 on Gleizes lived in retirement at Saint-Rémy-de-Provence, continuing to exert a marked influence, by his writings and lectures as well as by his paintings and his example, on many groups of young artists and artisans in the Rhône Valley. His last important work was the illustration of the *Pensées* of Pascal, consisting of fifty-seven original etchings.

**GOERG** Édouard (born in Sydney, Australia, in 1893). Goerg, who was of French and Irish parentage, soon left Australia and spent several years in England; then, at the age of seven, he moved to France. In 1912 he enrolled for a year's study at the Académie Ranson (*), where Maurice Denis was teaching. Goerg's predilection for Goya, Daumier and Rouault indicates that his art was inspired by realism, but he was to

GOERG. IMAGINARY PORTRAIT. 1929.
*Private Collection, Paris*

accentuate the sentimental note. 'What I love in art', said Goerg, 'is man . . . I well know that a painting has its laws, that it is a plane surface, a combination of volumes . . . but I say that that is not enough.' In that remark Goerg seemed to be condemning genuine plastic emotion and to be preferring the anecdotal. His work fell into a sort of naturalism, a characteristic aspect of which was the representation of nude young girls barely out of adolescence, accompanied by men in evening clothes, all enveloped in shadowy atmosphere relieved by conventional gleams of light. Georg has illustrated a number of literary works, such as the *Tales of Hoffmann* and Baudelaire's *Les Fleurs du Mal*, with engravings and lithographs in which his understanding of contrasts has enabled him to accentuate the dramatic elements very skilfully, with a certain stress on the macabre.

**GONTCHAROVA** Nathalie (born in the Russian province of Tula in 1881). She was descended from a noble Russian family, studied in Moscow, and began to exhibit in 1900. After that she visited the principal European countries. Upon returning to Russia she became acquainted with Larionov, whose lead she was to follow in the Rayonist movement (*see* Rayonism). From then on she did a great deal of stage scenery and designed costumes for ballets. At the same time she organized large exhibitions in Moscow, where her daring and variegated art caused a good deal of comment. She painted Rayonist pictures in green and grey, reminiscent of underbrush, canvases covered with letters and ciphers which are prototypes of a Russian Futurism and, notably, a remarkable canvas covered with black, grey and yellow streaks which she called *The Cats*. In 1914 she came to Paris with Larionov and exhibited with him. Apollinaire appreciated her work and introduced her, in his preface, as a disciple of the *avant-garde* French school. After making the acquaintance of Diaghilev, she devoted herself almost entirely to the *Ballets Russes* (*), for which she designed many décors, costumes and stage sets (*Le Coq d'Or, Le Tsar Saltan*, Stravinsky's *Noces*). Between the two

GONTCHAROVA. STUDY FOR 'LES NOCES'. 1923

exhibited a group of his Montmartre canvases at the London shop. Another Goupil related to the founder of the firm, was the author of a book on painting which was instrumental in Matisse's choice of career.

**GRIS** Juan (1887–1927). Born in Madrid; died at Boulogne-sur-Seine, near Paris. José Victoriano González, known as Juan Gris, was born of a Castilian father and an Andalusian mother. According to his sister Antonieta, his vocation was evident in early childhood, at the age of six or seven. Nevertheless, he received a general education and then enrolled at the School of Arts and Crafts in Madrid. His preliminary education was essentially scientific, and this is seen in his writings and pictorial theories. When financial ruin struck his family, he made a living by selling drawings to humorous papers in Madrid. It was not long before he devoted himself entirely to painting, entering the studio of an old academic painter, Moreno Carbonero, who,

wars she painted a series of *Espagnoles* (of which many reproductions have been made), as well as flowers and abstract compositions.

**GOUPIL** (Gallery). In the years around 1850 the Goupil Gallery, then located in the Rue Caulaincourt, was a small shop which sold principally engravings of the works of such painters as Horace Vernet, Paul Delaroche and Ary Scheffer. In 1877, with the third Impressionist exhibition, Goupil became interested in the new movement and from then on the growth of the gallery was rapid. Van Gogh worked in the branch in The Hague in 1869 and was later transferred to the Brussels shop, where he was replaced by his brother Theo prior to his transfer to the London branch. In 1875 Vincent worked for a while at the Paris headquarters, from which he was dismissed the following year. Later, he sent some of his paintings to his brother, Theo, still employed by Goupil, who tried to place them with the Gallery, but they were rejected as 'horrors'. In 1893 Toulouse-Lautrec

GRIS. THE SCOTSWOMAN. 1918.
*Private Collection, Paris*

he said, 'made him disgusted with good painting'. He lived among painters and writers, and took the name Juan Gris. At that time the more advanced artistic circles in Spain were becoming initiated into 'Modern-style', under the influence of German publications and reviews.

At the age of nineteen Gris decided to go to Paris, paying for the journey by selling all his possessions. Since he left without doing his military service, he was never able to obtain a passport, and this prevented him from ever

GRIS. STILL LIFE WITH DIE. 1922.
*Musée d' Art Moderne, Paris*

travelling out of France. He asked for French nationality, but he died without obtaining it. Attracted by the rising fame of Picasso, he settled at the Bateau-Lavoir *(\*)*, 13 Rue Ravignan, where he lived precariously by making

satirical drawings for newspapers and magazines. But he worked mostly for himself, and when he decided, after four or five years of endeavour, to exhibit his work, he gave up his old livelihood for ever. His first buyer was the dealer Clovis Sagot, and he first exhibited at the Salon des Indépendants of 1912, to which he sent a *Hommage à Picasso*. In the same year he showed his works in Barcelona, Rouen, and the exhibition of the *Section d'Or (\*)* in Paris. Kahnweiler, who had known him since 1907, became his dealer. He also became his best friend, and the book which he wrote about him in 1946 was the first definitive work published about him. Gertrude Stein, Léonce Rosenberg and Alfred Flechtheim acquired his works. These were still painted in the style of analytical Cubism. Cubism, reacting against imitation, had recourse at first to the analysis of objects, which it tried to grasp not merely in their changing appearances but in their successive aspects, in all their facets, even in cross-section, the result on the canvas being a juxtaposition of planes and lines that was often complicated but was particularly expressive. Gris's first works, especially his portraits, are always intelligible and well balanced. The Cubists very soon tried to introduce elements taken from everyday life into their compositions, to serve as guide-posts and explanations for the public: for instance, *trompe-l'œil* wood and marble, printed letters, and actual pieces of newspaper. Juan Gris used these ingenuous and empirical methods with great distinction, but he started a reform that was more profound and coherent, a truly scientific doctrine of modern painting. He played a decisive role in what has been called synthetic Cubism *(\*)*.

In the summer of 1913 Gris stayed at Céret with Picasso, who encouraged him, and with Manolo, with whom he had endless arguments on theory. From then on he strove to make Cubism clearer, more precisely defined, more irrefutable. The war found him again at Céret, in 1914, with Matisse and Marquet. On his return to Paris he set to work at once, helped by Léonce Rosenberg the art dealer, who held an exhibition for him in 1919. At the Salon des Indépendants of 1920 he participated in the last exhibition of the united Cubist group, which

GRIS. THE ALBUM. 1926.                    *Collection of H. Rupf, Bern*

was to break up soon after that. He was not very successful, and he saw himself disparaged, even by his friends, although he always showed them the greatest kindness. It disturbed him to see the meaning of Cubism distorted – its impetus had been broken perhaps by the war – and he decided to pursue alone his search for a 'grand style' suited to his time. Possessed by a sort of craving for knowledge, in which he seemed to seek compensation for the ineptitude against which he raged, Juan Gris would have been one of the universal men of the Renaissance had he lived at that time.

What was synthetic Cubism, according to Juan Gris? A certain discrepancy already existed between the structure and composition of the picture and its colours, for the latter were sometimes indicated only by a smudge. Thus, in the *papiers collés*, the details could be interchanged without any damage to the solidly established structure. This was the starting-point of Juan Gris's method. Kahnweiler has reported a talk on this subject in 1920: 'I begin', declared Gris, 'by organizing my picture; then I characterize the objects'. Another of his declarations – often

quoted and generally misinterpreted – states, even more precisely, that he went from the general to the particular, starting from an abstraction and arriving at a real fact. Yet the context is very clear. He began by saying: 'I work with the elements of the mind; with the aid of the imagination, I try to make concrete what is abstract'. And he continued: 'I want to arrive at a new set of characteristics, to create specific individuals by starting from a general type. . . . From a bottle, Cézanne made a cylinder, but I make a bottle from a cylinder – a certain type of bottle.' Because he spoke of the mathematical structure of a picture, it is assumed that he had a theoretical and abstract mentality which arbitrarily reversed all the normal processes of artistic creation, excluding from them every human element. It is sufficient to look at Gris's work to dismiss these legends and hasty interpretations. The basis of this new work is a sort of generalized drawing, charged with memories, concepts, ideas, all long meditated upon by the artist before they took form.

He chose consciously the geometrical architecture that emerges therefrom. Then, with his imagination and reason, he strove to make this construction objective, so that it should be communicated, and comprehensible, to the spectator. This process could justly be compared with the creative work of musicians and writers. It is not surprising, then, that Gris should appear a true classicist whose pure, noble, and austere art is fixed in the essential, from which everything peripheral has been excluded. At the end of his life Gris, a great admirer of the seventeenth century and particularly of Philippe de Champaigne, turned to the art of Pompeii, the Fontainebleau school and the work of David. His style is the result of a remarkable effort. He used a

GRIS. THE GUITAR. 1926.          *Collection Doetsch-Benziger, Basel*

process of reversal of forms which almost recalls the repetitions of rhyme and gives a curious undulation to his lines, creating the impression of volume. His art is a logical, complex, coherent system.

In 1920 Gris fell seriously ill with pleurisy and went to Touraine for a few months, then spent the winter in Bandol, on the Côte d'Azur. Diaghilev, who was at that time in Monte Carlo, suggested that he do the décor and costumes for a Spanish ballet, but this project did not materialize. Gris spent the following winter at Céret and

returned to Paris in the spring, apparently restored to health. He settled in Boulogne, just outside Paris. Musicians, painters, poets and critics came to see him on Sundays, and the evenings were gay, for Gris loved dancing. The week was spent in calm, reflective work. Diaghilev, returning to his old project, commissioned Gris in 1923 to design the décor and costumes for a Louis XIV ballet, *Les Tentations de la Bergère*, then the stage set for *La Fête Merveilleuse* which he was presenting in the Gallery of Mirrors in the Palace of Versailles, and a décor for *L'Education Manquée* by Chabrier. But the feverish, disordered atmosphere of the ballet, and the intrigues and jealousies that abounded there, exasperated him so that he refused to repeat the experience. On May 15th, 1924, Gris read to the philosophical and scientific study group at the Sorbonne his paper on *Les Possibilités de la Peinture*, which was published in French, German and Spanish, and had tremendous repercussions. Gris had even greater success in 1925, when he painted his serenest and most perfect works. But his health was gravely undermined. He spent his winters in the south – in Toulon in 1925, in Hyères in 1926. The climate at the latter place did not suit him, so that his health grew steadily worse, and he was brought back to Paris, where he died on May 11th, 1927.

**GROMAIRE** Marcel. Gromaire was born in 1892 in Noyelles-sur-Sambre, of a French father and a Flemish mother. From 1910 on he frequented the studios of Montparnasse and met the pupils of Matisse, whose academy had just been closed. He was wounded in the First World War in 1916, in the Battle of the

Somme. An opponent of theories, Gromaire has remained outside all schools. Nevertheless, his art has generally followed the lines of an expressionism that is far removed from the pathological form this movement has taken in Scandinavia and Germany; his is an expressionism that reflects the inspiration of the Romanesque and Gothic primitives. Gromaire has generally taken the subjects of his most significant compositions from the life of the peasant or workman. Although any strictly naturalistic expression is foreign to his canvases, the most moving of them show a very great decorative talent. And if he has often borrowed from Cézanne or Seurat, it is because he has tried primarily to make his art conform to strict rules of composition. Whether he paints smugglers or fishermen, beer-drinkers or card-players, Gromaire subjects his themes to exacting graphic formulas. Nothing is more significant in this respect than his canvas entitled *War* (1925), where, excluding the picturesque and scorning the anecdotal, he gives himself up to the vision of a monumental universe that is rigorously exact. In this sense his art approaches that of the fresco, and it is not surprising that Gromaire is

GROMAIRE. TWO BATHERS. 1953.
*Louis Carré Gallery, Paris*

among the contemporary revivers of tapestry (*The Four Elements, The Four Seasons*). Adapting his palette to the necessary synthesis, he has chosen sober, rugged, dramatic and powerful colours, with browns, ochres, greys and greens predominating, and more recently reds and grey-blues. In his latest works Gromaire seems to have freed himself from any remaining traces of stylization, and to be taking new liberties with a reality that is more and more detached.

GRIS. SELF PORTRAIT. 1920.

**GROSZ** George (German painter, born in Berlin in 1893). After studying at the Academies of Dresden and Berlin, Grosz drew for humorous reviews. Although he had already begun to paint before 1914, it is his drawing that is of chief interest. Grosz was haunted by actuality. At first, in 1916, it was the evil, absurd face of war; then, after 1918, the buffoonery of the post-war years that were depicted in his incisive drawing with its savagely aggressive social satire. He was trying to make his art a weapon in the struggle against the ruling classes, and he simplified his drawing for political action. A number of lithographs reveal his acrid, fanatically topical art. Whereas in 1918 Grosz was a member of the Dada *(*)* group of Berlin, which had a very pronounced political character, in 1925 he turned towards the realism of the *Neue Sachlichkëit*. In 1932 he was invited to teach at a New York art school, the Art Students' League, and he is still there today. In America a romantic and idyllic note has appeared in his painting, but his satire is still alive. He first directed it against the materialism of the middle classes; since the last war it has been on a broader, humanitarian basis, in visions of nightmares, like the fantastic series of *The Stick Men*.

**GRUBER** Francis. French painter, born in Nancy in 1912; died in Paris, 1948. Gruber's health was so delicate that he was incapable of sustained study. At a very early age he showed unusually precocious gifts for drawing and painting. He was guided by Bissière and Braque, who had neighbouring studios, and in

GRUBER. MODEL IN THE STUDIO. 1945

GROSZ. THE ENTRÉE. 1929.
*Private Collection, New York*

1928 he entered the Académie Scandinave, where he became the favourite pupil of Friesz and Dufresne. He was so successful at the Salons d'Automne and Salons des Tuileries that by the time he was eighteen he was one of the 'characters' of Montparnasse. His truculence and verve were as apparent in his *kermesse* paintings – he was a great admirer of Breughel, Bosch, Grünewald and Dürer – as in his voluble speech and his irregular existence. He was, however, an ardent and punctilious worker, with a passion for technique. Moreover, he had the courage to paint on the grand scale. There is not one of his works, from the vast mural composition he did for the Lycée Lakanal (*Homage to Le Nôtre, 1936*) to the least of his still lifes, which is not monumental in conception. His scenes from everyday life, studio settings, or groupings of familiar objects, are peopled with a whole mythology of figures, symbols and monsters, representing the palpable background of life, be it morbid or exalting. Each picture is the expression of a state of mind in which the painter's reasons for living, his obsessions, even the necessity for his death and destruction, are at stake. He dreamed of finding a great technique that would make art intelligible to all. In his last years of serious illness, his work became more and more austere and abstract. The greater his body's struggle against the tuberculosis that was draining its strength, the more his painting freed itself from the morbid and hallucinatory. His very last paintings attained a purity that indicated his approaching end. They were angular nudes shut up in a closed, stifling world that was reduced to the red hangings, the grey walls and the floor of a studio, or large canvases inspired by the movement of trees, with elongated young bodies in the midst of imaginary forests.

**GUILLAUMIN** Armand (1841–1927). French painter; born and died in Paris. Although he exhibited with the Impressionists from 1874 on, and was a close friend of Monet, Pissarro and Cézanne – the latter copied one of his landscapes – and the teacher of Signac, Guillaumin was able to withstand all influences. Barge-filled quays and landscapes of the Creuse Valley are frankly depicted by this Parisian who, whenever he touched the soil, seemed to recover the ruggedness of his peasant ancestors, whose stature and direct gaze he inherited. It can easily be imagined that his occasional abuse of reds, violets and mauves, and his raucous tone, which only just avoided commonness, as well as the absence of certain transitions in colour, shocked the public of 1874. With these reservations, how can one fail to admire the authentic and joyous lyricism that accompanies the river in its course, and gilds the woods with the autumn sun? Few of the landscape painters at the end of the nineteenth century were so straightforward, so free from sentimentality, or so frankly earthy.

While his work is uneven, and certain views of Agay and Le Trayas are rather harsh, some of his Sédelle valleys and impressions of autumn seem to foreshadow Cézanne. The tone of many of his portraits in pastel (he excelled in this medium) and of his still lifes is that of a virile painter who stands high above the secondary Impressionists with whom he has too often been confused. Moreover, towards the end of his life his art came singularly close to that of the *Fauves*.

**GUYS** Constantin (1802–1892). French artist; born in Vlissingen, Holland; died in Paris at the age of ninety, destitute. The modesty of Constantin Guys, who rarely signed his drawings and water-colours and wished to be mentioned only by his initials, has left historians without precise details of his stormy life. Until 1860 he was a correspondent for the *Illustrated London News*, and he sent his drawings from Spain, Italy, Germany, Turkey, Egypt or the Crimea, to be made into woodcuts. But this great traveller did not need to leave Paris to find something marvellous at every step. His studies of certain social *milieux* have, with time, taken on the value of documentary evidence of types and fashions. Baudelaire has described Guys at work, bent over twenty sketches, emphasizing

GUILLAUMIN. QUAY ALONG THE SEINE. 1887. *De Ruaz Gallery, Paris*

with water-colours a light
pencil outline, deepening certain shadows, brightening
certain lights and, like Daumier, composing only from
memory. His palette, at first
very intense, rich in reds and
saffron yellows, took on a
calmer tone as his touch became broader, and he put
more and more feeling into
his organization of values.
*War, Pomp and Solemnity,
Soldiers, Dandies, Women, Prostitutes, Carriages* – these classi-
fications handed down to us
by Baudelaire are still the
most convenient for Guy's
immense production, which,

GUYS. THE OUTING. 1865

though very uneven, raises him above the minor
masters. Sensitive to the slightest vibrations of
the present, interested in every kind of spectacle,
retaining only the essentials of a movement or a
character, reproducing faithfully individual traits
or deviations, he always subordinated anecdote to
style. Prostitutes transformed into dream girls,
carriages transformed into fairy coaches, every-

thing – even the very background which contributes so actively to the life of every composition –
escapes literal or prosaic transcription. Thanks to
Guys, the days of crinoline, tasselled shoes and
beautiful courtesans still live on. 'The painter of
modern life', as Baudelaire called him, he has
left us an idealized picture of his epoch, where
the annalist is even surpassed by the visionary.

# H

**HECKEL** Erich (born in Döbeln, Saxony, in 1883). German painter, one of the founders of the *Brücke (\*)*. The style of that movement is reflected in his painting, with its angular, pointed forms, influenced by wood-engraving, at which he was a master.

But these forms, in his case, convey intensity of feeling rather than an emphasis on structure. He is attracted by the invalid's quiet sadness, by a Dostoevskian anxiety (*Two Men at a Table*, painting 1912, woodcut 1913), by the enchanting transparency of light (*Translucence*, 1913). His wartime landscapes show the elements in conflict. Since 1920 the expressive force of his plastic language has diminished, and Heckel, drawing closer to Nature, has set himself to revealing the rhythmic grandeur of certain landscapes in Germany and Italy. The lyrical tenderness of his art is evident in his choice of colours, in the mat shades of his palette.

HECKEL. TWO MEN AT A TABLE. 1913.
*Wood Engraving*

**HODLER** Ferdinand (1853–1918) (born in Gürzelen, Canton of Berne, died in Geneva). Swiss painter. After a great success, a sort of European triumph, his fame has declined steadily since his death. At present this self-taught painter is overestimated by some, given insufficient recognition by others, no doubt because of the duality of a talent which turned from an all-pervading gentleness to hardness. It is a strange fact that the Impressionist movement raged for over a quarter of a century without having the slightest effect on the man or leaving the faintest trace in his work. Hodler jumped straight from the gentle painting of Corot – as it was taken over by the Barbizon painters – to the pedantic harshness of the Munich school. How can such a surprising break be explained? One must bear in mind the ideas and feelings that were then common among the Swiss. For them there were two schools of painting, the French and the German – Paris and Munich. As for Impressionism, they dreaded its fluidity, the subordination of line to colour; they were afraid of its daring ventures in colour. They thought the antidote was to be found among the professors across the Rhine, who, by stressing draughtsmanship, were producing Denners rather than Dürers.

At the age of nineteen Hodler entered the École des Beaux-Arts at Geneva, where he studied hard under Barthélemy Menn, a pupil of Ingres and friend of Corot. Hodler made his début with *The Schoolboy* (1875), a portrait in the manner of Holbein, which he painted at Langenthal during his holidays. While he was making portraits of labourers and artisans at work, such as cobblers, locksmiths, carpenters and watchmakers, he was at the same time painting in a very sober style on large, simple planes, landscapes that were luminous, limpid, perhaps a bit too precise yet never hard. But then came the break. In

HODLER. MONT BLANC. 1918

1891 Hodler exhibited *Night* at the Société Nationale du Champ-de-Mars. The following year, in his *Disillusioned Souls*, which was the principal attraction of the Salon de la Rose-Croix, he showed himself to be infected with the disease that was then befogging the minds of so many of the vanguard – Symbolism. To a rather rough-hewn man, initiation into Symbolism could be disastrous. That is what happened to Hodler, who, thoroughly at home in depicting everyday life, now set himself to painting *The Elect* (1894) – a little boy kneeling before a miniature garden and dreaming, under the protection of angels, clad in nightgowns and ranged in a semicircle – and *Eurythmics*, 1895. This rather ludicrous mythology, although it did not exactly ruin him, did at least give him a taste for grandiloquence, as practised by the Germanic artists. From that time on his work consisted of a succession of large pictures on historical subjects, ranging from *The*

*Retreat from Marignan* (1899) and *The Truth* (1903) to *Departure of the Jena Volunteers* (1908). Toward the end of his life Hodler painted lakes and landscapes in which the colours were more tastefully distributed. What was it that he lacked for creating work of a pronounced character? Somewhat like the Norwegian Edvard Munch, Hodler was exposed to conflicting influences and therefore produced work of uneven quality. And although he was a forerunner, in certain directions, of tendencies which were to appear after him, he was not capable of stamping his art with that profound spiritual life which communicates emotion. Reared in the hard school of Nature and poverty, Hodler was first and foremost a master of his craft. Perhaps the artisan in him was stronger than the artist. Some of his canvases have, none the less, a powerful significance. A sure draughtsmanship that is expressive and extraordinarily precise gives them lasting value.

# I

**IMPRESSIONISM** From April 15th to May 15th, 1874, a group of independent young French painters who had formed a *société anonyme* that included Monet, Renoir, Pissarro, Sisley, Cézanne, Degas, Guillaumin and Berthe Morisot, held an exhibition, apart from the official Salon, at the studio of the photographer Nadar *(\*)*. The exhibition caused an uproar, and a journalist named Leroy, writing in the satirical magazine *Le Charivari* of April 25th, jeeringly called the exhibitors 'impressionists', after a canvas by Monet entitled *Impression, Sunrise*. This name, accepted by the painters themselves, became very popular and was universally adopted. The meaning of the term, however, remained vague. The spontaneous Impressionism of the artists was superseded by the doctrinaire Impressionism of the critics, who turned a living ideal into a set system. Then successive reactions against Impressionism set its limits even more rigidly and distorted its scope. It is therefore quite difficult to recapture its actual climate and to mark out correctly the range of the movement which brought about a renewal not only of vision but of the whole of modern sensibility, and which united so many dissimilar artists. Each of them fulfilled himself according to his own genius, sustained in his freedom by the very principles which constituted Impressionism.

The Impressionist painters were born between 1830 and 1841 – Pissarro, the eldest, in 1830, Manet in 1832, Degas in 1834, Cézanne and Sisley in 1839, Monet in 1840, Renoir, Bazille, Guillaumin and Berthe Morisot in 1841. These young innovators, from different environments, came together in Paris about 1860. Pissarro, Cézanne and Guillaumin met at the Académie

BOUDIN. COMMERCIAL DOCK, HAVRE.      *Havre Museum*

MONET. IMPRESSION, SUNRISE. 1872.     *Musée Marmottan, Paris*

while through the foliage a thousand reflections of sunlight broke upon the moving surface of the river. It was in their endeavour to convey the dynamism and the joy of that spectacle, which constantly stimulated them, that they spontaneously discovered what were to become the technical principles of Impressionism: division of tone and shimmering spots of colour. A new vision was born, derived not from a theory but from on-the-spot observation of the reflection

Suisse *(*)*; Monet, Renoir, Bazille and Sisley at the Atelier Gleyre *(*)*. They soon escaped, however, to the Forest of Fontainebleau, where they began to paint in the naturalistic, compact manner of the Barbizon school. From there they went to the Seine estuary and the Channel beaches, which were to become, between 1860 and 1870, the cradle of Impressionism. It was in that light-and-water-saturated air that Monet, in contact with the two innovators, Boudin (1824–1898) and Jongkind (1819–1891), evolved a style of painting that became more and more fluid, ethereal and highly coloured. Pissarro and Sisley remained close to Corot. Cézanne and Degas, the one still under the sway of Romanticism the other still dominated by Classicism, had no part in this pre-Impressionist phase. Manet, through the modernity of his subjects and his *succès de scandale* in 1863 at the Salon des Refusés, became, perhaps in spite of himself, the standard-bearer of the young school that met at the Café Guerbois *(*)*. In 1869 Monet and Renoir, whose figures and open-air compositions had been inspired by Courbet, painted, at Bougival, a small village on the Seine, the picturesque wharf of the *Grenouillère*, a restless confusion of boats and gaily coloured dresses,

of sunlight along the banks of the Seine. Certainly their style had not yet attained unity, and it was not to become a truly conscious one until 1873, but the freshness of these first achievements was never to be surpassed.

The Franco-German war of 1870 dispersed the group just when their experiments were taking shape. Manet, Renoir, Degas and Bazille were called up and went to war; Bazille was killed in the battle of Beaune-la-Rolande. Monet, Pissarro and Sisley took refuge in London, where Daubigny introduced them to Durand-Ruel *(*)*, the dealer who was to become their chief defender. Their discovery of Turner and Constable hastened the evolution of their technique. In 1872 Monet at Argenteuil, near Paris, and Pissarro at Pontoise (Seine-et-Oise) began painting the new type of open-air landscape. Monet's work, on the grand, universal scale, dominated by the spell of water and by the phantasms of light, attracted Renoir, Sisley and Manet; Pissarro's, bucolic and earthy, with more stress on structural values, influenced Cézanne and Guillaumin. In 1873, with the conversion of Manet, Cézanne and, to a limited extent, Degas, to light-coloured painting, the Impressionist style spread and became more generally understood. The small brush strokes already used for reproducing reflections in water were now applied to trees, houses, sky, hills – all the elements of the landscape. The colours became systematically lighter and the shadows themselves were coloured. The transitional greys and browns used by Corot gave way to the pure colours of the spectrum, harmonized or contrasted according to the law of complementary colours. Coherence of vision brought in its wake unity of technique, the exaltation and vibration of light as the dominant principle, and consequently the abandonment of contour, of modelling, of chiaroscuro, and of over-precise details, the over-all composition retaining the vigour of a sketch, with the incomplete, unfinished look that so shocked contemporaries. The critic Armand Silvestre made a fine distinction between the three painters: 'Monet, the most skilful and the most daring; Sisley, the most harmonious and the most timid; Pissarro, the most true and the most naïve'. Renoir led his figures into the sunlight. In 1874, with the exception of Manet, who remained faithful to the official Salon, the group as a whole faced the public, under a barrage of insults and taunts. Seven joint exhibitions followed, at intervals, until 1886. In 1876 Duranty (*), the writer and art critic, published *The New Painting* – a significant title – and shrewdly analysed the orientation of the young painters: 'Going from intuition to intuition, they have gradually come to the decomposition of sunlight into its rays, its elements, and to reconstructing its unity by the general harmony of the iridescent colours which they spread on their canvases'. The year 1877 was perhaps the peak year of Impressionism, the moment of its most homogeneous and complete unfolding. On the

MONET. BRIDGE AT ARGENTEUIL. 1874.                    *Louvre*

occasion of the third exhibition, and at the suggestion of Renoir, Georges Rivière published a little periodical entitled *The Impressionist*, in which he commented intelligently and warmly on his friends' efforts: 'Treating a subject for its colours

PISSARRO. PORTRAIT OF CÉZANNE.
*Etching*

and not for the subject itself', he summarized, 'is what distinguishes Impressionists from other painters', thus emphasizing the victory of pictorial autonomy. The traditional representation of the 'subject', determined by mythology or history or bourgeois convention, was replaced by contemplation of the 'motif', a tree, a thatched hut, a horizon, detached from space and time, a universal source of values; the painting corresponded to its content, without any literary overtones. In 1878 there appeared a brochure, *The Impressionist Painters*, by the writer and art critic Théodore Duret *(\*)*; this work, together with Duranty's, constituted the first study of the movement as a whole. The defection of Monet, Renoir and Sisley in 1880, at the time of the group's fifth exhibition, revealed a profound crisis, both personal and aesthetic.

After a heroic decade of enduring contempt, and producing masterpieces, Impressionism, at the very moment that it began to gain recognition, ceased to exist as a spontaneous ideal. Each of its founders, having reached maturity, thenceforth went his own way, while retaining allegiance to the common cult that had brought them all together – that of Nature and of liberty.

The death of Manet in 1883 – by then a new generation has arisen (Seurat, Van Gogh, Gauguin and Lautrec), nourished on Impressionism but reacting against it – coincided with the complete breaking up of the original group, despite the efforts of Durand-Ruel. Geographical dispersion (Pissarro at Eragny, Monet at Giverny, Sisley at Saint-Mammès, Cézanne at Aix-en-Provence, Renoir alternately travelling and staying in Paris before finally settling in Provence) was accompanied by a divergence in their aesthetic principles. At that time, as Lionello Venturi puts it, 'Monet tended toward a symbolism of colour and light, Pissarro was attracted to pointillism, Renoir wished to assimilate elements of academic form, Cézanne concentrated on problems of construction, and Sisley took satisfaction in style'. Renoir and Cézanne, carried along by their genius, fulfilled themselves without faltering, in a continuous upward surge. Monet, Sisley and Pissarro, however, the three landscape painters most closely linked to Impressionism, and the most confused, had many vicissitudes, producing uneasy and uneven work, sometimes merely decorative, without being able to recapture the fine equilibrium and spontaneity of their beginnings. Certainly they were still achieving much, but a spirit of system and literary or scientific influences often restricted the freedom of their intuition. After 1895 Pissarro regained an astonishing creative vigour, and his last masterpieces, like those of Monet, Renoir and Cézanne, still derived from Impressionism in the broad sense of the

PISSARRO. RED ROOFS. 1877.                    *Louvre*

term, by reason of their cosmic sweep, vibration of light, and direct emotion before Nature.

Thus Impressionism was not a set group with a congealed programme or a master-disciple relationship; it was a privileged correspondence of taste, a living experience, a moment of brotherhood, shared by young artists indifferent to ideas but rich in sensations, who suddenly discovered the world and found it vast enough for each of them to draw upon it without constraint. And because painting for them was something spontaneous, not derived from a theory, they revolted against its traditional 'laws'. If almost all the artists of the *avant-garde*, different as they were in temperament, joined together, between 1860 and 1870, to contribute to the formation of what was to be called Impressionism, it was not as a result of their gradual submission to some uniform principle or technical prescription, but because of their impatient desire to free their own personalities for a dynamic contact with Nature and life, and to shatter – following Manet's lead – all official conventions, all academic fetters. 'The effect of sincerity', said Manet, 'is to give one's work the character of a protest, the painter being concerned only with conveying his impression. He simply seeks to be himself and no one else.' In point of fact, the Impressionist painter, guided solely by his intuition, could only rely on his own sincerity, and each of his paintings, being an act of 'creation', was a reaffirmation and rediscovery of painting. The world did not exist once and for all in a set form, but every glance rediscovered it in its renewed freshness, and the least of its aspects was part of its moving beauty. Such liberty could not but shock the people of that time, whose vision had been petrified by the École des Beaux-Arts (itself an expression of social petrifaction). To us, however, the Impressionist experiment appears to have fitted naturally into the pictorial tradition which has come down to us from the Renaissance, while pursuing more and more faithfully the optical expression

RENOIR. THE SWING. 1876.　　　　　*Louvre*

of reality. Under the dominant influence of Courbet, the Impressionists started out in a more or less realistic tradition, which they intensified to the point where it was overthrown, and replaced by the flight from reality of modern painting. Although the visible world that they offer us appears more real, or is perhaps a better likeness, than the objective data of Realism, it is important to realize that the two attitudes are much more in opposition to each other than they are a continuation of each other. The realistic painter still rests his work on an intellectual basis and adapts his emotions to his knowledge – that is, he fits them into traditional frames: respect for contour, the rules of anatomy and perspective, the primacy of chiaroscuro. Opposed to this realistic intellectualism is the sensualism of Impressionism; the unity of its style is founded on personal intuition, on an emotional choice unfettered by any theoretical data. The external universe loses its constraining power and, entirely transposed into anti-naturalist pure colours, becomes for the artist a 'theme', in the musical sense of the word, on which he can make variations to his heart's content. Delacroix comes to mind, but the freedom of Impressionism is both richer and more rigorous than that of Romanticism. Romanticism was, in fact, tinged with too much torment and day-dreaming, too many external elements that were often artificial, too many fantastic and literary suggestions. Impressionism delivered painting from the literary passion of Romanticism and from the social rhetoric of Realism, and restored its purity. Having won its autonomy, at the price of heroic struggles, Impressionism expresses none the less the moral vision of its period – straightforwardness, sincerity, an impetus towards individual liberty and social equality, poetry revealed in the most rustic themes, in humble, everyday life. This was the universal fraternity of light, as opposed to the 'select', the distinguished, the exceptional, the 'finished', as opposed to the hierarchical canons and false elegance of the *Salon officiel*.

It is obvious that Impressionism, even in its most homogeneous period, from 1870 to 1880, showed a variety of tendencies. After that date, with the coming of a new generation, other tendencies sprang up – Neo-Impressionism, Symbolism, Expressionism – that reacted violently against it, even though they derived from it. Nevertheless, in spite of the complexity of temperaments and movements, a vast spiritual unity, from 1860 to 1900, marks the whole of a period which may still justly be called Impressionist, when painting, thanks to an unparalleled constellation of geniuses, acquired full autonomy, at the same time bearing witness, in the most sensitive and truthful manner, to the life of the period and to its deepest aspirations.

SISLEY. REGATTA NEAR LONDON. 1874. *Louvre*

# J

**JAWLENSKY**   Alexej von (1864–1942). Russian painter; born at Souslovo near Tver; died at Wiesbaden. Giving up his career as an officer in the Imperial Guard to become a painter, Jawlensky studied from 1889 on in Moscow at the Academy and with Répine, and, beginning in 1896, in Munich at Anton Azbe's school, where he met Kandinsky. From 1902 on he worked alone. With Kandinsky, Kubin, Gabriele Münter and others he founded the New Association of Munich Artists in 1909. Though he did not join in the *Blaue Reiter (\*)* exhibitions, he was in close agreement with the aims of that movement. During the war Jawlensky lived in Switzerland (Saint-Prex, Zurich, Ascona) and, in 1921, settled at Wiesbaden. In 1924, with Kandinsky, Klee and Feininger, he formed the Four Blues Group, which exhibited in Germany and America. At Munich he was influenced by Western art. Cézanne and Van Gogh impressed him and spurred him on in his search for a greater, simpler and more expressive form. A stay, in 1905, in Brittany and Provence liberated his gifts as a colourist, and his meeting with Matisse helped him to find his way. So the composition of his pictures of 1909, with their large flat masses of pure, bright colour, is related to Matisse's work. But whereas Matisse's line is dynamic and active, Jawlensky's passively outlines the masses of colour with a rich, sensual building up of the *matière*. In his frank, exuberant art the colours seem to sing with an earthy force and expressive primitive violence which recall Russian folk art. Jawlensky painted some landscapes but, more often, heads and half-length figures whose powerful vitality, in the work he did between 1911 and 1914, is concentrated in an even simpler and more monumental form. During the First World War Jawlensky's art underwent a great transformation. The road which led from his pre-

JAWLENSKY. GIRL IN BLUE APRON. 1909.
*Private Collection*

war painting to the *Variations* on a landscape of Saint-Prex, in colours now more delicate, and from there to *Mystic Heads* (1917), to *Visions of the Saviour* (1919) and the *Abstract Heads* of later years, was that of spirituality. The human face became the only theme which interested him, and its essential architecture – the cross of the nose and the arch of the eyebrows, the mouth, the oval of the chin, the forehead – determined the symbolic composition of the picture, a new form of iconography stamped with a profound, mystical religious sense. 'Art is nostalgia for God', Jawlensky often said. Enclosed within the linear structure which it stresses, colour now burned with a rarer and more secret flame. Light and transparent until 1935, it darkened in his last works as the painter, in his life, as well as in his art, found once more the way to the faith of his childhood.

**JEANNERET** (*see* Le Corbusier).

**JOHN** Augustus Edwin (born in Wales in 1878). Augustus John studied at the Slade School from 1894 until 1898. When he left he was acclaimed the best draughtsman in England. He has remained first and foremost a draughtsman, and for many years his best painting drew its strength from its drawing. John was a true bohemian, living with gypsies and learning their language and tramping through Wales and France. Yet there are two aspects to his character: one of them has been grasped by Wyndham Lewis, who has written of John's 'fits of seeing' and has described him as 'a great man of action into whose hand the fairies stuck a brush instead of a sword'. The other aspect has rarely been touched upon but is manifest in several of his landscapes and his *In Memoriam Amedeo Modigliani*. John has fits of seeing, he is a visionary like El Greco (and, perhaps, Modigliani, whom he admired and who was also influenced by El Greco), and yet he is an intellectual who has absorbed the influences of Cézanne, Puvis de Chavannes and the *Fauves*. He can organize words almost as well as the materials of his art, as his autobiography clearly shows. His greatest portraits (Lady Ottoline Morrell,

Madame Suggia, W. B. Yeats, Viscount d'Abernon, among others) show a visionary power allied to great intellectual force; his landscapes and studies for large compositions show more of his intellectual nature. When these qualities are not satisfactorily balanced, his work suffers and becomes mannered. Yet when he is successful, few other painters of modern times give such a sensation of pure ecstasy and joy and effortless achievement. Long after his personality and wit have ceased to have a direct effect on the public, his art will exercise its great appeal, and his portraits, his gypsy types, his women and his landscapes will outlast the

JONGKIND. DUTCH LANDSCAPE. 1872.  *Private Collection, Paris*

mannered and popular work of some of his more fashionable contemporaries.

**JONGKIND** Johann (1819–1891). Dutch painter, born at Latrop, Holland; died at Grenoble. For a long time Jongkind was considered with Boudin as a precursor of Impressionism. It is clear that in his watercolours, and still more in his drawings, before Sisley and Monet, he knew how to translate the fluid atmosphere and distant horizons, the movement of trees and the glittering changeableness of water. But it is also true that his merits did not limit him to the role of forerunner. He has his own distinct value, as have his works, and the best of them give him a place among the great painters of the nineteenth century. His vision is acute, his drawing trembles with life, and the least of his sketches, done with a few strokes of the pencil, is intensely alive. Should we see in his Dutch origin the reasons for his exclusive taste for landscapes, for broad horizons where stretches of earth and sea are separated from sky by only a lightly curved, uncertain, extremely fine line: great flat landscapes, formed of horizontal lines, in which the masts of ships and the sails of windmills balance in contrast? Jongkind's art is, above all, an art of atmosphere; it does not pretend, as Impressionist painting did, to the pretext of scientific discoveries to justify an aesthetic doctrine. Jongkind simply set down the appearances of the moment. New as his technique and his vision were to his time, it is not exact to make everything begin with him and not to relate him to the past. There is a definite relationship with certain Dutch artists like Ruysdael and Van Goyen, but Jongkind seems to have a freshness of feeling and interpretation whose spontaneity recalls some of the drawings of Saint-Aubin. In a sense, then, he should be thought of as climaxing a certain tradition. If the whole of his work is considered, his painting, however, calls for some reservations, for a good many of the canvases were executed for commercial reasons and ill reflect his qualities. His night scenes, with light falling among the boats can, in most cases, be discarded in any search for the artist's true sensibility. Though freely and admirably expressed in the water-colours, it is sometimes less in evidence and less natural in the oils, yet even in this domain one must recognize certain masterly and subtle successes. There were strange contradictions in his destiny, an incomprehensible contrast between his serene, luminous art and his life, which was often miserable. Though his life was unstable and sordid, in Paris he had several faithful friends: the painters Isabey, Sano, Cals and, later, a Dutch teacher of drawing, Mme Fesser, whose life he

shared and with whom he succeeded for a while in leading a fairly calm existence, at times in Normandy and more frequently in the Dauphiné or in Provence. With her Jongkind settled, in 1878, at the Côte-Saint-André between Lyons and Grenoble. When he left this district it was to be taken to the lunatic asylum at Grenoble, where he died.

## JUGENDSTIL

The term *Jugendstil*, derived from the Munich review *Jugend* (Youth), founded in January 1896, designates in the German-speaking countries, in which it was particularly developed, the movement known in England under the name of 'Modern Style', in France under that of *Art Nouveau*, and sometimes just called 1900 Style, because of its extreme vogue in Europe about that time. It was a sort of essentially decorative baroque and romantic resurgence, characterized by an exuberance of decoration based on plants and undulating forms, and was related more to fashion and taste than to art itself. Its historical importance and implications have been too lightly dismissed in the reaction against it. Even though the decorative arts and architecture were affected most of all, its effect on painting and the graphic arts was greater than many care to admit. The expressive or decorative line, with its sinuous contours, clearly appears in the last canvases of Van Gogh and of Seurat; is found in the wood engravings of Gauguin and Vallotton; marks the entire work of Lautrec, and the early work of Munch, Hodler and Kokoschka, for example.

The artistic atmosphere of the end of the century was very complex, and it is difficult to isolate the specifically 1900 Style (which really first appeared in 1880 and did not really end till 1925). Symbol (*vide* Symbolism), décor and expression are the bywords of the Post-Impressionist generation, which returned to the practice of drawing, of engraving in all its forms, and which took up eagerly the new techniques of illustration. The hero of the Modern Style in England was the amazing young mannerist Aubrey Beardsley (1872–1898), illustrator of the Yellow Book. His success in Paris coincided with the prestige of Jacques-Emile Blanche and the rediscovery of Botticelli. In France *Art Nouveau* played an important role in the renaissance of the minor arts, thanks to the school of Nancy, directed by Emile Gallé (1846–1904), and which also included, besides decorators, a few painters of talent (Sellier, Friant, Victor Prouvé).

The Modern Style elements which can be detected in the last works of Seurat (*Le Chahut* and, above all, *Le Cirque*) and of Van Gogh (Saint-Rémy and Auvers-sur-Oise periods) are developed in the engravings and decorative compositions of Gauguin and the Nabis *(\*)*, and also affect certain canvases of Matisse and the *Fauves*. It is in the poster, the dynamic creation of the period, that the most significant and highest expression must be sought, carried to the point of perfection by Lautrec and his emulators, Steinlen, Chéret and Cappiello. In 1896, in the Rue de Provence, the dealer Bing opened his Galerie de l'Art Nouveau and soon exhibited the work of the Norwegian painter Edvard Munch. Munch frequented Mallarmé, designed the production of *Peer Gynt* for the Théâtre de l'Œuvre, and surrounded his pictures and drawings with allegorical and decorative borders in the spirit of *Jugendstil*, of which the most active centres were Barcelona, Munich and Vienna.

Barcelona, the centre of the Spanish cultural revival, where the fantastic architecture of Gaudi (1852–1926) was being created, with its ornamentation of plant forms, was deeply penetrated by Nordic and Germanic influences. It was in this 'modernist' atmosphere that the genius of Picasso was being formed. His first drawings appeared in *Joventut* and *Arte Joven*, periodicals which were inspired by the Munich review *Jugend*. His first journey to Paris took place in 1900 and his 'blue period' showed him still under the influence of Lautrec and Steinlen.

In Germany, whose two artistic capitals were Munich and Berlin, the *Jugendstil* helped to break the fetters of traditionalism and encouraged new trends. The Secession group in Munich was created in 1892 with Franz Stuck, Trübner and Uhde, spurred by memories of Böcklin (1827–1901), who had lived in Munich eleven years before settling in Florence. It was presided over

in 1897 by Max Klinger (1857–1920), whose engravings the French symbolist poet Laforgue found enchanting. In January 1896 Georg Hirth began publishing the *Jugend* review with the collaboration of the best German artists. In 1899 Erler, Jank and Putz formed the *Die Scholle* group (The Land), which had some influence on Kandinsky, when he came to Munich in 1896, before he opened his own art school. The influence of the *Jugendstil* was also felt by the future members of the *Brücke (\*)*. In 1899 the Berlin Secession group was founded under the presidency of Max Liebermann. From 1895 to 1900 the review *Pan* put out by Bierbaum and Meier-Graefe, published drawings by Beardsley, wood engravings of Vallotton, etchings of Munch, and lithographs of Lautrec.

But it was in the cosmopolitan and fastidious Vienna of the end of the century that the *Jugendstil* found its supreme expression. Its uncontested leader was Gustav Klimt (1862–1918), who executed the decoration of the University (1899–1900), and who remained, till 1905, president of the Secession, whence the name of Style of the Secession, which is still given to the Viennese version of *Jugendstil*. In January 1898 appeared *Ver Sacrum*, the Secession review. The group's exhibitions (notably that of Hodler in 1904) had a great success, and their headquarters, specially constructed in the taste of the day by Josef M. Olbrich, was opened on November 12th, 1898. The poets and musicians Hugo von Hofmannsthal, Peter Altenberg and Gustav Mahler were all part of this atmosphere of culture and aestheticism, which was evident also in the furniture, the jewellery and the objets d'art of the Wiener Werkstätte (Viennese Studio), created in 1903. Here, too, grew up the young Kokoschka (born in 1886), a fellow-pupil of Egon Schiele at the School of Decorative Arts, friend and protégé of the celebrated architect Adolf Loos. In 1908 Kokoschka exhibited the illustrations for his book *Die Traümenden Knaben* (The Boy Dreamers) in which can be recognized the double influence of Klimt, to whom the work is dedicated, and of Hodler, and which constitutes, by its refined sensibility of line and the decorative use of colour, perhaps the masterpiece of the *Jugendstil*.

# K

**KAHNWEILER** Daniel Henry (born in 1884 in Mannheim, Germany). When he was eighteen he went to Paris and spent three years there before arriving in London, where his uncle began to train him for a career in banking. But his passion for art history and painting soon made him neglect his work at the stockbroker's with whom he had been placed, in favour of long hours in museums. It was not long before he threw over his banking career. On his return to Paris in 1907, when Fauvism was triumphing at the Salon des Indépendants, he opened a picture gallery which rapidly became famous. The first painters who interested him were Derain, Vlaminck, Van Dongen, then Braque, Picasso, Léger and Juan Gris. In 1908 he exhibited Braque's first Cubist canvases after they had been refused at the Salon d'Automne. He not only materially supported the Cubist painters but also took up his pen in their defence. In 1909 he began his series of art books with Apollinaire's *L'Enchanteur Pourrissant*, with woodcuts by Derain, then *Saint Matorel* by Max Jacob, with etchings by Picasso. During the 1914–1918 war Kahnweiler retired to Switzerland. In his absence, his belongings were confiscated and his collection dispersed at an absurdly low price, despite the efforts of his painter friends. After the Armistice he returned to Paris, and with his friend André Simon opened a new gallery in the Rue d'Astorg. In 1920 Kahnweiler published three works: one by Vlaminck, another by Derain, and one in German, *Der Weg zum Kubismus*. Kahnweiler's house in Boulogne became an artistic centre frequented by *avant-garde* writers and painters. New artists were shown at his gallery: with the sculptors Manolo and Henri Laurens there were Masson, Beaudin, Suzanne Roger, Roux and Kermadec. During the Second World War Kahnweiler sought refuge in the unoccupied zone of France, after placing the management of his gallery in the hands of his sister-in-law, Louise Leiris. During the years 1939–1944 Kahnweiler wrote his book on Juan Gris, the standard work on the artist, which was published in 1946. In it he showed that knowledge, insight and faith which, throughout his career, he has put at the service of a cause of which he has been one of the most lucid and ardent defenders.

**KANDINSKY** Wassily (1866–1944). Born in Moscow, died in Neuilly-sur-Seine. His father was Siberian, born near the Chinese border. He began his studies in Odessa and then studied law and political economy in Moscow. In 1889 he was a member of a mission charged with studying legal customs of the peasant communities in a northern province. The decorative richness of the interiors of the village houses was a revelation to him. In 1896 he abandoned his law career to devote himself entirely to painting. In Munich he worked with Azbe, in whose studio he met Jawlensky, and then at the Academy with Franz Stuck. In 1898 he discovered Claude Monet, whose picture *The Haystacks* was being exhibited in Munich. He opened his own school of painting and drawing in 1902 and presided over the Phalanx group. After various journeys, to Kairouan in Tunisia in 1903, Holland in 1904, and Italy in 1905, Kandinsky settled in Sèvres, near Paris, in 1906, and spent a year there. He had exhibited at the Salon d'Automne since 1904. His Impressionist period, characterized by long strokes of colour laid on with a palette knife, and a concern for construction, was succeeded by a lively kind of Fauvism, which was better adapted to dream landscapes or imaginative themes than to realistic description. On his return to Munich at the end of 1907, after stays in Berlin and Dresden, where

KANDINSKY. UNBIEGSAM (INFLEXIBLE). 1929

he exhibited at the *Brücke (\*)*, Kandinsky founded the New Association of Munich Artists in 1909. In 1910 he painted his first entirely non-representational works and wrote his treatise *Concerning the Spiritual in Art*, which was published in 1912. He met Franz Marc, August Macke and Paul Klee. With Marc, he was responsible for the publication of the *Blaue Reiter (\*)* year book, which gave its name to the movement whose two exhibitions, in December 1911 and 1912, are landmarks in modern German painting. The appearance in 1910 of Kandinsky's first non-figurative work, *Abstract Water Colour* (*see* illustration, page 2), was the result of a long evolution whose stages he traced in his book *Glimpses of the Past*. 'I felt more and more strongly', he wrote, 'that it is the inner desire of the subject which determines its form ... The separation between the domain of art and the domain of Nature grew wider for me, until I could consider them as absolutely distinct, one from the other.' And he concludes: 'I knew then that objects harmed my painting'. In the two

so-called 'dramatic' periods, between 1910 and 1920, Kandinsky painted pictures characterized by their disordered, violent lines, and very vivid colours. But this chaos gave way to order in response to an inner necessity; it was not a matter of the liberation of automatism but of a concerted attempt to express cosmic forces which transcend the powers of the individual.

Kandinsky had his first retrospective exhibition in Berlin at the Der Sturm Gallery in 1912 (an album was published in 1913), and he retired to Switzerland at the outbreak of war. On his return to Moscow after the Revolution he occupied several important official posts at the Commissariat for Popular Culture and at the Academy of Fine Arts. He organized twenty-two museums and directed the Museum of Pictorial Culture. In 1921 he founded the Academy of Arts and Sciences and was elected its vice-president. In December 1921 he returned to Germany and, in 1922, became a teacher at the Bauhaus *(\*)* in Weimar. He met Klee, Jawlensky and Feininger again, and with them formed the Four Blues group. The Bauhaus moved to Dessau in 1925. Kandinsky did important work there in decoration, teaching and publications. He had his first one-man show in France in 1929 at the Zak Gallery. He made a journey to the Near East in 1931. In 1933 the Bauhaus, which had moved to Berlin, was closed by the Nazis. Kandinsky's canvases were confiscated and sold as examples of degenerate art. He then came to Paris, where he lived until his death, in 1944.

From 1920 to 1924 the so-called 'architectural' period maintained the dynamism of the 'dramatic' periods, but more precise forms began to emerge: dots, bundles of straight or broken lines, segments of circles, rectangles and lenticular forms. Circular, concentric or overlapping outlines characterize the so-called 'circular' period (1925–1928), the other elements being more particularly used in the following period, called 'romantic or concrete'. The plastic signs to which the painter clung were employed for their own sake, quite apart from any reference to the material world. When Uccello put a diagonal in his picture, it had to be a lance. Kandinsky confined himself to the line itself, to its orientation and its relationship to the other elements of the composition.

In this way he effected a liberation of form within a picture, which recalls what the *Fauves* did for colour when they freed it from any localization implied by the object represented. Kandinsky abandoned all reference to the real world and did not even make allusions of the kind found in Paul Klee's work. He deliberately tried to create purely unreal figures, detached from all representation. No doubt it was difficult for him to cut himself off from all memories, impressions or obsessions. However, he did attain that state in his last years; he seemed to move in an unknown world to which he had gained entrance by a combination of poetic intuition and a spirit of scientific deduction. That was the result of long research. In fact, when he began his abstract adventure in 1910 it was with a very romantic and lyrical enthusiasm. This Russian, half-Asiatic by ancestry, impregnated with Oriental arts and Slavic mysticism, had a supremely spiritual ambition. If he laboured to study scientifically the mechanics of painting and to rediscover quasi-mathematical laws for the use and meaning of colours, it was because, like Seurat, he counted on finding in this way meanings which had been unknown till then. The stricter his technique became the more his imagination freed itself. It was as a conscious act that he invented forms which had no precedent. These elements group and arrange themselves according to a rather mysterious and yet convincing order, one in which the artist had no need of dimension to attain the monumental.

**KIRCHNER** Ernst Ludwig (1880–1938). German painter born in Aschaffenburg; died in Davos, Switzerland. Kirchner was the dominant personality of the group of young artists who, in Dresden in 1905, joined together to found the *Brücke (\*)* movement.

The example of Munch as well as the discovery, in 1904, of Polynesian and Negro art, helped him to grow out of his first works and led him to simplify form and colour. Working together with his friends, especially from 1907 to 1909, he gave to this technique a still more systematic character. These painters sought to express plastically the immediacy of life in a music-hall, a brothel or a circus. Kirchner, above all, was haunted by the concentrated energy of athletes' bodies and by the animal freedom, the tremulous eroticism of nude women. In 1911 the members of the *Brücke* left Dresden for Berlin. From that moment Kirchner's painting – in portraits and street scenes – conveyed the acid flavour of the intense, artificial life of Berlin at the time. The plastic structure of his canvases become more solid, more dynamic, Kirchner having learnt from the new Cubist movement the concentration of spatial aspects and their translation by angular forms. Nevertheless, Kirchner did not follow Braque's and Picasso's method of representing volume in its entirety. What he wished, above all, was essentially the immediate presence of the human being with his vital energy, though at the same time he tried to give it transcendental significance. The passers-by in his street scenes, the *cocottes* and dandies in the electric atmosphere of his pictures look like half-closed gigantic fans. By

KIRCHNER. THE AMSELFLUH. 1923

this transformation he intensifies their power to communicate their solitude in the cold, crowded co-existence of city life. During the war, in 1916, unable to bear the hardships of military life, Kirchner fell ill: he had to leave Germany in 1917 to rest in Switzerland, at Kreuzlingen, then in the district around Davos, where he stayed until his suicide in 1938. Thus, at first against his will, he encountered a reality which moved him deeply – mountain scenery. In the life of the peasant bound to the grandiose rhythm in his surroundings, he found the image of man at peace with the forces of Nature. In his pictures the scenes of peasant life sometimes take on a monumental character. This theme is developed in great allegorical compositions after 1926. In the following years, inspired by the simultaneous representation in Picasso's work, Kirchner found new ways of solving his problems. Nevertheless, of all the work painted at Frauenkirch, it is the landscapes which are the most interesting. A mountain landscape as conceived by Kirchner is at the same time a representation and a symbolic reality. The village in the depths of the valley, the steep slopes, the ridges and summits, have at once a mystical and a symbolic quality.

Kirchner was not only a painter. His sculptures in different materials and, above all, his immense output of drawings and engravings, are no less important (*see* drawings, pages 97 and 98). Above all, Kirchner was a great master of the woodcut, and his illustrations for *Peter Schlemihl* by Chamisso (1916) and for *Umbra Vitae* by the expressionist poet Georg Heym (1924), rank among the best work in modern engraving.

**KISLING** Moise (1891–1953). Born in Cracow, Poland; died at Sanary, Var. Kisling's art presents rather clearly the characteristics of what is called the *École de Paris*, in the sense that he tried to associate the ideas of French art with those of his ethnic temperament. As a boy he was so gifted a draughtsman that his family wished to make him an engineer. But at fifteen he entered the Academy at Cracow, where his teacher was Pankiewicz, who opposed the Munich style of art then in fashion in Poland

and initiated Kisling into the art of the Impressionists he had known personally. On the advice of his teacher, Kisling went to Paris in 1910 and settled at Montparnasse, where his witty joviality, charming, sensitive nature, along with his talent, made him one of the most picturesque and likeable figures of the quarter. At the time of the 1914–1918 war he joined the Foreign Legion, was wounded in 1914, and then invalided out. He was one of Modigliani's closest friends and helped him till the very last. His art always

KISLING. PORTRAIT OF A BOY. 1937.
*Private Collection, Paris*

reflected a dynamism of coloured form, which he inherited from his Slav origins. Under the influence of the French sense of proportion, particularly that of Derain, he tried for a time to repress his sensual exuberance. Despite the apparent gaiety of his character, Kisling often painted female nudes and young boys' faces which show something of Modigliani's melancholy. This melancholy, often obscured by passages of bravura, is completely dispelled from his portraits of actresses and fashionable women, in which his *brio* and verve are magnified to enhance the effect of his brilliant colouring.

**KLEE** Paul (1879–1940). Swiss painter, born at Münchenbuchsee, near Bern; died at Muralto-Locarno, in the Canton of Tessin. No other painter of the last half-century, formed far from the Nabis, *Fauves* and Cubists, and owing nothing at all to the *École de Paris*, has exercised such a widespread influence. Even more than the variations of Picasso, whose genius recapitulates the history of forms, Klee's art opens on the future. His work is not easy to understand. There are no clichés to be found there nor anything that has been seen already – nothing, at least, that has already been fully expressed. At first glance his compositions seem hermetic and the drawing childish. But when they are looked at more closely, a hidden world reveals itself by stages. From the hidden mysteries of this art there suddenly appears a dream world, peopled by apparitions which seem to light up, one after the other.

Although he was born in Switzerland, the son of a music teacher of Bavarian origin and a Bernese mother, it was in Germany that he made his career. After briefly hesitating between music and painting, he decided for the latter. He studied

KLEE. FLOATING CITY. 1930.
*Private Collection, Bern*

at Munich at the Academy of Fine Arts under Franz von Stuck. After visits to Italy and Paris, Klee settled in Munich, where he married a pianist. Between 1908 and 1910 he discovered Cézanne, Van Gogh and Matisse. He was a friend of Kandinsky and Franz Marc, the founders of the *Blaue Reiter (\*)*, and he exhibited with them. In 1913 Klee spent almost a year in Paris before going to Kairouan in Tunisia. This journey was decisive in his evolution. Up to the age of thirty-five Klee was essentially a draughtsman and had painted only water-colours. In his Journal he wrote

KLEE. FAMILY WALK. 1930.

these particularly significant words, which testify to the new era opening in his life as well as in his art: 'Colour and I are one; I am a painter'. From 1920 on he taught at the Bauhaus *(\*)*, first in Weimar and then in Dessau. After a visit to Egypt in 1928, Klee was appointed Professor at the Academy of Fine Arts in Düsseldorf. Resolutely hostile to Hitlerism, he left Germany in 1933, settling in Switzerland, where he worked till his death.

Klee drew a great deal. That is one of the secrets of the profoundness of his art. The notes he took from Nature, before his subject, are full

KLEE. ANIMALS IN THE UNDERBRUSH. 1938

of shrewd insights. Their suggestive filigree is as personal as his non-figurative drawings, in which he creates his own world by twisting lines that sometimes recall honeycombs. Here and there he can be seen attempting a hieroglyphic, an indication of synthesized power, signs which are never static – hence this writing, which is so strange at first, labyrinthine, but in which new meanings keep appearing. These drawings have a rhythm based on associations, contrasts, balancings and interruptions. In them are found what might be called directional arrows (arrows frequently appear in Klee's work, in which every line points to the inner life of man and the elements). Houses huddled together in a village, vegetation springing upwards, the wake of fish in the water, flames

dancing, the rise and fall of waves, the formation of crystals, roads and encounters, comings and goings – Klee gives form to everything which perpetually puzzles mankind, and he succeeds in suggesting its perpetual activity. By his blue foregrounds and grey backgrounds he gives space and vibrancy to his coloured planes. Klee owes to Cézanne his conviction that Nature does not lie in its superficial appearance but in its depth, so that, on the surface, colours are the expression of this internal force. Colour is not just incidental for him; it is an integral part of the organization of the picture. Who can resist those shades of blue contrasted with vermilions verging on orange and mauve, those golden browns, yellows, the pale violet punctuated with bistre? Sometimes Klee used a *Fauve* palette, but not stridently. With his quiet reds and greens he evokes the tender radiance of the moon which, 'itself like a dream of the sun, reigns over the world of dreams'. His colour has the extraordinary gift of associating planes and giving rise to rhythms in the drawing. By modulating the extreme values of chessboard white and black and superimposing his shining spectrum on them, he creates the effect of distance and evokes the sense of movement.

Klee was in everything he did, not just superficially but by a projection of his physical being in a profound way. He actually becomes the amœba trembling in the depths of the water, the crumbling mountain peak, the plant growing towards its fulfilment. He was completely at one with Nature. He had the power of giving substance to shadow and of giving form to everything that was fleeting or evanescent, be it a flower, foam or smoke. He was perhaps the only artist of our time who, without resorting to Impressionism, could paint the ceaseless movement of the heavens as seen by a child lying in the grass and dazzled by the beauty of a fine summer's day.

Towards 1924 Klee set down his reflections on art in the form of notes, which were published in the following year by the Bauhaus under the title *Pedagogical Sketchbook*. His aesthetic system was only fragmentarily expounded there. His theories, which he employed in his lectures, were far from being the codification of a method; on the contrary, they forbade his having a pre-established vision and led him to seek new means of expression. When he set to work, Klee gained power from them to throw himself freely into the improvisation of his fantasies. Far from becoming a manufactured product, work was a process of rebirth for him. He knew well enough that the creation of a painting was not a logical matter. 'One comes to know a thing', he said, 'by its root. Thus one learns the prehistory of the visible. But that is not yet art at the highest level. On the highest level, mystery begins.' Klee arrived at this conclusion: 'Nothing can replace intuition'. Even though his draughtsmanship was extremely deliberate, Klee was fortunately able to forget all about method while he was creating. No doubt certain paintings do point to the pedagogue – he taught for over twenty years – but his poetic inspiration spreads everywhere. 'To make memories abstract', was his purpose. No other painter in the last thirty years has so subtly touched the emotions or diffused such bewitching and rare poetic feeling. Werner Haftmann, his biographer, has said: 'He was the primitive of a new sensibility'.

Why does his work give such a sensation of music and poetry? Klee did not deliberately strive to transpose these feelings from one medium into another.

That would have been a sign of weakness, an underestimation of the resources of drawing and colour. It is simply that, with an artist of Klee's importance, everything flows from visual expression and everything is suggested by it. Every impression takes form, instinctively, in lines, planes and colours which, in turn, give rise to a new range of perceptions. This was the secret of Klee's art. Nobody was quicker to perceive, more competent to suggest the primal movement of life. In the very act of creation Klee seized upon this life-force. He wrote: 'As a child plays at being a grown-up, so the painter imitates the play of those forces which created and still are creating the world'. Klee's ideas on the origin of these forces were somewhat tinged with Eastern mysticism. He delighted in the idea of metamorphosis. Almost all of his work was done on very small canvases and papers. What they lack in show, they gain in depth.

His work is strictly individual, but never set apart by egocentricity nor arrogantly superhuman. Klee's painting plumbs the most secret depths of the human soul and opens on mysterious paths. And yet it never loses its purpose, and its language always remains that of visual possibilities.

KLEE. LANDSCAPE WITH YELLOW BIRDS. 1923.
*Collection Doetsch-Benziger, Basel*

**KOKOSCHKA** Oskar. Austrian painter; born in 1886 in Pöchlarn. Kokoschka studied in Vienna, beginning in 1904. Vienna at that time was the capital of an immense, dying empire and the centre of great intellectual activity. The artistic movement most in evidence was the *Jugendstil (\*)*, marked by the affected, decorative art of Klimt. After being part of that movement, which inspired his book *The Boy Dreamers*, Kokoschka soon showed his independence. His painting, as well as the expressionist dramas he wrote, astonished and deeply shocked the public. Between 1908 and 1914, first in Vienna, then in Switzerland, and much later in Berlin, he painted some portraits, particularly of writers and actors, which are psychological documents of haunting accuracy. The colours are very gloomy – blacks and browns, sometimes shot with blue, sometimes touched with highlights of red. Nervous and feverish, the drawing does not trace in a normally reassuring fashion the external aspect of his sitters so much as the strange lines of their inner personality (*see* drawings, pages 97 and 98).

Kokoschka seems to have a gift of second sight that has allowed him to portray physical transformations which later actually show themselves in the model. He is haunted by his subjects. The problems of form have only a secondary importance for him. The interest of his paintings resides essentially in their visionary character. The psychological preoccupations which one notices in his early pictures transform themselves little by little into a more general passion for all the human realities. Kokoschka's conception is dramatic, and his work carries an echo of that tradition of dynamic and visionary baroque painting which was still strong in Austria before 1914. His major work before the 1914–1918 war was *The Vortex* (1914), in which two lovers, transposed as myth, become all the forces of Nature unleashed

Seriously wounded in 1915, Kokoschka had to wait for years before he was completely recovered. He settled in Dresden and, in 1919, became a teacher at the Academy. He was then influenced by the *Brücke (\*)*, particularly in his use of colour. After his gloomy portraits and the cold blue night of *The Vortex*, his Dresden paintings astonish by their frank colouring, even though colour is not always perfectly integrated into the structure. It was only much later that he solved this problem by using a dramatic Impressionism of feverish brush strokes. In 1924 Kokoschka suddenly decided to leave Austria, and for seven years he travelled through Europe, North Africa and Asia Minor. With the same passion he had shown in his portraits of men he now painted sites, mountains and, above all, cities. He generally chose a very elevated or distant viewpoint from which the principal features of his subject could be seen in a broad, rhythmical pattern. In this manner he portrayed Paris, Aigues-Mortes, Lyons, Marseilles, Jerusalem, Toledo, London, Amsterdam and Prague. In the visionary synthesis of the picture these cities appear to be living beings, with their legends, their stories and their secrets. In 1931 Kokoschka again settled in Vienna, but in 1934, after Dollfuss came to power, he left for Prague, and from there, in 1935, went to London. During these years, and also during the war, the ideological struggle gained mastery over his painting, and he composed a number of large allegorical and historical pictures (Loreley, Anschluss). After the war, painting gained the upper hand in his landscapes, streaming with colour, of the Valais and of Italy. In 1950, in London, in the decoration of an immense ceiling, Kokoschka used the myth of Prometheus in presenting a grandiose parable of the destiny of our civilization.

**KUPKA** Frantisek. Czech painter; born in 1871 at Dobruska, Bohemia. Kupka studied at the School of Fine Arts in Prague. To support himself, he gave lessons in religion and worked as a medium at spiritual séances. He was immersed in the thought of the French eighteenth century, and so was overwhelmed by an exhibition of the Impressionists in a Prague gallery. In 1891 he studied in Vienna and, in 1895, in Paris, where he has lived ever since. He studied from Nature and greatly admired Rodin and Toulouse-Lautrec. He undertook some important illustrative work: *Lysistrata*, *Prometheus* of Aeschylus and *Les Erinnyes* of Leconte de Lisle. He learnt Hebrew when commissioned by

KOKOSCHKA. LONDON, TOWER BRIDGE

Élie Faure to make drawings for a new translation of the *Song of Songs*. His studio had the calm atmosphere of a religious workshop. From 1906 on his painting changed profoundly; his technical development served an imagination which saw beyond appearances. In his landscapes Kupka sought the distortions of bodies in water and expressed them in cold, strident colours. He gave them a life of their own, independent of the subject and freed of the demands of reality. In a portrait of 1907 a yellow tone dominates the expression and even the features. The large *Nude* painted in 1909 and exhibited in the Salon d'Automne of 1910 marks a decisive stage: the body is cut up into severely constructed and brightly coloured zones of purple, orange, yellow, rose and dark green. A bridge had been thrown between a methodical Fauvism and a Cubism which was soon to rediscover the use of colour. A portrait of Kupka's wife is invaded by lines and only the face survives among the clean-cut verticals and diagonals. But this rather hybrid combination of contrasting elements is soon left behind and an interest in construction predominates: the image springs up amid the interplay of complementary planes, as if through a series of screens. In 1911–1912 Kupka painted the first totally abstract work: *Fugue in Red and Blue*, in which concentric rhythms in blue, red,

green and black are ranged on a white ground. He superimposed coloured masses, chromatic blocks which seem to emerge from one another (as in *Vertical Planes*, 1913), and from which shoot out isolated lines which sometimes recall graphic motifs.

Kupka joined with his neighbour Jacques Villon in the meetings of the *Section d'Or (\*)*, in which a whole group of young Cubists were seeking the ideal proportions of a new painting. He was mentioned by Apollinaire as being among the Orphist painters *(\*)* and the creators of the art of the future. In 1913 the *New York Times* devoted an article to him in which he was quoted as saying: 'To people who claim that one cannot create forms or colours, I will reply that man has created the Ionic column and the Doric column and that architecture has constantly created forms with well-proportioned and fully justified modifications. . . . Man expresses his thoughts in words . . . Why not create in painting and sculpture, independently of the forms and colours which surround him?' A little later, in the preface to an album of abstract woodcuts, he wrote: 'The work of art, being in itself abstract reality, needs to be made up of invented elements'.

During the 1914–1918 war Kupka joined an infantry company before becoming an officer in the Czech Legion. The French poet Blaise Cendrars, his comrade in battle, has described their experiences in *La Main Coupée*. After the war Kupka continued his experiments, his expeditions to the extreme limits of knowledge. In 1924 he exhibited his *Diagrams* and *Whirling Arabesques*. But his contemporaries did not appreciate him, and this pioneer of non-objective art saw himself almost ignored. Uncompromisingly, he continued with his work and attained a purity and balance which evoke a sort of philosophical architecture. In 1936, in a large exhibition at the Musée du Jeu de Paume in Paris, he arranged a vast panorama of his creations, in five sections: *Circulars*, *Verticals*, *Verticals and Diagonals*, *Triangulars*, *Diagonals*. But it was not until after the recent war that his work received the recognition it merits: first in Czechoslovakia, where an important retrospective exhibition was

KUPKA. BLUE AND RED VERTICAL PLANES. 1913.
*Louis Carré Gallery, Paris*

organized in 1946 for his seventy-fifth birthday, and from which fifty pictures were bought to form a Kupka Museum; then in Paris and New York, where it was recognized, because of its unity and logical development, as one of the key sources of abstract art (q.v.).

# L

**LAETHEM-SAINT-MARTIN** The school of Laethem-Saint-Martin was founded in the last years of the nineteenth century, when Valerius de Saedeler settled there, a few miles from Ghent, in a bend of the River Lys. The exceptional beauty of this district began to attract a number of Flemish artists, who formed a group around Saedeler – Gustave van de Woestyne, Alfred Servaes and the sculptor Georges Minne, among them. Laethem had already known an extremely gifted primitive painter named van den Abeele, a local government employee who at the age of forty had begun to paint modest but penetrating works inspired by local scenes and customs. Valerius de Saedeler, a great admirer of Breughel and the Flemish Primitives, particularly excelled in the treatment of snow seen through the black branches of dead trees. Servaes united Flemish realism with such personal power and originality that the clergy banned his religiously inspired works from the churches, including a *Stations of the Cross*, which had caused a scandal.

A few years later a second group of painters formed at Laethem, including Albert Saverys, Constant Permeke, Gustave and Leon de Smet, Fritz van den Berghe, Edgar Gevaert, Hubert Malfait, Jules de Sutter, Piet Lippens, and several others (*vide* Permeke, Smet). The artists met on familiar terms in the modest tavern they had chosen as their meeting-place. They were rather strongly opposed to the idea of Impressionism. Their villagers and peasant types were painted in a kind of healthy expressionism in a clearly Flemish tradition. They sought to express a full sense of life. A certain *joie de vivre*, a robustness of form, transfigured a reality which was no longer seen in the manner laid down by the old academic canons. The Laethem-Saint-Martin school was violently attacked by the Academy. But its final success confirmed its interest and its value, and the influence it has had on Belgian painting in general has been its surest justification.

**LA FRESNAYE** Roger de (1885-1925). French painter; born in Le Mans; died in Grasse. Descended from an old Norman family, Roger de la Fresnaye was reared in the best French tradition. His precocious childhood drawings show surprising precision, purity and directness. In 1903 he enrolled at the Académie Julian and followed the courses at the École Nationale des Beaux-Arts until he was tired of the pettiness of the teaching there. He then entered the Académie Ranson, where Maurice Denis and Sérusier were teaching. These two artists taught that painting, far from being a mere

LA FRESNAYE. STILL LIFE. 1918.

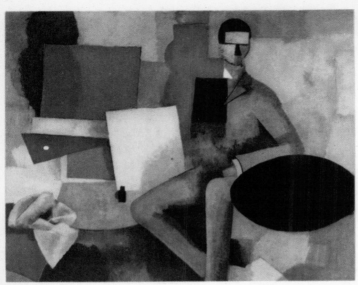

LA FRESNAYE. SEATED MAN. 1914. *Private Collection, Paris*

1911, at La Ferté-sous-Jouarre and Meulan, in *Man Drinking and Singing* (1910), *Cuirassier* (1911) and *Joan of Arc* (1912), those works in which, through Cézanne, La Fresnaye reached back to Géricault and Poussin, he succeeded in interpreting Nature by means of a strictly intellectual discipline. Energy under control, a direct and somewhat lofty tone, much nobility, despite a certain youthful sharpness – these are the characteristics of La Fresnaye's painting at this time. As an admirer of Cézanne, he could not ignore Cubism, and from 1913 on La Fresnaye joined Braque in this movement. More intellectual than Braque, he saw Cubism only as a method; less baroque than Picasso, he sought a classical basis in Cubism. La Fresnaye soon tried to check the splitting-up of form and the multiplication of planes which were the consequences of analysis. Probably he was the first to introduce the synthesis lately extolled by Gauguin into the Cubist experiment, to eliminate details and fussiness of every kind. In this spirit he painted *Seated Man* (1913), *The Conquest of the Air* (1913), *Married Life* (1914), and the beautiful series of *Still Lifes with Square-Rule, Diabolo, Bottle of Turpentine* and *Bottle of Port Wine*. In each of these works line and colour are so closely bound together, so marvellously combined that the composition has not a single flaw. From then on La Fresnaye heightened his tones, brightened his reds and blues (he who had used such austere colouring during his Cézanne period) while the other Cubists were impoverishing their palettes. La Fresnaye made only a brief foray into Cubism before the First World War interrupted his work.

copy of reality, was an absolute and convincing ensemble of forms and colours, that art was the concrete image of the inner life, the fruit of intelligence and discipline, that it was consequently natural to modify Nature and to obtain a new reality by deliberate distortion. Such was the theory of the Nabis *(\*)*. Nothing could have better suited La Fresnaye's own inclinations. He submitted to the influence of Sérusier, Maurice Denis and Gauguin for several years. A mixture of irony and tenderness, of mannerism and austerity, even a certain literary quality, give his first canvases, particularly his *Self-Portrait* (Museum of Modern Art, Paris), a definitely Nabist accent. Unlimited possibilities were soon revealed to La Fresnaye by Cézanne. The *Ève*, which he executed in 1910, was already more plastic than the works of the Nabis. However, he took only the construction of forms from Cézanne: cubes, cones, cylinders, fitted together to give solidity and density to the objects. His palette was reduced to ochres, browns, muted blues and greens. More preoccupied with volume than with space, he sought above all for right proportions. In the landscapes he executed in

He had never been very strong. But when war came, he enlisted, asked to be sent to the front, and distinguished himself there by his courage and self-effacement. When the troops were resting, he drew or painted water-colours. He came down with fever and was evacuated to a temporary hospital in Tours. Then began that doleful, restless sickbed life, which he bore without complaint, and in spite of which he continued his work. But his energy was sapped. In 1919, ill with tuberculosis, he settled in Grasse with his friend Gampert, a painter and engraver. He executed several portraits of Gampert, drawings, water-colours and gouaches. Stoically, he watched his strength and genius decline. He died on November 27th, 1925.

By 1918 La Fresnaye had said everything he had to say. His work of the following seven years – his last – was not without its importance, but one must remember the conditions in which La Fresnaye was obliged to work. Confined to his sickbed, incapable of sustained physical or in-

LA FRESNAYE. PORTRAIT WITH A PIPE. 1918.

LA FRESNAYE. PORTRAIT OF J.-L. GAMPERT. 1920.
*Musée d'Art Moderne, Paris*

tellectual effort, cut off from all contact with Paris artists, even obliged to abandon oil-painting, La Fresnaye could put only meagre means at the service of his talent. The few paintings he was able to turn out were inevitably marked by these conditions, but his drawings retained the same qualities of purity, sharpness of insight, and that characteristic aristocratic distinction of his, with occasional touches of preciosity. On December 29th, 1924, he wrote to one of his correspondents: 'In thinking of the common difficulties we have known for twenty years, of all those I have gone through, and of all that I should wish to do if I were in good health, I cannot help sighing when I consider the time and energy lost through lack of a guide or authority'. An admirer of Cézanne, a satellite of Cubism, he put grace and sobriety, boldness and moderation into his compositions. But unfortunately he never let himself be content with a single god. He worshipped Gauguin, Géricault, Ingres, and the Florentines of the Quattrocento. With his complex nature and whimsical mind, he often achieved real style, but he did not always maintain it. Despite his adventurous spirit, he was

LA FRESNAYE. STUDY. 1914.

Amid such an abundance of new roads and stupendous promises, La Patellière's work invited repose and meditation, and proved that there could be several solutions to the problems of the time. Today we see that his art, beneath its apparent calm, sought to resolve the same problems, and that the means he employed were not so very different from those which then appeared revolutionary. Like the Cubists, La Patellière returned to strictly constructed compositions, seeking a distribution of objects in three-dimensional space which still retained unity of surface, refusing the picturesque, using light to give rhythm to his compositions and not to transform the colours, limiting himself to simpler

really a classic, but today, whether because of his premature death or for some deeper reason, his work seems incoherent and incomplete.

One cannot help wondering where his talents would have led him after 1918 if his strength had remained unimpaired. 'The more I live,' he wrote, 'the more I believe that painting is not a question of intelligence; it is almost a physical discharge.' These are the bitter words of a sick man who cannot develop his capabilities and is aware of his plight. His masterpieces such as *Portrait of Guynemer* and *The Countryside at Hauteville* show that he possessed the artistic resources of a great painter. But for the onset of his illness he would no doubt have forged a coherent and original style of his own, and ceased to be an inspired eclectic.

**LA PATELLIÈRE** Amédée Dubois de (1890–1932). French painter; born near Nantes; died in Paris. La Patellière belonged to the generation of painters which, after the 1914–1918 war, found itself in a completely changed world in which the triumphant Cubist movement was imposing a new vision, a new order which had all the appearances of disorder.

LA PATELLIÈRE. STUDIO WINDOW. 1929.
*Musée d'Art Moderne, Paris*

forms and to a range of sober tones dominated by browns. This is equally true of the Cubists. However, in his strict observance of these principles, La Patellière wished to keep in close touch with Nature, with the inner reality of things, and so was able to use the poetic feeling which springs from a reverence for Nature; thus his work has a quiet poetry which harks back to the peasant inspiration of the Le Nain brothers. Through the sense of mystery which arises from this sentimental aspect of his work, La Patellière's contribution to modern painting deviates from more modern formulas, particularly those of Cubism; no doubt that is why he has been given a place rather outside contemporary painting, a solitary place, despite the admiration given him by the other artists who were his friends.

On the other hand, because his powerful personality did not exercise all the influence which might have been expected of it, because he died too soon, without revealing his full potentialities, and, finally, because his return to tradition was not a return to inertia, ignorance and mediocrity, but a quiet and deeply positive attitude, La Patellière's art has a value which extends beyond the modest place he is given at the moment.

**LAPRADE** Pierre (1875–1923). French painter; born in Narbonne; died in Fontenay-aux-Roses. Seven or eight years younger than Bonnard and Vuillard, Pierre Laprade is one of the most tender of modern 'intimists'. Dividing his life between his little house in Fontenay-aux-Roses and his studio in Paris, he lived without ambition or need. Like Corot, he loved to wander through the French provinces; there was not a cathedral whose bells he had not heard. Italy was his second home, and he brought back rich harvests of water-colours from there, like Claude Lorrain mixing French harmony and a sense of balance with classical memories.

He excelled in suggesting a poetic atmosphere by using the most familiar elements – a window opening on a town or on the sea, garden terraces, Chartres Cathedral rising above

LAPRADE. THE MUSICIANS. 1907.
*Private Collection, Paris*

harvest fields, Florence dreaming beside the Arno, or a young woman resting in a hammock as unsubstantial as a dream. It was not so much the actual forms as the colouring of the atmosphere in which they were bathed that he loved to paint. A kind of sad enchantment envelops all reality: ears of corn or yellow roses among blue pottery or among old books and masks, dusty puppets and pierrots, parks full of soft light. From youth Laprade used water-colour with mastery. At first his paintings were in monochrome, but they soon grew more colourful without losing those silvery tones with which his brush so successfully created the iridescent atmosphere of his dreams. This friend of poets was born to illustrate such works as the *Fêtes Galantes* of Verlaine. His delicate line is never insistent, sometimes even appearing uncertain; it does not so much describe an object or a particular landscape as a sentimental moment enveloped with deep or light greens with rose tints or blues dancing among the tender whites and yellows.

**LARIONOV** Michael. Russian painter born in 1881, at Tiraspol, near Odessa. He attended courses in painting, sculpture and architecture in Moscow, and from 1898 onwards took an active part in artistic activities there. In 1909, at the Society of the Free Aesthetic, he showed *The Glass*, a near abstract work which reflected the influence of the new Cubist movement. The following year Marinetti *(\*)* made a lecture tour in Russia, speaking on Futurism *(\*)*

LARIONOV. DIAGHILEV AND APOLLINAIRE AT A REHEARSAL OF THE 'BALLETS RUSSES'. 1917.

He was triumphantly received in Moscow and St Petersburg, and his influence was soon felt there. That same year Larionov launched Rayonism *(\*)* by showing, at the Kraft Studio, canvases which were entirely composed of spots and rays. The Rayonist manifesto did not appear, however, until 1913. Larionov was a friend of Malevitch and the teacher of Tatlin, whose portrait he painted in the Rayonist technique. He went to Paris in 1914 and held a retrospective exhibition with his wife, the Russian painter Nathalie Gontcharova. The introduction to the

Catalogue was written by Guillaume Apollinaire. In addition to his Rayonist works, Larionov did canvases representing soldiers or peasants, painted in a very primitive style. After making the acquaintance of Serge de Diaghilev, also in 1914, Larionov worked for many years for the Ballets Russes *(\*)* and almost completely gave up easel painting.

**LAURENCIN** Marie. French painter; born in 1885 in Paris. She attended the Lycée Lamartine until she was twenty. Of average ability, she received some rather discouraging advice from her drawing teacher: 'You would be better off learning to play the mandolin'. Nevertheless, she began to attend drawing classes at a municipal night school. Then she met Clovis Sagot, a small art dealer, who spoke to Picasso and Apollinaire about her; soon after, Gertrude Stein bought one of her canvases. She used to go to the Bateau-Lavoir *(\*)*, where painters and poets congregated. Though she took part in the feverish discussions which gave rise to Cubism, she was hardly influenced by this movement: in the group portraits she painted of Apollinaire and his friends there is that great simplicity and stylization of bodies and faces from which she never departed. Apollinaire wrote of Marie Laurencin's art of this period that 'it dances like Salome between that of Picasso, the new John the Baptist, who cleanses the arts in a baptism of light, and that of Rousseau, the Herod of the sentiment, magnificent and puerile old man, that love led to the very edge of intellectualism'. Her art has never changed its character and throughout her career she has sought the same dream of gentleness in the pathetic faces of women, filmy veils, feathers and flowers and delicate colours. Perhaps the only exception is Poe's *The Raven*, which she illustrated for Apollinaire with red and black lines and dots and which has remained unpublished. In the thirty works she later decorated with lithographs or water-colours, she returned to figurative representation. Among these were *La Tentative Amoureuse* by André Gide and *Alice in Wonderland*. She designed the décor of *Les Biches* by Poulenc (*vide* illustration, page 12) for the

LAURENCIN. PORTRAIT. 1913.
*Collection of J. Paulhan, Paris*

Russian Ballet in 1924, and the décors of *À quoi rêvent les jeunes filles* by Musset for the Comédie Française in 1928. She reads widely, and her best friends are the books which line the walls of her apartment; sometimes, too, their authors, for Marie Laurencin has always preferred the company of writers to that of painters. She has described herself in these terms: 'Loves luxury. Very proud of having been born in Paris. Likes neither long speeches nor reproaches nor advice, nor even compliments. Eats quickly, walks quickly, lives quickly. Paints very slowly.'

**LEBOURG** Albert (1849–1928). French painter; born ·in Montfort-sur-Risle (Eure); died in Rouen. Lebourg is one of those artists exactly described by the epithet 'minor master', with all that this expression conveys in the way of talent, refinement and reserve. He did not play the revolutionary role of the great Impressionists, but· he fully understood their poetic quality and the benefits they brought, especially to landscape painting. In his taste for landscapes seen through the rain and monochrome skies, he follows in the tradition of Boudin and Jongkind. His origins and also his education – he was a pupil at the Rouen art school – explain the harmony between his sensibility and the landscapes of the Seine valley. Between 1872 and 1877, during his stay in Algiers, he undertook, in the Monet tradition, to paint series of pictures exploiting the same theme (*Arab Fountain, Moorish Café*). Lebourg, however, remained on the margin of true Impressionism and did not draw from these series any of the extreme conclusions reached by Monet at that same time. His Impressionism is never provocative; it is, rather, a discreet harmony of half-tones with the vibration of light-filled atmosphere. In him Paris found one of its most sympathetic interpreters, because he knew how to remain scrupulously exact without being banal. He was the echo, in a minor key, of the great Impressionists; but however discreet his canvases might be, they were never impersonal. Subtle harmonies are to be found there; above all, a great freshness through the use of light colours, more often complementary than contrasting. By his work

LAURENCIN. THE SPANISH WOMEN.
*Etching*

LEBOURG. APSE OF NOTRE-DAME. 1899.
*Lorenceau Collection, Paris*

Lebourg proved the error of academicism in refusing the new benefits of Impressionism and becoming obstinately static. He demonstrated what a non-revolutionary conception of art rejuvenated by new ideas might have become.

**LE CORBUSIER**  (real name Édouard Jeanneret). Swiss painter and architect; born in 1887 at La Chaux-de-Fonds. We are not concerned here with the work of this original architect but with his important contribution to the ideas which have renewed contemporary painting. For five years, until he was eighteen, Le Corbusier was apprenticed to an engraver and was the pupil of L'Éplattenier at the art school in La Chaux-de-Fonds. When he began his architectural studies in 1905 he did not completely give up the graphic arts, and he was keenly interested in the first Cubist experiments. As an architect he did not feel that the new aesthetic doctrine agreed sufficiently with a discipline which had to be respected and cultivated if the picture was not to be debased to the level of a decorative ornament. Thus arose his idea of demanding from painting a total submission to the architectural setting destined to contain it. It was still understood, however, that the picture remained, above all, 'a machine to

work upon the emotions', and the work of art 'a game'. The paintings and drawings dated 1918–1919, still signed with the name of Jeanneret, already appeared as imperious calls to a new order founded entirely on numbers and geometry. When he founded *L'Esprit Nouveau (*)* in 1920 with Ozenfant, and gave birth to what was called Purism *(*),* it was essentially with the intention of preserving Cubism from the decorative tendency which threatened to engulf it. Nevertheless, Le Corbusier did not outlaw lyricism or attempt to repress the mysterious, intimate demands of sensibility. Beginning in 1929, the human face appeared in his painting alongside the still life, the only genre he had practised till then. From then on he seemed to let his plastic imagination go adventuring, in compositions in which nudes adopted violently dramatic attitudes. Le Corbusier saved from his old Purist discipline only an absolute rejection of bewitching arabesques or facile arrangements of tones which were more particularly suited to easel painting. His work gained frescolike characteristics and began to show a development of audacious and striking shapes specially adapted to mural painting. In 1936 he executed tapestry designs for the Aubusson workshops; in them he showed a tumultuous imagination always restrained by the notion of a plan which, he felt, helped 'to avoid waste'. In short, the profoundly human side of Le Corbusier as an architect is strengthened by his feelings as a painter. If he subjects his aesthetic emotions to rules, they are not those of mathematical canons but of norms proper to a feeling human being.

**LÉGER**  Fernand. French painter; born in 1881; died in 1955. Though he was of peasant stock and left the soil to follow his irresistible vocation, nobody remained more faithful to his humble origins than this robust, simple, generous man, this artist gifted with powerful instinct and unfailing good sense. In 1897 he became an apprentice in an architect's office in Caen. He went to Paris in 1900, did his military service at Versailles, and after a short spell in the École Nationale des Beaux-Arts, settled at La Ruche in 1905. He was first influenced by Cézanne. He met Picasso and Braque in 1910. He had just shown his *Nudes in the Forest* in the Salon des Indépendants. In the following year he joined with Gleizes, Delaunay and Metzinger in the first Cubist exhibition in the same Salon. He was mobilized in 1914, fought at the front, and made drawings of soldiers and weapons of war, the mechanical aspect of which had a profound effect on him. Between 1912 and 1914 Léger had painted objects reduced to their geometrical form – cones, cylinders, polyhedrons; the dy-

LE CORBUSIER. STILL LIFE. 1920.
*Collection of R. La Roche, Paris*

namic phase of his work began about 1917. He renewed his inspiration and choice of subjects from what he saw about him. While his friends – such as Braque, Picasso and Gris – chose such familiar objects as playing-cards, a packet of tobacco, newspapers and drinking-glasses as themes for creation, Léger used objects invented and constructed by industrial civilization: railway wheels, cogs and tugs. He introduced human figures, workers, acrobats, Negro chauffeurs and signalmen into his mechanical universe. He painted *Discs*, *The Town* and *Man with Wheel*. Broad planes and large areas of colour create rhythm and space in these pictures, which have the impersonal precision of machines. But these various elements are not arranged in a naturalist manner: that is to say, in combining them Léger had no intention of reproducing some aspect of reality. His works are images proceeding from direct experience, immediate sensation, stark, evident, familiar, banal reality, which we see every day without really seeing it because the veil of fiction intervenes between it and us. Up to 1921 the people he fits into his composition only form accessory elements – simple fragments of architecture, cogs of machines, machines themselves – and are, there-

LÉGER. JULY 14TH. 1914.

fore, devoid of humanity, physiognomy and name. From 1921 on, however, the human figure begins to dominate in his pictures, but it still appears as an automaton or puppet. Léger seemed to renounce movement in favour of a static art. His immobile forms, his machines are masses in repose. Up to 1924 he constructed a monumental art, peopled with proletarian gods, with a mythology both strange and common, unusual and concrete, majestic yet vulgar. Such famous canvases as *Fisherman, Women Holding Flowers, Man with Sweater, Woman with Vase* date from this period.

In the years that followed, his desire for stability and purity was accentuated, he returned to still life, executed mural, decorative, frankly abstract paintings which permitted him to liberate colour from form, to discover the value of coloured surfaces in modern construction. To create space with colour was perhaps the problem which most occupied Léger from then onwards. Already, in his *Woman in Blue* (1909), he felt it, and then, in *The Town* (1919), he clearly enunciated it. From 1924 to 1926 he brought out convincing solutions which he developed later in some still more

important works: *Sports* (Brussels Exhibition, 1935) and *Transport of Forces* (Palais de la Découverte in Paris, 1937). Since then it is no exaggeration to say that Léger's entire production was conceived in relation to a wall: whether real or imaginary, does not matter. What is important is that mural painting has a deep connection with the social life and aspirations of humanity.

After this abstract and constructive period Léger painted the series of pictures known under the generic title of *Objects in Space*, in which architectural elements are replaced by scattered objects, then the series of *Contrasted Rhythms, Divers* and *American Works*; he also produced paintings, tapestries, mosaics and ceramics. In spite of this, however, he always thought, while working, of the conditions of modern life, made up of violent contrasts, tumult, speed and tension; he always dreamed of the monument, the surroundings, the décor, the new space in which we are obliged to move. Léger never suggested this new space by colours alone but also by forms and their contrasts. Everything is contrasted in his art. There is a contrast of motifs: of flowers and mechanical elements, a figure and a bunch of

LÉGER. WOMEN WITH BOUQUET. 1921.

keys. There is a contrast of lines: a step and a wheel, a disc and a chessboard. There is a contrast of rhythms: a tree-trunk and a dancer, a thick plank and a rotating screw. The oddest objects find themselves united: the most static forms with the most dynamic. Léger only needed to intervene to arrange the most unexpected things, the most trivial and absurd, for them to acquire all the force and strength of truth. Léger belongs to his time; he speaks the language of his period. No art is more different from traditional art than his. He never entered a museum, he never copied, even in his early days, a picture by some Florentine or Flemish master. With him everything is new: the form, the space, the colours. He deliberately ignores the cultures and disciplines which have preceded him; he is at his ease everywhere: in the street, in the fields, in the factory, everywhere there is life. And it is precisely because he belonged so much to his period and his country that he created work with a lasting and universal character.

He was a decorator as well as a painter. The costumes and décors which he executed in 1921 and 1922 for the Swedish Ballet (*Skating Rink*,

*La Création du Monde*) have enriched theatrical art. In 1924 he created the first film without scenario: *Le Ballet Mécanique*, a kind of poem of pure movement. He created monumental ceramics, tapestries, mosaics (the church of Assy), and his stained glass for the church of Audincourt is one of the masterpieces of our time. No one has more profoundly marked his period than Fernand Léger, or in more diverse domains. And yet his fame has only lately been widely recognized. It is only today that we see him in all his grandeur. One wonders why this has been so. After the revolutions which have succeeded one another since Cézanne's time, total liberty has come to mean misunderstanding, uncertainty and unreasonableness. But in Léger's work our age has found a justification and a rallying-point. In a world of subtle analyses, of abstract ideas, acquired cultures, Léger is perhaps the only artist who has been a man among men, neither proud nor sad nor complicated. Would he have been less great if he had been more refined, less sure of his force and his instinct? He was a labourer of painting – a labourer gifted with genius. He was probably the only painter who

LÉGER. THE FINE TEAM. *Ink*. 1944.

neither took nor borrowed anything from anyone (with the exception of Cézanne, who influenced him at first). Themes, forms, colours, composition – he drew everything from the depths of his own being. He was the most modern of painters in the sense that he went beyond his own time and that his *raison d'être* lay in the future, not in the past. He invented a form, a space, a colour range, without rejecting the world; and he respected the beings and the things among which he had to live. And at last he brought us something new. Where can

his Adams and his Eves on the tympanum of a Romanesque church, his mechanics by the side of Uccello's armed men. And yet there is no trace of archaism in his painting, no references to history or to literature. Neither mystic nor lyric and still less Romantic, Fernand Léger was compound of the virtues – order, generosity, honesty, integrity and health. The American critic James Johnson Sweeney has called him the Primitive of modern times. That he was also the Classic is equally certain.

LÉGER. COMPOSITION WITH BRANCH. 1946.

one find the unyielding labour of the working man or the peasant, the rhythmic chant of the machine, the hearty fraternity of the factory, the simple joy of picnics, if not in Léger's work? But everyday existence is recalled only by a strict language of lines, forms and colours, a direct and living language which is joined by the inner road of the mind to that of the great civilizations of the past. His *Divers* could easily mix with the dancers in Tarquinia's tomb. One can imagine

**LEGUEULT** Raymond. French painter; born in 1898 in Paris. For years Legueult has belonged to that group of artists called 'painters of poetic reality', each of them being inspired by the same desire to preserve, in a rather conservative way, the direct inspiration of Nature filtered through his individual personality. Legueult has shown himself especially attracted by colour, which transforms all his compositions into an extremely subtle play of rainbowlike iridescence in which the volumes of forms count less than the areas they offer for the use of colour. His art is not much concerned with the space and volume of objects but is completely captivating in its delicacy and grace. Legueult's art is close to music through its subtle orchestration and rare harmonies. Not only in the drawings or the composition or the settings in which he places his people, but in the subtlety of the relationship between tones, his art gives the impression of certain Oriental painting. He introduces us to a poetry in which fantasy has the freshness and unexpectedness of a spring morning. The forms dilute themselves in this magical world in which everything has an equal density and, as in Bonnard's canvases, one has the impression of confusion, but little by little details appear to recompose the forms and thus to give to the poetry the added value of a secret language.

**LÉPINE** Stanislas (1835–1892). French painter; born in Caen; died in Paris. It would not be exact to place Lépine among the innovators of his time, and one can hardly compare

LEGUEULT. THE BLUE DRESS. 1952.

Courbet, long before anyone knew the more violent audacities of the Impressionists. The Impressionists needed to lean on the achievements of more modest figures such as Lépine and Lebourg, and perhaps the refined, quiet art of such painters was the most effective way of preparing the ground for public acceptance of the great masters. Lépine's art, however, was not just that of an intermediary. He has his own charm. His numerous views of Paris remain among the memories which can best evoke the atmosphere of the city at that period. They are valuable witnesses of the time, the more so because the artist never sacrificed anything to anecdotal details. Perhaps Lépine was one of those last artists to know how to make a landscape intimate, how to fix the secret soul of a city, a street or a river. His life was as discreet as his art, and practically nothing is known of him except that he died in such poverty that his friends had to make a collection to pay for his funeral.

him with the masters of Impressionism, even if one admits his gift for finding an inspiration of refined poetry in the representation of Nature, in changing skies and landscapes glittering with light. It would also be unjust to see him merely as a respectful follower of a careful academic tradition. Actually, Lépine is one of those artists indispensable in explaining the transitions of art. The history of art is not just a series of violent reactions, as one is tempted to believe in viewing the works of the great artists alone. It is the minor masters who discreetly stake out the progress of ideas so that developments result from forward steps and not contradictions. It is the minor masters, from Daubigny to Lépine, who make the history of French nineteenth-century landscape painting a logical process, far removed from revolt, dominated by Corot and

**LEWIS** Wyndham. Born in 1884 in Nova Scotia, of English parents. After studying at the Slade School *(\*)* he travelled widely in Europe, returning to London in 1909. Here he threw himself into the polemical battle for modern art with unparelleled exuberance. 'In art I was a *condottiere*' he was to write. Around him formed a circle of friends that included Ezra Pound, Jacob Epstein, T. E. Hulme,

LÉPINE. PLACE DE LA CONCORDE.     *Collection of Arthur Sachs, Paris*

Richard Aldington, Gaudier-Brzeska, and it was these names that were to be associated with the Vorticist movement which Lewis founded in 1914. Vorticism derived in part from Cubism, in part from Futurism. More than anything, however, the movement was a weapon, dynamic and aggressive, explosive as the title of its review *Blast (\*)*, and it set itself to hustle Britain into step with the European *avant-garde*. Wrote Lewis later: 'Really all this organized disturbance was Art behaving as if it were Politics. But I swear I did not know it'.

The war failed to inhibit his activities. 1914–1915 saw the completion of his first major novel *Tarr*, the publication of a folio of twenty drawings entitled *Timon of Athens*, his first portrait of Ezra Pound, the first Vorticist exhibition and the second number of *Blast*. In 1917 he was seconded as an official war artist to Canadian Corps H.Q. at Vimy Ridge; in 1918 appeared *Time and the Western Man*; in 1919 he held his first one-man show at the Goupil Galleries. For some years from this period, date a great number

LEWIS. THE SURRENDER OF BARCELONA.

of those incisive, marvellously constructed pencil portraits which show his powers of visual analysis at their most lucid. In 1924 appeared another review *The Tyro*, and in 1930 perhaps his best-known book *The Apes of God*. All his life in fact, Lewis has alternated between painting and writing, has continued to wield a savagely satirical pen – as a novelist, as critic and as pamphleteer. In his books he lashes out at the grotesque incomprehension of actuality evidenced by a society based on outmoded values; as a critic he is remarkable, penetrating and accurate in his analysis of contemporary art; as a pamphleteer he is prophetic and oracular.

It must be faced that Lewis is equally at home with the brush or the pen, but he is not therefore to be grouped with those English painter-writers whose background is chiefly literary and whose painting is more or less a side issue. Lewis is a born painter, whose dominant characteristic, both in his non-figurative works and in his portraits and other more naturalistic compositions, is an innate sense of construction. Most of his works are built on a vertical axis with a precise framework, somewhat metallic; occasionally they seem cold at first glance, but they are generally redeemed by their qualities of strength, dignity, and clarity. After 1914 his work is hardly ever entirely abstract. A painting by Lewis may strike one as pre-eminently a kind of geometrical or rhythmical speculation; yet it will invariably have, in addition to its sculptural qualities, a totemic character which makes of it a sort of magical object with a soul and a life of its own, as in the case of *The Contemplator* or of his drawings for *The Enemy*. *Sunset in the Atlas*, on the other hand, Cubist in structure but fluid in atmosphere, sums up rather well the characteristics of the Vorticist movement. Two paintings in the Tate Gallery are representative of his art: *Red Scene*, a composition of sombre, flat tones and a masterly geometric construction, and his *Portrait of Edith Sitwell* (1921), vertical, metallic, powerful. His *T. S. Eliot* has the same characteristics. Lewis must indeed be regarded as one of the foremost portraitists of the present century.

**LHOTE** André. French painter and theoretician; born in 1885 in Bordeaux. He exhibited in the Salon des Indépendants beginning in 1906 and the Salon d'Automne in 1907. With such surprising works as *The Widow*, he could not be disregarded. He was fortunate enough to be appreciated at once by the critics and poets. Generally it is difficult to forgive a painter who writes or a writer who paints. Lhote is the exception, however. As an art critic – he contributed to the *Nouvelle Revue Française* until 1940 – and as a writer of such books as *Treatise on Landscape, Treatise on the Figure, Writings on Art, Egyptian Painting in the Valley of Kings,* Lhote has raised outstanding questions, analysed the aims of art and explained matters of technique which no writer before him had even dared to touch.

LHOTE. RUGBY. 1917.        *Musée d'Art Moderne, Paris*

He has exercised a lasting influence on the younger generation, not only by his writings but also by his example, by the teaching he has done in the school he founded in 1922, and by the advice he has never withheld from the young people who have asked him for it. André Lhote joined in the first Cubist activities without becoming lost in that movement. His cult of Cézanne, his admiration for Picasso, have not prevented him from expressing himself, from unequivocally becoming a painter devoted to analysis and construction.

A picture such as *Rugby* (1917) is a good example of his method and ideas: the geometrical transcription of figures or objects, the clear articulation of planes through contour and colour, subtle composition, emphasis on movement and intelligibility of style. Always searching for perfection, Lhote tries to put everything into his pictures: form, light, space, intelligence and sensibility, energy and stability. He attempts the absolute. And every one of his works seems like a demonstration rather than an outpouring. His is an integral, supple, reflective art which offers all the genres and all the themes. Lhote today is still as lucid, charming, active and keen as in his youth. He is indifferent to nothing connected with the art of forms – surely the explanation of his influence on contemporary painting.

**LIEBERMANN** Max (1847–1935). German painter; born and died in Berlin. Liebermann's studies in Berlin and Weimar were completed from 1873 onwards by long periods of study in Paris and at Barbizon. After that, he worked in Munich and in 1884 settled in Berlin, where he remained until his death. Every summer, from 1879 until the First World War, he spent several months in Holland. Liebermann's painting continued the Berlin tradition, the tradition which had culminated in Menzel. However, he was the first in Germany to feel the influence of the great currents of foreign painting, from Naturalism to Impressionism. His early canvases were genre scenes. But the example of Courbet and, above all, of Millet, helped him, from the time of his first stay in Paris, to find a personal language which was colder and less sentimental in its realism than that of the French masters. As subjects for his largest compositions he took groups of men or women at work. *Plucking the Geese* of 1873, his first large canvas, created a scandal; he was accused of making himself the apostle of ugliness. Liebermann took a great step forward several years later, when he came into contact with Dutch art. From then on he saw men and objects in an atmosphere impregnated with dampness and light, just as the great Dutch masters had painted, in particular Frans Hals, whom he studied and copied. His works of this period – scenes from orphanages or old people's homes – and those which follow, are more monumental in their

LIEBERMANN. STREET IN AMSTERDAM. 1907

construction. In them Millet's influence predominates, and they are technically more finished. Their principal quality, nevertheless, remains a rather cold cautiousness, and they have that sobriety in the evocation of Nature which seems to correspond to the puritanism of the Berlin tradition. In 1873, during his stay in Paris, Liebermann had not recognized the importance of the Impressionists. It was only after 1890 that he discovered Manet and submitted to his influence. His palette became lighter, his painting gained in light and movement. His landscapes,

his street scenes (especially those of the Jewish quarter of Amsterdam) and beach scenes acquired a new unity of tone and colour. But with Liebermann, Impressionism was only a process by which light was added to naturalism without totally transforming it. The colouring remains sober, varied only in its values. A few years later, Degas's influence appeared in the drawing, which became more dynamic and nervous, and in the bolder arrangement of his figures. In the last thirty years of his life Liebermann evolved a discreetly refined work in which, alongside views of his garden at Wannsee, portraits and self-portraits occupy a prominent place. Liebermann's work is of capital importance for Germany. Through it and through the struggle of Liebermann and other pioneers for the recognition of French art, German art came in contact with the main currents of European painting. This contact was essential for all the pictorial movements which were to be born after 1900.

**LISSITZKY** El (1890–1941). Russian painter; born in Smolensk; died in Moscow. He studied engineering at the Darmstadt technical school from 1909 to 1914. He then returned to Russia, where he was influenced by Malevitch and the Constructivists. In 1919 he began a series of drawings and paintings to which he gave the generic name *Proun*, a term he applied to all his work thereafter. In 1921 he was named professor at the Moscow Academy, but because of the growing hostility of the Government towards new art, he left his homeland in that same year for Germany. There he met Moholy-Nagy, with whom he became friendly, and on whom his influence became important. In 1922, in Berlin, he made the acquaintance of Theo van Doesburg, who published in Holland several months later a very curious *Story of Two Squares*, a set of six drawings that Lissitzky had composed in Russia in 1920. He worked with Hans Richter and published with him, in 1922 and 1923, the review *G* (*Gestaltung*). Then he went to Switzerland, where he created the group and review *ABC*. In 1925, in collaboration with Hans Arp, he published *The Isms of Art*. From 1925 to 1928 he

LISSITZKY. COMPOSITION FROM 'THE STORY OF TWO SQUARES'. 1920.

was in Hanover at the invitation of the Kaestner-gesellschaft. It was at this period that he did the interior decoration of the Modern room at the Landesmuseum, later destroyed by the Nazis. He then returned to Moscow, where he occupied himself mainly with organizing exhibitions of international art and publishing books for children. Lissitzky's very personal art (*Proun*) is based on a composite conception of space, of three-dimensional forms mingled with flat forms. No other Russian artist among those who were active in Central or Western Europe exercised such a radical influence on the course of art. This influence was felt, first of all, at the Bauhaus *(\*)*, through the teaching of Moholy-Nagy, who was named professor there in 1923.

## LONDON GROUP

'The London Group' wrote Roger Fry, 'has done for post-Impressionism in England what the New English Art Club did, in a previous generation, for Impressionism'. To a greater extent than the NEAC however – indeed, more than any other British exhibiting society – the London Group has contrived to avoid that hardening of the critical arteries which comes to affect most such societies with the passing of the years; of all those in Britain it remains the most broadly representative of all that is best in non-academic painting and sculpture. Founded in 1914, its origins lie a decade further back. When Sickert *(\*)* returned to London in 1905 he at once became the centre of a group of painters – most notably Lucien Pissarro, Harold Gilman, Charles Ginner and Spencer Gore – who looked to Gauguin and the other post-Impressionists rather than to the watered-down Impressionism of the NEAC. These artists met regularly at Sickert's studio at 19 Fitzroy Street; they stood for urban and 'low life' subject-matter, for a light palette and a high colour key, and opposed the jury system of exhibition selection. The Allied Artists Association, which also subscribed to the latter viewpoint, held a first exhibition in 1908 at which over 3,000 works were shown. Considering this scale of operations so vast as to defeat its own objects, the Fitzroy painters finally founded, in 1911 (the year following Fry's first post-Impressionist exhibition), the Camden Town Group, which held its first showing at the Carfax Gallery under the presidency of Gore. Among the original sixteen members, besides Sickert, Pissarro, Gilman, Ginner and Gore, were W. Baynes, R. Bevan, J. D. Innes, A. John *(\*)*, H. Lamb and J. B. Manson. In

LUCE. ROTTERDAM. *Etching*. 1908.

1914, under the presidency of Gilman, the Group amalgamated with several smaller groups – notably the Vorticists – to form the London Group (the name was suggested by Epstein), showing as such in the same year at the Goupil Gallery. Among the new members were D. Bomberg, Sylvia Gosse, W. Lewis *(\*)*, J. Nash, C. R. W. Nevinson and E. Wadsworth; other names which became associated with the London Group within the next few years were those of V. Bell, D. Grant, M. Gertler, B. Meninsky and P. Nash *(\*)*. Today the membership stands at about ninety, and embraces painters and sculptors of every creed from the most realistic to the completely non-figurative, quality and integrity being the Group's only concern. Participation in its annual exhibitions is open to non-members and it is thus to the London Group that many young artists look for their first showing.

**LUCE** Maximilien (1858-1941). French painter; born and died in Paris. Luce was only a minor artist, but his simple, sincere nature was satisfied with such a role, for he had an inborn disdain for honours, and his only desire was to paint. He sought neither to innovate nor to dazzle but, with the conscientiousness of an artisan, devoted his long, retired life to painting. 'It was no easy task', wrote his friend George Besson, 'to make a name at twenty at the moment when Monet was painting his *Gare Saint-Lazare* and Renoir his *Moulin de la Galette*, or to hope for notoriety at thirty with only the will to do good work to pit against Gauguin's genius for the picturesque, or at seventy, with only disdain for M. Dali's bluff.' However, Luce was not entirely indifferent to the artistic trends of his day, and he joined the group around Signac and Seurat for a few years, until finally his poetic sensibility could no longer submit to the inflexibility of their system. On abandoning Divisionism he came under the influence of his friend Camile Pissarro, and his work tended towards Impressionism: fixing the fugitive effects of Nature in subtle, delicate tones, he produced paintings which were both poetic and powerful.

In his youth Luce was an anarchist, and in 1894 was implicated in the celebrated 'Procès des Trente'. Acquitted at the trial, he left prison and continued all his life to paint steadily, taking part in no group activities and never abandoning his independence of mind and pride in his working-class birth. Apart from his landscapes, some of Luce's best paintings represent the humble, arduous life of the people: labourers, dockers or masons at their daily work. His art, which has its own highly individual side, has its place between that of Pissarro and Bonnard.

When Signac resigned from the presidency of the *Société des Artistes Independants* in 1934, Luce was elected to succeed him – the only worldly honour he ever accepted.

# M

**MACKE** August (1887–1914). German painter; born at Meschede in the Ruhr; died at Perthes, in Champagne, during the war. After a childhood spent in Cologne and Bonn, Macke studied at the Academy of Düsseldorf. During visits to Paris after 1907, he came in contact with French painting: the Impressionists, then the *Fauves*, and later Cubism. In 1909–1910 he met Franz Marc and Kandinsky in Munich, and in 1911 he took part in the preparation of the *Blaue Reiter (\*)* almanac. Breaking off a stay at Hilterfingen by the Lake of Thun in the spring of 1914, he went on a trip to Tunisia along with Klee and the Swiss painter Moillet. A few weeks after his return to Bonn, he left for the war and was killed shortly afterwards.

Because Macke was associated with the *Blaue Reiter*, it is tempting to consider his work only in relation to that movement. But his position was quite different from that of Kandinsky or Franz Marc. Whereas Marc turned toward direct expression of a spiritual reality, Macke always remained deeply concerned with visual experience. His sensitivity allowed him to benefit more than any other German painter from the lesson of French painting. It is possible that the spirit of the Rhineland, where he spent nearly all his life, made this contact easier for him. As early as 1910 his painting, which had undergone the influence of Impressionism and then of Cézanne, developed a broader, freer rhythm inspired by the works of Matisse. In fact, the painting of his friends of the *Blaue Reiter* confused him more than it helped him find his way.

It was the influence of Cubism, to some extent of Futurism, and, above all, of Delaunay, that helped him as early as 1908 to find his own idiom. He was enthusiastic about Delaunay's *The Windows* (reproduced on page 7), and paid a visit to the painter in Paris; the latter came to see him in Bonn with the poet Guillaume Apollinaire. While the influence of Cubism simplified Macke's form, Futurism suggested a means for more complete representation of life. This representation he meant to accomplish by the use of light and colour in 'simultaneous contrast', after the example set by Delaunay. In this way his painting found its own form. In just about a year, at Bonn and Hilterfingen, in Tunisia, and again at Bonn, a body of work of luminous colour and perfect grace and distinction was born. Some small abstract compositions, in 1913–1914, reveal Delaunay's influence, but, unlike the abstractions of Franz Marc, Macke's did not indicate the general direction of his work. Macke's painting,

MACKE. GIRLS UNDER TREES. 1914.
*Private Collection, Austria*

163

on the whole, remained representational: strollers by a lake, children, girls under trees, women before a milliner's display – such are the subjects he preferred. The figures are quiet in the midst of motion, or as they wait, and the moment becomes fixed in a hazy space created by pure and luminous colours. From the Tunisian trip Macke brought back, in addition, water-colours of crystalline structure.

**MAGNELLI** Alberto. Italian painter; born in 1888 in Florence. After having studied in technical schools, Magnelli devoted himself to painting, away from all academies and professors. In 1913 he associated with the

MAGNELLI. DISTURBING VISION. 1947.

Futurists Boccioni, Carrà, Marinetti, Papini and Soffici, but without belonging to their movement, and his own experimentation stemmed from other preoccupations. During a stay in Paris, from February to June 1914, he made friends with the poets Apollinaire and Max Jacob, and the painter Fernand Léger. He painted a series of large still lifes and compositions of very simplified human figures in Florence. This synthesis of severe forms led him, in 1915, to his first complete abstractions, in which bright colours were applied flat. After

this period of extreme severity, he returned in 1918 to a semi-representational way of painting, very violent both in colour and in form. From 1920 to 1930 he painted several series of figures and landscapes, extremely architectural in composition and clear and sober in colour. In 1931 he reverted to abstraction with a new style, which had long been ripening, opening with the so-called 'stone' period, in which his forms recalled shattered rocks. He arrived in 1933 at a total abstractionism, resting upon no theory but still based upon imagined figures. During the Second World War he stayed at Grasse, in the south of France, together with Arp, Sophie Taeuber-Arp and Sonia Delaunay.

Magnelli's art strives to rediscover the pure and archetypal forms which lie behind superficial sense-impressions. If he brings to mind the ideal abstraction of mathematical figures, he always provides sensory and plastic equivalents, for he does not think that a picture can be only a blueprint. In him there is a creative will as far removed as possible from the fortuitous, and a health and natural strength that prevent even his most enigmatic forms from ever being meaningless or literary.

**MAGRITTE** René. Belgian painter; born in 1898 at Lessines, in Belgium. In 1925, after a short glance in the direction of Futurism and Cubism, Magritte joined the ranks of the Surrealists. He lived for five years in Paris, where he made friends with the poet Paul Eluard. While most Surrealist painters were making use of automatism, paranoia or the exploration of dreams, on the basis of the 'purely interior' standard that their leader, André Breton, suggested to them, Magritte was more interested in the world about him and its objects.

He wanted to reveal their existence by means of a representation that was realistic but poetic nevertheless, making painting both a way to knowledge and a means of moral liberation. From 1924 to 1936 he applied himself to producing surprise effects by bringing together incongruous objects, creating new ones, and transforming familiar ones. By means of exchange or opposition, he enlightened us about them: stone-burned, the sky was wooden or cracked, the bells of horses became dangerous flowers. Some ten years before, Chirico had already made use of unexpected combinations of elements unrelated to one

MAGRITTE. SUMMER STEPS. 1937. *Private Collection*

another, to create an atmosphere of mystery and bewilderment. Magritte's dryness, his precision, and his will to paint 'anti-painting' sometimes recall the style of Chirico. From 1936 to 1940, expanding his field of investigation, Magritte no longer juxtaposed dissimilar objects, but instead explored the affinity that the object, isolated, could have with itself. The question was to discover the relation of the encompassing and the encompassed – the relation of the tree and the leaf, the landscape and the picture, the shoes and the feet, the sky and the bird. This problem, solved a hundred times with astonishing imagination, made Magritte a wonderful inventor of images. Each of his canvases, admirably painted, was a discovery in which intelligence and sensitivity mingled. At the same time his tonality lightened. It passed from brown to green, from grey to blue. This metamorphosis announced other research in a sphere where colour would play a role of primary importance. Although very much questioned, the Impressionist period of Magritte, which dates from the Second World War, should not be a surprise. Painting being for him only a means of deepening his knowledge of the world, every technique, even an old one, was useful in

so far as it made us reconsider the object from an angle and in a light that the painter could dictate at will. On the other hand, it is regrettable that this flood of colours was accompanied by only a few discoveries about the object itself. The aspect of the canvases changed; the content became less rich. Toward 1946, in the final *volte-face* of an amazingly independent man, Magritte returned to his former manner. His ideas are without doubt less numerous and his hand less sure, but *Scheherazade*, a woman's face outlined with pearls, is an enchanting find. Above all, he repainted two celebrated pictures, the *Madame Récamier* of Gérard and *The Balcony* of Manet, replacing the figures with coffins. Recreating masterpieces or remaking objects is the same process. In both cases the aim has been to teach us to see. Magritte is a great visionary.

**MALEVITCH** Casimir (1878–1935). Russian painter; born in Kiev; died in Leningrad. Malevitch was first influenced by the Post-Impressionists and the *Fauves*. Later he made friends with Larionov and the more advanced Russian poets. The latter, in 1915, helped edit his Suprematist manifesto (*vide*

Suprematism). As a member of the Jack of Diamonds group in 1911, he exhibited works of Cubist inspiration; and he became the leader of the Russian Cubist movement, to which his wife Udalzova belonged as well. In 1912, after a trip to Paris, he began to paint in the manner of Léger, although he emphasized straight lines and clean geometrical figures slightly more (*The Scissors-Grinder*, *Woman Carrying Water*). This step brought him to the threshold of complete abstraction, and in Moscow at the end of 1913 he exhibited a black square on a white background, making a great sensation. The square, whose area was painstakingly filled in with black pencil, was the first element of Suprematism. It was soon joined by the circle, the cross, and the triangle. During the next few years, with these basic shapes, Malevitch painted a number of compositions, most of them quite simple, the shapes themselves being created by clear colours upon a white background. The acme of simplicity and delicacy was reached in 1919, when he painted his *White Square on a White Background*, exhibited in Moscow in the same year (now in the Museum of Modern Art, New York). He was then appointed professor at the first National School of Applied Art in Moscow. A few years later, when modern art fell into disrepute with the Soviet Government, he was transferred to Leningrad, where he could nevertheless keep on teaching until his death. Until the end he was surrounded by the discreet admiration of a number of friends, but it is not known whether he continued to paint after the opportunity to exhibit was over. He was granted permission, however, to go to Germany in 1926, in order to prepare his book *Die Gegenstandslose Welt* (The World of Non-Representation), an elaboration of the Suprematist manifesto of 1915, for publication at the Bauhaus (*). Along with Mondrian and Kandinsky, Malevitch is one of the pioneers and most important representatives of Abstract Art (*). As in the case of Mondrian, the starting point for his discovery of abstraction was Cubism; but what Mondrian gained as the result of a slow and gradual evolution, Malevitch grasped in a sort of sudden revelation that led him immediately to the most absolute result – the famous black square on a white background – which he afterward devoted years to achieving dialectically.

MALEVITCH. SUPREMATIST COMPOSITION. 1914–1916. *Private Collection, Stuttgart*

**MANET** Édouard (1823-1883). French painter; born and died in Paris. Manet belonged to the upper middle class, and his existence was bound to that class; he remained attached to the privileges it enjoys, wished to receive the honours and recognition it confers, and at the same time gave rise during his lifetime to the most violent scandals and unwittingly produced through his painting a complete revolution. He brought a taste for liberty that did correspond to the aspirations of the time but was not yet admitted in its consequences. Academic art was still dominated by what was thought to be a tradition but in fact consisted of no more than the impoverished remnants of superannuated formulae. At the beginning Manet probably had no intention of playing the part of a revolutionary leader. He had very prudently begun by setting out upon a more conventional career. Yielding to family insistence, he started out in 1848 as a student pilot on a training ship, having failed in the competition at the Naval Academy. But to follow his calling as an artist he enrolled a few months later in the studio of the painter Thomas Couture. His independence brought him into immediate conflict with his teacher. He did not, however, approach the profession with preconceived ideas, sure of inventing a personal technique. He frequented the Louvre very assiduously, his lessons left him unsatisfied, and the example of

MANET  LUNCH ON THE GRASS. 1863. *Louvre*

masterpieces convinced him that he had more to learn from the masters and from Nature. His character as a painter therefore derived from his stays in Fontainebleau and from his admiration for Tintoretto, Titian and Velasquez. In his first works, already stamped by these influences, an inclination can be discerned for clear colours, a free touch, and large vibrant flat areas. His visits to Holland, Germany and Italy reinforced this tendency, in which he was reviving the freedom and dash of Frans Hals and the Venetians of the Renaissance. In the *Portrait of a Spanish Musician*, which he exhibited at the Salon of 1861, he revealed the attraction held for him by Spain, which he had just discovered in a play given by a troupe of travelling singers and dancers. To this chance is due the famous picture of *Lola of Valencia*, the 'pink-and-black jewel' celebrated by Baudelaire. The affinities between Manet's art and Spanish painting were once thought so obvious that a critic described Manet as a 'Parisian Spaniard', and Courbet, on the occasion of the 1865 Salon, where *Olympia* was exhibited, said: 'This young fellow had better not try to pull Velasquez over our eyes'. However, it was not until that year that Manet finally went to Spain to see the masters

by whom he was supposed to have been influenced. His admiration for Velasquez was strengthened and he discovered Goya.

From the beginning, then, Manet was astonishing and bewildering. The first violent reactions of the public dated from 1863, when he exhibited *Le Déjeuner sur l'Herbe* at the famous *Salon des Refusés*. The scandalousness attributed to this picture is difficult to understand today. It seemed indecent because it represented a naked woman sitting on the grass between some young men in contemporary dress. At the time nudes were tolerated only in allegorical scenes, when the figures were supposed to represent gods. Actually it is very likely that the technique was even more shocking than the subject. With its freshness and vivacity of colour and its broad execution, the canvas seemed to have been painted on the very spot rather than in the studio. All this indicated on the part of the young artist an inexcusably warped character, an audacity which made him exceed the limits of decency. The rejection of convention, the boldness of the elements employed had at the time an aggressive character, which, in drawing the opprobrium of the righteous bourgeoisie down upon him, made

MANET. THE FIFER. 1866.        *Louvre*

Manet the leader of the young painters. His attitude became even more apparent at the Salon of 1865, where he exhibited *Olympia*. Zola found it the pictorial counterpart of the theories he was himself beginning to elaborate. He felt in the work, in its reaction against accepted standards, a frankness and certainty revealing an art already liberated and sure of itself, leaving all hesitations and gropings behind it. The public was offended by the presence of a black cat at the foot of the bed, and the Negress offering a bouquet of flowers seemed out of place. The critics, for their part, deplored the lack of shading, the brutality of the drawing, and the crudity of the light, when they did not go so far as to insult. Jules Clarétie, very categorical in his denunciations, typified the attitude adopted by the antagonists: 'What is this odalisque with the yellow belly, some indecent model picked up

God knows where, presuming to represent Olympia? Olympia? What Olympia? A prostitute, beyond a doubt. M. Manet will never be reproached for idealizing the foolish virgins – he'll drag them all through the mud, more likely.' The model Clarétie so grossly insulted was the pretty Victorine Meurend, the central figure of *Le Déjeuner sur l'Herbe* before she became *Olympia* and who was to be *The Fifer* the following year. Today *Olympia* seems to us one of the finest achievements of modern art. In it one admires the unexpectedness of the pose, the firmness and purity of outline, the sincerity of the expression, and the consummate mastery of the composition. Enclosed in its abstract but still living whiteness, seldom has a woman's body known such nudity.

The painters a few years younger than Manet who were soon to create Impressionism did not underestimate the importance of these experiments. They recognized in Manet a precursor behind whom they could gather to renew painting more drastically than the art of a Courbet or a Corot had undertaken to do, much as they admired those painters. Manet benefited in turn from the good feeling of the younger men: having set them the example of his mastery and youthful boldness, he found them, with their glorification of light colour, a stimulus and a new source of inspiration. Although he did not participate in the Impressionist exhibitions organized after 1874, he felt the appeal of this renovation, as his lightened palette testifies. However, he did not become devoted to landscape for its own sake: his outdoor scenes always contained figures, which were the occasion for him to arrange, among the blue and grey reflections with which he surrounded them, dark colours that were set off by the contrast. While he shared with the Impressionists the desire to express sense impressions in all their immediacy, he never resorted to the systematic breakdown of colour. Unlike his young friends, he had no horror of black – quite the opposite. Black was to him, as to Frans Hals, a real colour, which he often used, and which gave an extraordinary brightness to many of his compositions. Neither was he haunted by plastic problems like Cézanne, or obsessed with drawing like Degas. Manet did not attempt to set up a system: less a theoretician than a painter, instinctively inspired and gifted, he wanted, above all, to re-create on canvas the vividness and intensity of what he experienced. No doubt he was always surprised by the scorn he encountered in academic circles. For a long time he persisted in exhibiting at the Salon and ended by being awarded a secondary medal that put him out of the running. But this was in 1881,

MANET. OLYMPIA. 1863.

*Louvre*

and his career was already fulfilled – so much so, in fact, that the next year he was made Chevalier of the Legion of Honour (through the intervention of Antonin Proust, his fellow student at the Collège Rollin, who had by then become Minister of Fine Arts).

The art of Manet is an introduction to the future, in its freedom of handling and the importance accorded to colour. Even when he applied the pigments flat and refused to tone them down,

his colour retained spatiality, and this was probably his most characteristic contribution to the art of his time. The importance he gave to colour made him sometimes summarize the surface of a volume in a few essential planes and sometimes, on the contrary, adopt broad, uniformly coloured surfaces, as in *The Fifer*. It was in connection with this canvas that Daumier accused him of wanting to reduce painting to the 'faces on playing cards'. This was a failure to recognize the boldness of Manet's experiment; for thus to plant a figure in vivid and brilliantly coloured dress against the emptiness of a monochrome background suggested by Valasquez without allowing such extreme simplification to end in a total lack of life, called for the very surest kind of hand. Although every shadow has disappeared and become concentrated in the vibrancy of outline round the form, it is astonishing that this mysterious process has not allowed either the fluidity

MANET. LA RUE MOSNIER. 1878.

MANET. MAXIMILIAN'S EXECUTION. 1867.
*Tate Gallery, London*

of outline or solidity of form to diminish. The art of Manet, in spite of all innovations in technique, is nevertheless bound to tradition, because of the influences it has felt, and especially because of the over-all concept of a picture that it presupposes. Like the very greatest artists, Manet was able to take a hackneyed theme and give it such life that it seemed new. Without proof, an unsuspecting person would not think of Rubens behind *Le Déjeuner sur l'Herbe* or Titian behind *Olympia*, and yet the relationship is indisputable. *La Pêche* (*Fishing*) mixes elements found in two works of Rubens: *The Rainbow* and *The Park of the Castle of Steen*; also from Rubens comes *The Nymph Surprised*, a reversed fragment from *Susanna at the Bath*. *The Dead Toreador* is a replica of *The Dead Warrior* of Velasquez, and *The Execution of Maximilian* a pendant to Goya's *The Second of May*. These are neither imitations nor plagiarism, but real creations starting from an external and independent reality, whether it be an object, a person, or another picture. No matter what the theme selected, Manet fits it to the measure of his own personality. There is no less intensity or life in the canvases inspired by classic works than there is in *The Bar at the Folies-*

*Bergère*, the subject of which was taken from an episode in contemporary life; and this composition conforms to laws no less severe than the others do. Throughout all his changes Manet preserved a surprising unity. No doubt the ability of some men to invent a new vision, so unexpected that it comes as a surprise, and yet so perfectly in accord with still unformulated aspirations, that its style immediately compels recognition, is a sign of genius. Works like these are of lasting value; when they can no longer surprise they become classics, for the feeling of life they diffuse bears witness to their truth.

Free as it may seem, the art of Manet is not improvised; his compositions are not the product of chance but are rigorously and purposefully constructed. He was not so entirely detached from the subject as might be believed, at least not so detached as his successors. He was easily tempted by large historical compositions, not only in his youth, as the works discussed above reveal, but also when he was in complete control of his powers: *The Execution of Maximilian* furnishes an example. In 1879 he even proposed to the Prefect of the Seine to decorate the Hôtel de Ville with compositions depicting Paris life:

MANET. PORTRAIT OF IRMA BRUNNER.
*Pastel.* *Louvre*

MANET. THE MODEL OF THE BAR AT THE FOLIES-
BERGÈRE. 1881. *Dijon Museum*

the markets, the railways, the bridges and the race-track. Finally, in 1881, he produced a picture on the escape of Henri de Rochefort from the Noumea penitentiary, which illustrated an event hardly seven years old. One can conclude that he did not have the reticence about anecdote, or even the distaste for it, that began with Impressionism, and was to become one of the principles of modern art. The interest he took in human subjects made him one of the best portraitists of the nineteenth century. The numerous portraits he did of Berthe Morisot, particularly the one with the black hat, and those of Proust, Clemenceau, Théodore Duret, Zola, Irma Brunner and Nana, not to mention one of the finest, that of Stéphane Mallarmé, should not be forgotten. Toward the end of his life, when he began to feel the onset of paralysis, he took

up pastels, easier to handle, and produced portraits of Parisian celebrities that are among his finest accomplishments. The natural elegance of his work permitted him to be a precise and exact observer, who never fell into the slightest vulgarity. Although he always remained on the fringe of the Impressionist group and did not give up work in the studio for outdoor painting, as later artists did, Manet deserves the position of leader that is usually granted him in the history of Impressionism, for he was the first, and for years the only, painter to fight for a new art that sought a renewal of inspiration and technique in direct observation of Nature and contemporary life.

**MANGUIN** Henri Charles (1874-1945). French painter; born in Paris; died at Saint-Tropez. Manguin's work can best be described as joyful painting: what it expresses is neither a burst of self-astonished happiness nor the exuberant joy of a moment or of a sequence of exceptional moments but a tranquil fulfilment conveying a feeling of duration. Bright but not violent tones, coloured harmonies without contrasts, everything blends in a serenity attained freely and effortlessly. To Fauvism *(\*)*, in which he ranks just below the great leaders, Manguin brought a vividness free from anxiety. One has only to analyse the means employed to see that this state of mind is apparent in every technical detail: the drawing is firm, without ever being stiff or brutal, the straight line is virtually proscribed, and every theme is resolved into flowing arabesques. The angles of the volumes soften, the object is not sharply isolated, everything harmonizes and interconnects, and the colour suggests and outlines the forms, whose relief calls for another set of colours rather than any real shadow. Certain nudes or still lifes are related to those of Matisse, but with less austerity and severity. Manguin never gives the impression of a will bent upon reaching a difficult goal. His charm is largely due to an air of facility, which one soon realizes to be the result of a thorough craftsmanship that allows extreme flexibility. Manguin's great merit is that he did not attempt to exceed his limits. In a period when a young

MANGUIN. JULY 14TH AT SAINT-TROPEZ. 1905.
*Lucile Manguin Collection, Paris*

artist was easily tempted to try to outdo his
fellows, he was able to preserve enough calm to
keep to the work that suited him; in a region
where Nature offered the appeal of extreme
colour (Manguin lived a great deal in the south
of France), he could retain sufficient control to
obey the dictates of his own taste. Thus his
paintings still appear the harmonious result of
the artist's expressing himself without reticence.
Manguin belonged to the group of painters who,
before the First World War, gave the Salon
d'Automne in particular such a distinctive
character, countering the austerity of Cubism
with the vision of a joyously coloured world.

**MARC** Franz (1880–1916). German painter;
born at Ried in Bavaria; killed at
Verdun. Marc was the son of a Munich painter.
In 1900 he decided to become a painter also and
enrolled in the Academy. But his attainment of a
style that was truly his own was to be long and
arduous. He experienced years of deep depres-
sion. As early as 1903 a stay in Paris brought him
in contact with Impressionism. The *Jugendstil (\*),*
the most advanced movement in Munich, helped

him state more clearly the problems of form. On a
second visit to Paris, in 1909, he was strongly
impressed by Van Gogh. In 1910 he met Macke,
who was to remain his best friend, and a little
later Kandinsky, with whom he was to fight for
the new painting and publish the *Blaue Reiter (\*)*
almanac. In 1911 he came into his own. Between
then and 1914, when he left for the war, he
produced his best work. Although problems of
form occupied him, they were subordinated to
his desire to express himself. He felt an almost
religious need, as did Kandinsky, to find through
the work of art an objective and spiritual reality
beyond the deceptive illusions of Nature. He
freed himself only slowly from the wholly subjective sentimentality of his early work. His first
step in this direction consisted in the choice of his
subject – animals; beings involved in the universal harmony, capable of bringing the painter to a
more objective realization of the world. Marc
studied them for years before acquiring a
thorough knowledge of their movements. This
knowledge enabled him to find the essential form
(*Wesensform*) in which all their tenderness,
innocence and nobility could be contained. Thus
*The Blue Horse* in its youthful vigour, *The Roe*
cowering in a hollow of the wood, the beautiful
and dangerous *Tiger* become, like *The Dog before
the World*, the centre of a universe peculiar to
themselves, and thereby they take on the force
of symbols, the symbols of communion and
peace.

After Pointillist experiments, Marc, having
come in contact with Kandinsky and his friends,
used colour in a free and expressive manner
that recalled the *Fauves*. But for Marc nearly as
much as for Macke the most important influence
was Delaunay. In 1913 the coloured forms in his
pictures, animals in their setting, began to inter-
penetrate, the colours brightened and grew more
transparent, the forms more crystalline. All living
things drew closer and entered into the primal
harmony. The large pictures of 1913 attain a
mythic force which recalls the painting of the
Douanier Rousseau, for whom Marc had a profound admiration. *The Destinies of the Animals*
and *The Tower of the Blue Horses* are among the
most important works of this period. However,
the forces conflicting in the cosmic struggle of

the large landscape *The Tyrol*, begun in 1913 and taken up again in 1914 had no further need of animal form to achieve expression. From then on Marc's course led toward an abstractionism bordering upon the play of the pure forces in a still undivided Nature. In the short time that remained before the war he finished a series of abstract compositions, profoundly lyrical (*Broken Forms, Serene Forms*).

**MARCOUSSIS** Louis (1883–1941). His real name was Louis Markous, transformed into Marcoussis– after a village near

MARC. TYROL. 1913–1914.      *Bavarian State Museum, Munich*

Montlhéry, outside Paris – by the poet Guillaume Apollinaire. He was born in Warsaw and died at Cusset, in the Allier, in central France. After his arrival in Paris in 1903 he exhibited at the Salon des Indépendants and the Salon d'Automne. Until 1907 he painted in the Impressionist style. Later he took part in the experiments of the first Cubist painters and in 1912 was active with the *Section d'Or (\*)* group. Even though he gave a vigorous structure to his landscapes and still lifes, his style retained a poetic lightness, evident in subtle passages of colour and in an elliptical and sensitive line. His art, based upon a graceful balance, always evokes a season, the charm of a faintly seen light, a real and emotionally experienced atmosphere of tender, restrained lyricism. This obedience to the beauties of Nature and this understanding of the aerial density of space came only as the result of an inspired search for the secret rhythms that animate the universe. Marcoussis presents a curious mixture of sensitivity, reason and submission to the supernatural, to signs and messages. The poet Max Jacob, one of his oldest friends, has told of Mar-

coussis' superstitions, his continual interpretation of events, the protection he invoked of 'benevolent' monuments, his communion with the dark forces of the earth and his sense of portents. Indeed, toward the end of his life Marcoussis devoted his final collection of dry-points to the theme of *Soothsayers*. In his painting, which always resembles a poetic or musical interpretation, he avoided the stylizations into which so many post-Cubist painters lapsed. He never strayed from the natural order, even when he strove to incorporate into it the notion of a beyond; but neither was he ever content with realistic description: until the end his severe landscapes and sober still lifes revealed a vision of constantly renewed freshness.

**MARIN** John (1870–1953). American painter; born in Rutherford, New Jersey. Inevitably the name of John Marin is linked to the vanguard in American painting that developed once Alfred Stieglitz *(\*)* had established his '291' gallery in New York in 1907. Also associated with this project were such rebels

MARCOUSSIS. THE PORT OF KÉRITY. 1927.
*Musée d'Art Moderne, Paris*

painting reveals a play of colours not dissimilar to that of the *Fauves*, though actually their work had touched him but little. Majestic and violent spectacles kindled him, and he resorted for motifs to the lines and volumes of skyscrapers and bridges, and the more tumultuous aspects of sea and mountain. Great magnitude, in short, could compel him, though he strove endlessly for force and high expression, as well as for intensity of colour, which he would heighten by outbursts of lyricism sometimes almost ecstatic. He concerned himself somewhat less with the resolution of more strictly plastic problems, his object being to liberate the

and forerunners as Marsden Hartley, Max Weber and Alfred Maurer, who likewise broke with the academic and sought new freedom. After some uncertainty, Marin had become an apprentice architect and then, in the mid-90s, had opened his own office. In 1899, relinquishing that career, he enrolled at the Pennsylvania Academy of the Fine Arts in Philadelphia. Here he profited from the teaching of Thomas P. Anschutz and Henry Breckenridge before shifting to the Art Students' League in New York and then to France, the land of his paternal ancestors. After some study in various Parisian *ateliers* he applied himself to the craft of etching, which he learned largely by consulting the prints of Rembrandt and Whistler, whose stroke and shading appealed to his nature. He exhibited ten etchings in the Salon d'Automne of 1910. Then, after nearly six years of residence in France, he returned to the United States, exhibiting annually at '291' and participating, in 1913, in the New York Armory Show, which included such other innovators as Arthur Dove, Hartley and Weber. In 1936 the Museum of Modern Art in New York organized an important retrospective of his work, and in 1950 the Venice Biennale devoted two of its rooms to a fairly comprehensive showing of it. Marin's

emotions ne experienced before Nature and his other motifs. Yet, whatever his propensity for idealization, he never narrowed himself to a literal depiction of what gripped him. He endeavoured rather to transpose all such matter into some more tuneful substance, scoring it meanwhile with stenographic notations which he did not hesitate to push to the very limit of abstraction.

**MARINETTI** Filippo Tommaso (1876–1944). Italian poet; born in Alexandria, Egypt; studied in Paris. Although he made a name by writing a play in French, *King Bombance*, which was produced at the Théâtre de l'Œuvre in 1909, his real title to fame is to have invented the word 'Futurism' for that movement, whose first manifesto he published in the newspaper *Le Figaro* on February 20th, 1909. In it he wrote: 'Until now literature has glorified pensive immobility, ecstasy and sleep; we want to exalt aggressive movement, feverish insomnia, the quickstep, the somersault, the slap in the face and the punch'. But this was still only literature, and it was not until Marinetti met the Italian painters Carlo Carrà, Umberto Boccioni and Luigi Russolo in Milan that painting in turn became involved in the movement.

**MARQUET** Albert (1875–1947). French painter; born in Bordeaux; died in Paris. Arriving in Paris as a young man, Marquet, like his friend Matisse, was, from 1897 on, a pupil of Gustave Moreau. His beginnings were particularly difficult. To make a living he worked with Matisse on the Modern Style decoration of the Universal Exhibition of 1900. A year later he painted landscapes and nudes that already showed his originality and independence. At the Salon des Indépendants in 1903, the Salon d'Automne and the Berthe Weil Gallery his canvases hung next to those of Matisse. For this reason he has been considered as one of the original *Fauves*. But he was really not allied to any group, although he was one of the young rebels who, at the turn of the century, made the last assault on the Impressionist stronghold. His alleged Fauvism was no more than the effect of an attack of fever transmitted by a band of

MARIN. MAINE ISLANDS. *Water-colour.* 1922

boisterous artists, for never, even when he painted the *Sergeant of the Colonial Troops* (1907), the *Fair at Havre* (1905) or *Sainte-Adresse* (1906), did Marquet regard colour as an end in itself or as a means of relieving emotions. Between 1909 and 1910 he worked occasionally at the Académie Ranson, where he met Jourdain and Manguin. In 1912 he accompanied Matisse on his trip to Morocco. The fever having abated, and each *Fauve* retired to his cage, Marquet followed his own inclinations. He who had painted portraits and nudes of such firm design and vigorous touch devoted himself entirely to landscape: the Seine, its quays and tugboats; the harbours of Fécamp, Honfleur, Algiers and Naples, of Hamburg and Stockholm; repeating untiringly the same themes and the same subjects: the Pont Neuf in various seasons, the Pont Neuf at dawn, at midday, at night, always the same Pont Neuf, but never the same picture. He did not make the slightest attempt to humour his public; the man who had refused the Legion of Honour, membership in the Institut de France and every other official recognition, who lived in simple, dignified solitude, working for his own pleasure, unconcerned with critics, art dealers and collectors,

SEVERINI. PORTRAIT OF MARINETTI.

MARQUET. COLONIAL ARMY SERGEANT. 1907.
*Private Collection, New York*

eye. One will remember his contempt for lyrical effusions, the concision of his style, and the sobriety of his means, although some will less readily accept another aspect of his classicism, a sometimes excessively bridled imagination and a temperament that modesty often restrained to the extreme. Marquet, in fact, had no other ambition than to set forth a faithful image of Nature. It was before Nature and in the midst of it that he felt happy. He experienced an ever-renewed pleasure in reproducing it. In this way he forgot man, who eventually disappeared from his work. At the beginning he showed promise of becoming a great portraitist and a great figure painter. One is inclined today to see in him only a specialist of harbours, beaches and bridges. Rather indifferent to humanity, whom he regarded without indulgence, he devoted all available emotion to Nature. At most he allowed himself to reduce it on his canvas to a simplified image. No daring transpositions, no marked distortions, but always the natural light, local

was above making any concession. A master draughtsman, Marquet reduced drawing to quick notations, concentrated it to the extreme and subordinated it to plain and limpid colour, seemingly monotonous, but varied in gradations. A picture by Marquet asserts itself by its harmony, its balance, its solidity and its stability, but has nothing that is heavy or strident. Masses, compact forms, a dense atmosphere, an almost solid light: all this appears nevertheless clear, imponderable, alert, so nervous is the execution, so quick the decision, so direct the painter's vision. A few horizontals, colour applied in thin layers, skilful composition, a refreshing spontaneity, a sure craftsmanship, along with taste, elegance, will and a quick intelligence – all these things are sufficient explanation for this landscapist's renown. Marquet gave the landscape and the seascape that intelligibility, simplicity and poise which the Impressionist works of a Monet or a Pissarro so lacked. It is gratifying, moreover, that he did not fall into the trap of facile picturesqueness and insipid sentimentality. Marquet's judgment was, in fact, as sure as his

MARQUET. WOMAN WITH A PARASOL. 1901.

tone, free-and-easy perspective character-ize his landscapes; and it was always to his astonishing dexterity that he resorted rather than to the daring of speculation and instinct. A realistic painter, Marquet can no longer be regarded as a *Fauve*, even a repentant one. His credo was that of Poussin, of Corot, of Courbet. He was a master of line. His hasty pencil sketches, his drawings, which recall the strength of suggestion of the Japanese compel admiration. 'He is our Hokusai', Matisse said of him. It is perhaps into this minor part of his work that Marquet put the best of himself, his rigour, his fine sensitivity and the sharpness of his mind.

MARQUET. QUAI DE CONTI. 1947.

**MASSON** André. French painter; born 1896 at Balagny, in the Oise. After having studied at the Academy of Fine Arts in Brussels, Masson, following the advice of the Belgian poet Emile Verhaeren, came to Paris in 1912. His meeting with Kahnweiler (*) in 1922 enabled him to devote himself entirely to painting. His work underwent the influence of Cubism and of Juan Gris. During the winter of 1923 he painted his first deliberately symbolic picture, *The Four Elements*, which attracted the attention of Surrealist leader André Breton when it was exhibited at the Galerie Simon in the spring of 1924. Masson met Antonin Artaud, Miró and Max Ernst, and until 1928 took part in the exhibitions of the Surrealist group. Particularly sensitive to the fundamental drama of existence and to the interdependence of all particles of the universe, he always placed men or animals in a kind of architectural framework, while probing their very insides to discover what makes them move, act, love and suffer. His *Fights of Fishes* symbolizes the hand-to-hand combat of human beings. The austere and undisguised cruelty of the fishes suggests the motives of love, of an eroticism without obscenity. For him the earth exists only in fusion, its substance in a state of decay upon which future germination feeds. Even when he gave himself over to automatic writing (*vide* Surrealism), his hand kept the habit of giving matter a shape and forcing it into significant form. Thus, against the dull colours he used, browns or greens, against a ground of sand or ashes, the line stands out, deep, shaded with thin and thick strokes. In this way he has forged a whole symbolism, not accidental or childish but nourished upon the ancient and curious myths with which he characterizes his philosophical interpretation of man's destiny. Since settling in Provence in 1947 he seems to have discovered a new secret of the elements, through his contact with the Southern light on objects, beings and landscapes. His art has lost what may sometimes have been abrupt and grating, to be enriched by a more flexible vocabulary and more complete expression. One could not be further removed from the Cubist concept of the object in itself, or from the revelation by means of accidentals that was fostered by Surrealism. At the final point in its evolution the work of Masson culminates in a rediscovery of heretofore unsuspected magic in the visible world, whose changes are infinite on the groundwork of eternal fixity.

**MATISSE** Henri. French painter; born in 1869 at Le Cateau, in the north of France; died in Cimiez near Nice in 1954. Matisse's father was a grain merchant and his mother an amateur painter of some talent. After having finished his secondary studies he was employed as a clerk in a solicitor's office at Saint-Quentin. His interest in art was awakened in 1890 during an illness, when he read a treatise on painting by Goupil. At this time he painted his

MASSON. AMPHORA. 1925.
*Louise Leiris Gallery, Paris*

first picture, a still life with a tobacco jar. He took evening courses at the Quentin de la Tour Municipal School and finally obtained his father's permission to go to work in Paris, first at the Académie Julian (*) and then at the École des Beaux-Arts, where he enrolled in the studio of Gustave Moreau. There he made the acquaintance of Rouault, Camoin and, especially, Marquet, with whom he was to remain particularly friendly. His teacher urged him to study both Nature and the masters. Acting on this advice, he made many drawings from Nature and haunted the Louvre, where he executed numerous copies from Philippe de Champaigne, Poussin and Chardin. At this time his art was extremely conservative and traditional: an example can be found at the Museum of Modern Art in Paris in the *Breton Weaver* of 1896. In this painting, greys, so frequent in French painting from Louis Le Nain to Corot, are used with extreme subtlety, and re-create beautifully the dark, soft atmosphere of the room in which the craftsman is at work. It was natural, then, that Matisse should participate in the very official Salon of the National Society of Fine Arts, where he exhibited canvases such as *La Desserte* (*The Sideboard*) of 1898. His discovery of Impressionism at this time was the beginning of his adventurous and triumphant career. The influence is apparent in the seascapes he painted in 1898 at Belle-Isle in Brittany, where Monet had already worked, as well as in the landscapes executed in Corsica and on the French Riviera. His palette grew brighter and more varied, the drawing became less conventional and revealed a more definite personality; an effort to portray the brilliance of light was evident. But he had already parted ways with the Impressionists: whereas they intended to transcribe the atmosphere that envelops objects, softens forms and veils colours, he chose to express a light that heightens tones, asserts contours and clarifies forms by simplifying them. The fact that he preferred the landscapes of Southern regions, more highly coloured, more regular, more constructed, to those of the Île-de-France and Normandy, is in itself significant. Little wonder, then, that he should have undergone successively the influence of various painters who, while connected with Impressionism, had tried to go beyond it: Cézanne, on the one hand, and the Neo-Impressionists on the other. The influence of Cézanne, one of whose *Bathers* he purchased and later gave to the Petit Palais, is apparent in a series of pictures, especially still lifes and nudes (*Models in the Studio* sequence, 1900; *Carmelina*, 1903). Here the colour is intense but rather dark, the drawing vigorous, the form built up with broadly simplified planes. On the other hand, he drew his inspiration from the Neo-Impressionists in various Parisian landscapes and in a few compositions which he painted according to the Divisionist technique. It is characteristic that Signac should have bought one of these, *Luxury, Calm and Voluptuousness*, 1903.

Fortified by his experiments and research, which showed his methodical but wilful genius, he was ready for the peremptory assertion of his personality and art that would be shown in his Fauvist manner, about 1905–1908. In contrast to Vlaminck, Fauvism *(\*)* for Matisse was less a question of heightened sensation than an attempt

MATISSE. OPEN WINDOW, COLLIOURE. 1905.
*Private Collection, New York*

to reduce the whole art of painting to colour and a few other fundamental elements, chiefly line and rhythm, the necessary and sufficient resources with which the painter can realize himself. 'You are going to simplify painting', Gustave Moreau had predicted to him, and in fact Matisse jettisoned all the impedimenta which since the sixteenth century had encumbered its course, to rediscover the ease and mobility of the traveller without luggage, ready for any adventure. No more 'passages', those pictorial equivalents of the transitions that poets and novelists were giving up at the same time: colours were laid on openly one against the other, and frequently collided, if the combination served to heighten them; but if this was to be avoided, a thick black line around the forms separated them or the white of the canvas was left visible. 'Values' were also abandoned: instead of diversifying the tones by a minute mixture of light and shadow, Matisse unified them and spread them out in large sheets, finding other means to express light and model form. These, or rather *this*, other means was colour and relations of colours. In fact, by choosing his

MATISSE. STUDY.

MATISSE. GOLDFISH. 1914.
*Private Collection, New York*

were, along with colour, Matisse's fundamental resources during his Fauvist period. That time witnessed an abundant flowering of masterpieces, such as the *View of Notre-Dame* (reproduced on page 100), *La Joie de Vivre* (1905), *The Open Window* (1905), *The Red Carpets* (1906, Grenoble Museum), *The Young Sailor* (1906), *The Sideboard* (1908), *The Manila Shawl*.

But the influence of Cézanne was beginning to be felt more and more strongly by young painters: first Derain, then Dufy, Vlaminck and Friesz developed a feeling for construction; Braque went as far as Cubism, soon followed by Picasso and then Léger, Gris, Lhote and La Fresnaye. Matisse, who had been in touch with Picasso, was not the last to give up Fauvism (a trip to Morocco in 1911–1912 particularly accelerating his evolution) to practise a kind of painting that was, if not Cubist, at least so Cézannesque that it sometimes verged on Cubism. *The Three Sisters* of the Paul Guillaume collection, *The Dance* and *Music* (1909 and 1910) in the Museum of Western Art in Moscow, *The Red Studio* (1914), *Goldfish*

tones and establishing relations between them, the painter transcribed the colour of the object (itself a synthesis of the local tone in combination with light), the form of the object, the luminosity of space and depth. Refusing the techniques of *trompe-l'œil* and perspective – for he did not want to hollow out the picture and conceal its nature as a plane surface – he resorted to oppositions of tones: behind the coloured figures, for example, he spread out zones of various colours which, in their relation to one another and to the figures themselves, give an impression of space, a space full of light, without hiding the fact that the picture is a plane covered with colours. This was a rediscovery (unpremeditated, in fact, not an imitation) of the solution of the Romanesque painters; the stripes of various colours that can be seen, for example, in the frescoes of the Oberzell and the Niederzell on Lake Constance find their equivalent in those which Matisse introduced into his picture *Luxury, Calm and Voluptuousness* (1907), the only difference being that he used them with a representational intent, making them suggest the beach, the sea, the mountains, the sky. Rhythm and the arabesque, toward which his line often tended,

MATISSE. LITHOGRAPH. 1936

MATISSE. RED STUDIO. 1916.                    *Museum of Modern Art, New York*

(1914), *The Moroccans* (1912), and finally the series of *Studios on the Quai Saint-Michel*, of which the Museum of Modern Art in Paris possesses one of the finest examples (*The Painter and His Model*, 1914), reveal the painter given over to an austere chromatism in which blacks, greys, ochres, and forms harder and stricter than those of the Fauvist manner predominate. The sinuous arabesques have given way to straight lines that break into segments and assemble in right or acute angles. The rhythms are jerky, syncopated, and elliptical. The transcription of Nature is still bolder and the interpretation of space more radical. The art of Matisse adopted a slightly contorted look, revealing an inner tension in the painter, the tension that brings about new investigations and the need to transcend oneself.

Every period of tension is necessarily followed by a period of release. A sequence of favourable circumstances, just after the First World War, brought about this release in the art of Matisse: the euphoria of victory, the discovery of Mediterranean nature (he then established himself at Nice, which became his adopted home), and

finally success. For about ten years he had undoubtedly taken on the appearance of the head of a school and had seen a flock of pupils, particularly foreigners, hurrying to the Academy that he had founded in Paris at the former Couvent des Oiseaux. But it was a success felt only by the few. After 1919, however, he won international and universal renown. It is not difficult to understand, therefore, why he should have drifted toward a more amiable art, especially since the same development can be observed at that time in nearly all the painters, from Dufy and Derain to Braque and Picasso. A return to bright colours, less intense and bold than in the days of Fauvism, but fresher and sprucer, in which reds play a leading part; a return to a flowing line of enveloping flexibility, an introduction of very light modelling in the figure, which does not break the unity of the surface; a recourse, to obtain a decorative effect, to certain artifices, such as the representation of hangings with large designs, of tiles, flowered textiles, and Oriental rugs in the background: it is by these various characteristics that the manner in which Matisse

MATISSE. GIRL IN A WHITE DRESS. 1941.  *Private Collection*

worked between 1919 and 1927 can be defined. His favourite theme was the *Odalisque*. Two words describe the works of this period adequately: ease and grace – ease at having mastered the craft to the point of such assurance that he could be allowed to rest, and grace in the creation of a universe of children, young women, precious fabrics, flowers, leisure, luxury, and light. Matisse enjoyed his success for a while and, as a result, was able to create abundantly, without effort, without anxiety. But he soon grew tired of this oasis of facility and, as early as 1928, he resumed his investigations and again moved toward grandeur and strength. In the *Decorative Figure on an Ornamental Background* of 1928 (Museum of Modern Art, Paris) one sees straight lines meeting at right angles, lines broken into short segments, a hard and powerful form whose bold synthesis bears witness to daring invention, majestic construction (echoed the same year in *The Sideboard*) and the clearly stated will to make things severe, grandiose, and new. But this time Matisse did not renounce the characteristics of his former manner: richness of the palette, suppleness of arabesques, decorative sumptuousness, and glorification of the sweetness of life.

The synthesis of the complementary tendencies of his genius thus achieved was afterward evident in all his works, particularly after the execution of a vast decoration on the theme of *The Dance* at the Barnes Foundation in Merion, Pennsylvania (1931–1933), had obliged him to summon up all his resources and take his bearings. For him this was an opportunity to set out again more resolutely than ever. He demanded more of colour than he ever had in the past, either by risking tonal harmonies of unheard-of violence (*The Rumanian Blouse*, 1940) or by establishing a chromatic unity, often red, across his whole canvas, as in the *Still Life with a Magnolia* of 1941, or in *The Large Interior in Red* of the Museum of Modern Art in Paris (1948), or even in a successful attempt to make black a colour radiating light and almost insupportably intense (*Bed Jacket on a Black Background*, 1938). The drawing became both more flexible and more rigorous and synthetic, more abstract and suggestive and, finally, so bold that it shrank before no interpretation of Nature and the human figure (*Asia*, 1944; *The English Girl*, 1947). The form, flat once more, had none the less great power (*The Plum Branch*, 1948), and this power is due as much to the line surrounding the form and the tones that suggest its mass as to the rhythms that animate it with a candid and imposing simplicity (*Girl in a White Dress*, 1941). The universe of Matisse, composed invariably of young and beautiful women, exotic plants, flowers and fruits, birds, luxurious objects, idleness and sun, testifies to an ever bolder daring of imagination, the fruit of liberty acquired by the painter through mastery of his art and his constant efforts to renew, surpass and enrich himself, always by simplifying himself more radically. If the starting-point for this final synthesis was the decoration of the Barnes Foundation, its climax was the chapel of the Convent of Dominican Nuns at Vence, finished in 1950. There Matisse not only said his last word as a painter, a painter who renounced colour to content himself with white and an ochre verging on black, but also brought to a conclusion the investigations that he had pursued for a long time in the other arts.

One cannot pass over in silence Matisse's activity in fields other than painting: as an engraver he executed a great number of plates and illustrated ten books or so, from the *Poems* of Mallarmé (1932) to the *Poems* of Charles d'Orléans (1950), by way of the *Amours* of Ronsard (1948) and *The Letters of a Portuguese Nun* (1946). As a sculptor Matisse has to his credit an imposing number of works, which constitute one of the most important monuments of contemporary sculpture, both on account of their intrinsic beauty and because of the lesson of invention and renewal that they provide. Finally, a special place belongs to the cutouts, which occupied the artist a great deal in his last years, and with which he created masterpieces

MATISSE. PLUM TREE BRANCH ON A GREEN BACK-GROUND.          *Private Collection, New York*

like *The Negro Boxer* (1947) and *The Sadness of the King* (1952). Never, indeed, had he manifested such imagination of design; the scissors seem to have allowed him to bestow upon colour an inventive composition that surpassed in daring the chromatism of his former work. A triumph of arabesque and pure colour, his *papiers collés (\*)* are perhaps the supreme expression of his genius, while at the same time they represent his discovery of a new domain: there is, in fact, nothing in common between those he did and what the Cubists had produced in 1911–1914.

Important because of the diversity of his work and the new horizons he opened to art, Matisse is no less so because of the example of his powerful personality. In complete opposition to Picasso, he remained close to the tradition of French art and the French spirit, to the line of lucid and determined artists who created with 'clear and distinct' ideas deliberate, conscious and long-thought-out works. It is not surprising, then, that a man of his stamp should have written some of the most pertinent observations on painting – and notably on his own – that have

MATISSE. SAINT-DOMINIC. 1941.
*Vence Chapel*

come from the pen of an artist (cf. his *Notes of a Painter* published in the *Grande Revue*, December 25th, 1908). What characterizes his art is first an admirable logic, as witnessed the care he always took to use his most varied tools and techniques in conformity with the requirements of their nature. If he drew with the pen, it being the nature of the pen to trace a precise and clean line, he made use of the line and the line only to express everything – contour, form, light, even matter. If, on the other hand, he used charcoal, whose property is to crumble, and thus to permit the indication of values and shades, he executed drawings in which form grew exclusively out of the play of blacks, greys, and whites. Matisse was logical, lucid and determined. Nothing in his art was left to chance. He wrote: 'The composition that must reach expression alters with the surface to be covered. The artist who wants to transplant a composition from one canvas to a larger canvas must conceive it anew to preserve the expression.' Matisse made no brush stroke or pencil line that was not actuated by reflection. But nothing could be freer or more natural than his art, and these qualities it owes to his method of work. Having prepared for his important works by a great number of drawings, sketches, and studies, he often executed the final work in a single session, so as to preserve all the life of a sketch. Thus the movement of passion joined the equilibrium of thought to make this refined art a creation of inexhaustible richness and salutary complexity. Essentially modern, although rooted in the oldest French tradition, an echo of our present experiments and the fruit of an ancient culture as well as of a spirit that has survived, unchanged, alterations in aesthetics and civilization, the art of Matisse, a bridge between yesterday and tomorrow, constitutes one of the most important expressions of the painting of today, and will doubtless dominate and fertilize that of tomorrow.

MATISSE. THE YOUNG ENGLISH GIRL. 1947.
*Private Collection*

**MERZ** Invented by the German painter Kurt Schwitters *(\*)* in 1919, this term seems to derive from a part of the word *kom*merziell, torn from a newspaper, which appeared glued in one of his first *Merzbilder* or *collages*. From 1923 to 1932 Schwitters published a magazine under the name *Merz*, with the co-operation of Arp, Lissitzky, Mondrian, Van Doesburg, and many others. Nothing could better describe what Schwitters meant by *Merz* than the definition of the word *nature* that he copied from a German dictionary, to have it printed in large red letters on the cover of an issue of his magazine (April–July, 1924): 'Nature, from the Latin *nasci*, means to become, to come from; that is to say, all that through its own force develops, forms and moves'. The same issue further reads: 'The modern world is the other half of nature, the half that comes from man'. Thus Schwitters took all the cast-off things of everyday life and made them into abstract works, which had no other purpose than to continue Nature through man, but which are moving in their humility, in all the human delicacy they contain and unknowingly communicate. Schwitters' *collages* and compositions (*Merzbilder* or Merz-Pictures) are among the most curious and rare productions of the Dada *(\*)* movement.

**METZINGER** Jean. French painter; born in 1883 in Nantes. He began to paint at fifteen. The emotion he experienced before a picture by Ingres was at the root of his desire to paint. While continuing his studies, he achieved success in local exhibitions, and this incited him to devote himself entirely to painting and settle in Paris. He attended various academies, where the instruction disappointed him because it made painting dependent upon imitation of Nature or of the old masters. For Metzinger there could be no real relationship between the object that the picture constitutes and the other object it represents; the picture had no other value than the particular pleasure produced by its combination of forms and colours. In his search for the laws that govern these relations and control their effectiveness, Metzinger was first influenced by the Neo-Impressionists and then by the *Fauves*, who were occupied with the chemistry of colour and attempted to influence the aspect of the pictorial image. But desiring a more coherent construction, he endeavoured to discover the structure of objects. He joined the young painters who, from 1908 onwards, were working along similar lines in the wake of Picasso and Braque. At first Cubism was their common need to emerge from the old ambiguity and restore primal purity to artistic creation. Metzinger took part in the famous Salon des Indépendants of 1911 and in the meetings and exhibitions of the *Section d'Or (\*)*. With Gleizes, in 1912, he published *On Cubism*, the first theoretical work on the movement to be written by painters who participated in it. He took care, however, to avoid a purely abstract manner, endeavouring to express the general harmony of the model by emphasizing characteristic details. He helped to create one of the styles of the period, in which objects rendered by their surfaces are surrounded by a kind of halo that becomes a plane in itself. His work, which he has continued on the same principles until now, aided by a very

METZINGER. STILL LIFE. 1917.

sure technique, maintains remarkable unity and remains an example of what a sensitive human artist was able to draw from the Cubist experiment.

**MIRÓ** Joan (born in 1893 at Montroig, near Tarragona). Miró is a native of a province that, more than any other part of Spain, has always been the favoured spot of arts and artists. After having served as a bridge between East and West, Catalonia was the cradle of the Romanesque Style. Workshops of illuminators and famous fresco painters flourished there in the Middle Ages, and finally modern art recruited some of its boldest pioneers there. From Catalonia came Miró and Dali in particular, two of the chief creators of the Surrealist movement. At fourteen Miró entered the School of Fine Arts of Barcelona. Later he attended courses at the Gali Academy. In 1915 he felt official teaching did more harm than good, and he decided to work alone. He had the good fortune to be taken up by Dalmau, the perspicacious manager of an important art gallery in Barcelona. It was Dalmau who, in 1918, organized the first exhibition of his protégé. At the time Miró's works,

MIRÓ. SNOB EVENING AT THE PRINCESS'S. 1944.

first definitely subjective and unrealistic picture, *Turned Soil*. At the same time he signed the first Manifesto of Surrealism published by André Breton. In November 1925 he participated in the first exhibition of the Surrealist group at the Galerie Pierre. In collaboration with Max Ernst, he designed the settings and costumes of *Romeo and Juliet* for

such as *The Chauffeur* and *Landscape with a Donkey*, were clearly influenced by Van Gogh. After a short stay in Paris (1919) his painting caught the beneficial germ of Cubism, although it remained definitely representational, if not imitative. The drawing was dry, planes sharply evident, the colours light without intensity. In 1921 the critic Maurice Raynal presented at La Licorne Gallery in Paris, which no longer exists, an important group of Miró's canvases. Connoisseurs did not fail to observe the incompatibility of Cubism with the temperament of the Catalan painter, with his instinct, his native ingenuousness, his fundamental anti-intellectualism, and his already asserted passion for colour. It was not among painters or through study of the works of the masters that he came to recognize his calling but by associating with poets and the young rebels who were preparing to set off the bomb of Surrealism. No one was, in fact, less suited to speculation and less willing to tolerate restraint and discipline than Miró. An anarchist by birth, naturally hostile to any tradition or cult, either of Nature or of museums, his enthusiastic enlistment in a movement that proclaimed the bankruptcy of the intellect, contempt for reality, and the sovereignty of intuition can be easily understood. For two years, dividing his time between Barcelona and Paris, he continued to execute landscapes and representational still lifes (*The Farm, The Ear of Corn*). In 1924 he finished his

the *Ballets Russes (\*)* of Diaghilev. From this period dates *Harlequin's Fair* (1925), in the Albright Art Gallery of Buffalo.

His works were already very characteristic of his art as we admire it today. All of Miró is in them, with his schematic forms, his powerful, heavy 'spots', his patiently prepared grounds, and also his fantasy, his humour, his freshness of emotion, his innate affinity for the craftsmen of the African jungles or the American prairie. These are complex works, overburdened but already containing the repertoire of signs that Miró had only to amplify, particularize and accentuate in order to achieve the paradoxical mastery that makes the value and originality of his current work. In 1928 he visited Holland. He exhibited for the first time in the United States at the Valentine Gallery in New York. In 1930 he showed his *papiers collés (\*)* to the Parisian public. In 1931 the Ballets de Monte Carlo commissioned the settings and costumes for *Jeux d'Enfants* from him. He executed a large mural decoration for the Paris Exhibition of 1937. In 1940, obliged to leave France, he returned to Catalonia and soon settled at Palma de Majorca. Withdrawn from the tumult of arms, he continued to paint, took up lithography and, in collaboration with Artigas, ceramics. He returned to France in 1944, and from then on he has worked either in Paris or in Barcelona. His reputation has grown and his activity also. He has tried his hand at media other than painting, with equal success. In the space of a few years, personal as his art may be, his renown has become universal.

His career, clearly enough, offers nothing to captivate amateurs of the picturesque and unforeseen. Besides, he has not made the least attempt to ornament it or bestow the romantic touch of which the public is so fond. It offers neither comment nor confidence: Miró is a silent man. Even though his work is diagged into the limelight by his admirers, he himself remains in the background, reserved, unobtrusive and unnoticed. No one has solicited or intrigued less to assert himself and to make himself known. But no one has ever asserted himself and become known in less time. How can this be explained, if not by the fact that his painting came to fill a gap, to satisfy a need and to offer something that other painters, even the greatest among them, have denied?

What is there in a picture by Miró that casts such an irresistible spell over the spectator? Is it form? There are no forms, only elements, embryos of forms, rudimentary figures like the *graffiti* that children scratch on walls, signs that recall those engraved in caves by prehistoric man. Is it colour? With Miró, to be sure, the lyricism of colour recovers 'its significance at the point where the *Fauves* and Matisse had left it', as Maurice Raynal has said. Observe, however, how restricted Miró's palette is: a few elementary colours, blue, vermilion, yellow, green, black, used sparingly but with assurance and infallible accuracy. Nor is it composition. Miró seems to throw lines and spots nonchalantly on to his canvas, unconcerned with their interrelations, or the requirements of space and depth. Blood-red or electric-blue crescents, black masses softly spread, cells holding their nuclei like targets, childish silhouettes daubed with artificial carelessness, hairy placentas entangled in their cords: a whole world, unexpected, whimsical, droll, larvae, madrepores, spasmodic amœbas, long and sinuous filaments, vagrant lines ending in a kind of cup-and-ball or kite. It is a dreamworld transcribed by a master technician. One can understand, therefore, why André Breton could write in 1928: 'Miró is probably the most Surrealistic

of us all'. Miró is a Surrealist quite naturally. without recourse to artifice or attitudinizing, with sincerity and humility. He is, in fact, the only Surrealist painter with no contempt for the resources of his art or the constraints of his profession. Although there is neither subject nor object, neither volume nor logical construction in his painting, it is undoubtedly plastic. And because of its plasticity it has survived the breakdown of Surrealism *(\*)*. But this is not enough to explain the fascination it exercises. Tired of studio experiments, aesthetic demonstrations and rhetoric, we find in Miró's work a fresh spring water to dispel our fever and clear our head. Here at last is a painter who poses no problems, for he is aware of none; who resorts to the conveniences of tradition no more than to the calculated extravagance of the professional

MIRÓ. FRAGMENT OF A TRIPTYCH. 1939.
*Private Collection, Paris*

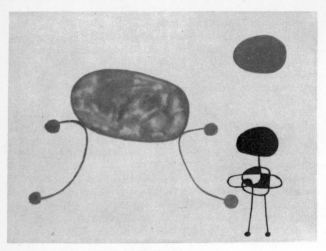

MIRÓ. PERSON LOOKING AT THE SUN. 1942.
*Private Collection, Basel*

**MODIGLIANI** Amedeo (1884–1920). Italian painter; born in Leghorn; died in Paris. The widow of a ruined banker, his mother recognized her son's calling early and never opposed it. She acquainted him with all the Italian museums and sent him to work at academies in Florence and Venice. Finally, in 1907, he arrived in Paris. Handsome, aristocratic in appearance, but already a prey to tuberculosis, he soon became one of the eccentric young men of Montmartre, where he lived for six years, taciturn, prodigal, moving incessantly from lodging to lodging, wandering from café to café, but also participating in aesthetic battles, drawing, sculpting, painting pictures. He took part in the discussions at the Bateau-Lavoir *(*)*. His tall, languid figure could be seen in the same places that had been frequented by Toulouse-Lautrec, whose work he admired at the time. The offspring of the upper middle class, he showed humanitarian tendencies. His love of the

*avant-garde*; who refuses the legacy of his predecessors and does not try to outdo anyone. He does not reinvent painting, he invents it, like primitive man or a child. He does not speak any of the idioms current in our time, but the time is nevertheless grateful to him for speaking a language it has forgotten but still longs for. A poetry of the unutterable, of the unreal, of germinations and beginnings, is the secret of his power. He will never be the head of a school or the advocate of a trend. Unclassifiable, unassimilable, inimitable, in complete simplicity. complete innocence, he holds a place apart in contemporary art. It is not the highest place, but it is the least disputed.

**MODERN STYLE** A term for the movement that developed toward 1895–1910, called *Jugendstil* in Germany and, in general, the *Style 1900* (vide *Jugendstil*).

MODIGLIANI, HALF RECLINING NUDE.

humble people, the pity he had for the outcasts of fortune, he expressed in his actions, his work and his choice of models: the daughter of his concierge, sickly children, girls of the lower classes. Like so many other painters, he discovered Cézanne (1909). He made friends with the sculptor Brancusi, who introduced him to Negro sculpture, which thereafter exercised a profound influence on his drawing. From his contact with Brancusi he felt a need to carve stone himself. He is the maker of statues that were, unfortunately, never finished. To be sure, plastic art was less his medium than drawing. In 1913 he left Montmartre and transferred his anxiety and drunkenness to Montparnasse, a prowler, miserable, full of alcohol, drugs and talent, wasting his gifts as he did his money. He never, in fact, had enough money to live. He used to sell his admirable drawings for a few *sous*, drawings jotted down with a disconcerting sureness, and his portraits and nudes for a few francs. He was frequently to be seen on the terrace of the *Rotonde*, or the *Dôme*, drawing portraits with an acute, rapid stroke, and then offering them to his chance models in exchange for a drink. Then he worked in the studio of Kisling. Soutine and Pascin were his friends. He drifted from café to café and from attic to attic, occasionally finding a haven or a compassionate soul. An English woman poet, Beatrice Hastings, supported him for some time; Zborowski sheltered him later and denied himself necessities in order that his protégé might paint. He met a young girl, Jeanne Hébuterne, married her and fathered a child. Consumed by fever, overwhelmed by tuberculosis, he entered a hospital, where he died on the 25th of January, 1920, in his thirty-sixth year, murmuring 'Cara, cara Italia!'. On the day of his funeral, which was organized by André Salmon and Kisling, and made something of a sensation, his wife jumped from a fifth floor and was killed.

The compatriot of Duccio, Castagno and Botticelli, Modigliani was, above all, a linearist, a draughtsman and a mannerist. Colour adds nothing to drawing in his pictures, although it is applied with accuracy and is both resonant and enjoyable. Nevertheless, Modigliani, loyal in this respect to the Tuscan tradition, expressed

MODIGLIANI. LITTLE GIRL IN BLUE.
*Private Collection, Paris*

himself entirely through drawing, in the flexible, subtle, melodious line which for a time was perhaps excessively prized. Elegant and frail, supple to the point of preciosity, with what indulgence it curves in upon the oval of a face, turns round a shoulder, excessively lengthens a neck, accentuates a hip! And how it dominates the form and suffices for volume and space! Modigliani answered in his own way the question raised by the Cubists. The Cubists tried to render the object in its totality by multiplication of the points of view. Modigliani was aware of the experiments of Picasso and Braque, but he was neither a constructor nor a synthesist. His intelligence was not adapted to organization and reflection. He was therefore prudent enough to refuse to join the Cubist band. He resorted to distortion rather than to invention and to techniques rather than to a coherent system.

MODIGLIANI. PORTRAIT OF ZBOROWSKI.
*Private Collection, Paris*

Although, like the Cubists, he was indifferent to light, atmosphere and *sfumato*, and aspired to express tactile values and the solidity of volumes, he had at his disposal only limited means: simply and solely line. He paid tribute to modern art by adopting its canon of abstraction and inflicting upon forms the elongation, distortion, contraction, disruption of axes and overlapping of planes that constitute his 'expressionism'. Observe the bent heads, sloping shoulders, swan necks, interminable arms, and the disproportion between torso, legs and head, and, in the head itself, the nose thinned to the extreme, the almond-shaped eyes, close-set and hollowed out, the thin and pinched mouth; observe further the nudes with frail limbs, high waist, and sinuous arabesques: everything contributes to the impression of delicate and precious distinction, rare and somewhat unhealthy, of a *morbidezza* that would

not have been disowned by Botticelli. Modigliani can therefore not be regarded as one of the founders of contemporary painting. He found a style, both graphic and decorative, an idiom that was on the whole rather restricted, but self-sufficient and not without effect. The curves, spirals, elongations, the austerity in the midst of gentleness, nonchalance in the midst of fragility, purity in the midst of the suggestive, the Italianism adapted to satisfy the modern mind, the mannerism saved by a proud gravity, and finally the Expressionism held in check by a certain sense of dignity and aristocratic reserve: these are sufficient reasons to admire Modigliani but also to wish him no descendants. Modigliani belonged to the *École de Paris*, the largest number of whose painters, foreigners, are characterized by the fact that their works betray a certain sickness of life. Modigliani, however, who suffered more than anyone, made it a point of honour to hide his pain. His laconic style did not always succeed in repressing an irremediable pessimism. But an innate pride, nobility and dignity preserved him from excessive lyricism as well as from shoddy craftsmanship. An anxious, tense intellectualism, which he shared with numerous other Jewish artists of his day, gave his work a disillusioned tone. Rather than a new idiom, Modigliani contributed to his time a new sensation. He had in him something dark, irrational and complicated that his drawings and paintings put within the reach of a generation eager for vivid sensations and acrid pleasures.

**MOHOLY-NAGY** Ladislaus (1895–1946). Born at Bacsbarsod in Hungary; died in Chicago. Inducted into the Austro-Hungarian army in 1914, he was severely wounded on the Russian front in 1917. During his convalescence at Odessa, then at Szeged, he began drawing portraits and landscapes in a very personal, undulating style that he did not resume later. Upon his discharge from the army, he returned to Budapest, where he obtained the degree of Doctor of Law (1918). He met Lissitzky in Düsseldorf in 1921 and produced his first abstract paintings, which were exhibited in Der Sturm Gallery in Berlin. In Vienna in 1922, in collaboration with the Hungarian poet Lajos Kassak, he published a kind of anthology of the new art: *Buch Neuer Künstler*. In 1923 he met Walter Gropius, who, impressed by his personality and enthusiasm, appointed him a professor at the Bauhaus *(\*)*. His activity in this famous school of fine and applied arts was very important from 1923 to 1928. In particular, he edited the collection of *Bauhausbücher* there, publishing several of his own works, which show the novelty of his ideas and experiments with materials and various techniques. While continuing to paint, he was chiefly known at the time for his photograms and photomontages. Under the pressure of political developments in Germany, he left the Bauhaus and travelled throughout Europe (Hungary, Switzerland, Finland, Norway, France, Greece, Italy). He was in Amsterdam in 1934, in London in 1935. It is there that he published several volumes of documentary photographs and began the series of his painting-sculptures or painting-objects which he called 'space modulators'. In 1937 he went to the United States, where he founded an autonomous school, the School of Design, which met with great success. At the same time he developed his experiments with space (sculptures in plexiglass in combination with other materials) but also continued to paint. In 1946 he published *The New Vision* in New York. He died of leukemia the same year. In 1947 a posthumous work called *Vision in Motion* was published in Chicago, condensing in non-technical form the sum of his experiences and concepts of art. Moholy-Nagy is the most authentic type of the experimental artist.

His works must be considered as pure experimentation; otherwise one could easily be indifferent to his plexiglass sculptures or studies of transparency of colours. In transferring his investigations to new spheres, Moholy did not always avoid dispersion, but he feared nothing more than petrification in a closed theory. His plastic works seldom achieve greatness, but his didactic works contain an inexhaustible wealth of ideas, documents, examples and original propositions of interest to all students of modern art and everyone engaged in independent research.

**MONDRIAN** Piet (1872-1944). Dutch painter; born at Amersfoort, in central Holland; died in New York. Mondrian came from a strict Calvinist family. His father, a schoolteacher himself, brought him up to teach. Eventually the son turned down this career, and having earned two degrees to teach drawing in state schools, he enrolled in the Amsterdam Academy (1892), where he was a studious pupil, well thought of by his teachers. Then he went through a difficult period, painting a great deal, selling little, gaining his livelihood by copying museum pieces or making scientific drawings. He worked chiefly in the vicinity of Amsterdam and often returned to the same motif: a farm at Duivendrecht, for example, which he repainted many times from the same vantage point. The colour was often delicate, although grey and dull green predominated; the style was direct and the handling full of assurance. A long stay, about 1903, among Catholic peasants in Dutch Brabant seemed to open new vistas to him.

MOHOLY-NAGY. CONSTRUCTION. 1922–1923.
*Jeanne Coppel Collection, Paris*

# MONDRIAN

MONDRIAN. COMPOSITION. 1936.
*Kunstmuseum, Basel*

Religious matters fascinated him, and he read books published by the Theosophical Society, of which he became a member a few years later. At this time he preferred to paint isolated houses or mystical undergrowth in mauve and grey. His first stay at Domburg on the island of Walcheren, in the summer of 1908, changed his manner entirely. Light appeared in his palette; mauve faded gradually to make room for light blues, whites, pinks, and golds (the sequences of *Dunes* and of *The Towers of Westkapelle*, 1908–1911). Friends urged him to go to Paris. The Dutch painter Kickert lent him a studio in Montparnasse, and he left late in 1911. Influenced at once by Cubism, he painted the famous *Trees* series, successive abstractions of a given theme that remain unique in the painting of the century. Two weeks before the outbreak of the First World War he returned to Holland to see his sick father. The war caught him in Amsterdam, and he was unable to get back to Paris until after the Armistice was signed. During these four and a half years he stayed at Domburg, Scheveningen, Amsterdam and the village of

Laren. He continued his research in abstractionism – themes of *The Sea, Cathedral Façades* – which resulted in 1915 in rhythms of horizontal and vertical lines (canvases later called *plus* and *minus* series), and which constituted an immediate prelude to Neo-Plasticism *(\*)* or pure plastic art.

Afterward he made the acquaintance of Theo Van Doesburg *(\*)*, and together they founded the magazine *De Stijl (\*)*. At this time Mondrian wrote more than he painted. He published lengthy doctrinaire essays in *De Stijl*, some of them under the form of dialogues. One of these, *Natural Reality and Abstract Reality*, can be considered one of the cornerstones of Abstract Art *(\*)*. Returning to Paris in 1919, Mondrian continued his long meditations upon the Neo-Plastic horizontal-vertical theme, meditations which were terminated only by his death twenty-five years later. The backgrounds he used were at first grey and then blue, but beginning in 1922 they remained uniformly white. Often compositions were repeated with slight changes, like the series of square canvases produced between 1929 and 1932. Among colours, red held his preference. Some of the works of this central period contain a red rectangle that occasionally takes up two-thirds of the painted surface. The painter exhibited little, sold only to a few collectors, and lived modestly in a studio organized and painted according to Neo-Plastic principles. He made very little stir but was known the world over. The significance of his work spread far beyond the borders of his native country. For a time Léger and Baumeister, and later Ben Nicholson and Max Bill, were influenced by his ideas. He had disciples: among them Miss Moss and Jean Gorin. In 1925 the Bauhaus *(\*)* published his book *Neue Gestaltung*, an expanded German translation of a booklet that had appeared in Paris in 1920 under the title *Le Néo-Plasticisme*. The significance of Mondrian's art is due, above all, to his search for plastic purity through reduction of means to a simple expression of the essential relation of two straight lines meeting at a right angle. He proscribed not only the curved line and spatial illusion, but also every trick of the brush and every treatment reminiscent of the

Impressionist technique. The result was a kind of mystical pursuit of the absolute that made a *tabula rasa* of the world of appearances. The canvas being a plane, the paint applied to it was also on a strict plane and was to be the vehicle of a concept outside both space and time but presiding over them: the relation. But Mondrian always desired this relation to be dynamic and to express an asymmetrical balance.

In September 1938, sensing the approach of war, he left Paris for London and went on to New York in September 1940. There he resumed work, encouraged by the interest of numerous admirers. Canvases begun in London, or even in Paris, were finished in New York with the addition of squares and lines of colour to alleviate the oppressive effect of the black lines that had grown so numerous. The last two years of his life brought him more satisfaction than had the fifty preceding years of incessant labour. His material comfort was reflected in his works by a greater spiritual ease. Black was proscribed. *New York City* contains only yellow, red and blue lines. In *Broadway Boogie-Woogie* the lines tend to split into small rectangles, as if keeping time to a happy pizzicato. Finally, with the unfinished *Victory Boogie-Woogie*, he achieved joy, in a symphony in which measure and freedom, restraint and exaltation dissolve into perfect unity, of which the Neo-Plastic horizontal-vertical basis remains the law. The importance of Mondrian in this century's painting is considerable, not only on account of his slow, gradual progress from Naturalism to the most severe Abstractionism, but also on account of the quality of the work at each progressive step. At no moment of its development does this painting leave one indifferent: it takes full responsibility and knows no compromise. On the most arid summits of abstraction something still vibrates behind the canvas, warming, humanizing and making it inimitable.

**MONET** Claude (1840–1926). French painter; born in Paris; died at Giverny. Claude Monet is the most Impressionist of Impressionists, and his work is the symbol of the movement. It is appropriate that one of his pictures, exhibited in 1874 and called *Impression, Sunrise* (reproduced on page 126), should have led a Parisian columnist to baptize the new movement. The title of the picture was in itself significant. It revealed the artist's will to transcribe his own feeling rather than to represent a particular landscape; and such an act was revolutionary in its time. This was the point at which modern art broke with that of preceding centuries. It is likely that the persons concerned did not fully appreciate the radical change that their new attitude constituted; they did not foresee its consequences, but kept enough faith to continue their efforts in spite of the greatest difficulties. In his youth Monet had met Boudin at Havre and then made friends with Pissarro at the Académie Suisse (*), where the two of them worked. A few years later he entered the Atelier Gleyre (*), where he met Renoir, Bazille and Sisley. Thus, Fate brought together fortuitously the men who would soon shatter the formulae

MONET. HÔTEL DE LA PLAGE. 1870.
*Private Collection, Paris*

MONET. ARGENTEUIL BRIDGE. 1874.                    *New State Gallery, Munich*

landscape. Pictorial problems were important enough in themselves for Monet not to want to complicate them still more. He experienced too much trouble in finding his own medium, and even more in having it accepted, to think of adding new difficulties.

The year 1874 saw the Impressionist group's first exhibition, which gave rise to mockery and malevolent comments. To the stiff and static art, manufactured in studios, that was then in favour, Monet opposed a fluidity captured from Nature: not only the fluidity of movement but also that, much more subtle, of environment and atmosphere. Had he been content to seek lifelike postures for figures, like those revealed in a candid photograph, his theories would no doubt have been accepted, but what he wanted to paint was the glow of light, the shimmering of water, the transparency of the atmosphere, the scintillation of foliage. His idea of the instantaneous concerned not forms in motion but an arrest of time: a landscape is not the same at dawn and at twilight, in autumn and in spring. He wanted to paint the sun, the cold, the wind, the mist. These ideas were new and came as a revelation. Oscar Wilde later remarked of him that Nature certainly imitates art, since although nobody before Claude Monet had ever discovered that fog becomes iridescent around the London bridges, nobody could afterwards see London fog without thinking of him.

Thereafter Monet confined himself almost exclusively to landscapes, and mostly to those in which water adds an element of movement. Channel ports, the banks of the Seine, England, Holland, and Venice furnished him with

in which official art was imprisoned. For several years, however, they were not so uncompromising as is thought today. Monet sent works to the Salon that were not always refused. The first painting he sent, in 1865, was accepted, and even enjoyed some success. Furthermore, he was admitted several times in later years, although of course with more difficulty. In addition to his landscapes, Monet executed a few figure studies at this time, first a large composition, *Le Déjeuner sur l'Herbe*, which he destroyed after it had been criticized by Courbet (an admirable sketch for it survives in the Frankfurt Museum), then *The Lady in the Green Dress*, which attracted much attention at the Salon of 1866, *Women in the Garden*, in the Louvre, and *Lunch in an Interior*. These canvases, together with a few portraits executed at various periods, are almost the only works in which he gave himself over to the representation of the human figure. This indifference may seem surprising and be regarded as a sign of insensitivity, but a more accurate interpretation suggests that for an artist as scrupulous as Monet – and scrupulousness is characteristic of the Impressionists – the portrait added psychological problems to purely pictorial ones, and that he preferred the more neutral theme of the inexhaustible themes until his death. Today it is difficult to understand that this art, full of freshness and youth, sensitive to the charm of all seasons, luminous as a song of joy, could have raised storms and brought many years of poverty to its apostle. But his tenacity succeeded in convincing the unbelievers and, about 1880, Monet began to see hostility subside. Calm entered his life little by little and, later, comfort and even wealth with the fame that crowned his old age. However, the crown was not untarnished, for if Alfred Sisley had died too young to see the beginnings of his success, Monet lived to witness the new assaults that triumphant Impressionism was to undergo, this time not from official or academic artists but from the members of the new generation who, making use of the freedom won for them by the Impressionists, rejected them to explore other paths toward other feats of daring, other concepts, even other repudiations. The Impressionist technique, carried to the point Monet finally reached, can undoubtedly be criticized for giving less importance to forms than to the atmosphere enveloping them. But an artist cannot be denied the right to think his thought through to the end. Monet was not afraid to seek out this finality. Already in the series of *Cathedral of Rouen* one finds no concern for suggesting effects of mass, but only a desire to observe light in all its intensities. It was mainly at Giverny, in the garden that he arranged himself, that Monet achieved his dream in a magic art free of any concern for stable form. His garlands of wistarias, reflected in the shifting mirror of the lake, his sheets of water lilies floating on the changing water, provided him with a whole dazzling play of coloured mirages that were their own justification, like certain variations in music, whose theme is nothing more than a pretext and a place to start. The whole development of Monet's work was toward a complete liberation that allowed him, near the end of his life, to arrive at an art as independent of reality as that of the most abstract painters of today. The astonishing mural ensemble inspired by *Water Lilies*, which occupies two rooms in the Musée de l'Orangerie in Paris, demonstrates the attainment of a poetical world rid of all concern with form, a

MONET. ROUEN CATHEDRAL. 1894.
*Rouen Museum*

world in which the evocation of reality is no more than a vague pretext. A curious magic emanates from it, but also the certainty that a point has been reached that cannot be passed, a point where the artist, at the height of his powers, has discovered a purity beyond which he cannot go without dissolution.

This extreme experiment could not have been attained if Monet had not previously undertaken many times to paint the same landscape seen at different hours, in different seasons, under different lights, with the sole purpose of extracting new effects from the same subject. The views of *The Gare Saint-Lazare* (1876–1878), of *Rouen Cathedral* (1892–1894) and of the garden at Giverny (1905–1908) are among the most celebrated, but there are other sequences, *The Ice Breaking* (1880), *Haystacks* (1891), *Poplars on the Bank of the Epte*, and the views of London and Venice, that deserve being equally known. Those fortunate enough to have seen several canvases on the same theme, assembled and exhibited by the artist at the Durand-Ruel Gallery, realized the interest and appeal of such a grouping. In them Monet demonstrated that no absolute colour exists in Nature, only light; and that since the appearance of all objects changes perpetually, the art of the painter should consist in choosing one moment in preference to any other, in order to fix its individuality in a definitive image. The demonstration is convincing, although Impressionism would have been justified even without it.

It is easy to understand why this art, which at the beginning won the support and encouragement of Naturalists in literature, who regarded it as an illustration of their theories of objective reality, was later disowned by the same writers. It was, in fact, not so much a Naturalist expression that Monet sought as a poetry of suggestions in which imprecision and the absence of clear figures leave a large place for dreaming and a constantly renewed play of colour. Monet's art, as it appears to us today, claims no ancestry in the past, even though some of the painters of the eighteenth century seem to have been its forerunners. One predecessor of Monet can be found in the English painter Turner, although his is an art of pure imagination and magic. The art of Monet, in fact, remains closer to Nature; and if a divergence seems occasionally to exist, the explanation is that the painter's eye has succeeded in catching what previously seemed impossible to seize. He is quite distinct from some of the other painters classified as Impressionists. He has almost nothing in common with the rigorous draughtsmanship of Degas, except when Degas, in later years, indulged, in his pastels and particularly for his dancers, in similar iridescences; his construction was entirely different from Cézanne's, and he had real kinship only with Sisley and Pissarro, although he has more assurance than they. Jongkind and Boudin paved the way for him and succeeded in transcribing similar wet atmospheres in their own manner, but without achieving the poetical quality that remains the unique achievement of Monet.

**MONTICELLI** Adolphe (1824–1886). French painter; born and died in Marseilles. The offspring of an old Piedmontese family, Monticelli was, as a painter, the direct

heir of the great Venetians. In 1846 he left Marseilles for Paris, studied there for three years, went back and then returned to the capital in 1863, where he lived until the war of 1870. Then he returned to his native city, on foot, and did not leave it again until his death. His last ten years were the most fruitful and original period of his career, a period of exaltation and certainty, of lucid entrancement, although it is the least known. Up to 1870 Monticelli was influenced by the art of museums and of his illustrious contemporaries, by that of Watteau, Veronese, Rembrandt, and also of Diaz, Delacroix, Courbet. Personal as it may be, his painting was then precious, brilliant and mannered. This is the painting that would tempt forgers: *The Courts of Love* and *Scenes of the Park* and *Scenes of the Opera*, of which there are innumerable imitations. After 1870 he did not give up scenes of the park and the opera, but from then on it was in his dreams that he saw the masquerades, balls and *fêtes galantes* and pursued their scintillating illusions. He also painted flowers, portraits and travelling shows. He had conquered his idiom and he enriched it with all the technical means his instinct suggested: thick layers of paint, varnish, mixtures of tones, shading, glaze. In this oily, kneaded, tormented mixture forms seem to bog down, colours to vanish. And then, as the attention persists, the forms reassemble, and the colours emit vivid glows. Golden yellows, midnight blues, reddish shadows, sumptuous blacks sprinkled with touches of emerald and a few drops of vermilion: everything that would be a thick pudding with others is, with him, an alchemist's secret. 'Monticelli taught me chromatism', Van Gogh said later, with gratitude. In preparing his mixtures and reactions, Monticelli was aware of the wonders time would work with them; he knew that one tone would dim, another intensify; that the years would bring out an unnoticed form and an unsuspected contour; that his work would live and relive, changing, multiple, giving off here a nugget, there a gem, hitherto buried in the affectionately mixed paste. 'I paint for fifty years hence', he prophesied. He worked with frenzy, executing landscapes that dripped with light and were saturated with warmth;

portraits, flowers, fruit, whose shifting splendours hide none of the admirable draughtsmanship, figures and objects cast in a kind of lava of melted gold and silver. The trees devoured by slow combustion are almost the same ones that Van Gogh was to set on fire. These woods along a rough slope of hills in Provence seem to reappear in the canvases of Soutine, but devastated by a violent tornado.

Monticelli announced modern Expressionism, and he can also be re-

MONTICELLI. THE ACROBATS' PARADE. 1877.
*Grobet-Labadié Museum, Marseilles*

garded as a precursor of Impressionism. Were not air, light and atmosphere his chief preoccupations? Nevertheless, instead of reproducing natural light and its fugitive variations, he put an invented light, a pictorial light, into his works. And this light is not only a personal, absolute medium, it is also a sign of spiritual elevation. He said of his discovery: 'I am the luminous centre; it is I who light'. That part of his production is open to criticism, there is no doubt. However, it cannot be denied that Monticelli was one of the great French painters of the nineteenth century. Delacroix singled him out. Cézanne was fond of him. We know from letters how much Van Gogh admired him. There are more powerful painters, of harder and more sonorous metal. But no one attempted this learned and bold painting before him.

A belated and fertile genius – he accumulated over eight hundred pictures in less than ten years – Monticelli seems an innovator in direct line of the baroque artists who, from the Romantic Delacroix to the Expressionist Van Gogh, practised what can be called a painting of temperament.

**MOORE** Henry (born in 1894 in Castleford, Yorkshire). After studying at the Leeds School of Art and, later, at the Royal College of Art in London, Moore won a scholarship which enabled him to travel in France and Italy. He has been a member of the London Group and of the Seven and Five Group, and has exhibited at home and abroad with the Surrealists. During the Second World War he made a remarkable series of drawings of London Underground stations in their function as air-raid shelters. In 1934, in a manifesto published by Sir Herbert Read, Moore defined his position in the following terms: 'Beauty, in the later Greek or Renaissance sense, is not the aim of my sculpture. Between beauty of expression and power of expression there is a difference of function. The first aims at pleasing the senses, the second has a spiritual vitality which for me is more moving and goes deeper than the senses'. In response to this conviction, Moore has attempted to give his sculpture a power based on his working out of the sculptural problem rather than on the subject portrayed, while, technically, his purpose has been to form a bridge with the great archaic traditions of Mexico, Egypt and even pre-history. He has sought to attain these ends through respect for his material, feeling that stone, wood or metal – hard and compact as they are – should not be made to lose their identity by attempts to make them look like flesh. In all his work from 1930 onwards there is a growing sense of the material being pushed from within by its own inner energy, an aspect perhaps of Moore's increasing pre-occupation with the opening-up of the sculptural mass. 'A hole', he has said, 'can itself have as much shape-meaning as solid mass. Sculpture in air is possible, where the stone contains only the hole which is the intended and considered form.' From this conception of truth to material, of the outer forms and surfaces of sculpture resulting from the pent-up energy within, of the penetration of the sculptural mass, have sprung Moore's most typical sculptures. Tunnelled and eroded like some ancient landscapes in miniature, his biomorphic forms are related to that same vision which has led Paul Nash and Graham Sutherland to create 'object-personages' – double-image metaphors for landscape – in paint. Moore has acknowledged his particular debt to the organic processes of nature as exemplified in the forms of pebble and rock, shell and tree and bone. He has said, 'I would rather have a piece of my sculpture put in a landscape, almost any landscape, than in, or on, the most beautiful building I know'.

In idiom, Moore has ranged from the sweetly formalized naturalism of the *Madonna and Child* commissioned for St Matthew's, Northampton, to completely non-figurative exercises in spatial relationships. Best-known are his long series of reclining figures, but among his more notable commissions since the war have been the *Three Standing Figures* in Battersea Park, London; the abstract screen for the roof of the *Time-Life* building in London; and the *King and Queen* group at Middelheim, Antwerp. Moore's central position between realism and abstraction, and the slow working out of his thoughts over a long period, have combined to give great stability to his development. He has worked with stone, wood and bronze with equal ease, and has also experimented with cement and terracotta. His sketches and drawings form a considerable body of work by themselves and are important in their own right: they include not only preparatory studies for his sculptures, but works of independent value in which Moore elaborates new forms and techniques. Moore's work is now to be found in museums throughout the world; he has executed commissions for public monuments and buildings, schools and parks in Britain and other countries; in 1948 he won the International Sculpture Prize at the Venice *Biennale* and five years later the equivalent prize at the São Paulo Biennal.

MOORE. LYING FIGURE. *Study for a Sculpture in Wood.*
*Sir Kenneth Clark Collection*

**MORANDI** Giorgio. Italian painter; born in 1890 in Bologna. Morandi's first landscape dates from 1911. He is one of the few Italian artists never to have been to Paris, although he underwent the Parisian influence in his first works. An aloof and lonely artist, he was to complete successfully the metaphysical cycle of Italian painting in 1918 and 1919, far from Ferrara where Chirico and Carrà had just painted their most famous works. As Chirico put it, Morandi 'sanctifies' Metaphysical Painting *(\*)* by reducing it to a kind of linear magic. The intelligence and sensitivity with which he

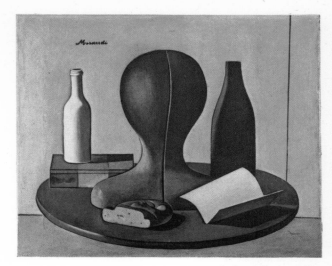

MORANDI. STILL LIFE. 1918.          *Jucker Collection, Milan*

recreates objects are more an engraver's than a painter's. Although he has painted a few beautiful landscapes, only a very few figure studies by him are known, among which is one self-portrait. His universe is the very humble world of still life. He gave up spheres, regular shapes and metaphysical polyhedrons, and a few familiar objects sufficed him: cups and salad-bowls, long-necked bottles that he imprisoned in a very chaste line to produce a strange and rarefied atmosphere. Later, having gradually softened the rigour of his contour, he succeeded, halfway between Cubism and Impressionism, in finding his own personality in a delicate compromise between form and colour. Like Léger, he is capable of creating an atmosphere with three tones; but while the three tones of Léger have become more and more vivid and dazzling over the course of years, Morandi's modulations have been further toned down, as if he wanted to reduce painting to the semitones of etching. His tonal 'intimism' had great influence upon the Roman School (Scipione, Mafai, Cagli, Capogrossi), which was the most valid artistic expression on the peninsula under Fascism. The work of Morandi is perhaps the best that contemporary taste has produced in Italy.

**MOREAU** Gustave (1826–1898). French painter; born and died in Paris. Gustave Moreau plays, in the history of contemporary art, only an episodic part. He has the merit of having been, at the École Nationale des Beaux-Arts, the teacher of Rouault, Matisse, Marquet and Jean Puy – the group of young men from whom Fauvism would spring. One is grateful to him for having preserved the personality of his pupils and thus prepared the blossoming of an essential movement in contemporary art. But there would be some injustice in seeing him merely as a teacher. We should like to see him placed at the source of Surrealism, for more than any other painter he possessed the secret of an unexpected magic. He knew that the object contains a mystery and can express a whole unknown world beyond appearances, and that forms and colours are a language. He may be reproached for a somewhat artificial fantasy and an excessively literary mythology, but in this field, too, he is a forerunner of the Surrealists. Excluded from modern painting, in this way he has his justification as a precursor. He was not only concerned with the plastic problems that form the basis of contemporary art, he was also the master of an extremely elaborate technique.

MOREAU. SALOMÉ.
*Gustave Moreau Museum, Paris*

He wanted to introduce a notion of magic into painting, a part of the incomprehensible and unconscious world in which everything could become a symbol. Considered in this light, the art of Gustave Moreau acquires a significant value. There was religious feeling in his mind, less involved with the Catholic faith than attracted by a curious pantheism. He made his fabulous heroes – the Sphinx, the Chimera, Salome – live in a glitter of gems, in the glow of sumptuous clothes and strange lights. His admiration for Delacroix and especially for Chassériau could not save him from certain excesses and bondage to a pseudo-poetry whose artificiality is transparent today. What appears to us the bric-à-brac of cheap fantasy is none the less the work of a thoroughly sincere artist quite free from morbid obsessions.

**MORISOT** Berthe (1841–1895). French painter; born in Bourges, where her father was a high government official. Berthe Morisot was brought up in cultivated but traditional middle-class surroundings. Nothing in those surroundings would have led one to predict that from the very outset she would be drawn towards the best artists of her time. Her temperament asserted itself at once in the reticence with which she met the mediocre teaching of her first instructor, Chocarne, in the profit she was able to draw from that of the second, Guichard; and further in the desire she expressed to work with Corot. It was under his guidance that she painted from 1862 to 1868. She assimilated his lessons perfectly, and to them she owed a great deal. Their influence is apparent until about 1874: *The Harbour of Lorient* (1869), *On the Balcony* (1872), *The Butterfly Chase*, *At Maurecourt* (1874). But attracted by the art of Manet, she made his acquaintance in 1868, and his influence, in addition to that of Corot, was especially apparent in the years 1875–1876: *Woman at the Mirror, Le Déjeuner sur l'Herbe*. However, having joined the Impressionist group at its beginning, she drew Manet toward light colours and outdoor painting. It was between 1877 and 1879 that she forged her own style, which began to crystallize during this period (*Young Woman Powdering Her Face*, 1877; *Behind the Blind*, 1878; *Summer Day*, 1879). She did not resort to the systematic divided stroke but to large strokes very freely applied in all directions, which gave her canvases an aspect characteristic of herself alone. The familiar interior or open-air scenes she painted are bathed in radiant and iridescent light, in which silvery tones mingle in harmonies of a rarely achieved delicacy and sensitivity. Extremely characteristic of her genius, these paintings are feasts of light, of aerial mobility and lightness, of a spontaneous freshness, constantly renewed from 1879 to 1889 (*Eugène Manet and his Daughter at Bougival*, 1881; *The Veranda*, 1882; *The Garden*, 1883; *On the Lake*, 1884; *Reading*, 1888). This very free, personal manner seemed particularly to suit her temperament, which found in it a medium made to order. However, towards 1889 she became disturbed by the danger inherent in the

Impressionist vision, which was too exclusively attached to the atmospheric aspect of the world and she sought greater unity and respect for form. She assumed a long and flexible stroke that followed the form without encircling it, but shaped its mass and luminosity: *The Mandolin* (1889), *Young Girl Asleep* (1892), *Young Girl with a Fan* (1893), *The Two Sisters* (1894). This is her final manner, for she died early in 1895. Without separating it from the rest, the important place that water-colour occupied in her work should be stressed, as this medium corresponded particularly

MORISOT. AT MAURECOURT. 1874.       *Private Collection, Paris*

well to her nature as a painter and is one of which she made masterful use. A few simple, limpid spots, applied with extreme audacity, were all she needed to express herself completely. Specifically a painter, Berthe Morisot was responsive, above all, to the play of light upon the world which surrounded her; she drew her emotions from it, and in its pictorial interpretation she expressed her nature as a woman and an artist. She allowed no ideology or spirit of system to impair the spontaneity of her art, at whose service she put only purely plastic means. As a woman, she excluded brutality, preferring delicacy and subtlety, and she found her most favourable climate in the intimate atmosphere of family scenes animated by the simple gestures of life, from which she could extract poetry.

**MUNCH** Edvard (1863–1944). Norwegian painter; born at Löten; died at Ekely, near Oslo. After passing his early years and studying in Oslo, Munch spent almost twenty years abroad, in Paris, in the south of France, in Italy, and later in Germany, travelling a great deal and frequenting literary *avant-garde*

circles. Often he spent the summer in Norway and, after recovering from a serious nervous crisis, he returned for good to his homeland in 1908. During the thirty years that passed before his death he worked in the country, in the jealously guarded solitude of his homes at Aagaardstrand, Kragerö, Ramme and Ekely. In Munch's painting there appears the ancient face of the Nordic world, a world animated by forces which still remain extremely close to their source. The unreality of dream mingles with the reality of an imposing and awesome Nature. Like the Scandinavian writers of the same period, he saw the life of man first on the psychological plane. But transposing this frequently too literary vision, Munch conferred a mythic power upon it through his art. Thus he created real symbols that far surpassed the allegories of a Boecklin or a Hodler. Plastic problems were only secondary and remained subordinate to the requirements of expression. His work underwent the influence of Impressionist painting chiefly after his first stay in Paris in 1885. In 1890, in Paris again, he admired Van Gogh, Gauguin, Seurat and Toulouse-Lautrec. His colours became more clear and expression was concentrated in large

MUNCH. GIRLS ON THE BRIDGE. 1901.
*National Gallery, Oslo*

forms with simple and rounded contours. The expressive density of the pictures of this period seems due to the painter's obsession with certain subjects: death, which had made an impression on him when he was still a child, painful loneliness, melancholy terror before the immensity of Nature (*The Scream*, reproduced on page 96), and especially love, which appeared to him a terrible and threatening power. For him, woman personified the Vampire who, in the world of Strindberg, triumphs over man. The principal pictures after 1890 belong to an ensemble he called *The Frieze of Life*. This frieze was meant to be 'a poem of life, love and death', in which the suffering and joy of each man would meet. *The Dance of Life* (1899–1900) is in the centre of the frieze. There the painful loneliness is overcome, and man's destiny, in its misery as in its joy, is intimately linked with the great forces of Nature. Munch's landscapes express, without allegory, a similar understanding. Dark blue trees of simple, dense forms stand out

against snow with the power of primitive signs; a naked peninsula, green and ochre, a gigantic paw of earth, crawls towards the water of the fjord and, in the starlit night, the spell is at last complete. The picture of *Girls on the Bridge* (1901) is in the same spirit. For the University of Oslo, in 1909–1911, Munch painted mural decorations, in which a huge sun, the symbol of force and light, stands out in the centre. These murals belong to the second period of his work, which is characterized by an increasingly greater freedom and light, revealed in other decorations that he undertook in 1921–1922 for the dining hall of a factory. From then on colours became bright, almost 'Fauvist'. Munch was increasingly liberated from his obsession with the terrible forces of Nature, and the mystery of life, round which his work continued to be organized, seemed to become a mystery in broad daylight. This is particularly clear in the poignant series of self-portraits done in his last years. Many of his pictures exist in several versions. This is partially due to his habit of making a replica for himself of each canvas that was sold.

The great themes of Munch's painting occur again in his engraved work, which is particularly important. Both in black-and-white and in the simplified colouring of lithography and woodcuts Munch frequently achieved a concision that gave the image a strength sometimes surpassing that of his painting. Munch's art, with that of Van Gogh and Ensor, was the first great manifestation of Expressionism *(\*)* on a European level. He can indeed be reproached with being dominated by preoccupations that go beyond the limits of painting.

However, he was filled with a desire to make a synthesis of modern form and symbolic expression; and his influence was felt in the development of art wherever such a synthesis was being sought after. In Germany, for example, the Expressionism of the *Brücke (\*)* arose out of contact with Munch's work.

# N

**NABIS** (The). It was in the last days of September 1888 that Sérusier had his decisive encounter with Gauguin at Pont-Aven *(\*)*, and upon his return could show his fellow-painters at the Académie Julian *(\*)* the famous 'talisman' painted in the Bois d'Amour in juxtaposed pure tones upon the lid of a cigar-box. The exhibition of the Impressionist and Synthesist Group (Gauguin, Bernard, Laval) at the Café Volpini early in 1889 completed the revelation. Converted to the new gospel were Bonnard, Ibels, Ranson and Maurice Denis, who were soon joined by a number of fugitives from the École des Beaux-Arts: Vuillard, Roussel, Piot and, a little later, Verkade, Vallotton, the sculptors Lacombe and Maillol, and the latter's friend, the Hungarian painter Ripl Ronai.

The Nabis, so baptized by the poet Cazalis with a Hebrew term meaning 'prophets', met every month for dinner at *l'Os à Moelle*, in the Passage Brady in Paris, and every week in the studio of Ranson, who found a picturesque nickname for each of them: Bonnard, 'The Nipponizing Nabi'; Verkade, 'The Nabi Obelisk'; Vuillard, 'The Zouave'. They also assembled at the art dealer Père Tanguy's *(\*)*, in the rue Clauzel, where they discovered Cézanne and Van Gogh; at their own art dealer Le Barc de Bouteville's, who devoted several exhibitions to them from 1891 to 1897; or at the Théâtre de l'Œuvre, founded by their friend Lugné-Poë, for whom they designed settings, and on the premises of the *Revue Blanche (\*)*, which was also frequented by Lautrec, whose friendship they made along with the acquaintance of all the celebrities of Symbolism in literature. To these numerous contacts and to the momentarily dominating influence of Gauguin were added that of Puvis de Chavannes, Odilon Redon, folk images and Japanese etchings and, to a lesser extent, of Gustave Moreau and the English Pre-Raphaelites. The Nabis' doctrine was summed up, according to Maurice Denis, in the Theory of the Two Distortions: 'The Objective Distortion, based upon a purely aesthetic and decorative concept, upon technical principles of colour and composition, and the Subjective Distortion, which brought into play the artist's own perception . . .' They applied these principles not only to easel painting, 'a plane surface covered with colours brought together in a certain order', but also to a series of decorative techniques whose spirit they revolutionized, such as painting on cardboard, tempera, stained glass, lithography, posters, theatre settings, and book illustration. The variety of their experiments and increasing exchanges between the worlds of art and entertainment characterize the end of the century, which bore the Nabi stamp in all fields

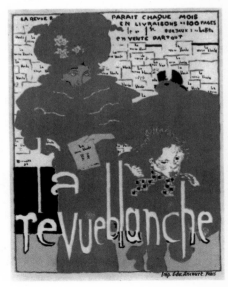

BONNARD. POSTER FOR THE 'REVUE BLANCHE'.
1894

(cf. the articles on Bonnard, Denis, Sérusier, Vallotton and Vuillard).

Bonnard, Vuillard, Denis and Lugné-Poë, the latter three schoolmates at the Lycée Condorcet, shared a studio for a time in 1890, in the Place Pigalle. Then Denis, Sérusier and Verkade – the latter became a monk at the famous Benedictine monastery of Beuron in 1893 – drew together in a certain neo-classical mysticism vaguely derived from Pont-Aven, while Bonnard and Vuillard, the sensitive Intimists, by far the most gifted of the group, unamenable to the theories of Sérusier, soon separated from Gauguin and formed with Roussel an actual group within the group. During this period Vallotton practised chiefly wood-engraving in black-and-white. He made the doctrine and the art of his friends known in Switzerland, but after 1900 his tense, severe style developed into an extreme realism close to German expressionism. The Nabis exhibited

RANSON. WOMEN IN WHITE. *Circa* 1890.
*Tapestry Cartoon*

together for the last time at the Durand-Ruel Gallery in 1899, in tribute to Odilon Redon, but by then each of them had already gone his own way. In 1908 Paul Ranson opened an Academy *(\*)*, which his premature death the following year prevented him from managing long, but which was maintained by his widow with the assistance of the former Nabis, especially Maurice Denis and Sérusier, both of whom were the authors of the group's doctrinal books, Denis of *Theories* and *New Theories*, and Sérusier of *An ABC of Painting*.

**NADAR** Pseudonym of the pioneer French photographer Felix Tournachon (1836–1910). A friend of painters and writers, he left portraits of both, and these portraits make him a true precursor of modern art. Recalling his own difficult beginnings, as well as those of his friends, Claude Monet once said: 'Nadar, the great Nadar, as good as gold, lent us the place . . .' It is not the least of his glories that the famous photographer lent his studios to the future Impressionists, who organized there (from April 15th to May 15th, 1874) the first of eight exhibitions of the 'Painters, Sculptors and Engravers Company'. It was at this event that the word *Impressionism* was spoken for the first time by a critic who had burst out laughing in front of Monet's canvas *Impression, Sunrise* (reproduced on page 126). Admission was charged. The entire *avant-garde* was represented, all the painters rejected by the official Salon. In addition to Boudin, Lépine and some others, who had been invited at the suggestion of Degas, and who were to serve as a sort of guarantee, the future Impressionists, Cézanne included, were present in full strength. Manet alone was absent. Besides the picture previously mentioned, Monet exhibited the *Boulevard des Capucines* and *Boats Leaving the Harbour of Havre*. Renoir was represented by, among others, *La Loge*, Berthe Morisot by *The Cradle*, and Cézanne by his *Modern Olympia*, and particularly *The House of the Hanged Man*. Pissarro, Sisley and Guillaumin were present. It was, with Press and public alike, an unprecedented scandal, but 'the good Nadar' was exultant, although he had certainly not suspected the historical importance of his generous gesture. All his life Nadar had the luck and the intelligence to do the right thing. His name will always be inseparable from those of the great artists of his time, of whom he has left unsurpassable portraits. Other than his own *Baudelaire*, no painted portrait has exceeded in psychological interest his feverish *Delacroix*, his disquieting *Constantin Guys*, his Assyrian *Courbet* or his majestic *Monet*. With the same felicity he brought out the cautious finesse of Manet, the sensitive good nature of Corot and the moving melancholy of Daumier. In his attentive search for expression, Nadar always obeyed a strict discipline, which contributed in great measure to the perfection of his results. Thanks to him, photography sometimes equalled painting in the psychological interpretation of characters and faces.

NASH. AFTERNOON ENCOUNTER. 1936.
*Private Collection*

**NASH** Paul (1889–1946). Born in Dymchurch, Kent; died in Boscombe. Studied at the Slade School, then joined the London Group and the New English Art Club. In 1933 he was one of the founding members of the group of painters, sculptors and architects called 'Unit One'. Nash was an official war artist in both world wars, and during the period between his stark, angular records of the Western Front and his more visionary records of the Battle of Britain, his gentle yet disturbing romanticism made him a dominant figure in British painting. Although Nash underwent a number of influences – first Cézanne, later Surrealism and Constructivism – he remained essentially true to his origins, and his concept of art was profoundly marked by a Nordic and Celtic strain. He felt that his destiny was to find his way back to the sources of English art. Technically his roots may be found in Cotman and Turner: his colours were the soft colours of the moisture-laden atmosphere of England and even his oils maintain a fluidity and lyricism which relate him to the best traditions of the English water-colourists. Poetically his roots were in the work of Blake: he had the same tireless imagination, tinged with mysticism, which drove him constantly to search in new directions. His painting suggested a sort of druidical rite inspired by his contact with Nature and its overtones of history and memory. When he erected sinister, obsessive monoliths in a moon-bathed desert landscape, he was only responding to the call of a magic symbolism which can be found at the origin of all primitive arts. He was acutely aware of analogies and correspondences. The sea of German aircraft destroyed in the Battle of Britain suggested to him the waves of a sea of death, and he called it *Totesmeer*. For him the tree trunks in *Monster Field* blasted by lightning had entered another existence. 'We are not studying two fallen trees that look like animals', he wrote, 'but two monster objects outside the plan of natural phenomena.' The association of, or 'encounter' between, objects in different elements fascinated him, and several of his last paintings are built around the mutually echoing forms of sun and sunflower. In any landscape Nash sought the active element, the drama – but it was always a drama of the inner eye. The most striking image in the Bible, he once said, is the sentence 'Why leap ye, ye high hills?' because it ascribes a power of movement to inanimate things. It is just this same animistic force upon which Graham Sutherland *(\*)* and Henry Moore *(\*)* have since drawn. Nash is represented in numerous British museums; in addition to his painting he carried out a good deal of book illustration, some textile and poster design, and some theatre décor.

**NEO-IMPRESSIONISM**  A movement whose members were Seurat, Signac and the group of painters who followed their principles, the scientific study of colour and the systematic division of tone as they had been practised instinctively by the Impressionists. The term is supposed to have been created by the painters themselves, in homage to their elders, or by their friend and interpreter Félix Fénéon *(\*)*, who used it for the first time in the Brussels magazine *L'Art Moderne*, in the issue of September 19th, 1886. It was taken up by Arsène Alexandre, who is usually credited with originating it, in his review in *Événement*, December 10th, 1886, of Fénéon's famous pamphlet *The Impressionists in 1886*. The term was definitely consecrated by Fénéon in May 1887 in the decisive essay in *L'Art Moderne* on 'Neo-Impressionism', in which he set forth with accuracy and rigour both the aesthetic and technical tenets of the movement.

The dispersion of the Impressionist group in 1880 was accompanied by a tightening of method and a return to classical discipline. In the same year, in the magazine *Art*, David Sutter published an important series of articles on *The Phenomena of Vision*, defined in 167 rules that seem to forecast the Neo-Impressionist programme, and ending with a statement of the validity of the link between art and science. Rules, he declared, do not hinder spontaneity of invention or execution, despite their absolute character; science liberates from all uncertainty, allows free movement in a very wide area; it is thus unfair both to art and to science to think that the one necessarily excludes the other. Psychology and physiology of vision, problems of optics, and analysis of light and colour were the order of the day. Recent experiments by the physicists Helmholtz (1878) and Edouard Rood (1881) completed the previous discoveries of Chevreul, whose work, *The Law of Simultaneous Contrast*, published in 1839, was reprinted at the expense of the State in 1889 for the centenary of the birth of the scientist, who was still alive. In this atmosphere of theoretical fervour Georges Seurat (1859–1891) was reaching artistic maturity.

His experimental works of 1882 were already characterized by little spots of colour and long even strokes of vibrant luminosity. In the spring of 1884, along with the artists refused by the official Salon, he founded the Salon des Indépendants, to which he sent his first large composition, *La Baignade*. Also among the numerous exhibitors – without knowing each other as yet – were Paul Signac, Henri-Edmond Cross, Charles Angrand and Albert Dubois-Pillet, who were similarly oriented. He made friends with them, and in June constituted, on the basis of regular by-laws and under

SIGNAC. BEACHED SAILS. 1902

SEURAT. SUNDAY IN SUMMER AT THE GRANDE JATTE. 1884–1886.
*Art Institute, Chicago*

the presidency of Odilon Redon, the Société des Artistes Indépendants, within which they became the most active group. Their aim was to rationalize the expression of light with pure colours and to substitute a scientific method for the empirical one of the Impressionists. At the first show of the new Société des Indépendants, in December, Seurat again exhibited his *La Baignade*, based on 'contrasts of shades', which, in a still flexible handling, achieved his purpose: to reconcile the eternal and the fugitive, architecture and light, figure and landscape, Impressionist vibration and classical stability. Signac, four years younger, dynamic and pugnacious, himself given to the same investigations, was enthralled by this canvas and became an eager proselyte. In 1885, at Guillaumin's, he met Pissarro, whom he introduced to Seurat, and who enthusiastically took up the new discipline, which met his need for order and structure; Pissarro interested his eldest son Lucien and the latter's fellow student Louis Hayet in the movement. Between 1884 and 1886 Seurat executed his second large composition, *A Sunday at the Grande Jatte*, based upon 'contrasts of tones', in accordance with his now fully established technique, the methodical fragmentation of stroke that he called 'Divisionism' and carried as far as 'Pointillism'.

'To divide,' explained Signac, the theoretician of the group, 'means to secure all the benefits of luminosity, colouring and HARMONY: (1) by optical fusion of pigments pure in themselves (ALL THE SHADES OF THE SPECTRUM AND ALL THEIR TONES); (2) by separating various elements (local colour, colour of lighting, their reactions); (3) by balance of these elements and their proportions (according to the laws of CONTRAST, GRADUATION AND IRRADIATION); (4) by the choice of a stroke proportionate to the size of the picture.'

In March 1886 the art dealer Durand-Ruel went to New York with three hundred Impressionist canvases, to which he added works by Signac and Seurat, including *La Baignade*. The same year the *Grande Jatte* was the chief attraction at the eighth and last Impressionist exhibition, May 15th–June 15th, which marked the breakup of the original group, impending since 1880, and the official appearance of Neo-Impressionism or, in Pissarro's terms, the separation of 'Romantic Impressionists' and 'Scientific Impressionists'. Monet, Renoir and

Sisley withdrew. Degas accepted the participation of Seurat, Signac and Lucien and Camille Pissarro exhibiting in the same room, but asked that the word 'Impressionist' be eliminated from the poster, and rejected the works by Angrand and Dubois-Pillet as inadequate. At this time Fénéon made the personal acquaintance of Seurat and his friends. He was to remain their faithful advocate and official interpreter. He devoted a series of masterly articles to them in *avant-garde* magazines, articles which were collected in a booklet at the end of the year. The Neo-Impressionists made an appearance as a group at the second Salon des Indépendants at the Tuileries (August 21st–September 21st, 1886), where Seurat showed his *Grande Jatte* again. Pissarro exhibited at Nantes in November and succeeded in getting Seurat and Signac accepted with him. These three painters were invited to exhibit in Brussels by 'The Twenty', an independent group courageously led by Octave Maus. Signac and Seurat were present at the opening in February 1887. Though admired by Verhaeren, the *Grande Jatte* attained only a *succès d'estime*, but it won several Belgian artists over to Divisionism, among them Henry van de Velde and Theo van Rysselberghe. In France new Divisionists appeared: H. Petitjean, Maximilien Luce, and, a little later, Lucie Cousturier, to mention only the more important. The movement also spread to Italy, with Segantini, Previati, and Morbelli, who appeared for the first time in Milan in 1891. Finally, three of the principal artists of the late nineteenth century, without belonging to Neo-Impressionism, underwent Seurat's influence and practised Divisionism for a time: Gauguin in 1886, Lautrec in 1887 and Van Gogh during almost his entire Parisian period (1886–1888), when his relations with Signac and Seurat were particularly fruitful.

The methodical enterprise of Seurat culminated in two great compositions: *Le Chahut* (1890) and *The Circus* (1891), based upon 'contrasts of lines', in which his will for style turned to stylization and touched Modern Style. He died at thirty-two on March 29th, 1891, exhausted by work but having delivered his message. Pissarro, who was asked to assume leadership of the movement, refused, chiefly because he had just

given up Divisionism to return to the freer handling of his initial manner. Only Lucie Cousturier, Cross and Signac, who in 1889 published the doctrinal work that has since become a classic, *From Eugène Delacroix to Neo-Impressionism*, attempted to remain true to the spirit of the method that had been for some no more than a recipe, but through which the architectonic genius of Seurat had been able to crystallize its fervour. In 1899, and even more in 1904, the Fauvism of Matisse was prepared by a Pointillist stage, through contact with Signac and Cross, at whose side he worked in the summer at Saint-Tropez, and the large Seurat retrospective at the Salon des Indépendants in 1905 brought on Cubism (cf. the articles on Cross, Fénéon, Luce, Pissarro, Seurat and Signac).

**NEO-PLASTICISM** The doctrine of pure plastic art derived by Mondrian (*) from Cubism, and consisting in the exclusive use of the right angle in a horizontal-vertical position and of the three primary colours in conjunction with the three 'non-colours', white, black and grey. Mondrian's development of the concept of Neo-Plasticism was the result of five years of research and active meditation, brush or pen in hand (1912–1917). Theo van Doesburg (*) was his first follower (1916). From their meeting in Amsterdam was born the magazine *De Stijl* (1917–1928), in which Mondrian could express his ideas at leisure, and which was, until 1924, the organ of radical Neo-Plasticism produced with the collaboration of the painter Huszar and of the painter and sculptor Vantongerloo (*vide Stijl*). Later, Mondrian continued alone but untiringly until his death to apply the law of Neo-Plasticism, so that his name is almost synonymous with the term. Besides writing numerous articles in *De Stijl*, he developed his ideas in a booklet, *Neo-Plasticism*, which appeared at the *Effort Moderne* Gallery of Léonce Rosenberg in Paris in 1920. A German version of this essay appeared in 1925, in the series of books published by the Bauhaus, under the title *Neue Gestaltung*. Finally, as *Plastic Art and Pure Plastic Art*, Mondrian's essays in English were published in New York in 1945.

**NICHOLSON** Ben, born in 1894 at Denham, Buckinghamshire, son of the painter Sir William Nicholson (1872–1949). He studied at the Slade School, then in Tours, Milan, and Pasadena, California. In 1933–1934 in Paris he exhibited with the Abstraction-Creation group and during the inter-war period was one of the foremost links between Great Britain and the modern movement in Europe. He is considered

NICHOLSON. STILL LIFE. 1948.
*Private Collection*

the leading English non-figurative painter. The creator of abstract compositions – sometimes treated plastically as bas-reliefs – and of highly stylized landscapes and still-lifes, Nicholson seeks above all to express static, architectural themes of great simplicity of form. His art is a kind of exact, refined geometry, controlled always by exquisite judgement and heightened by a range of colours that is best described as chaste. The same objects borrowed from everyday life – a pitcher, a table, a glass – serve as the basis for an infinite number of variations which, through subtle modulations, result in an increasingly complex series of linear rhythms and constructions. Within the fastidious limits imposed by his intellect and his sensibility, Nicholson has

been drawn, now towards the classical, now towards the romantic ideal. He started from a basis of clear-cut reality and gradually, after a period of increased schematization, reached in his white plaster reliefs of around 1935 a culmination in the organization of static relationships. His evolution did not stop there, however, with these pure distillations of the circle and the rectangle, but has come full cycle to a renewed, even more purified concept of reality. In this more recent work are resolved the two sides of his nature, represented by his respect for Mondrian and his admiration for Alfred Wallis, the old Cornish primitive. Nicholson has written '. . . so far from "abstract" art being the withdrawal of the artist from reality (into an "ivory tower") it has brought art once again into common everyday life . . .', and '. . . the problems dealt with in "abstract" art are related to the interplay of forces and therefore, . . . any solution reached has a bearing on all interplay between forces: it is related to Arsenal *v* Tottenham Hotspur quite as much as to the stars in their courses.' Nicholson's contribution to the abstract movement is a highly individual one. In spite of the severity of his style and the rigour of his geometrical conception, his work retains an intensely English character. A certain gentleness and discreet lyricism relate him to the English water-colourists, as do the lightness of his touch and the transparency of his colour. He is represented in museums all over the world. In 1952 he was awarded the first prize for painting at the 39th International Exhibition at the Carnegie Institute, Pittsburgh.

**NOLDE** Emil. German painter; born 1867 at Nolde, in Schleswig. His real name was Emil Hansen and he was born of a Danish-Frisian family. About 1904 he changed his name to that of his native village and from then on signed his canvases Nolde. A teacher of drawing, he devoted himself entirely to painting from 1898 on. He studied in Munich, Paris and Copenhagen. In 1904, after Impressionist beginnings, his touch became stronger and more free, and colour played a more active part in his work. In addition to landscapes of his native region, its sea, swamps, and gardens, fantastic and grotesque figures began to appear in his canvases. From 1906 to 1907 he participated in the *Brücke (\*)*, but later, being of an unsociable and solitary nature, he remained outside all groups. In 1908 his art attained its most monumental form, and colour charged with expression burst out in unrestrained force. As early as 1909 he produced large religious compositions: *The Last Supper*, *Whitsun*, *Joseph Tells His Dream*; also figures from a personal mythology, such as the *Old Pasha* or *The Warrior and His Wife*. At the same time, masks, primitive statuettes and exotic textiles appeared in his still lifes. In 1913–1914 he was a member of an ethnological expedition that travelled to Russia, China, Japan and reached Polynesia. What he discovered in the latter area was not so much the more authentic life that Gauguin had sought as an elemental demoniac essence in the attitudes of the primitive beings that he studied with keen interest. Later, Nolde was bitterly attacked by the Nazis, who went so far as to forbid him to paint. As a watercolourist and engraver he did important work (etchings, lithographs, woodcuts, from 1905 to 1922), which is among the most exciting in contemporary German art. A demon chained to earth, Nolde seems to have shaped the landscapes, flowers and the savages or girls he represents with their luxuriance of flesh from the very earth itself. And the colours he generously spreads out on his canvas are opaque and dazzling, like earth on fire. Colour does not represent, it *is* the magic presence of things and men on the canvas, and thus their primitive

NOLDE. MARSH LANDSCAPE. 1916.                    *Kunstmuseum, Basel*

being is unmasked before the spectator with a sudden shock. Mystical in his way, Nolde discovered a religiosity in the very heart of the most primitive sensuality.

## NOUVELLE ATHÈNES

About 1877 the Impressionist painters dispersed. Starting from this period, certain painters, whose names remain none the less linked with Impressionism, began to frequent the Café de la Nouvelle Athènes, in the Place Pigalle. Later on writers were in the majority; the English novelist George Moore has left a lively first-hand account of these evenings in his *Confessions of a Young Man*. Manet and Degas could still be met there. Renoir came seldom, Cézanne even less often, and only when brought by his curious friend, the musician Cabaner. Increasingly estranged from their Impressionist friends, as they had always had loose ties with the movement, Manet and Degas eventually became the only clients of the establishment.

# O

**OROZCO** José Clemente (1883–1949). Born in Zapatlan, Mexico. Along with Diego Rivera, Orozco can be considered one of the initiators of the Mexican painting of today. Less influenced than Rivera by European painting, probably closer to Aztec tradition, Orozco appraised perfectly the requirements made by the immensity of the American continent. He did not accept the limits suggested to European artists by the will inherited from the ancient Greeks to reduce plastic arts to human scale. As he worked out cartoons for his frescoes, Orozco no doubt thought more of skyscrapers than of houses and monuments in Mexico, although the Maya or Aztec pyramids could have justified his choice. His resolution to put his art at the service of his political opinions was certainly more decisive. Every work was to illustrate a grievance of contemporary man. This tendency led him to give to his work the character of an appeal, a message, and therefore to arrive eventually at a poster style. In this field Orozco's virtuosity is incomparable. His art not only solicits, grips the attention of the passer-by, but also attempts to make him react, and succeeds in doing so. Aesthetically, this will of the painter has not failed to create serious misunderstandings. It is, nevertheless, true that the work of Orozco has enabled contemporary painters, Mexican in particular, to escape from affectation, free themselves of their repressions and broaden their vision. In some respects Orozco was a renovator. He showed that modern painting could be directed toward a field deliberately neglected by the painters of the late nineteenth century, who had forgotten the example and lesson of Delacroix. In spite of the definitely local, deeply Mexican character of his painting, Orozco has been recognized by many inhabitants of the Western Hemisphere as one of the first painters to have expressed the spirit of a new civilization. It is, moreover, indisputable that not only the dimensions of his work but even the very light in his painting correspond to those of the cities of the New World. No wonder, therefore, that European artists, borne upon frequently contrary currents, find it so difficult to accept the genius of Orozco. None the less, this painter

OROZCO. ZAPATISTAS. 1931. *Museum of Modern Art, New York*

211

offers them one of the most precious means for escaping the impasse to which a number of them have come. The influence of Orozco is at present undergoing an eclipse, for today his art appears to be too faithful to a certain period in the history of his country. But it is likely that justice will be done in the future to the powerful and incontestable personality of this artist.

**ORPHISM** A word used, from 1912 on, by the poet Guillaume Apollinaire, particularly in the lecture he gave in Berlin at the time of Delaunay's exhibition at the Der Sturm Gallery, to designate the movement in the new painting of the time, which proclaimed the primacy of pure colour in pictorial construction. Realizing the extent to which these manifestations of vitality reflected a will to escape the severe harmonies of Picasso and Braque, Apollinaire prophesied the disruption of Cubism; then, invoking the name of Orpheus, under whose patronage he had just placed the poems of his *Bestiary*, or *Cortège of Orpheus*, he compared the experiments of Delaunay, Kupka and the young painters surrounding them to the poetic and musical games whose fancy delighted him. According to Apollinaire, Delaunay believed that when a primary colour does not determine its complementary, it shatters in the atmosphere and produces simultaneously all the colours of the spectrum. After having stressed his attachment to the pure colours of Ingres and praised Seurat's major creation, the contrast of colours, Delaunay claimed that behind all pure expression in modern painting there would thereafter be Simultaneous Contrast, the sole means of securing dynamism of colours and their arrangement in the picture. This exaltation of the dynamic mission of colour brought forth an entirely new art, with its own laws of creation, capable of emerging from any objective, visual representation of Nature.

**OUDOT** Roland. French painter; born in 1897 in Paris. Oudot belongs to the group of artists who, without trying to shock, have asserted themselves between the two wars and been given the name of 'painters of poetic reality'. They are generally considered as the final product of Impressionism. This has meant giving Impressionism and its consequences an interpretation that the movement certainly did not have at the beginning; and it is not because these painters have taken the landscape as an essential theme that they should be credited with Impressionist descent; Oudot's art has, in fact, a fixity that contradicts the mobility of Impressionism. His large blue skies, his dominant greys, his slate tones are the opposite of scintillating light; he seeks stability rather than instantaneity. After having very strongly felt, until about 1920, the influence of Cézanne, Oudot turned toward Fauvism and Cubism, but without allowing himself to be diverted from close contact with Nature. At first interested by the landscapes of the Île-de-France, he has recently taken up those of Provence, whose austerity suits his temperament. His dominant grey is far from being monotonous;

DELAUNAY. PARIS. 1937. AIR, IRON AND WATER

OUDOT. PEN-AND-INK SKETCH. 1954

it gives a mineral resonance to his very intense reds and hard blues, which are softened by the contact. Even though his landscapes maintain an austerity from which man is nearly always absent, Oudot introduces into his compositions a note of calm fantasy, of sober and reserved elegance. His compositions attest a rigorous sense of balance, and a nice disposition of elements allows him to adjust his style to the requirements of mural composition without recourse to systematic formulae. He is one of those who remain true to a very classical conception of art, in which an always controlled emotion admits of no facility. Nature remains his inspiration under all circumstances, but it is Nature conceived anew, seen through a tense, penetrating sensitivity that is never lacking.

**OZENFANT** Amédée. French painter; born in 1886 at Saint-Quentin. After studying the classics in Spain, Ozenfant returned to Saint-Quentin, where he attended an art school. He was given the La Tour pastels to copy and noticed with surprise that in his big box of clear colours none was suitable; he ascertained, for example, that 'sky blues or the flesh tones are neutrals transfigured by tones even more neutral'. The painter was to remember this lesson when he taught his disciples, 'Painting starts where reality ends, where illusion begins'. From 1915 to 1917 Ozenfant laid down the principles of Purism in his magazine *L'Élan*. In 1917 he met Charles-Edouard Jeanneret, the future Le Corbusier, and made him part of the movement. In 1919 they published together *After Cubism*, a manifesto of Purism (*). Ozenfant's work then consisted of compositions of simplified forms, organized according to a set of strict rules, strictly followed in order to avoid 'facility' and force the imagination to exert itself fully. While Juan Gris at the same period was proceeding from the abstract to the concrete, Ozenfant started from real or possible objects and moved toward abstraction, eliminating everything variable or accidental from each object, to retain only constants. The Purist rules of organization have often been compared to those imposed upon the fugue by J. S. Bach, and it is quite natural that certain paintings by Ozenfant bear the name of *Chord* or *Fugue*. From 1921 to 1925 Ozenfant and Jeanneret published their magazine *Esprit Nouveau (*)*, which enabled the boldest and most diverse tendencies in contemporary art to express themselves. From 1925 to 1928 the whole activity of Ozenfant tended toward the renewal of mural painting; the central work of this period is the vast composition in the Paris Museum of Modern Art, *The Four Races*. In 1928 he published *Art* (I: *The Balance Sheet of Modern Arts*; II: *The Structure of a New Spirit*), which is now a classic and has been reprinted many times in several languages. In 1931 he began a vast composition called *Life*, in which over a hundred figures handled in the Purist manner lyrically sing human solidarity, and he worked on it for seven years. This work now belongs to the Museum of Modern Art in Paris. From 1935 to 1938 he published *Journey Through Life*, his diary for the years 1931–1934, in which he recorded all events, whether general or personal, in so far as they influenced the work in progress,

*Life*. Since 1938 Ozenfant has been living in New York, where he founded the Ozenfant School of Fine Arts. Developing his theory of 'Pre-Forms', he has endeavoured to show that great works of art, like all truths, exist necessarily, potentially, in humanity's subsconscious before being revealed by an 'inventor'. While his work before the important composition *Life* was dominated by a will for economy, to say as much as possible with a minimum of means, since 1950 the artist seems to have set himself the goal of 'giving as much as possible to be seen'; in fact, his recent works appear quite simple from a distance, but on closer inspection, series of details are revealed.

OZENFANT. STILL LIFE. 1925.
*Collection of R. La Roche, Paris*

# P

**PAPIERS COLLÉS** This is a technique as old as Time. But what was originally only a children's game has become a genuine and undeniable art form in this century. What is its origin, and who was its inventor? While *collages* appeared in the work of both Picasso and Braque at the end of 1912, it is apparently the latter who first had the idea and was the first to apply it. In fact, by introducing, in 1911, a typeset phrase into his picture *The Portuguese*, Braque discovered a new plastic element, which his fellow Cubists were quick to adopt. At this time Cubism was already loosening its ties with reality and drifting toward abstraction. The subject tended to be eliminated; the picture was not so firmly constructed. The question was less one of representing the object in its concrete totality than of considering it as an ensemble of pure signs, of exclusively graphic or pictorial effect, as an intellectual and often hermetic creation. Thus at the time when Synthetic Cubism was being substituted for Analytic Cubism, it is not surprising that painters in general, and Braque in particular, should have sensed the dangers of an art divorced from the world of appearances. It must not be forgotten, moreover, that Braque had never ceased being a craftsman, and a craftsman in the French tradition. Consequently, typographical characters and, after this, imitation wood and marble, the *trompe-l'œil* effects that he had seen used and had used himself during his childhood in his father's workshop, appeared in his work as reminders of external reality. From *trompe-l'œil* painting to the use of the very materials reproduced was only one step, and one which was soon taken by both Braque and Picasso. Evolving Cubism lent itself to the new technique: there were no more intricate architectures, entangled lines, minute strokes or monochrome colour, but only plane surfaces, large flat areas, lighter and less uniform tones.

PICASSO, PAPIER COLLÉ. 1914. *Private Collection, Paris*

Braque glued pieces of printed or decorative papers or of newspaper to cardboard or canvas, and then applied either ink or pencil lines or touches of gouache or oil paint to them (see *Aria de Bach* reproduced on page 37). Picasso's procedure was not much different in his *Still Life with a Fruit Bowl*. Soon both incorporated into their pictures sand, pieces of cloth or wood, odd objects like playing-cards, boxes of matches or wrappers from tobacco packages. While Picasso sought unexpected effects of contrast, Braque succeeded in revealing the relations between the concrete elements employed and forms mentally conceived, to achieve an intimate poetry of exquisite appeal. The common, inert, dead substances had only to be incorporated by human ingenuity into a picture to take on artistic life.

As early as 1913 Juan Gris made harmoniously rhythmic *collages* of selected materials, juxtaposed

GRIS. BREAKFAST. *Papier Collé.* 1914

with the melancholy, somewhat haughty lyricism peculiar to him: pages of books, musical staves, decorative flowered papers, old-fashioned engravings. Between 1914 and 1918 the French sculptor Laurens executed numerous compositions which mark the high point of the Cubist *papiers collés*. But the experiments that Jean Arp, another sculptor, made at the same time revealed entirely different preoccupations. Arp, a deliberate and reflective artist, concerned, above all, with sobriety, if not austerity, of expression, cut out from paper with great precision plain forms that he had only to glue upon a ground to obtain simple and straightforward rhythms. Italian Futurists, in turn, experimented in the technique practised by the French Cubists: Balla, Boccioni, Carrà, Prampolini, Severini. The Dadaists made use of it also, but in a spirit that was different from, if not opposed to, that of the inventors. Whereas the latter desired to accentuate the plastic value of the image, the boisterous followers of Dada used the same technique to destroy the traditional concept of a picture, to

exhibit in the most extravagant juxtapositions their contempt for logic and reason. In the *collages* of a Max Ernst or a Schwitters, for example, with their incongruous contrasts and their challenging metaphysical and literary allusions, it would be fruitless to look for a new dialectic of form, colour and space. Nevertheless, the humour and fantasy of these artists could not fail to influence the Surrealists Miró, Tanguy and Magritte about 1928. Russian Constructivists, Germans from the Bauhaus *(\*)*, Neo-Plasticists, and the Futurist Magnelli also made uses of the *collage* technique. Today, in the work of non-representational painters, interesting efforts are to be seen, in particular those of Jeanne Coppel and Karskaya (*see* studies on the history of *papiers collés* by Mme Wescher in *Art d'aujourd'hui*, 1953 and 1954).

Finally, comes Matisse, whose experiments were the most important since that of the Cubists. It was, in fact, Matisse who revived *collage* as an idiom and endowed it with an inimitable vocabulary, syntax and style. The *papier collé* was the happy culmination of his art and life. Barred by illness and age from easel painting, he gave up the brush for the scissors and paint for coloured paper during his last ten years. Cut and glued paper came to be his sole medium. He mastered it so completely, made it a tool so obedient to his will, so suited to his gifts, that his *papiers collés* illuminate his entire past and justify all his previous experiments. His constant effort, continued during half a century, to increase the emotional value of the arabesque and the sonority of tone, to create an increasingly acute feeling of pictorial space, could not fail to lead to the cut and glued papers to which his book *Jazz* introduced us in 1947. There is indeed little difference between his pencil drawings and the designs he made with scissors; indeed he said himself 'scissors can achieve more sensitivity than the pencil'. As he preferred to apply colour on his canvases flat, he had prepared himself for a long time to substitute paper for paint. Moreover, by cutting out sheets of coloured paper with scissors he could simultaneously associate line with colour and contour with surface. This was the most unexpected, although quite predictable, consequence of the new experiment for Matisse's art: in resorting to new tools and consequently new principles, in submitting to a craftsman's discipline, he was forced to give to form the same opportunity he had previously given to colour. This is why, completing the Cubist experiment, Matisse was able to make *papiers collés* an autonomous medium, an idiom as authentic, as alive as the weaving, enamel and stained glass of the past, Thanks to him, *papier collé* has become a completely convincing and irreplaceable form of art, and it may stand as the modern equivalent of medieval illumination. What was originally an innovation of only secondary importance has become an incontestable, autonomous art form, an art in itself. The history of *papiers collés* has begun again.

**PARIS** (School of). 'L'École de Paris' was the name given to a group formed after the First World War by a number of foreign painters, brought to Paris by similar needs and

MATISSE. NEGRO BOXER. *Cutout*. 1947

MODIGLIANI. PORTRAIT OF KISLING.

united by similar affinities. Since then the name has acquired a looser meaning. Originally, the School of Paris consisted of Modigliani, Pascin, Chagall, Kisling, Soutine (q.v.): an Italian, a Bulgarian, a Russian, a Pole and a Lithuanian. To these can be added the names of Leopold Gottlieb, Eugene Zak, Krémegne, three Poles; Mintchine, a Ukrainian; Max Band, a Lithuanian. All these painters were of foreign birth, and however diverse their ideas, temperaments, ways of life, they were brought together by common bonds of age and race. They belonged to the same generation, all having been born between 1884 and 1900, and they were all Jews. These uprooted ones liked France and drew from French sensibility, thought, and art the elements they needed to bring their gifts to fulfilment. But as painters they did not succeed in making themselves French. Contemporary with the Cubists, they did not espouse their theories nor follow their example. They always remained lyricists, romantics, expressionists and passionate individualists. Looking out upon the world through tormented souls, they rendered it with a

PASCIN. GINETTE AND MIREILLE. 1929.
*Petit Palais, Paris*

subtle and disenchanted grace like Modigliani, or, in a burst of desperation, like Soutine. Whatever their individual style, all shared the same disquiet, the same moral suffering under different forms. These Expressionists were very different from the French, German, Scandinavian or Flemish Expressionists. It is possible, therefore, to speak of a school, but to speak of a School of Paris is less accurate. Besides, these three words have acquired an increasingly wide meaning.

For many the 'School of Paris' tends to include all the immigrant painters who have settled in the shadow of the Eiffel Tower since the beginning of the century: Picasso, Juan Gris, Van Dongen and Foujita as much as Chagall, Kisling and Pascin. For several years opinion outside France has tended to identify the School of Paris with all the innovating activity of modern painters who work in Paris, the artistic movement that develops and feeds on all the contributions and personalities attracted by the universal prestige of French painting.

In short, for most people today the School of Paris is synonymous with the vanguard of contemporary painting.

**PASCIN** Pseudonym of Julius Pincas (1885–1930), a painter born in Vidin in Bulgaria; died in Paris. The son of a Spanish-Jewish father and a half-Serbian, half-Italian mother, Pascin did his early work in Vienna, Berlin, and Munich, where he collaborated while still very young on the satirical paper *Simplicissimus*. He came to Paris for the first time in 1905. Adopted very soon by America, he became the perfect example of 'internationalism', as Pierre MacOrlan has written. Having hobnobbed in all cafés of the old and new worlds with painters of every school, he was fond of camping in Paris, in the midst of the greatest disorder, among dusty sofas on which he made his models sit or lie, suggesting to them the least chaste poses. Although success came to him, he was found hanged in his studio on June 20th, 1930, the opening day of his exhibition at the Georges Petit Gallery. Like Toulouse-Lautrec, Pascin asserts himself above all as a great draughtsman even in his paintings, most of which were done after 1920. Colour often enhances only slightly, with exquisite restraint and delicacy, meanings that have already been brought out by the drawing. The life of the various planes is suggested with an authority and a charm that recall the great masters of the eighteenth century, whom he particularly liked. A supernatural atmosphere bathes his prostitutes, with their short legs and vague eyes. Alone or in pairs, they look like prostrate or passive little girls killing time. Sometimes there is a sort of mystical note in this acute and tender eroticism, occasionally mixed with Biblical reminiscences (*The Prodigal Son, Salome, The Judgment of Solomon*). From this voluptuous art emanates a kind of irremediable despair.

Pascin drew everywhere, and with passion. A line, at once fine and heavy, often impressed through sheets of carbon paper, nervously accentuates rhythms and contours. Modelling is achieved by shading light greys with a finger as voluptuous as Renoir's. The heightenings in water-colour are hardly felt. Illustrations of books and sketches brought back from Tunisia and Florida reveal Pascin, whose portraits have such subtlety, as one of the best witnesses of life between the two wars.

## PEINTURE MÉTAPHYSIQUE

(Metaphysical Painting). It is Giorgio de Chirico who must be credited with the invention of Metaphysical Painting. It was born in Paris between 1910 and 1915 and was, above all, a reaction against the Futurist dynamism. It revived a longing for antiquity, exalted the dream, discovered the mystery of apparitions. 'Around me', Giorgio de Chirico wrote, 'the international gang of "modern" painters was making a foolish commotion in the midst of worn-out formulae and sterile systems. I alone, in my dismal studio in Montparnasse, was beginning to glimpse the first traces of an art more complete, more profound, more intricate and more *metaphysical*.' During his stay in Munich, Chirico had read Nietzsche, Schopenhauer, Weininger. Otto Weininger had said 'the arc of a circle, as an ornament, can be beautiful; it is capable of completion: it still leaves room for imagination'. In Turin, before the eighteenth-century porticoes and arcades, Chirico must have thought of Weininger. And Schopenhauer had urged his countrymen not to put statues of their famous men on columns or high pedestals, but instead on low stands, 'as it is done in Italy, where marble men seem to be on the level of the passers-by and to walk among them'. Metaphysical painting would be lacking an essential element of its aesthetic doctrine if the 'mannequins' that populated Chirico's canvases were not there. The idea of 'mannequins' was suggested to him by a poem of his brother Alberto, a painter, poet and musician known as Alberto Savinio. The objectives of Metaphysical Painting could not be better described than in this sentence by Chirico himself:

'We who know the signs of the metaphysical alphabet know what joys and sorrows are present in a portico, on a street corner, within the walls of a room, or inside a box'. To Cubism Chirico owed 'at least the suggestion of chromatic composition, which became freer, more rhythmical, more dancing about 1913' (Giorgio Castelfranco, in *Pittura Moderna*).

Although Metaphysical Painting was born in Paris, it was in Italy, at Ferrara, during the First World War, that it became not a movement, like Futurism, but a 'school', which could have adopted the mannequin as an emblem. Chirico and Savinio had been called up and assigned to the Ferrara depot. Chirico's *Metaphysical Interiors*, which were painted in this city, were suggested to him by certain shops in the ghetto, 'in which one could see cakes and biscuits of extremely

CHIRICO. ENIGMA OF AN AUTUMN EVENING. 1910.

metaphysical and odd shapes' (*vide* Chirico). The first to undergo Chirico's influence was the painter Carlo Carrà, who was also an infantry soldier and a former Futurist. With less fantasy, Carrà painted the same objects as Chirico: mannequins, copper fishes, biscuits; he placed them in a three-dimensional space, transporting them from the oleograph that inspired Chirico to the ideal climate of Giotto, for both form and colour. With Carrà objects are no longer metaphysical signs, as in the works of Chirico. For him the painter's imagination must express itself 'through lines and colours', through the relation 'it discovers between light and shadow, the full and the void'. In short, Carrà employed the language of a painter not of a poet, as Chirico did. His paintings exercise a less fascinating but more profound magic than Chirico's, which were to influence the Surrealists (*vide* Surrealism) so strongly. Alberto Savinio, the theoretician of Metaphysical Painting, maintained that it was 'total representation of spiritual necessities within plastic limits – power to express the spectral side of things – irony'. Surprisingly enough, it was Carlo Carrà who fulfilled the third condition, irony, perhaps unconsciously, by clothing the pensive mannequins of Chirico in tunics with folds and putting tennis rackets and balls in their hands (*vide* Carrà). 'We metaphysical painters have sanctified reality', contended Chirico. For us the painter who seems to have actually sanctified reality is Giorgio Morandi: 'closing the triangle of Metaphysical Painting', he brought it to its purest expression. With three tones and a few very simple lines, Giorgio Morandi creates mystery, as Chirico himself admitted when he wrote in *Valori Plastici*, the magazine of Metaphysical art published by Mario Broglio, 'He sees with the eyes of a man who believes; and the inner framework

CHIRICO. ENIGMA OF THE TIME. 1811.          *Mattioli Collection, Milan*

of things that are dead for us, because motionless, appears to him under its most comforting aspect, under its *eternal aspect*' (*vide* Morandi). Metaphysical Painting did not survive the First World War, which confronted artists with new problems, but it has proved to be one of the key periods of twentieth-century painting.

Its collapse may be said to be due to overelaboration of design and obscurity of intention. Lines and perspectives multiply in all directions, weird figures stripped of life and sexuality are no more than mannequins. The movement played itself out and was attacked by its own creator, Chirico, who from 1930 onwards has denied his former pictures and has painted in an orthodox style which bears no relation to his earlier experiments; Morandi now prefers the world of Nature.

**PERMEKE** Constant (1886–1951). Belgian painter; born in Antwerp; died at Jabbeke, near Bruges. Permeke attended courses at the Academies of Bruges and Ghent before settling in Laethem-Saint-Martin (*), the cradle of Flemish Expressionism, in 1909. He belonged to the second Laethem group with Servaes, van den Berghe and the Smet brothers. Severely wounded at Antwerp in 1914, he was evacuated to England. He returned to Belgium after the hostilities. He worked successively in Antwerp, Ostend and finally at Jabbeke, where he spent the last twenty-five years of his life. At first influenced by Impressionism (*Winter in Flanders*, 1912), his work drifted toward the baroque as early as 1913, the baroque peculiar to a generation of Belgian artists, among whom Permeke was the central figure. His English landscapes, seascapes of Ostend, harbour scenes, fishermen's homes, studies of peasants, views of Flanders, nudes, all bear the stamp of his plebeian temperament, rough, jovial and powerful. No one has represented Flemish Expressionism better than Permeke: by his physical health, his muscularity, his dynamism, as well as by his elemental, monumental vision of Nature and man. There is nothing artificial, studied or cerebral in canvases such as *The Caravan*, *The Harvester*, *Green Seascape* and many others, in which the artist placed rough, full forms, titanic figures, encircling them with a thick stroke, colouring them on a very sober scale of heavy, dark tones. Indifferent to light, he wanted to exalt the human and, in the human, the vigour of muscles, the vitality of the people, everyday toil, all that man receives from the soil: the strength of instinct, generosity of the heart, humble and patient devotion. And this with the resources of the earth, the colours of earth. Passionately devoted to the plastic, he was quite naturally led to sculpture, beginning in 1936. But his modelling is no more than the solid, massive, summary forms contained in his canvases transposed into clay. Permeke was the faithful interpreter of his race, his native country, in a period of artistic renewal. He was a Flemish painter with absolute sincerity. He was an Expressionist painter without preciosity, without mannerism, with great naturalness. This is why his proletarian giants, his colossal effigies, his huge constructions, achieve a virile, wholehearted grandeur. One therefore pardons him his total lack of finesse, elegance, charm. He was a proud workman of painting, one of the very few Expressionists to have spared us a display of their sufferings or their despair.

**PEYRONNET** Dominique (1872–1943). French painter; born in Talence, a suburb of Bordeaux; died in Paris. Peyronnet, a printer, came to painting rather late and brought to it his craftsman's conscience, his love of precision, of work well done, of a well-learned trade. He was almost fifty when he began to paint, with the patient honesty he had acquired in printing coloured pictures. He judged his achievements with as calm a certainty as when he made an exact adjustment on his machine. He did not fear to tackle the greatest subjects in Nature; the sea was his favourite theme, and he did not hesitate to think that no one could represent certain subjects better than he. It is true that this pride was genuinely naïve; it is also true that he painted with a concern for never falsifying reality, and thus he succeeded in extracting from familiar subjects a secret life that certainly does not have the grandeur present in the works of Rousseau, but is not devoid of mystery. His art is somewhat frigid, but never dry. In his very special way of isolating every object, making it a whole in itself, he recalls the Gothic Primitives. In his faithfulness to his subject there is a fervour, put to the service of Nature, that exalts reality and doubles

PERMEKE. THE FIANCÉS. 1923.
*Musée des Beaux-Arts, Brussels*

its intensity. Thus he has created an immobile world in limpid air, whose poetry is outside all the present problems of painting.

**PICABIA** Francis (1879–1953). Of Spanish origin, Picabia was born and died in Paris. He spent his life changing residences, friendships, ideas and styles, fighting for a cause and then against it, in favour of a new one that he abandoned in turn. An anarchist by atavism and temperament, a prolix and subversive artist, making fun of everything and of himself, fond of disparaging ideas, institutions, men, sceptical to the point of dogmatism, a lover of freedom to the point of libertarianism, much less concerned with making a career than with creating a scandal, Picabia nevertheless left his stamp on his time as an artist and, even more, as an individual. A pupil of the École Nationale des Beaux-Arts, he painted definitely Impressionist pictures until 1908, and then compositions influenced by Cubism. In 1911 he joined the *Section d'Or (\*)* group but left it the following year, to come over to an Orphic concept of painting. The same year he painted one of his best canvases, *Procession in Seville*. In 1915 he came into contact with Marcel Duchamp in New York and, in co-operation with him, laid the foundations of the Dadaist rebellion. Picabia was in Barcelona in 1916 and founded there the magazine *391*, which sparkled with his verve and sharp irony. The magazine appeared until 1924, irregularly to be sure, in Barcelona, then in New York, Zurich and, finally, Paris. In 1918 he joined forces with the Dada group *(\*)* in Switzerland. Returning to Montparnasse, he served as a link between the German Dadaists in Zurich and the French Dadaists.

'It was from this moment', noted Ribemont-Dessaignes, who became the historian of Dadaism, 'that Dada was really born.' Picabia took part in the sensational events that scandalized the Parisian public and composed his famous 'ironical machines', which stood as a manifesto and a challenge. The baroque, the droll, the preposterous were the means he used to destroy traditional dogmas, laws and accepted formulae, the established order. He signed a tract of February 5th, 1920, as 'The Joker', and baptized one of his pamphlets *The Unique Eunuch*. In 1921 he quarrelled with his friends, to follow the poet André Breton when the latter founded the Surrealist movement. For the *Ballets Suédois (\*)* he created the settings and costumes of the ballet *Relâche* (1924), and exhibited with Miró, André Masson, Max Ernst, and Dali. Suddenly, he turned his back on Surrealism and reverted to representational art. Finally, in 1945, he took up abstract painting again, which he had been one of the very first to practise, as early as 1909 (*Rubber*). These erratic shifts reveal a man curious but unstable, enthusiastic but ineffective. Pursuing his researches in all directions, he indulged in the most gratuitous experiments, contradictions and provocations, cultivating, not without humour, a rhetoric of the absurd, more as a poet than as a painter. However, his gifts

PEYRONNET. MEDITERRANEAN. 1942.          *Private Collection, Paris*

as a painter are incontestable, as are his high standards. Did he not destroy a portion of his work more than once? But his love for jest and his desire to astonish never left him even with age. In 1949, under the name of 'sur-irrealist' paintings, he exhibited purely abstract compositions which he entitled: *You'll Never Sell It, Upside-Down, I Don't Want to Paint Any More, What Do You Call That?* He was then seventy, but still as aggressive and spontaneous as a student. This is why he was surrounded by young men full of admiration for his disinterestedness, and his independence. But if he exercised an influence, it was, above all, as an animator and an inspirer. Besides, he never wanted any other title to fame.

PICABIA. OPTOPHONE. *H. P. Roché Collection, Paris*

**PICASSO** Pablo (born 1881, in Malaga). Spanish painter. Although he has participated in all the adventures of French painting for half a century, Picasso has remained inalienably Spanish. The sumptuous, tragic and ponderous Spanish legacy he carries within himself, in his thought and his mood, and he

PICASSO. YOUNG MAN WITH PIPE.

squanders it without ever exhausting it. However, to find in his work, his vocabulary, his syntax and his themes solely this composite and sumptuous Spain, nourished on the myths and forms of Oriental civilizations, barbarian contributions, Greek and Gothic reminiscences, would be a vast oversimplification. In the formation of his genius it was the Spain of Góngora and Goya, of the baroque architect Gaudi, of Catalan anarchism and insurrectionism, a very special Spain, ardent, subversive, violent, passionate, that played the most important part. Be this as it may, no living foreign artist working in France has allowed himself to be less absorbed by the customs and spirit of France; no one has more asserted his loyalty to his origin. For everything is contradiction in Picasso, his life, his character, his work.

He was born of a Basque father, José Ruiz Blasco, who was a teacher of drawing, and a Majorcan mother of Genoese origin, María Picasso. At an age when most children are still playing with marbles, he had already painted pictures worthy of figuring in a museum. In 1900 he came to Paris. He admired the pictures of Van Gogh and the Montmartre scenes of

PICASSO. THE BANDERILLA DANCE.                    *Lithograph.*

in the Bateau-Lavoir (*), 13 rue Ravignan, in Montmartre, as early as 1904, and his studio became a meeting-place where artists and writers worked out the principles of a new aesthetic doctrine. The poets Apollinaire, Max Jacob, André Salmon, Pierre Reverdy, the painters André Derain, Van Dongen and Juan Gris frequented this place or even lived there. After 1907 Georges Braque, introduced to Picasso by Apollinaire, could also be met there. Fernande Olivier has left the following striking portrait of Picasso at this time: 'Short, dark, stocky, disturbed, disturbing, with dark, deep, piercing, strange, almost immobile eyes. Awkward movements, a woman's hands, badly dressed, unkempt. A thick lock of hair, black and shiny, gashed the intelligent forehead. Half Bohemian, half

Toulouse-Lautrec. The latter's influence is noticeable in the paintings he executed at the time, and also in those of the 'Blue Period' (1901–1904). Poor and sick people, outcasts of life, were the objects of his attention. These themes, dear to Spain – poverty, solitude, sadness – he took up, but in a spirit influenced by French art and with means refined by contact with Montmartre draughtsmen. He drew single or grouped figures with increasing precision, but he elongated or narrowed them to stress their tragic expression; he painted them almost in monochrome, in a blue tonality, the blue of mystery and night. Picasso was then twenty-three, but already his name was known far beyond the narrow circle of friends who surrounded him. He established himself

PICASSO. TUMBLERS. 1905

PICASSO. LA SAISIE. 1902–1904.
*Private Collection, Paris*

luxuriant vocabulary, and bold abstraction. And when, in 1907, in his dilapidated studio in the Bateau-Lavoir, he showed his disconcerted friends the *Demoiselles d'Avignon* (reproduced on page 64), a page of history had been turned. The composition of this famous canvas lacks unity, the colour is hard and dry, the figures gesticulate, have no relief. But the lines, the angles, the slope of the planes, announced a new direction in modern painting. The Cubist revolution was not far off. The *Demoiselles d'Avignon* is not only a picture, it is also an event, a date, a starting-point, as much as were in other times the *Mystic Lamb* of the Van Eycks, the *Battles* of Uccello, *Dante's Barque* of Delacroix.

Fauvism was already drawing its last breath. In it the century had sown its wild oats, but had pulled itself together rather quickly, and the artist, sobered, had begun thinking. Confined in his studio, he attentively observed the objects that surrounded him, the table, the decanter, the glass, the package of tobacco, the newspaper. He observed them with so penetrating an eye that they appeared unknown to him. He entered

workman in dress, he had long hair that swept the collar of his worn coat.'

With his 'Rose Period' (1905–1906) Picasso seemed to soften, even to mellow. Nudes, itinerant players, harlequins, circus scenes offered him the opportunity of lightening his technique, making his line more supple, accentuating distortions. His works recalled those of the Japanese painters of phantoms. They are characterized by a morbid feeling, something elusive and floating, a rather troubled charm, finally by almost flat forms, sparingly coloured and without firm foundations. But he was not long in reacting. Probably under the influence of Negro sculpture, he executed statues, drawings, pictures in which his plastic preoccupations stand out. How could he not be won over by the monstrous distortions of the African fetishes that were then being revealed to Europe? Distortions? Were they not rather invented forms, volumes charged with emotional power? Be this as it may, Picasso fell under the spell of these primitive works; he certainly admired their sensitivity, rawness,

PICASSO. MA JOLIE. 1913.
*Private Collection, Paris*

PICASSO. STUDY. 1925.

into them as the novelist enters into his characters. He settled into them with the aid of a sympathy that was neither love nor passion but total consent and total respect. Thereupon things revealed to him their form, their structure, their top, their inside, their underside. When he represented them with his new vision, Cubism (*) was born. Gauguin was deserted for Cézanne. The real was rediscovered and essentially, in the real, volume and space. A prey to his contradictions, Picasso saw in this transcendence of realism a means of resolving them. He countered the sensualism of the *Fauves* by an intellectualism that writers were undertaking to explain and encourage at the same

moment. As early as 1908 he assumed leadership of the movement with Braque. The question for them was to introduce the illusion of volume on a plane surface without resorting to modelling, chiaroscuro, linear perspective and other outmoded conventions. They succeeded in doing so through the breakdown of planes and representation of the object under several angles simultaneously. From then on they painted not what they saw but what they represented to themselves through analysis. In 1911 Cubism ceased to be analytic; it renounced contemplation of Nature and drifted toward an authoritarian conceptualism. At last tamed and dismantled, the object was subordinated to forms imagined *a priori*. While their companions went off in other directions, Picasso and Braque exploited their discoveries. Thanks to the new manner, between 1908 and 1915 Picasso executed works that revealed an unsuspected rigour of conception. He created objects freely, he accounted for reality, but by destroying it and substituting for it a subjective reality, autonomous, absolute. The picture became for him an object in itself. Indifferent to light, he concentrated all his faculties upon the transposed expression of forms, in order that the forms might suggest to the spectator images different from their counterparts in the world of appearances. But there came

PICASSO. DRAWING IN INDIA INK. 1923

a moment when Cubism lost through its own excesses the strength it had drawn from the excesses of Fauvism. It was a prisoner of still life, of a closed room. It had not opened the door upon life. Impersonality of handling, poverty of colour, bleak and dreary materials. On the other hand, it had restored to drawing and form a necessary and sometimes tyrannical predominance. As a result, painting had returned to linear purity, geometry, exactness of proportions, rigour of composition. However, Picasso soon saw the limitations of the doctrine he had been the first to set forth and illustrate. And he who had been its most ardent instigator became its least faithful practitioner. No sooner did he see that he was followed than he took another path. The painter of angles, cubes, geometrical architectures, applied himself to the study of the old masters. This was the period when he worked for the *Ballets Russes (\*)* and executed settings and costumes for *Parade* and *The Three-Cornered Hat.* He resumed his old themes, acrobats, harlequins, dancers. Then, influenced by Greco-Roman art, he begot a race of giants, of heavy women, drawn and modelled in an entirely classical way. Until 1923 his production was characterized by calm, balance and an exceptional health. One would not believe the same Picasso had practised the technique of the *papier collé (\*)* a few years before. Nevertheless, he who had gathered together on his canvases pieces of newspaper and boxes of matches and indulged in *trompe-l'œil* for love of realism, could not fail to be led to paint like Ingres in moments of relaxation. On the other hand, a man so torn by different, if not opposing, needs, so sensitive to the currents of his time, so given to every kind of daring, could not remain indifferent to the explorations of Surrealism *(\*)*. Besides, in this insurrectional movement there was a taste for challenge and a will for destruction that could not fail to stimulate his fundamental nihilism. But Surrealist art resorted to means so poor, so worn, so unplastic that Picasso neglected them deliberately. He retained from the experience only the ferment capable of renewing his inspiration. After a short Romantic period, during which he painted folk scenes and bull-fights in the spirit of Goya (1923), he tried to make explicit his

PICASSO. HARLEQUIN. 1915.
*Museum of Modern Art, New York*

dreams and impulses. While his countrymen Dali and Miró were obeying the metaphysical-literary directives of the Surrealist poet André Breton, Picasso let crop up in his pictures the madrepores and larvae that stir in the depths of the unconscious (1926–1935). Fantastic forms, without significance, swarmed under his brush. These forms are strongly schematized, feebly coloured, with very dense volumes, that stand out, absurd and comic, in a space without depth. Towards 1932 the straight lines disappeared in favour of long, flexible curves, the summary structures gave way to exuberant arabesque, colour took on a heavy and acid lustre. He painted the series of young girls at the seaside, whose physical rapture is transcribed by extraordinarily bold drawing.

In 1935 the latent expressionism of Picasso

reappeared, exasperated by the tragedy that was drenching his motherland with blood. The line twisted or swelled, the colour heightened, the emotion burst out and, at the climax of a pathetic crescendo, reached its paroxysm in *Guernica*. This large composition in black and white is certainly one of his masterpieces, if not his masterpiece. For while he expressed in it the horrors of war in apocalyptic images, for his purpose he called only upon form and contrasts of shadow and light. Instead of describing, as did Goya or Delacroix, for example, a certain military episode or scene of slaughter, Picasso succeeded, for the first time in the history of Western painting, in terrifying the spectator merely by a plastic transcription of an actual event and convicting him of guilt by combining, with shrewdness and passion, specifically pictorial values. The tragic and the burlesque, sarcasm

investigations ever farther, now casting anchor in the peaceful river of Humanism, now venturing in full sail among Romantic storms. However, since 1948, that is to say since he has settled on the Mediterranean coast, near the sea that has soothed and enchanted so many bold spirits, he has been rediscovering old legends and spells, fauns, centaurs, nymphs; he has been resuming all his old themes, portrait, landscape, still life, applying himself in particular to the representation of animals: the dove, the owl, the toad, the horse, the bull; taking in turn as models his wife, his children; painting, engraving, sculpting, turning pottery, all this with his usual impetuosity and an unusual love of life. And whatever his subjects, his motifs, he always metamorphoses them, gives them a life similar to his own, an ill-restrained violence, a desperate note, something wild, troubled, disquieting. He

PICASSO. DRAWING IN INDIA INK. 1936

is curious and unsatisfied, irritating and fascinating, generous and avaricious with his feelings, laden with fame and wealth, continuing nevertheless to work like a slave, the slave of his impatient genius, but also the master of his forces, of his faculties, prodigiously active, never at rest, knowing no weariness, always seeking in the world an ever-elusive joy and meeting only with anguish, doubt, fury. The age he seems to be is not his real age. He works, conceives, feels, hates and loves as at twenty. It is there-

and pity, imprecation and irony, the palpitation of life and the immobility of death, a tumult of thoughts and emotions spring from this agonizing picture with an intensity that is at the limit of human endurance. After this, Picasso explored courses he had already followed, carrying his

fore difficult to study his production without studying his life, so inextricably are the two mixed. All the facts, all the events in which he has been an actor or a witness are registered in his various works. He has nourished his art with his loves, his contempts, his torments, his whims,

PICASSO. STILL LIFE WITH ANTIQUE HEAD. 1925.    *Musée d'Art Moderne, Paris.*

revolts, his presumptions, not without complacency, not without trickery, with a sometimes embarrassing insistence. An heir of the Humanist tradition, an individualist by temperament, an anarchist by race, his actions and reactions are always unpredictable, sudden and brutal. An unbeliever, he believes only in himself. A revolutionary, he baffles his followers. Always the contradiction.

There is neither unity nor continuity nor stability in his work, as there is none in his life. Inconstant, multiple, fiery and irascible, amiable or insolent, sincere or affected, charming or uncivil, he can be one or another according to his mood or the moment, and yet remain unfailingly true to a single passion: freedom. He wants to be entirely free, free to remake the world to his liking, free to exercise his omnipotence – no rules, no conventions, no prejudice. From Naturalism to Expressionism, from Expressionism to Classicism, from Classicism to Romanticism, then to Realism and to Abstraction, to revert to Naturalism and resume his indefatigable quest, grace alternating with horror, elegance with the monstrous, he goes to and fro, he begins again, remaining an inveterate baroque in spite of his incarnations. When he wants to

be classical, he startles less and does not move. He is too individualistic, too anxious to surprise and hurt, too hostile to all restraint and to any serene vision of the universe, to put up with limitations, discipline, humilities. Freedom alone suits him, absolute freedom, even if it has to take on the forms of the bizarre, of chaos, of the hideous. Picasso is a baroque by atavism, by principle, by inclination. And as one gets used to everything, to the exceptional, to extravagance, to strangeness, even to horror, he is naturally led to outdo his previous violence; hence his immoderateness and his recklessness, but hence also the percussive force of each of his creations, his violent drawing, aggressive forms, hurried and tense composition. In this he has no rival. It is by virtue of this that he dazzles, upsets, intoxicates and convinces. Electricity runs along his line; there is dynamite in the hollow of his objects.

Prodigious as his vitality may be, Picasso does not express happiness, hope, or joy of living, but mostly an incurable disquiet, the drama of man at grips with Nature, of man in revolt against his destiny – his own drama. When he is playful or facetious, when he wants to please or to charm, it is rare that the mask succeeds in concealing entirely the wan face of Death. His laugh is more like a sneer, his exultations sound like blasphemies, his banter like sarcasm. Wisdom, renunciation, serenity, naturalness, he has none of these in him. It is with his resources alone that he wants to substitute for the world of permanence his personal and therefore fragile, ever-

PICASSO. CANDLESTICK, JUG AND ENAMEL SAUCEPAN. 1945.
*Musée d'Art Moderne, Paris*

threatened world. Picasso is an individual who strives to extend the borders of his empire in order to go farther, ever farther; who tends to absorb everything, no doubt because he needs to be absorbed himself. Is there today an artist more profoundly an innovator, more determined to reject the fictions and forms of the past? Who has attacked more intrepidly the courters of tradition, all those who live punily on formulas, recipes, convention? The weapon he brandishes is the very weapon forged by the adversary: the outdated Humanism that has to be destroyed, the Humanism that, with Picasso, has borrowed its extreme form from obsession or frenzy. Picasso is, in fact, the last representative, the most passionate, the most terrible, of the Greco-Latin tradition. He is the prodigal descendant of Goya, Velazquez, Michelangelo, Uccello. One will, then, perhaps understand why this paradox should have resounded with such

painful echoes in a body of work with which no other can be compared.

This body of work is immense. It has to be accepted as it is, with its failings, its lightning-flashes, its imperfections, its grandeurs. In it one can count many sketches, experiments without conclusion, but also ardent confessions, incontestable successes. It is not a question of masterpieces; Picasso has never been concerned with producing eternal masterpieces. As a result, he has always appeared indifferent to the materials he employed. He draws and paints on anything: a paper tablecloth, cardboard, wood or plywood, fibrocement. He does not concern himself with the preparation of his canvases, the quality of his colours, the improvement of his tools. As a sculptor he uses earth, wood, cloth, broken pieces of hardware, which he often covers with wide strokes of the brush. But the waste of his abundant production can be forgotten for his having been capable of creating works like *Ma Jolie, Young Girl with Mandolin, Woman in Green*, among the high spots of Cubism; like *Guernica, War* and *Peace*, in which Expressionism attains an unbelievable perfection; *Still Life with Antique Head* and *Still Life with Enamel Saucepan*, in the Museum of Modern Art in Paris. Add to these the large paintings in the Antibes Museum, in which Picasso has not only displayed his inventive power but also, to an unusual degree, work, patience, reflection. Never has technique been for him an end in itself, despite his fabulous dexterity. But never has such dexterity stopped him from exploring new paths, nor has his boldness ever given way to virtuosity. He does not scorn effect, but to obtain it he commits himself entirely, with his sincerity and his guile, his resolution and his uncertainty, his confessions and his malice, his discoveries and his artifices – all of him.

His finds have often been taken up by the new generation. It is certainly easy to discern here and there in contemporary painting a sign, a form, a technique that bears his stamp. But these are superficial borrowings, fragmented and unassimilated imitations. For art, like Picasso's individuality, is autonomous, incommunicable, intransmissible, a closed world. 'I do not search, I find', he once announced. His person cannot serve as a model, his life as an example, or his work as a lesson. Picassos are not born in every century. And who does not feel that without him our century would have been flatter, duller, less worth living in?

We must be grateful for his boldness and inventiveness, and the shocks he administers to sluggish ways of thinking and seeing. He is the most original creative genius of our time.

PICASSO. PENCIL DRAWING, ANTIBES. 1946

PICASSO. SPHINX. 1953.    *Private Collection*

**PIPER** John (born in 1903 at Epsom). Studied at the Royal College of Art and the Slade School. Attached to the Army as a painter during the Second World War, he executed a series of paintings of streets, houses and monuments demolished by bombardments, notably the House of Commons and the City of Bath. Piper came to painting rather late, and began as a landscapist, painting the picturesque southern coast of England. About 1933, as a result of his contacts with certain painters of the École de Paris – Braque, Helion and Arp, among others – his style changed, and he turned to two-dimensional abstract compositions based most frequently upon vertical arrangements of flat colour. His scale of values was again revised, however, and in the late 'thirties he began working in a more realistic vein, which nevertheless retained from his earlier discipline an austere sense of composition and was often superimposed upon an essentially abstract-expressionist colour scheme. Now began that long series of dramatic, even melodramatic, portraits of castles and great houses under lowering skies that is most readily associated with his name. In these architectural themes Piper's sense of topography and history – perhaps too his long interest in

PIPER. ST. MARY LE PORT,
*Tate Gallery, London.*

medieval stained glass – have found their fullest scope: his crumbling patinated façades, painted in rich, warm tones with all the variety of texture that oil paint is capable of, are imbued with true poetic feeling. Increasingly with the years, Piper has felt himself drawn to the traditions of English eighteenth and early nineteenth century Romantic landscape painting; he has returned to the self-same scenes beloved of Richard Wilson and James Ward – to the frowning crags and fearful sublimities of the Welsh mountains and Gordale Scar – and has depicted them with an ever-greater 'rough and scumble' in his handling. That one who sees landscape so greatly in terms of the theatre backcloth, should have found himself directly engaged in décor is scarcely surprising. Piper has become well known for his work as a theatre and ballet designer; in particular his name is associated with the operas of Benjamin Britten, for which he has produced settings of striking and affecting power. He has also undertaken a good deal of graphic work, and has written with sympathy about the visual arts.

**PISSARRO** Camille (1830–1903). Born at Saint-Thomas in the West Indies (then a Danish possession); died in Paris. 'Of all painters,' said Cézanne, 'Pissarro was nearest to Nature.' His entire life was devoted to observing the changing effects of Nature, which he succeeded in capturing in innumerable oil paintings, water-colours, drawings and engravings. He never tired of studying the same village church, the same fields in different seasons, a market place, the Paris boulevards, and he infused a rare poetic quality into these subjects. He had a long struggle with his parents – a French father and a Creole mother – before obtaining their consent to leave the West Indies to study art in Paris, and had reached the age of twenty-five when finally he arrived in France. His first enthusiasm was for Corot, and he started work under his supervision – with permission to style himself 'pupil of Corot'. But his aged tutor disapproved when in 1865 Pissarro joined up with Monet, Renoir and other young artists grouped around Manet, though Daubigny and Courbet (whose influence is evident in some of Pissarro's early work) accepted the newcomers with goodwill. In 1870 Monet and Pissarro fled to London to escape the Prussian occupation, and there found Daubigny, who gave them valuable help and advice and introduced them to the young French art dealer Durand-Ruel *(\*)*, whose name has since become firmly linked with that of the Impressionists. Durand-Ruel bought Pissarro's work first in London and then on a larger scale in Paris; little by little he became the regular dealer of Monet, Pissarro and all their friends, sharing their setbacks as well as their painfully slow climb to fame. In England Pissarro studied Turner and Constable. On his return to France he found his house looted and his canvases (nearly a thousand) destroyed. But his joy at being back in France lent him courage, and he settled in Pontoise, where Cézanne came to work with him (1872–1874) and profit from his advice. Pissarro made regular trips to Paris, thus keeping in touch with his friends. With them, in 1874, he countered the official Salon's systematic refusal to hang their work by organizing the first independent picture exhibition. A hostile critic writing about this exhibition first applied the word 'Impressionist' to their work. The following eight exhibitions organized by the Impressionists between 1874 and 1886 – which met mainly with ridicule and insults – were due in large part to Pissarro's indefatigable initiative and his gift for reconciling adverse factions. He was the only member of the group to exhibit at each show, and he was alone in offering his friendship to the younger

PISSARRO. MARKET GARDENS WITH TREES IN BLOSSOM, 1877. *Louvre, Paris*

painters of promise. In 1880 he interested himself in Gauguin and introduced him to the group. Later he joined up with Seurat and Signac in their efforts to reconcile art with science, and he insisted on their being included in the final exhibition of 1886.

Pissarro, senior by two years to Manet and by ten to Monet, was the eldest of the group. Without exception, all the painters and writers included in his circle felt a profound esteem for this kind and gentle man, who united an innate goodness with an indomitable fighting spirit. A convinced atheist, Pissarro was also a socialist tinged with anarchist ideas, and he considered the artistic struggle as inseparable from the question of the artist's role in modern society. But however radical his views, they were free from hate and imbued with a disinterested integrity which commanded general respect even among those less socially conscious than he. Everyone knew of his personal difficulties, his continual fight to provide for his family of six children, and they could not but admire the composure and complete lack of bitterness with which he discussed the essential artistic or political problems of his day. Pissarro never ceased to

advocate humility before Nature, though he refrained from imposing his ideas on others. The advice he gave to Cézanne and Gauguin must have been similar to that given to his children, to whom he wrote in one of his admirable letters: 'Beware of trusting to my judgment! I am so anxious to see you succeed that I don't hide my opinions from you; but only accept what corresponds to your own feeling and way of understanding. What I most fear is that you should resemble me too much. So go ahead, and work!' To this respect for the individual he added a rare gift for pedagogy. 'He was so wonderful a teacher', said Mary Cassatt, 'that he could have taught a stone to draw correctly.'

Pissarro's artistic development can be divided into various phases. His early work shows the influence of Corot and Courbet: a poetic conception of Nature is expressed in hardy strokes of the palette knife and his colours are often as dramatically sombre as those in Cézanne's first paintings. Little by little his colours grew lighter and he stressed the solidity of masses in subtle but opaque shades, greys often dominating. 'As early as 1865', Cézanne tells us, 'he eliminated black, bistre, sienna browns and ochres.' It was

PISSARRO. AVENUE DE L'OPÉRA.  *Belgrade Museum*

Seurat's rigid theories with his own poetic temperament. This effort was doomed to failure; in 1890 Pissarro began to realize, as he put it, 'the impossibility of following my sensations, and consequently of expressing life and movement and rendering Nature's marvellous but fugitive effects, of giving individuality to my drawing'; so he abandoned the Pointillist technique 'to retrieve with difficulty and by

just before the 1870 war that he took the decisive step towards light colouring and the analysis of shadow, and the study of English landscape painters during his exile in London encouraged him to pursue this course and confirmed his conclusions. The outcome was the series of intensely vital, lyrical canvases painted between 1870 and 1880 – his truly 'Impressionist' period of open-air painting and discoveries in the use of colour. Light itself became a 'subject' – the principal element in his picture. The artist was attracted by golden and silver effects, vast stretches of green, delicate foliage, trees in flower, corn-fields, streams and mottled skies. He studied all these first around Pontoise, then at Osny and Éragny-sur-Epte near Gisors, where he settled in 1885. With these lighter colours he worked in small commalike brush strokes, which enabled him to depict the brilliance of light without breaking up the forms on which it shone. By 1884 Pissarro began to feel dissatisfaction with this technique, finding it too crude, and it is not surprising to find him attracted in the following years to Divisionism (*see* Neo-Impressionism) in an attempt to reconcile

hard work what I had lost, without losing whatever I may have found'. Pissarro spent the last years of his life in the search for a new liberty of expression. His efforts were astonishingly fruitful and in his views of Rouen and Paris he succeeded in uniting exquisite sensibility with a superbly vigorous technique. Profiting from his Impressionist and Divisionist experiments, his art became powerful yet subtle, firm of line and rich in colouring. Though mainly a landscape artist, Pissarro also painted portraits, still lifes and nudes. 'If we examine Pissarro's art as a whole,' wrote Gauguin in 1902, 'in spite of a certain unevenness, we find not only a tremendous artistic will which is never belied, but also an essentially intuitive, pure-bred art. He took from everyone, you say? Why not? Everyone, though denying him, took from him too.

**POINTILLISM**  This term, or 'Divisionism', refers to the technique perfected and carried to its extreme consequences by the advocates of Neo-Impressionism *(\*)*. It consisted in juxtaposing small strokes of pure colours on the canvas.

**PONT-AVEN** (School of). Pont-Aven is a picturesque little town in Brittany, frequented since 1873 by artists drawn there both by the archaic charm of the country and the celebrated inn of Marie-Jeanne Gloanec. It won fame through Gauguin's visits and gave its name to the school of painting created around him, the principles of which were revealed to him in Brittany. 'When my clogs strike this granite ground', he used to say, 'I hear the low, dull, powerful sound that I seek in painting.' However, his first lonely stay, from June to November 1886, was merely an introduction without immediate importance. In Concarneau, in August, his friend Schuffenecker met a young painter and poet of eighteen, Émile Bernard (1868–1941), precocious, open, cultivated, full of mystical ardour and passion for the country that he explored on foot in every direction. Schuffenecker introduced him to Gauguin; but the latter's rather cold reception cut the meeting short. Gauguin's second stay in Pont-Aven, from June to October 1888, was to be decisive. He took lodgings at the Gloanec boarding-house, where he was immediately recognized as leader. Around him, in the small room of the inn, an increasing number of disciples drawn by his personality and new ideas grouped themselves: the faithful Charles Laval (1862–1894), his companion on the trip to Martinique the preceding year; Henri de Chamaillard, Moret, Maufra, Jourdan, Grouchi-Taylor, Sylvain Depeige; the Swiss Cuno Amiet; the American O'Connor; and others. The big room was reserved for students at the Beaux-Arts and orthodox painters, among whom a certain G. de Maupassant, supposed to be the father of the writer, was the most hostile to the innovators. Early in August, Émile Bernard, this time cordially greeted by Gauguin, with whom he was to have fruitful exchanges and whose technical evolution he advanced, arrived from Saint-Brieuc with his sister Madeleine, who was to become the 'mystic muse' of Pont-Aven. Under the stimulus of Bernard, Gauguin executed *The Vision after the Sermon*, which marked the beginning of his new manner, characterized by Cloisonnism and Synthesism. Cloisonnism (inspired by cloisonné enamels) consisted in surrounding vast plain surfaces of pure colour, juxtaposed without transition, with sinuous, heavy arabesques. The new use of pure colour – to which, he said, everything had to be sacrified – without the nuances of light peculiar to the Impressionists, led to glorification of the decorative plane surface, the lifting of the horizon, and the suppression of naturalistic perspective and space. Thus it is that in this picture the meadow, daringly rendered in red, invades the entire sky, while the figures stand out flatly like Chinese silhouettes. Synthesism was the direct consequence of this process of simplification and resulted from the need to work no longer from the subject but from memory, no longer 'before the thing' but 'entertaining it in the imagination', which eliminates details and retains only the essential form, the 'idea'. Synthesism and Cloisonnism constituted the aesthetic framework of Symbolism *(\*)* in painting. Émile Bernard, with great acrimony, was to claim credit later for inspiring the movement; but this periodically revived quarrel is absurd, for if Bernard seems indeed to have been the precursor for certain technical processes he evolved together with Anquetin as early as 1887 – processes which were, anyway, in the air (because of the influence of Japanese prints, stained glass, folk images, primitive art) – Gauguin's genius alone was able to draw masterpieces and an original vision from these techniques. At the end of September Sérusier, then a pupil at the Académie Julian, staying at Pont-Aven among traditional painters, was introduced to Gauguin through Bernard and painted under his direction the famous landscape of the *Bois d'Amour*, a small board covered with 'pure colours assembled in a certain order', which he brought back triumphantly to his comrades, the future Nabis *(\*)*, as the 'talisman' of the new doctrine. This was for them a decisive revelation, reinforced by the first public show of the Pont-Aven Group, held early in 1889 at the Café Volpini in the Place du Champ-de-Mars in Paris on the grounds of the Universal Exhibition: it bore the name 'Exhibition of Painting of the Impressionist and Synthesist Group' and comprised, together with seventeen canvases by Gauguin and twenty-three by Bernard, works of Laval, Anquetin, Schuffenecker, Fauché,

G. Daniel, L. Roy, all framed with white laths that made a sensation.

In the meantime, Gauguin stayed two months with Van Gogh at Arles, a visit that was tragically interrupted by the drama of the amputated ear. In April 1889 he returned to Pont-Aven, but soon exasperated by the throng of painters and tourists, he moved to a neighbouring and quieter hamlet, Le Pouldu, in October, and took lodgings in an isolated seaside inn kept by Mlle Marie Henry, called 'Marie the Doll'. He stayed there from October 2nd, 1889, to November 7th, 1890, with the Dutchman Meyer de Haan, his admirer, patron and most gifted disciple. Charles Filiger, another person of unusual temperament, joined him in July 1890. Laval, Sérusier and Seguin spent part of the summer there in shifts. Moret, Maufra, de Chamaillard and Jourdan, who remained faithful to Pont-Aven, came often as neighbours. The small inn was entirely decorated, from window-panes to ceiling, with paintings, frescoes, drawings, ceramics, lithographs and sculptures and adorned with inscriptions like *Honni soit qui mal y pense* or *I Like Onions Fried in Oil*. The front door was ornamented with the famous canvas jokingly imitated from Courbet, *Bonjour, M. Gauguin*, and on the communal tobacco jar one could read the rallying cry *Long Live Synthesis!* It was in this 'retreat' of Le Pouldu that Gauguin, now master of his style, had his longest, happiest and most fruitful stay in Brittany, surrounded by his most fervent disciples; and had he not, as can be seen, taken with some irony his role as leader of the group, it would no doubt be more correct to speak of a School of Le Pouldu rather than of Pont-Aven.

While 'the School of Pont-Aven', according to Maurice Denis, 'stirred up as many ideas as that of Fontainebleau', and renewed the aesthetic current of the end of the century, the gathering of the artists who formed it was due only to the prestige of Gauguin and hardly survived his departure. Only Charles Filiger and Armand Sequin, whom Gauguin was to encounter again during his final stay at Pont-Aven in April to December 1894, between his two trips to Tahiti, remained obstinately faithful to the Breton land and to the principles of Pont-Aven and Le Pouldu.

**PORTINARI** Cándido. Brazilian painter; born in 1903 at Brodowski in Brazil. It may seem surprising that the climate, the vitality, the exuberant landscapes of Brazil should not have induced a more widespread urge to paint. One artist, however, has recaptured the intensity of the twilights of Rio de Janeiro: Portinari.

After having been an attentive pupil at the School of Fine Arts in the Brazilian capital, he came to Paris. It is clear that he felt out of his element there, and Pascin alone seems to have exercised a lasting influence upon his vision. On his return to Brazil, Portinari drifted away very soon from everything he had learned at school and came under the spell of the atmosphere of the Rio suburbs, a city of contrasts, where light struggles day and night with shadow, where the sky threatens to conquer the earth at any moment. He forgot Paris and its mirages to fall in love with the tones that make mountain slopes iridescent and with the clouds that crowd in on the bay of Rio. Turning his back on the excessive lyricism of Brazilian cities, he caught the fascinating mystery of the existence of those who were called by Franklin D. Roosevelt the forgotten men. They taught him, with music on their lips, what is most authentic and intense in the atmosphere of the tropics. Thus, capable of resisting the excesses of the Brazilian climate, Portinari assented to being a painter of semitones, of subtle colours; and he makes us discover the magic of twilight, reminding us that this hour preceding sleep and dreams is the one which men of all times and all places have both dreaded and preferred. And this paradox can furnish us an explanation of the strong spell cast by Portinari's art. Allied both with Europe, in its most artificial aspects, and with prehistory, this art has victoriously passed the test of the American Continent, and the painter has successfully replied to the requests of the architects who urged him to paint frescoes on the scale of ambitious and oversized buildings. One does not know what to admire most in his works, his composure or his virtuosity, or the fact that he was able to meet the challenge and impose his personality when the conditions he faced might have stifled him.

**POUGNY** Jean. French painter; born in 1894 in Finland, near Saint Petersburg. Contemporary painting, dominated by the great Cubist and Fauvist movements, has nevertheless made room for a few individualists, but on condition that they discover their own means. Thus, Pougny, who can be connected with no school, presents an example of a discreet art in which everything is brought back to personal feeling, a form of intuition that transforms every subject. Pougny's art is appealing and easy of access, and his canvases, all small in size, are as intimate and tender as melodies. Interior scenes and views of beaches assert themselves with moving precision at first sight; but when one looks for motifs or examines the execution in detail, they escape analysis and seem based on a secret technique which is difficult to define. The drawing is imprecise, line absent, the touches of colour shapeless, but the relations are so right, the juxtapositions so live that the subject falls together without the aid of logic or the laws of probability. It is an art that seems totally improvised, but that none the less never conveys a feeling of dispersion or carelessness. Pougny has sometimes been compared to Vuillard, but the comparison is justified only by his mat finish and the muted harmony of tones, discreetly blended with greys to set off the freshness of the modulations in yellow, green and red. There is no attempt to represent reality in this minute art but only to suggest the feeling left by the figure or the landscape. In fact, in recent years no painter has expressed atmosphere better than he, not the luminous atmosphere of the Impressionists but a sentimental atmosphere. The sincerity of this art and the simplicity of the means employed, allowed Pougny to discover very early the formula that suited him and achieve his perfection.

**PRIMITIVES OF TODAY** Outside all the great artistic and cultural currents of the last centuries, there has developed a craftsman's painting – decoration of furniture, shop signs, ex-voto offerings and the art of country portraitists – characterized by the

PORTINARI. COFFEE PORTERS. 1903. *Private Collection, New York*

supreme importance given to minute enumeration of things, beings, and facts, at the expense of a true representation in pictorial space, which as a result obeys only partially the laws of perspective. These 'naïve' methods have been revived by painters of a new kind, the Primitives of today, who appeared when craft painting came to an end. Far from the teachings of the Fine Arts, and from all contact with contemporary art, these painters have acted upon a genuine vocation. Of folk origin, they remained – because of the circumstances of their life and the frequently belated flowering of their art – outside the artistic and spiritual culture of their time. But this isolation, which deprived them of all cultural exchanges, enabled them, on the other hand, to preserve their primitive vision of the world intact and to express it fully in their painting. This vision is that of the man of the street (hence the phrase 'popular masters of reality' sometimes used in reference to these

POUGNY.
CANNES BEACH.
1950

artists): pathetic subjects, allegory, official 'views' often taken from post-cards, occupy a large place in it; but – more important – their vision was strangely close to the one that man could have formed of the world before entering upon the age of individualism. In France the most outstanding of these 'Neo-Primitives' are the Douanier Rousseau, Vivin, Séraphine, Peyronnet, Bauchant and Bombois. Their work achieves effortlessly the pure miracle of primal poetry, the expression of an intimate and ancient communion between man and the world. Their painting, done with humility and sometimes with real piety, retains extraordinary purity and serenity. In its deeply original character, its often rigorous and logical development (especially in Rousseau and Vivin), it differs both from that practised by earlier naïve craftsmen and from children's or madmen's paintings, although it shares with them certain manners of representation and a primitive vision of things. It is wrong to consider these primitives as 'Sunday painters': by virtue of the technique they invented instinctively, they are real 'professionals' of painting.

The discovery of the naïve painters, and especially of the Neo-Primitives, was made by artists, poets and a few collectors. The importance of the Douanier Rousseau was recognized about 1905 by Apollinaire, Jarry, Picasso and Robert Delaunay, and also by the German critic Wilhelm Uhde, who discovered Séraphine in 1912. Le Corbusier and Ozenfant chiefly defended Bauchant. The public's taste for the art of these new primitives, although often attracted by the sentimental or picturesque side of their life and works, continued to increase after the great group exhibitions that took place in Paris in 1927, 1932, 1937, in Zurich in 1937, in New York in 1938, in Bern in 1949, and brought to light other primitives, French, Italian, American, German and Swiss. These painters seem to find their place in the history of modern art quite naturally: thus the Douanier Rousseau, the humble creator of a magnificent succession of pictures in which man's imagination and the world's reality miraculously coincide, appears as one of the great forerunners at the source of modern art; he takes his place not far from Cézanne, Gauguin and Van Gogh, his contemporaries. Similarly, one could no doubt detect today profound correspondences between the instinctive or conscious experiments of contemporary painting and the individual adventure of the primitives of today (cf. the articles on Apollinaire, Bauchant, Bombois, Peyronnet, Rousseau, Séraphine, Uhde and Vivin.)

In the United States, in spite of the important role naïve painters and sculptors have played in the development of American art from its beginnings, it is only within recent years that there has been any great general interest in them. As was the case in France, it was the modern painter and sculptor who sensed their true artistic value and paved the way for a more widespread acceptance. Louis Eilshemius, Morris Hirshfield, John Kane and Joseph Pickett are among the best of the modern primitives. With the American public Grandma Moses holds a unique position by virtue of her considerable output, its unvarying quality, and the near-universal appeal of her quiet, nostalgic charm.

**PURISM** The manifesto of Purism, the work of Amédée Ozenfant and Edouard Jeanneret, who, under the name of Le Corbusier, became one of the great architects of the twentieth century, was published in 1918 under the title *After Cubism*. Ozenfant and Jeanneret maintained in this work that having laid a solid theoretical foundation for the art of painting, Cubism *(\*)* seemed to forsake its initial discipline to revert to a kind of Impressionism, and in particular to indulge in decorative art. Their aim was to restore art to soundness. Purism wished to forbid in painting all fantasy and preciosity, with a view to restoring objects to their architectural simplicity and their authenticity. As a plastic symbol the Purists adopted the machine, an object of absolute perfection because all trappings unnecessary to its function are eliminated. Purist works were therefore to reject every accident harmful to the architectural balance of form. Moreover, the composition of a Purist picture required absolute objectivity; any too individualistic touch was to be rejected. It was in the magazine *Élan* (1915) and then in *L'Esprit Nouveau* (1920–1925) that Purist theories were developed and opposed to the various aesthetic doctrines current at the time. However, Purism led to no development in painting, no doubt because of its excess of rigour. Only in the architecture of Le Corbusier and his disciples did these theories find a valid field of application (cf. articles on Le Corbusier, Ozenfant and *Esprit Nouveau*).

## PUVIS DE CHAVANNES

Pierre (1824–1898). French painter; born in Lyons; died in Paris. It is no longer customary to consider Puvis de Chavannes among the important painters of modern art. However, in his time he was, like the greatest,

rejected by the jury of the Salon, and misunderstood by critics. He sided with the most original artists, and was considered in his way as a reformer, a painter whose art brought something new; and if he finally enjoyed official honour, it was without making the slightest

PUVIS DE CHAVANNES. THE POOR FISHERMAN. 1881. *Louvre, Paris*

concession, and with the approval of those who were considered revolutionaries. In fact, he escaped all classification and influence of schools; he cannot be situated within Impressionism or any of the currents that derived from it, but neither can he be regarded as a champion of the academic. It is true that his audacities seem timid to us today and are surpassed by the violence with which contemporary art has evolved. At the end of the nineteenth century, when the art of the Impressionists began to dominate, and easel painting gradually became the only medium, Puvis de Chavannes wanted to defend the principles of mural painting. He knew that rhythms are not only valid for the exteriorization of feelings but can also be put to the service of necessities outside oneself without losing their value. He was, with Gauguin, perhaps the only painter of the time to have a presentiment of the grandeur of mural painting; and Gauguin was never indifferent to his art. But whereas Gauguin meant to glorify the real, seeking intensity of colours and a harsh nobility of basic forms in the exotic, Puvis de Chavannes desired something similar, at the other pole of refinement, in a calm poetry inspired by history and the legends of Western civilization. What Gauguin thought of obtaining through violence, Puvis de Chavannes wanted to find in tenderness. Thus the two are both profoundly opposed and very closely related, if only by their simplification of modelling in the representation of the human body, the calm and tranquil gravity of their figures, their disposition of figures in the foreground against a backdrop of landscape which covers a great part of the picture and, lifting the horizon very high, leaves little room for the sky. The marked taste of Puvis for fragile elegance can no doubt be regretted, but his large compositions cannot be denied plastic qualities that raise him as a painter far above the pseudo-classicism to which some attempt to confine him today. And the long, slightly too linear silhouette of his figures has not only plastic value. The artist meant to include a number of other meanings in it. He had a liking for symbols and varied imagery, through which his austere and tender poetry could be expressed. To be more precise, with Puvis de Chavannes symbol is not a secret vocabulary and a language for the initiated, but an effort to endow form and gesture with the maximum of human significance. In this respect his picture *The Poor Fisherman* is typical.

**PUY** Jean. French painter; born in 1876 at Roanne. It is customary to classify Jean Puy with the *Fauves*, and it is fitting to respect this custom, as he belonged to the group that created a scandal at the Salon d'Automne in 1905. Jean Puy painted in bright colours even before 1905; canvases of his exist dated 1902 and 1903, of such daring and frankness in drawing and colour that it is possible to trace Fauvism *(\*)* back to that period. Puy's association with Matisse and Derain dates from about 1900, when he was attending courses at the Académie

PUY. NUDE. 1920.      *Lorenceau Collection*

Carrière *(\*)*. Fauvism had no name then, but it already existed. In spite of this, is Jean Puy exactly a *Fauve*? It seems that he did not arrive at this style or conform to its successive evolutions to obey theories or a system evolved in studio discussions. His work is dominated much more by instinct than by reasoning, the instinct of a painter who experiences a sensuous joy in spreading out and harmonizing colours, in making a form emerge. Sensuousness inspires his nudes, full of robust vitality; a sensuousness based on the hearty appetite, apparent in the still lifes, a sensuousness that commands simplified forms, dictates relations of clear tones in landscapes, animates and transfigures his snow studies. But this instinctive expansiveness never leads to lack of restraint. In his abandon, Jean Puy retains distinction, a natural characteristic with him, that proves his art more controlled than it seems. Nevertheless, if it preserves something spontaneous in all its aspects, it does so because it has never lost contact with Nature. Whatever the subject of the canvas, Puy always conveys an impression of remaining attached to immediate sensation. However, he adopts neither the small stroke nor the division of tones of the Impressionists. He employs mostly a broad, open technique.

# R

**RAYONISM** This Russian movement, launched by Michael Larionov in 1911–1912, seems to have derived partially from Futurism. At least the lectures given by Marinetti in Moscow and St Petersburg in 1910 were not alien to its development. Larionov went farther than Futurism in a movement that he baptized Rayonism (*Luchism* in Russian). However, the manifesto of this movement was not published until 1913. In it one reads that a Rayonist canvas must give the impression of gliding out of time and space to convey a feeling of a fourth dimension, and that to achieve this end the painter must resort to parallel or crossed beams of colour. The canvases of Larionov and Gontcharova are among the first really abstract works painted in this century, without any reminiscences of traditional visual reality.

**REALISM** Current confusion between Naturalism and Realism aside, there can be a realism on the level of appearances, as in Impressionism, or a realism on the conceptual plane, as in Cubism. Every great artist creates his own 'reality' – external and internal – which he must transcribe in an autonomous and personal idiom, although two fundamental attitudes are to be distinguished: one that leans toward representation of reality, the other toward suggestive expression of it through metaphor or abstraction. Modern art has resolutely adopted the latter course, so frequently described as non-realistic. After the revolutionary audacities of the beginning of the century and its extraordinary creative outburst, a period of release and reaction occurred at the close of the First World War. This was only a matter of returning to order, to Nature, to traditional realism. The best representatives of this tendency, whose force was felt by all artists for a time, are Dunoyer de Segonzac, Jean Marchand, Luc-Albert Moreau, André Mare, Yves Alix, Boussaingault and La Patellière. Sincere and honest artists of considerable talent, some of them former participants in the exhibition of the *Section d'Or (*)*, they retained of Cézanne only his simplified arrangement of volumes and made up for their lack of plastic invention by masterful craftsmanship and a somewhat ostentatious sensuousness of texture. Sound in its principles but sterile, their attitude revealed a legitimate distrust of intellectualist excesses and a profound longing for good workmanship (*vide* Dunoyer de Segonzac, Boussaingault, La Patellière). A similar phenomenon occurred again in 1945, when the 'painters of poetic reality' (*vide* Brianchon, Legueult, Oudot) formed a group around Brianchon, this time under the banner of Bonnard rather than of Cézanne.

**REDON** Odilon (1840–1916). Born in Bordeaux; died in Paris. Born in the same year as Monet, Redon belonged to the Impressionists' generation but preferred to make his way alone rather than join their movement, which he found too limited in scope. From the start he insisted on the role of imagination in art, and as early as 1868, when Courbet and Naturalism were at their height, he gave his opinion clearly on the subject: 'There are those who want to confine the art of painting to reproducing only what they see. Whoever remains within these narrow limits restricts himself to an inferior ideal. The great painters of the past have proved that the artist, once he has mastered his medium and found in Nature his means of expression, is genuinely free to take his subjects from history or the poets, or to seek it in his imagination.' And he declared that 'while I recognize the necessity of the thing *seen* as a base, true art is in

REDON. ANEMONES. 1908.
*Private Collection, Paris*

incredible beings live according to credible laws, in placing the logic of the possible at the service of the invisible'. Thus Redon succeeded in translating that disturbing dream world which for him partook of reality into a purely plastic language of mysterious lines, subtle contrasts and harmonious colours. He was not interested in probing its meaning; his one aim was to express himself in luxuriant, vigorous colours or in delicate contrasts of black and white.

Redon worked for many years without attracting any attention, or even trying to make a name for himself. His first album of lithographs (*In a Dream*) – a medium he was to choose for some of his most original and important work – was not published until 1879, when he was nearly forty, and his first small exhibitions in 1881 and 1882 passed almost unnoticed. But as Symbolism in literature developed and reached its peak in 1886, Mallarmé, a close friend of Redon's, and the other poets of the movement were quick to recognize affinities between the painter's work and their own trend. Mallarmé, in a letter to Redon, expressed the pleasure a study of his lithographs gave him: 'The impression received never diminishes, so powerful is your sincerity of vision as well as your capacity for transmitting it to others'. But if it was Symbolism that created the climate necessary for an appreciation of Redon's work, it was not only men of letters who admired his work. The new generation of painters soon came to accept him as of importance to them; Gauguin was proud to be known as his friend, Émile Bernard was unsparing in his admiration, and did all he could to make his work known, while the young *Nabis* – Bonnard, Vuillard and Maurice Denis – came to him for advice. Henri Matisse, attracted by the intense colours introduced by Redon into his painting about 1890, called on the artist to express his admiration. But Redon's role as precursor was not widely acknowledged until after his death, when the Surrealists broke in on the world with their fantastic art – often far more literary and intellectual than that of their great predecessor.

reality *felt*'. These early convictions remained his creed all his life. He loved Nature and studied her closely, but his precise drawings led him to develop a personal style appropriate to the strange world of his dreams. Little by little the reality seen blended in his vision and work with the reality felt. Redon himself explained this double inspiration in a letter to a friend: 'I have always felt the necessity for copying small, fortuitous, individual objects from Nature. Only after an effort of will faithfully to reproduce a blade of grass, a stone, a branch, part of an old wall, am I fired with the urge to create something imaginary. Nature thus accepted and transformed, becomes my inspirational source. My best works have been the outcome of this approach.' Redon always insisted that his imagination had its roots in the observation of Nature and that his fantastic creations, demoniacal visions in black and white, belonged to a world never wholly divorced from reality. In his own words: 'My originality consists in making

Redon's art is not easily accessible; as with Delacroix and Goya – whom he admired without imitating – there is an 'obvious' side to his work which is easy to grasp but also a 'hidden' side,

REDON. SAILING BOATS IN VENICE. 1906. *Private Collection, Paris*

feeling for texture, the same sensuousness in the volumes, the same frankness. However, association with Claude Monet led him, in certain canvases, to practise the division of the coloured stroke that was to be one of the achievements of Impressionism, and to this we owe the two astonishing versions of *La Grenouillère*, dated 1868–1869. In 1870 Renoir was mobilized; he met his comrades again after the war and participated in the famous exhibition of 1874 at the photographer Nadar's *(\*)*, where Impressionism was born. Renoir, who exhibited

an inherent poetry, a masterly control, and a true harmony only visible to the initiated.

**RENOIR** Auguste (1841–1919). French painter; born in Limoges; died at Cagnes in the south of France. Beyond Impressionism, of which he was one of the chief initiators, Renoir joins the line of artists who, from Titian and Tintoretto to Rubens, from Fragonard to Delacroix and Courbet, have seen in painting a kind of pagan and sensual celebration of the glory of woman. The son of a tailor, Renoir began his artistic life as an apprentice, prudently painting small bouquets of flowers on porcelain plates, and then decorating, with the same care, fans and shades for missionaries. However, he had greater hopes. Having saved some money, he gave up being a workman to become a pupil and enrolled, in 1862, at the Atelier Gleyre *(\*)*, where he met Monet, Bazille and Sisley; the nucleus of the future Impressionists was thus constituted. The following year, leaving the Atelier, he went with his new friends to the forest of Fontainebleau to paint from Nature. He was at this time under the influence of Courbet, and this influence can be discerned as much in a work like *The Sisley Family* (1868) as in the *Bather with Griffon* (1870): there is the same

*La Loge*, was one of the painters who incurred the most acid criticism. This was, however, the period during which he produced works of such disconcerting beauty as *The Moulin de la Galette* (1876), *The Swing* (reproduced on page 129), or *Road Climbing Through the Grass* (1875). He was reproached,

RENOIR. THE END OF THE LUNCHEON. 1879.
*Staedelsches Kunstinstitut, Frankfort*

RENOIR. THE PATH UP THROUGH THE FIELD. 1875. *Louvre*

among other things, with covering his figures with mould when he painted sun filtering through foliage. Now that we are accustomed to coloured shadow and purple tonalities, it is difficult to imagine what a great innovation a canvas like the *Moulin de la Galette* was. The chief characteristic of Renoir's Impressionist period is that he succeeded in adding a sentimental atmosphere to the representation of Nature and seemed to be just as charmed by a tender interlacing of his figures as by the play of foliage or of water. Although he never yielded entirely to anecdote, it is evident that the subject of the canvas remained infinitely more important for him than for any other painter of the new school. While his friends were chiefly attracted by landscape, his own preference was for group studies and portraits. Having sung the joy of the popular country cafés with music and dancing, he devoted himself to producing some of the most sumptuous images of Parisian society that have been left to us by his period: for example, the portraits of the *Henriot Family* (1876), of *Madame*

*Charpentier and Her Daughter* (1878), of *Jeanne Samary* (1879). A painter of manners, Renoir apparently could not do without the human presence to give measure to his work and express the kind of feeling he wanted to put into it. Whereas Cézanne tended to reduce everything to the impersonal level of the object and to exercise the same calm impartiality for a face as for an apple, Renoir seemed, quite to the contrary, to bring everything into accord with his vision of man. In his work a flower, a fruit are coloured, savoury and palpitating with life, like a human body beneath whose skin one can tell that blood circulates. Cézanne looked and reasoned; Renoir saw and felt. The same opposition is evident in their colour, in the red, or warm, dominants of Renoir, and the blue or green, cold dominants of Cézanne.

But Renoir's Impressionist period proper was approaching its end, and the *The Canoeists' Lunch*, which he conceived during the summer of 1880, while frequenting the café of Mère Fournaise on the island of Croissy, near Paris, was one of the last canvases in which he was to express and sum up the ideal of his youth in a particularly demonstrative synthesis. He was forty and felt the need for renewal. Nothing troubled him more than the facility, the systematic spirit into which Impressionism threatened to lapse. Renoir, like Cézanne a few years earlier, gained a fresh grip by returning to the classical tradition. He left Italy in the autumn of 1881. After a stay in Venice, he went on to Rome, where he paused long before the frescoes of Raphael at the Villa Farnese, and then proceeded to Naples, where he discovered Pompeian painting. Of this period he would later say, 'A break occurred then in my work. I had gone to the limit of Impressionism and was arriving at the conclusion that I could neither paint nor draw. In short, I was dead-locked.' Under the influence of Raphael he was henceforth to adopt a much smoother manner. Reacting against the dispersion and scattering of colour in juxtaposed strokes, he gave a deliberate and rather surprising dryness to forms, which he encircled with a pure and precise line. For what had won him over in Italy, especially in Raphael's work, was the quality of the drawing, which,

under a seeming coldness, lingers over the modelling of forms with a keenness and a concentration in which the roles played by the senses and the mind are difficult to separate. Remembering that drawing represents the intellectual element in painting and colour the sensory, it is not a little surprising to see a painter like Renoir adopt such a manner for a time. He who had previously required colour to suggest form, to be its own design, would now imprison it in the severe frame of an increasingly minute and precise painting. This period, which has been called 'Ingresque' – Renoir called it more justly his 'harsh manner' – was characterized by a partiality for cold tones and acid colours, for a smooth, dull surface. A transitory stage in his work, it was nevertheless decisive in so far as it represented an admirable effort of discipline and corresponded to one of those critical moments in the life of an artist when he questions everything and thinks out his art again from its very fundamentals. From this discipline, so contrary to his nature, Renoir was able to extract the best results in numerous canvases about 1895, notably in *Les Grandes Baigneuses* and *The Braid*. However, he

RENOIR. BALL AT THE MOULIN DE LA GALETTE. 1876. *Louvre*

RENOIR. MME HENRIOT.
*Private Collection, U.S.A.*

more spontaneity and naturalness than those of Degas. Here Renoir has given the full measure of himself. These canvases achieved recognition very slowly, and even today many collectors consider them inferior to his earlier ones. It is certain that the big nudes that make up the essential part of his production after 1900 represent, when compared to works like *La Loge* or the *Moulin de la Galette*, an art much more difficult to accept, for, liberated of all constraint, the new manner proved capable of transcribing Renoir's feeling with a boldness that was not yet discernible at the time of Impressionism. The choice of themes is in itself significant. Renoir was not afraid of giving up what had made his success; when his personality was beginning to assert itself in society portraits, he rejected this theme to tackle either group studies, nudes or still life, with which he could not be sure of conquering a new public. This attitude resulted more from his character than from an aesthetic doctrine. 'For me', he liked to say, 'a picture must be a pleasant thing, joyous and pretty – yes, pretty! There are too many unpleasant things in life for us to fabricate still more.'

It was inevitable that the physical pleasure in form and texture that Renoir felt to an intense degree and that made him, in his own words, 'pet a picture, stroke it with the hand', should draw him toward sculpture. This he undertook

did not long endure this constraint, under which his genius was visibly not developing normally, and reverted soon to his characteristic coloured texture. He returned to it with greater vigour than at the time of Impressionism. His experience left him with more self-confidence but, above all, with the capacity to be no longer strictly dominated by reality and to impose upon the subject treated the will of his creative genius.

With his last 'manner' one witnesses an unprecedented flowering. In a rediscovered unity of colour and line, volume and light, Renoir would untiringly sing woman's body, the centre of the universe, an ever-renewed creation of our desire. Nudes filled his landscapes to the point of occupying the whole canvas, and red, infinitely modulated, became the dominant colour in which all the others were consumed, in the same way that woman in her eternal youth would be born again every time in Gabrielle, his faithful servant and favourite model. The compositions of this period are unusual in that under the appearance of total freedom they retain infinitely more will than those of Monet or Sisley, but

RENOIR. NUDE.     *Art Institute, Chicago.*

RENOIR. BATHING. *Pastel.* 1890

beginning, who had lived in Montmartre and met the young women of the quarter, nice working girls, models, with light heads and susceptible hearts, was to be received later in families of the Parisian *haute bourgeoisie*. But, in both cases, whether he painted the ball at the *Moulin de la Galette, The Swing, The Canoeists' Lunch*, or executed portraits he had been commissioned to do, it was first his own sensibility that he expressed, more than just the depiction of the sentimental atmosphere of his works, and, needless to say, it was to himself above all that he meant to be true. Thus his emotions as a painter were in harmony with his feelings as a man and, as a result, an exemplary unity was established between his works, in spite of their differences. Neither was there a sharp break when he gave up too specific subjects almost entirely and preferred to paint bathing women with naked torsos in the innumerable portraits of

at a time when, unfortunately, physical disability no longer allowed him much suppleness. He secured the assistance of a young sculptor to work under his constant direction. The only sculpture entirely from his own hand is the portrait of his son Coco, which was executed about 1907–1908. Later works were done by the sculptor Richard Guino, but Renoir's authorship of them cannot be denied; not only do they reveal a close relationship of form and spirit with his painting, but also what Richard Guino executed out of Renoir's presence cannot compare with them. The large *Venus* and the large *Washerwoman* are masterful works that can take their place among the masterpieces of contemporary sculpture.

Renoir's is a happy art, for as a man he was without bitterness and without jealousy. His work obeyed an inner logic; it was in harmony with a perfectly balanced life able to accept itself at every moment of its development, even the most painful, when illness had deformed his limbs and in order to continue painting he was forced to have his brush tied to his wrist. The impecunious young man he had been at the

RENOIR. GIRL WITH HAT AND VEIL. *Pastel.*
1876–1879

RENOIR. NUDE IN THE SUN. 1900.
*Louvre*

Gabrielle, this being his own way of creating pure painting. For here again it is clear that love of painting and admiration for woman were indissolubly linked in him and were only the double aspect of his single passion for a clear and healthy life.

**REVUE BLANCHE** (La). This was the first literary review to seek from painters a collaboration that was not occasional but that, on the contrary, based on very subtle affinities, was to be maintained during the twelve years that the magazine existed – a long time for an *avant-garde* review, and perhaps unequalled. The *Revue Blanche* was founded by the brothers Alexandre and Thadée Natanson in October 1891. Among the contributors who were interested in the plastic arts were, along with Thadée Natanson himself, Octave Mirbeau, Jules Renard, Alfred Jarry, Tristan Bernard, Félix Fénéon, Félicien Fagus and Guillaume Apollinaire. Regular meetings took place on the premises of the magazine, attended by Toulouse-Lautrec, Sérusier, Bonnard, Vuillard,

Ranson, Roussel, Maurice Denis, Steinlen, Vallotton and others. It was during these gatherings, often tumultuous and generally conducted by Sérusier, that a number of new artistic theories first were aired. The participants would be first Synthesist, then Neo-Impressionist or 'Neo-Traditionalist', and also Mystic. However, on the whole the tone of the *Revue Blanche* reflected a taste for detailed observation, but was always careful to avoid the excesses and facility of Naturalism. One of the issues that created a scandal was that of May 1900, in which Thadée Natanson, attacking the official Salon des Artistes Français, opposed to it the work of the painters grouped about the magazine, 'intelligent painters' as he said. These words, which the author had chosen for the title of his article, resounded like a challenge and took on the aspect of a manifesto. In 1901 Fagus, in the first article devoted to this artist in France, discovered the Picasso of the 'Blue Period'. Bonnard composed a series of lithographs in colour for the magazine in 1893, and in 1894 his celebrated poster (reproduced on

BONNARD. LITHOGRAPH FOR THE
'REVUE BLANCHE'

page 203). Vallotton adorned the review with portraits of writers and artists, frontispieces or drawings, for which Jules Renard sometimes wrote commentaries. As early as 1896, when Bonnard exhibited for the first time at the Durand-Ruel Gallery, Thadée Natanson published an excellent study of him, and articles on Lautrec in 1893 and 1901. Maurice Denis spoke of Renoir in 1892. Fénéon became the interpreter of Neo-Impressionism *(\*)* and of the *Nabis (\*)*, and he organized on the premises of the magazine itself two famous exhibitions, the retrospectives of Seurat in 1892 and 1900. The first exhibition of Vuillard also took place at the office of the *Revue Blanche* in 1891; and it published the famous manuscript of Gauguin, *Noa Noa*, in 1897. It was in the issue of April 15th, 1903, that Fagus announced the end of this publication which, in its boldness and its fidelity to its initial views, had reflected an artistic period whose originality and interest could not fail to make history.

**RIVERA** Diego. Mexican painter; born in 1886 in Guanajuato. After taking courses at the School of Fine Arts in Mexico City, Rivera freed himself of Spanish academicism (which no longer was related to Velasquez or Goya and was still strong in Mexico) by living in Paris and becoming one of the Montparnasse painters who have been grouped under the name of School of Paris. A friend of Modigliani, recognized by Guillaume Apollinaire, Rivera adopted, contrary to most of the painters of the period, an attitude of reserve, almost that of an observer. He followed attentively, but without participating in it, the evolution of the painters of the Bateau-Lavoir *(\*)* – Picasso, Braque and Juan Gris. However, he benefited from their research. But he clearly did not feel at ease in Parisian circles. He returned to Mexico and set out to discover his country. Profoundly influenced by the ancient art of the Mayas and Aztecs, he was also moved by the revolutionary spirit that was still strong throughout Mexico. These two appeals were so powerful that his formerly reserved personality underwent a real metamorphosis. He rejected the influences that he had accepted only

RIVERA. ARUMS

with the tip of his brush during his stay in Paris, and succeeded in becoming a revolutionary painter by adopting the traditions of a remote past. He waged an active campaign in Mexico City which led to the creation of a purely Mexican school of painting. With the assistance of the authorities, who gave him important commissions and supported his efforts, he worked out vast frescoes for public buildings, inspired by the political and social history of Mexico, particularly the history of popular uprisings. The attempt was decisive both for himself and for other Mexican painters. For the impulse had been given and the Mexican school created. From then on every fresco was a manifesto and a challenge. Rivera's art was explosive, and in turn caused a series of explosions. Can one maintain that this painting, which accepted European methods, techniques and procedures, was actually a modern expression of the prodigious art of the ancestors whose tradition it claimed to continue? Perhaps not. What is more evident is that, thanks to Rivera, Mexican art has proved one of the most dynamic movements in the painting of our time. One of the aspects of Rivera's art that should not be underestimated remains to be mentioned: what may be called its will to be a folk image. The colours as well as subjects of the frescoes are popular in intent. Rivera desires to meet the needs and strivings of the masses and does not care much for the élite. Certainly he prefers to address himself to the greatest number, but nevertheless he takes care to create a style.

**ROUAULT** Georges. French painter; born in 1871 in Paris. His father was a cabinet-maker; his aunts did china painting. At fourteen he was apprenticed to a stained-glass painter. He worked on the restoration of medieval windows. From this work he retained a taste for iridescences and colours encircled with a vigorous black line. It developed in him, moreover, a craftsman's integrity, examples of which he had already seen among his family. Of the masters of his time, Rouault possesses the soundest craftsmanship in the traditional sense, both in draughtsmanship and the conventional techniques that once ruled official art, and in the preparation of colours. During his apprenticeship he attended courses at the Paris School of Decorative Arts. In 1891 he entered the École Nationale des

ROUAULT. AT THE MIRROR. 1906.
*Musée d'Art Moderne, Paris*

Beaux-Arts, where his teacher was Gustave Moreau. The latter was a man of great culture and extremely broad minded. His work, unfortunately spoiled by excessively literary preoccupations, was related to the Symbolist movement and devoted to the evocation of a legendary and hieratic past, smothered in precious fabrics and jewels. The solid technical foundation he gave his pupils respected the originality of each. More than a teacher, he was a real friend to Rouault, whom he encouraged and to whom he gave self-confidence. But Rouault did not find himself immediately. His master had predicted a difficult career for him, perceiving his taste for rich and powerful pictorial material at the expense of linear precision. These tendencies existed even in Rouault's first works, where he treated religious subjects in a still traditional style. In 1893 he painted *Samson Turning the Millstone*; in 1895 *Christ Dead Mourned by the Holy Women*, both for the Prix de Rome, which he did not win. Here certain figures recall those of Leonardo da Vinci and of some of his disciples, Solario or Ambrogio da Predis. An admiration for

ROUAULT. SELF-PORTRAIT.
*Lithograph*

Rembrandt is apparent in *Christ and the Disciples of Emmaus*. After a period of material difficulties and moral crisis, following the death of Gustave Moreau in 1898, and coinciding with an estrangement from his family, Rouault participated in the foundation of the Salon d'Automne in 1903. At that time he was already painting the landscapes of suburbs and bleak countrysides that are found throughout his work – the earliest of these is *The Work Yard* of 1897. In 1904 and 1905 he exhibited works in which other themes appeared, themes that he has also taken up incessantly: prostitutes, clowns, pierrots. These canvases were done in a very dark tonality that disconcerted the public. The Catholic novelist Léon Bloy inspired certain subjects Rouault treated in 1905, like *Monsieur et Madame Poulot*, the strange couple of *The Poor Woman*. Bloy hardly understood the real problems of painting, and his nature made friendship difficult; however, the influence of his vehement oracular manner was evident. Rouault put extraordinary violence into the tribunal scenes, prostitutes and clowns he represented. Bestiality and stupidity are displayed on the faces that dark zones delineate cruelly with their black lines, accentuating the grotesqueness of the moral misery and physical ugliness. The horror of this fallen humanity fascinated Rouault; but he painted it with a kind of sensitive irony, dispensing light touches of bright colours, pinks, celestial blues, ardent reds.

In 1907 he worked at ceramics and met Odilon Redon, who was then making his most poetical transcriptions of coloured reveries. Rouault continued to treat social themes: peasants, workmen, individuals isolated or placed in their family surroundings; his characters transcend their station and become mythical figures. Rouault renewed his technique completely, reducing his drawing to essentials that took on a life of their own, giving up shadows, elaborate gradations, successive perspectives and planes, to portray the model directly in its hallucinating truth, created with colours chosen only for their greater expressive value. To reach the essential more directly he had only to block in a figure with large, rough strokes of colour that stand out against the shadow. His works contained the germ of tremendous power. They were starting a life that would be continued in all the painter's future creations. In 1917 Ambroise Vollard *(\*)* became his dealer. The artist undertook for him, until 1927, a whole series of etchings to illustrate various works: *The Reincarnations of Père Ubu*, *The Circus* and *The Flowers of Evil* of Baudelaire, a project that was abandoned but for which a number of plates were engraved, and finally *Miserere* and *War*, published only in 1948. In these plates, which are of exceptional dimensions, form is simplified to the extreme; all the sometimes caricatural picturesqueness of the previous works has disappeared in favour of a vehement expressionism of silhouette and a dramatic opposition of whites and blacks. Form is not only accentuated by dark zones but often uniformly encircled with a vigorous line that recalls the leading of stained glass. After a mechanical transfer to the copperplate of a composition drawn in India ink, Rouault undertook his work as engraver, with all possible tools: an etcher's needle, a roller, a file, a scraper, sandpaper, which he used according to his inspiration, discovering new techniques like the application of acid with wide strokes of the brush.

ROUAULT. THE APPRENTICE. 1925.
*Musée d'Art Moderne, Paris*

ROUAULT. THE HOLY FACE.
*Frigerio Collection, Paris*

human sins. Upon this gigantic enterprise, in which the painter mixed acid-like pigments, did violence to metal and put his powerful stamp upon everything, the technique of black and white imposes its harsh and strange discipline. Features stand out, hard, absolute. There is no complacency in the satire, nothing flabby or inflated in the rendering of the horrible. The effect achieved is of a richness, a depth that makes Rouault the greatest visionary of modern times.

In spite of his activity as an engraver, in which should be included the execution of settings for Diaghilev (*vide* Ballets Russes) and various literary texts, Rouault has pursued his work as a painter. It was especially after 1932 that the main part of his production again came to be in this field. Clowns and judges continued to supply him with themes, but he no longer kept the violence of his first works: anger had given way to pity. Wide, immense eyes, in the midst of livid faces, seemed to transcribe an inner emptiness or the vision of a beyond. Religious subjects grew more numerous and were integrated into the suburban landscapes; imprecise silhouettes stood out against towers and houses whose doors and windows suggested mouths and empty eyes. Scenes were bathed in a strange light, both warm and almost nocturnal, that seemed to radiate from within the forms. All these canvases Rouault kept taking up again, reworking them, never satisfied and never ready to part with them. From 1937 on he hardly ever signed his works and no longer dated them. In 1947 a suit was brought by him against the heirs of Ambroise Vollard. After a verdict that set a precedent, he was allowed to keep all the works still in his studio that he considered unfinished. He burned 315 of them, which he thought too far from the perfection he had glimpsed, and undertook a definitive perfecting of his work within self-assigned limits. It is in the large religious paintings, which compel everyone's esteem, that this great work reaches its peak, solitary but none the less entirely turned towards love for one's fellow man, passionate with fury but also with affection and pity. Rouault has drawn up an indictment of humanity that can be compared with the most terrible, those of Goya and Daumier. Then, by a sort of generosity, he has

Unsatisfied, he took up the subject indefinitely, producing up to twelve or fifteen successive states. The plates are accompanied by titles or captions of a rare power of visual evocation. They are not the prodigious philosophical and moral epitomes of Goya, but rather incantations or magic formulas suggested by the requirements of a mysterious inner rhythm. One finds in these etchings the gallery of figures invented by Rouault to represent human misery and the appetites of the flesh: crooked judges, kings and those in high positions wearing frightening masks, so-called women of pleasure, the clown with a pointed hat topping his sad face. There are landscapes in which lines converge toward a powerful light, peaceful countrysides devastated by ruin and fire, empty streets expressing the solitude of cities. However, the artist has moments of poignant gentleness when he paints certain women's or children's faces – in the most grimacing Daumiers, too, there are miraculous faces of young girls – or when he tells of the sufferings of Christ and of the Virgin to redeem transcended the misery to reach the eternal myths. He paints the flaws of societies, the decrepitude of the institutions that men of all times have established; but he fulfils himself in a burning communion with the holy figures and the saints.

**ROUSSEAU** Henri, called the Douanier (1844–1910). French painter; born at Laval in Mayenne; died in Paris. At eighteen he enrolled in the Army and was assigned to the 52nd Infantry Regimental Band, where he played the saxophone. After he left the Army he married, in 1869. In 1871, after having taken part in the Franco-Prussian war, he entered the customs service as a clerk: hence his name. He allowed people to think that he had participated in the Mexican campaign, but there is no evidence to support this idea. When he was about forty he retired and began painting steadily. In 1886, introduced by Signac and

ROUAULT. CHRISTIAN NOCTURNE. 1952.
*Musée d'Art Moderne, Paris*

Luce, he exhibited at the Société des Artistes Indépendants, to which he sent work regularly from then until 1898, and again from 1901 to 1910. Beginning in 1905, he exhibited also at the Salon d'Automne. He associated with Gauguin, Odilon Redon and Seurat. Through the poet Alfred Jarry, also of the town of Laval, he made the acquaintance of Rémy de Gourmont, who, in the magazine *L'Imagier*, published *War*, a lithograph based upon Rousseau's picture, exhibited the previous year. Having lost his wife, Rousseau remarried in September 1899 upon the completion of a drama in five acts, *The Revenge of a Russian Orphan*, which was unsuccessfully produced at the Théâtre du Châtelet in Paris. In 1903 his second wife died. He lived in the rue Pernel, in the Plaisance quarter of Paris, and, to make a living, he gave lessons in painting, diction and harmony. He made portraits of neighbouring shopkeepers, and when

ROUSSEAU. SELF-PORTRAIT

ROUSSEAU. PERE JUNIET'S CART. 1908.      *Private Collection, Paris*

he died on September 2nd, 1910. Seven people, among them Paul Signac, followed the hearse. He was buried in a common grave at the Bagneux cemetery outside Paris. The painter Delaunay and the caster Queval, owner of the house in which Rouseau lived, put up the money to buy a thirty-year concession at the cemetery, and the Douanier's remains were transferred to a decent burying-ground. Here, with a medallion by Armand Queval, was set a tombstone on which Apollinaire wrote in pencil the famous poem-epitaph that Brancusi and Orthiz de Zarate engraved in the stone the next year, following the poet's handwriting precisely.

Rousseau's attention was drawn only by the

he drew them he took their measurements, like a tailor. In 1907 he met Wilhelm Uhde *(\*)*, who wrote the first monograph on him (Paris, 1911). The following year his friends organized a banquet in his honour at Picasso's studio in the Bateau-Lavoir *(\*)*. In 1909 he painted his two portraits of Apollinaire. Wilhelm Uhde, Ambroise Vollard and Brummer were his first buyers. Baroness Ottingen (Roch Grey), Ardengo Soffici, the sculptor Hoetzer and Robert Delaunay bought pictures from him. He exhibited *The Dream* at the Salon des Indépendants. But he was driven by the desire to marry again. Turned down by the woman he wanted to marry at any cost and whom he had pressed with increasingly urgent proposals, his spirit broke. He was admitted to the Necket hospital, where

PHOTOGRAPH OF THE JUNIET FAMILY AND THE CART.

freshness of things. For him dream was never severed from reality. The most everyday events were bathed in enchantment. In Plaisance concierges saw him pass by in his big art student's hat, violin-case or paint-box under his arm. In his tiny studio he lived on the hundred francs of his monthly pension, which he stretched out as he could. There he occasionally gave his *soirées*. The studio contained a table in unstained wood, three chairs, a chest for wood, and a make-shift bed concealed behind a curtain. He interrupted his painting from time to time to eat bread soaked in wine or milk. He led the life of a forgotten man, a rather miserable one. He said he had 'suffered much in the heart'. But he was rich, alive with a world of colours and forms, a world impatient to be born, and which found its most appropriate idiom in painting. This idiom, springing from the very surge of life, from the beat of the heart, has its miraculous expression in his painting. He never had to make an effort to convey a sudden emotion. There is nothing reheated in his work. He gave himself totally, without a struggle. 'It is not I who paint,' he said to a friend, 'but someone else who holds my hand.' How did this essentially plebeian art achieve such distinction? Most of what we know of folk art has a direct but often monotonous savour. There is nothing of the kind here. Rousseau had found instinctively the quality of the style that strikes us in those whom we call Primitives. From all the Douanier painted emerges a unique form, a unique harmony of colours, a unique way of treating the detail of the foliage of trees and of subordinating even the tiniest fragments to the monumentality of the whole. A primitive intuition led him to paint weddings, family reunions, the old dreams of the Dream Book. He had the childlike gift of believing in the magic reality of his creations. Those who knew him assure us that he experienced sudden terrors while painting his tiger hunts. Rousseau's production extends over a period of twenty-five years. But works of his exist done before 1886, the year of his first appearance at the Salon des Indépendants. We know that in 1884 he was issued a copyist's card for the Louvre. What old masters could he have interpreted? We do not know. Of his work we know only a

part. Besides the 140 or so paintings exhibited at the Salon des Indépendants and the Salon d'Automne and the works recognized today, many canvases were destroyed through ignorance or ruined through neglect (they were in the possession of concierges or at the houses of workmen, who often took no care of them). Without expecting numerous discoveries, it may be hoped that other Rousseaus will still be found. The themes he treated can be grouped into six categories:

(1) Scenes referring to the life of the Douanier or of his relatives, of people whom he knew: self-portraits, ceremonies, weddings, baptisms, family reunions (self-portraits, 1888–1890; *To Welcome the Baby*, 1903; *A Wedding in the Country*, 1905; *The Cart of Père Juniet*, 1908).

(2) Landscapes of Paris and its suburbs, with strollers and fishermen, which often give off something euphoric (*View of the Foot Bridge of Passy*, 1895; *In the Parc Montsouris*, 1895; *Cabs on the Quai d'Austerlitz*, 1896; *The Chair Factory in Alfortville*, 1897; *The Alley in Saint-Cloud*, 1903; *Malakoff*, 1905; *View of the Quai Henri IV*, 1909).

(3) Exotic scenes: evocations of the virgin

ROUSSEAU. PORTRAIT OF PIERRE LOTI. 1891.
*Kunsthaus, Zürich*

forest, big game hunts, bloody fights (*The Negro Assailed by a Leopard*, 1904; *The Lion Devouring the Antelope*, 1905; *Practical Jokers, The Apes*, 1906; *The Monkeys in the Orange Grove*, 1907; *The Snake Charmer*, 1907; *Exotic Landscape*, 1908)

(4) Military, patriotic or sports scenes (*The Gunners*; *War*; *The Republic*, 1885; *The Centenary of Independence*, 1892; *The Football Players*, 1908).

(5) Allegorical scenes (*Present and Past*, 1907; *The Muse and the Poet*, 1909; *The Dream*, 1910).

(6) Bouquets of wild and garden flowers.

How did Rousseau work? 'As an embroideress embroiders', say those who knew him. If the man sometimes had the excessive simplicity of naïve persons, the artist was rather ingenuous. He painted with a natural and graceful frankness, adding freedom to his native gifts. Thus his technique had nothing summary to it. He could render details without impairing the unity of the whole in his small canvases. Works of greater dimensions he treated differently, with large planes of even colours. Whence came the monumentality that his landscapes almost always possess? From his way of presenting the plant world. Like Poussin, the Douanier enlarged greenery and branches, whose leaves he shows us as if through a magnifying-glass, taking care to distinguish every species. His palette of deep blacks, the colour of slate, is cut by yellows, browns, purplish greens; it has the delicate, almost acid, tones of the Christmas rose. Rousseau drew little, but with an extraordinary sense of plastic values. Usually he described contours directly with the brush, and in colour, but without harshness. Before painting with the very precise density that characterizes him, he sometimes made sketches that approach, though rather distantly, the Impressionist manner. This naïve and gentle man, something of a mythomaniac, ridiculed, scolded by his wife, bullied by his daughter, knew nevertheless that only the fittest survive, that Nature is a jungle full of ferocity, that the child is not always good. But, with his whole being, he sided with the underdog, the defenceless animal, the victim. In his painting the quality of universal commiseration almost always impregnates the fruits of observation. Beyond reality, this ingenuous man opened paths invisible to the naked eye and had a presentiment of encounters that escape logic.

There exist innocent beings to whom it is

given to see farther than others who are of more complex organization but conform to the common measure. Nothing discourages these ingenuous ones. In them hope springs eternal. Some day, they know, it will be 'different'. The little painter, the 'angel' of the Plaisance quarter, belongs to their family. Rousseau put up with poverty, but without too much resignation. He acknowledged it. He courageously claimed his place, his right to woman and to art, to freedom and Sunday calm. No doubt at the bottom of his heart he vaguely felt joy in having freed himself from the slavery of assigned work. With the resources granted

ROUSSEAU. THE SNAKE-CHARMER. 1907. *Louvre*

him, the degree of intelligence fallen to his lot, this child, who had been given more love than knowledge, was conscious of his humble victory as a man who remained true to his first dreams. Hence the kindness of heart and mind that his painting often conveys. At the threshold of our century this 'simpleton' came as a pioneer. At a moment when humanity is wondering whether mechanical distortion has not stifled its creative capacity, the work of the Douanier Rousseau, an antidote to our technical civilization, is still as fresh as prophecy.

**ROY** Pierre (1880–1950). French painter, born in Nantes; died in Milan. The offspring of a middle-class family, related to that of Jules Verne, he was deeply impressed as a child by Verne's stories, which were told to him by the writer's brother. His repressed ambition was to become a sailor. Instead, his secondary studies finished, he entered an architect's office. From this period, which did not last long, he retained a taste for precise, neat draughtsmanship, plans, worked and inalterable materials: stone, wood, rope, metal. Paris attracted him. He first enrolled

at the École Nationale des Beaux-Arts and then attended the Académie Julian (*) and the École des Arts Décoratifs. About 1910 he came in touch with the *Fauves* and the group of writers surrounding them: Salmon, Max Jacob, and especially Apollinaire. He wrote and illustrated with coloured woodcuts the volume *Comptines*, which was not published until 1926. An heir of the Neo-Impressionists, he changed his manner after the First World War. In 1920 he made friends with the future Surrealists and participated in their first two exhibitions (Pierre Loeb Gallery, 1925; Surrealist Gallery, 1931). Launched and in demand in the United States, he visited America every year and organized large exhibitions. In 1939 he went as far as the Hawaiian Islands and brought back in his work an element of sensitive exoticism and, in comparison with his pictures of the 1925–1935 period, a shade of affectation, except in his portraits, which remained realistic and vigorous. As a decorator he worked for the *Ballets Suédois* (*) of Rolf de Maré; and as an illustrator he produced a series of lithographs for *The Child of the High Sea* of Jules Supervielle (1946). It was on his way to an exhibition in Bergamo, where he was showing some of his

ROY. L'ÉTÉ DE LA SAINT-MICHEL. *Circa* 1932.    *Musée d'Art Moderne, Paris*

the startling in composition. He took pleasure in assembling heterogeneous objects–pieces of reed or wood, even logs, hair, ribbons, birds' eggs, artificial flowers, small pebbles, seeds, cardboard castles, shells, wool and silk, wicker baskets, and sometimes simple machines (the wheel, for example, the central motif of several of his pictures) – somewhat in the way that children in their games make up displays or counters, his set purpose being to suggest through transposition of meaning and unexpected juxtapositions, both a new significance and a sort of strange poetry, revealing a thirst for escape and an inner freedom comparable to that of writers and poets.

work, that he died suddenly in Milan on September 26th, 1950. Curious about everything, a fine scholar, a sure, keen critic, he brought to everything the rigour that made him both solitary and classic. In spite of inevitable affinities, his work remains isolated in its time. Its distinctive features are minute care, refinement, finish, realism to the point of *trompe-l'œil*, a rendering of materials comparable to that of the old Flemish and Dutch masters, and – in deliberate contrast – the unusual,

**RUSSIAN BALLET** (*see* Ballets Russes).

# S

**SCHLEMMER** Oskar (1888–1943). German painter; born in Stuttgart; died in Baden-Baden. After studying at the Stuttgart Academy with Adolf Hoelzel, Schlemmer came into contact with modern French and German painting in 1911, in Berlin. After the war, in 1920, he entered the Bauhaus *(\*)*, where he was chief of the sculpture and theatre sections. In 1929 he taught in Breslau and in 1932–1933 in Berlin, until his dismissal by the Nazis. Then he retired to Eichberg in Southern Germany, where he led a difficult life, exposed to attacks of the Nazi authorities. If at first the influence of Cézanne drew him near to Cubism, the example of Marées and Seurat soon became more important. Schlemmer's idiom was reduced to a geometry of straight lines and curves as early as 1915. By creating reliefs after the war in mortar and later in wire, he enriched his positions with spatial values. These reliefs organized and invigorated architectural space. At the same time he created ballets, and devoted himself to theatrical production. In a renewal of the theatrical idiom he sought elements of a synthesis of the arts, in which the human figure, the measure of a humanized universe, would recover its primal purity. During Schlemmer's years at the Bauhaus, his painting grew in scope; later (in Breslau) stressed diagonals enriched the dynamism of his composition: the picture *The Staircase at the Bauhaus* (1932) stands as a synthesis of his research during this period. He felt the influence of his friend the Swiss painter, Otto Meyer-Amden, a promoter of whose work he became, chiefly after Meyer-Amden's death in 1933. At Eichberg, Schlemmer's colour darkened and figures emerged from a background in which the strokes of the brush were more visible. From then on a more accentuated mystical meaning appeared in his work, as in the abstract compositions he called *Symbolics* (1936) and the series of *Windows* (1942), in which the human figure reappeared, but more remote than before and seen from outside, as though dematerialized by the windowpane.

A contemporary of Paul Klee and Kandinsky at the Bauhaus. Schlemmer was a painter of integrity and refinement. His early death, hastened by his maltreatment at the hands of the Nazis, robbed the world of a fine artist.

SCHLEMMER. FIVE WOMEN AND A PASSER-BY.     *Water-colour.* 1925

**SCHMIDT-ROTTLUFF** Karl. German painter; born in 1884 at Chemnitz-Rottluff. Schmidt-Rottluff was one of the founders of *Die Brücke (\*)* together with Kirchner and Heckel. The development of his painting during the years 1905–1910 (Dresden period) was closely linked with the formation of the first *Brücke* style, born of work done in common. Lithography, to which he introduced his friends, and especially woodcuts, influenced his painting, in which simple forms, applied flat and in pure colours with red predominating, are united in a vigorous rhythm. Schmidt-Rottluff was of a more robust character than Kirchner or Heckel, and within the group his works stand out by reason of their architectural quality. He had a more elemental, more earthy force, which made him a link between them and Nolde. After 1910, in Berlin, the differences between his art and that of his friends became more marked. This was partially due to his practice of producing the illusion of space by perspective, unlike Kirchner in particular. During the very steady development of his painting, Schmidt-Rottluff has obstinately sought a synthesis between this perspective and a powerful and solid organiza-

tion of surface. Throughout his life he has executed numerous large water colours, but his most valuable production is his woodcuts, and in particular those of the Brücke period. Here blacks and whites, in masses, points and ridges, meet violently; the expression is simple yet powerful.

**SCHWITTERS** Kurt (1887–1948). German painter; born in Hanover; died at Ambleside, England. After his studies at the Royal Gymnasium in Hanover, Schwitters attended the Academy of Dresden for six years. For a long time he painted portraits to make a living and never looked down on this academic work. Mobilized during the First World War, he was so absent-minded a soldier that his superiors finally preferred to limit him to office work. There his mind, Dadaist before the word was coined, found a chosen field in the search for deserters. He succeeded in scrambling the files so thoroughly that in most cases all traces of the fugitives were lost. However, the job was done with such care that he was never suspected. Returning to Hanover after the Armistice, he was first influenced by the work of Kandinsky and Franz Marc, and a little later he began publishing the *Merz (\*)* magazine, both Dadaist and Constructivist, of which a score of issues appeared between 1923 and 1932. At the same time, at home, he undertook the first *Merzbau*, a sort of column erected in the middle of a room, to which he gave a surprising architectural form and which he decorated or gradually developed with all kinds of odds and ends, many of them picked up in the street. *Merzbau* was to sculpture what *papier collé (\*)* is to painting: ready-made elements were superimposed and combined, sometimes alternated, the only concern being for the plastic effect of the whole. Schwitters worked for ten years on the structure, which finally pierced the three floors of the house. Unfortunately it was destroyed during the Second World War. In 1922 he accompanied Van Doesburg on a Dadaist tour through Holland. At the Bauhaus (\*), in 1924, he recited for the first time his *Sonata in Primal Sounds*, a work that was not published until 1932. He stayed briefly in Paris in 1927; he collaborated on numerous reviews, notably, after 1919, the famous Berlin magazine *Der Sturm*, to which he contributed a number of poems and stories full of placid humour. At the same time he published *Anna Blume* and wrote fairy tales for a local paper. During all this time he did not give up *collage*. When Nazism came to power in Germany, he settled in Norway. At Lysaker, near Oslo, he began a second *Merzbau*, interrupted when the Nazis invaded Norway a few years later. He went to England, where he was interned for some time as a German citizen. Liberated and finding some support (the Museum of Modern Art of New York made him a grant), he undertook a *Merzbau* for the third time in an isolated farm near Ambleside, in the Lake District. This time it was death that interrupted his work in January 1948.

Schwitters was childhood recaptured. He seemed to play with everything. To compose a poem or a picture, he resorted to the most trivial sentence, the most futile object: a used tramway ticket, a cork, valueless elements that, a scavenger of a new kind, he collected anywhere. Thereupon he transfigured these despised objects and showed that nothing is despicable. The tramway ticket glued in a certain way beside other cast-off things was no longer a ticket; it became part of a work whose value is literally inestimable. Touched by the artist's hands, objects suddenly changed their size and atmosphere. The whole animated them, gave them a soul. The artist was a kind of a miracle-worker whose touch transformed everything.

Schwitters himself condensed this idea into a seemingly exaggerated phrase: 'Everything the artist spits is art'. It would be difficult to find an apter illustration of this truth than in his own life and work, for no one has shown better than he that art is indeed anything, if done in a certain way.

SCHWITTERS. COLLAGE IN BLUE AND WHITE.
1926. *Private Collection*

**SECTION D'OR** (The Golden Section). The year 1912 marked the passage from Analytic Cubism to Synthetic Cubism and witnessed the movement's widespread propagation. Gleizes and Metzinger published the first doctrinal work devoted to the new movement. In the course of the autumn, the historic exhibition of the *Section d'Or* at the La Boétie Gallery in Paris gathered together in one vast collection all Cubism's adherents – with the sole exception of its two creators, Braque and Picasso, who showed their works only at the Kahnweiler Gallery. The exhibition included not only Juan Gris, Léger, Gleizes, Metzinger, Lhote, Delaunay, Marcoussis and Roger de La Fresnaye, but also Marcel Duchamp, Jacques Villon, Raymond Duchamp-Villon, Dumont, and Agero. Many of these painters retained only the superficial appearance of Cubism, the geometrical fragmentation of the painted surface, and later turned in opposite directions, some going back to traditional formulae, while others were borne away by abstract currents or Dada experiments, but the unity of their search was based on a common admiration for Cézanne and his constructive lesson. The initiative and the title of this exhibition, which created a considerable stir, were due to the painter and engraver Jacques Villon. In his studio at Puteaux, near Paris, a number of artists passionately interested in problems of rhythm and proportion met on Sunday afternoons, among them the two theoreticians of Cubism, Gleizes and Metzinger, Picabia, Léger and La Fresnaye, as well as the poets Paul Fort, Ribemont-Dessaignes, Jean Cocteau and Joachim Gasquet. Villon developed his theory of vision by pyramids, taken from Leonardo da Vinci, and suggested during these meetings the title of 'Section d'Or', borrowed from the treatise of the Bolognese monk Luca Pacioli, *The Divine Proportion*, published in Venice in 1509 and illustrated by Leonardo himself. Formulated by Vitruvius and taken up again during the Renaissance, the golden section or divine proportion (or gate of harmony) is the ideal relation between two magnitudes, expressed numerically as

$$\frac{1}{0 \cdot 168} = \frac{1 \cdot 618}{1}$$

and demonstrated in many masterpieces of different arts, applied consciously or, more often, by instinct. 'There is,' Voltaire said, 'a hidden geometry in all the arts that the hand produces.' Although the golden section was not the only constant to which the Cubists referred for the mathematical organization of their canvas, it reflected the profound need for order and measure that they felt more through sensibility and reason than as a result of calculation. Distorted by the incomprehension or bad faith of critics, the 'Section d'Or' exhibition met with immense *avant-garde* success in France and abroad, and constituted a general rally under the sign of Cézannian architecture and geometrical discipline.

**SEGONZAC** (*see* Dunoyer de Segonzac).

**SÉRAPHINE** (1864–1934). Séraphine Louis, sometimes called Séraphine de Senlis, French painter born at Assy in the Oise. After a childhood spent as a shepherdess she came to Senlis, where she worked as a char-woman, forced to do what she called 'black jobs'. Almost nothing is known of her life or of how she began to paint. Later, when she was almost

famous, she always guarded the secret of her prodigious enamelled technique. It was Wilhelm Uhde *(\*)* who discovered her in 1912. He had rented a small apartment in Senlis for a rest and had hired an old woman to do the housework for him. In a middle-class household nearby he discovered a still life of apples lying on a table, and was deeply impressed. Enquiring about the artist, he learned that it was the servant Séraphine. The first works of hers that he acquired at this time were confiscated and sold at the beginning of the war, and they have disappeared. It was not until many years later that having established himself in Chantilly, he again saw pictures by Séraphine at an exhibition of regional artists in the town hall of Senlis. Struck by the scope of these new works, he sought out the old woman, who lived shut up in a poor room where a small lamp burned day and night before an image of the Virgin. Séraphine, 'small and withered, with

SÉRAPHINE. COMPOSITION. *Circa* 1930.
*Private Collection*

a fanatical look and livid face framed by dis-
coloured locks', devoted herself entirely to
painting. With the help of Uhde, who supplied
her at last with the vast canvases her overflowing
imagination required, she achieved a work of
unique spiritual significance within a few years.
She painted nothing but flowers, leaves and
fruit, but hers bear little relation to their natural
counterparts. Descriptive or decorative purposes
were completely foreign to her art of mystical
effusion, which can be compared only to the
most lustrous Persian ceramics. The great
stained-glass flames in the churches of Senlis,
the only possible sources of inspiration of the
pious Séraphine, perhaps gave her the idea for
the ascending rhythms that activate her large
canvases. The details of these works give access
to a strange inner world: leaves, whose centre is
a fruit or upon which eyes open and lips appear,
fringed with lashes, recall peacock's plumage and
the wings of the rarest birds. The precision and
sureness of these imaginary forms should be
emphasized, as well as the magic richness of the
colours employed and the balance and harmony
of the canvases, which are related to no natural
order. Despite evidences of certain obsessions –
Séraphine died in a lunatic asylum – her works
are never repetitions; they are perhaps the most
direct attempt at expression of a soul.

SÉRUSIER. THE SHOWER.   *Private Collection, Paris*

**SÉRUSIER** Paul (1863–1927). French painter;
born in Paris; died at Morlaix.
Sérusier the theoretician overshadows Sérusier
the painter, a victim of his fondness for ideas.
Before meeting Gauguin in Brittany, he had
already assembled his comrades of the Académie
Julian (Maurice Denis, Bonnard, Vuillard,
Roussel, Ranson, Piot, Ibels) into a group, in
which philosophy and aesthetics were discussed.
This was the origin of the *Nabi* movement, as
much a gathering of friends as an aesthetic
current. In 1888, when Sérusier brought back
from Brittany Gauguin's theories about painting – synthesis and the symbol – he found ready
recipients for the message (*vide* Nabis). To the
art of the Impressionists, directly inspired by
nature, Sérusier opposed the logic of his reasoning and demonstrations; to improvisation and

intuition he replied with intelligence. His painting
fed upon intentions. The simplicity of his drawing and composition was not naïveté. Unceasing self-control marked all of his work, and
his sensibility is evident in it, although restrained,
as if hidden behind the screen of austere discipline. One would often wish he had a little less
constraint, for intellectual honesty, refined taste
and craftsmanship are insufficient for the construction of a masterpiece. Sérusier's ideas are
more convincing than his works, but seeing the
works one cannot help thinking of what they
might have been if their author had not confined
his gifts within such rigid barriers. As it is,
Sérusier's work is an indispensable link in the
chain of contemporary painting. Sérusier the
painter explains a 'moment' – incomprehensible
without him – in the art of today, and avoids a
break in continuity. He reconciles what would be
contradictory between the Impressionists, Gauguin, Maurice Denis, Bonnard and Vuillard.
Sérusier was born a few years too early. His
fondness for poetry corresponded to the Symbolist movement. Had he been born some fifteen
years later, he would have participated in the
enthusiasm of the young when Cubism was

born. His taste for deliberate construction, composition within the framework of purely linear design, simple and expressive volumes, would have found in Cubism a most favourable environment, and his wish to take part in the development of a valid system would have been satisfied and have realized itself more amply.

**SEURAT** Georges (1859–1891). Born and died in Paris. Seurat's life can best be summed up by dates corresponding to his paintings rather than to events, for the only remarkable facts of his short life are the large canvases to which he devoted all his time and immense creative powers. They represent progressive stages in a drive which led him to heights reached by only a few. Like Van Gogh and Lautrec, who both died under forty at the end of the nineteenth century, Seurat worked feverishly and unceasingly, as though realizing that he was to be allowed only a few years in which to express himself. After attending a muni-

cipal drawing school, he endured two years' instruction at the École Nationale des Beaux-Arts before serving a twelve-month term of military training at Brest. Next he spent his time studying such masters as Ingres, Delacroix and Veronese in the Louvre, and reading the works of Charles Blanc, Chevreul, Sutter, Rood and other theoreticians of colour. Blanc's assertion that 'colour, reduced to certain definite rules, can be taught like music' impressed him deeply, and he examined in detail Chevreul's law governing the simultaneous contrast of colours.

In 1882 and 1883 Seurat devoted nearly all his time to drawing, devising a highly individual language in black and white – the language of form rather than line, of skilfully balanced contrasts, of light and shade stripped of any incidental detail. He confined familiar forms within new profiles and raised them to an unforeseeable summit of poetical expression. Rejecting line as a means, he composed in masses. On rough-grained Ingres drawing paper he blocked in black masses in pencil, leaving clear forms to emerge

SEURAT. FISHING FLEET AT PORT-EN-BESSIN. 1888.     *Museum of Modern Art, New York*

in the intervening white. By shading and perfectly balanced contrasts he revealed unthought-of resemblances. He captured light and colour and transposed them into velvety blacks and expressive whites, thus creating a new world in which plastic forms emerge from dark shadow, the light parts breathe mystery, and the greys, blending black with white, disclose an intense inner life. Flowing arabesques counterbalance one another, forms melt into or emerge from shadow, light shines forth through the mass of his pencil strokes. It was an entirely new conception of drawing; later Signac described them as: 'drawings dependent on values; mere sketches, yet revealing so fine a perception of contrast and shadow that one could paint from them direct without the model'.

Having thus systematically mastered the problem of black and white, Seurat devoted a year's work to his first great painting, *Une Baignade*, for which he did numerous preparatory drawings and colour sketches. The picture was refused by the jury of the 1884 Salon, and their particularly uncompromising attitude that year led to the formation of the Société des Artistes Indépendants, which was to organize annual exhibitions without jury or prizes. Seurat collaborated with Signac, Dubois-Pillet and Redon in drawing up the rules of the new Society and the first Salon des Indépendants opened its doors in May 1884. Seurat exhibited his *Baignade*. Signac was immensely struck by it, but while admiring the keenly observed laws of contrast he was astonished by the dull colouring.

It was Signac who now introduced Seurat to the works of the Impressionists, explaining their efforts and pointing out the advantages of pure colour, sunlight and the interplay of colours. with small, short brush strokes to interpret local colour, sunlight and the interplay of colours. Next they adopted a technique in which instead of mixing their colours on the palette they worked in tiny dots of pure colour, to obtain better balance and a closer interpenetration. Seen from a distance these myriad dots revealed the colour intended. From this time on Seurat's art was essentially based on the laws of simultaneous contrast (to which he later added research on the symbolic significance of line direction),

SEURAT. THE PAINTER AT WORK. 1882–1883

the use of small dots in pure colours, and optical blending. In accordance with these theories he proceeded to paint a series of large compositions and a number of landscapes. He explained to his friend Verhaeren that he spent the summer of each year by the sea or near Paris painting landscapes, to rest his eyesight by contact with nature, whereas in winter he worked indoors on large canvases, trying out and if possible resolving the problems he set himself. In his studio he undertook successively: figures out-of-doors (*Un Dimanche à la Grande Jatte*, 1886) (*see* illustration, page 207); a reunion of people in the open air, the artificial quality of light combined with horizontal forms producing an effect of gloom (*La Parade*, 1887–1888); nude figures in the studio (*Les Poseuses*, 1888); dancing figures under artificial light, with vertical lines accentuated to express gaiety (*Le Chahut*, 1889–1891), and the unfinished *Le Cirque* (1890–1891). Just before his death he produced his only portrait – *Jeune Femme se Poudrant* (1889–1890) – a painting of his mistress Madeleine Knobloch (his friends knew of this liaison only after his death). Originally this canvas showed the reflection of

Seurat's head in the mirror on the wall (his only self-portrait); but one of his friends, ignorant of the intimate relations between artist and model, having remarked that this might lead to dubious jokes on the part of the critics who were nearly all ill-disposed towards Seurat, the painter replaced his image with a pot of flowers.

Indifferent to the heated polemics which followed the exhibition of each of his works, Seurat withdrew more and more into himself, spoke little except when questioned on his theories, confided rarely even in his few intimate friends, and adopted an almost disdainful attitude towards the new recruits attracted to his circle by Signac's tireless propaganda. He showed openly that the enthusiasm of these painters, who adopted his system and profited by his discoveries, clashed with his desire 'to create something new'. However, a limited nucleus of friends gradually formed around Seurat, respecting him as their leader, and the art critic Félix Fénéon wrote articles explaining the theories of those henceforward to be known as the Neo-Impressionists (see *Neo-Impressionism*, also *Fénéon*).

SEURAT. PORTRAIT OF SIGNAC. 1890.
*Private Collection, Paris*

In the summer of 1890, as though realizing that his days were numbered, Seurat agreed to sum up and commit to writing his theory of the concordance between tone characteristics (dark, light), colours (cold, warm) and lines (rising, descending – gay, sad). He formulated his code in the dry, precise style of a man of science rather than in the idiom of a painter:

AESTHETIC – Art is harmony. Harmony consists in the analogy of contrary and the analogy of similar elements of *tone, colour* and *line*, considered according to their dominants and under the influence of light, in gay, calm or sad combinations. The contraries are:

For *tone*, a more luminous (lighter) for a darker.

For *colour*, the complementaries, that is to say a certain red opposed to its complementary, and so on (red-green; orange-blue; yellow-violet).

For *line*, those forming a right-angle.

Gaiety of *tone* is rendered by the luminous dominant; of *colour* by the warm dominant; of *line* by lines rising from the horizontal.

Calm of *tone* is the equality of dark and light; of *colour*, equality of warm and cold; calm of *line* is given by the horizontal.

Sadness of *tone* is given by the dark dominant; of *colour* by the cold dominant; of *line* by lines descending from the horizontal.

TECHNIQUE – Taking into account the phenomena produced by the duration of a light-impression on the retina, synthesis necessarily follows as a result. The means of expression is the optical mixing of the tones and colours (local colour and that resulting from illumination: sunlight, lamplight, gaslight, etc.), that is to say the mixing of light and its effects (shadows), in accordance with the laws of contrast, gradation and irradiation.

In March 1891, a few months after having formulated these principles, Seurat was struck down by a fatal fever. 'At the time of Seurat's death,' said Signac later, 'the critics acknowledged his talent but considered that he left no body of work behind him! It seems to me that on the contrary he gave superbly all he had to give. He would certainly have gone on and produced more, but his task was finished. He had investigated and demonstrated all his principles: black and white, harmony of line, composition, contrasts, and colour harmony. What more can be asked of a painter?'

Seurat would undoubtedly have been delighted by the dry obituary notice in which his loyal friend Félix Fénéon recorded the principal dates of the artist's life: 'Seurat died, on the 29th of March, at the age of thirty-one. He had exhibited: at the Salon in 1883; at the Groupe des Artistes Indépendants in 1884; at the *Société des Artistes Indépendants* in ·1884–5, 1886, 1887, 1888, 1889, 1890 and 1891; at the *Blanc et Noir*, Amsterdam, in 1886. His work comprises: 170 small wooden panels, 420 drawings, 6 sketchbooks, and about 60 canvases (figures, seascapes, landscapes) among which five measuring several square metres (*la Baignade, Un Dimanche à la Grande Jatte, Poseuses, Chahut, Cirque*), and, probably, many a masterpiece.'

SEURAT. YOUNG WOMAN POWDERING HERSELF. 1889–1890. *Courtauld Collection, London*

**SEVERINI** Gino. Italian painter; born in 1883 in Cortona. In Rome, in 1901 he met Boccioni, the future theoretician of Futurism, and in the following year Balla, who became his first master. In 1906, coming to Paris, he found in Seurat an inspiration and an example. He settled in the studio where later Dufy, Braque, Suzanne Valadon and Utrillo were to work. He painted his most important pictures there, among them *The Boulevard* and *Pan-Pan at the Monico* (1909–1911). In Montmartre he made friends with Picasso, Max Jacob, Pierre Reverdy and Apollinaire, who was a witness at his marriage to the daughter of the poet Paul Fort. In 1910 his name figured among the signers of the Futurist manifesto (*vide* Futurism), and in the following year he brought about a meeting of Boccioni, Carrà and Russolo with Picasso, Braque, Juan Gris and Apollinaire in Paris. He participated in the first Futurist exhibition at the Bernheim-Jeune Gallery. His picture *Pan-Pan at the Monico* is considered the masterpiece of Futurism. Raymond Escholier writes in his book *La Peinture au XXe Siècle* that the Cubists, after having seen these canvases painted with the pure colours of Seurat, gave up chiaroscuro and returned to the colour and bright tones of Neo-Impressionism. In this justly famous picture Severini attempted to introduce a feeling of movement into space by multiplying the frenetic rhythms that isolate form while still pursuing it. Later he felt a need to counter Picasso's frenzied individualism with an art liberated from the tyranny of personality, and his research brought him close to the work of La Fresnaye, Léger, Juan Gris, Metzinger and Gleizes. His subsequent works and studies on the *Section d'Or* led him from Cubism to Classicism. In 1922, in a series of frescoes executed for Montegufoni Castle, near Florence, he painted masks from the Italian *commedia dell' arte*, a motif that can also be found in his canvases. But at this time he was already beginning

SEVERINI. THE BOULEVARD.                                  *Estorick Collection, London*

to be more interested by mural art than by easel painting. Invited to Switzerland, he decorated several churches in Semsales, La Roche, Fribourg and Lausanne with frescoes and mosaics. He also executed mosaics in Italy and then in France. He has published notable works, in both Italian and French, as well as a volume of memoirs.

**SICKERT**  Walter Richard (1860–1942). English painter; born in Munich of an English mother and a Danish father. His father, O. A. Sickert (1828–1885), who had settled in England in 1868, and his grandfather, Johannes Sickert (1803–1864), were also painters. He studied at the Slade School *(\*)* in London with Alphonse Le Gros and then became a pupil of Whistler. Later he fell under the influence of Degas and became a close friend of his. In 1911 he helped found the Camden Town Club to promote an independent art. With Steer *(\*)*, Sickert was the most influential of the English Impressionists. His family originally dissuaded him from becoming a painter, so Sickert spent several years in the theatre – a *milieu* with which he remained in contact all his life. In 1883 he visited Paris, sent by his teacher, Whistler, to

deliver to the Salon the famous *The Artist's Mother*, now in the Louvre. About 1900, Sickert settled in France, where he lived for five years. He worked often at Dieppe, drawn there by his admiration for Degas, whom he considered the greatest painter of his day.

A bit of a misanthrope, he divided humanity into two categories: patients and nurses. He enjoyed depicting incidents, sometimes sordid, of the everyday life of poor districts. He grew critical of Whistler's surface brilliance and facility and began to work in a slow, thoughtful manner, using a smooth, rich-toned palette. From Whistler he retained sombre shadings and a sober, restrained style. Prudent and cautious, he never let himself be carried away by what he considered the too facile charm of the light palette of the French Impressionists. Sickert owed a good bit of his popularity to his extraordinary personal dynamism – much as Whistler and Degas did theirs – but he was the undisputed master of that hollow period in English painting between the death of Turner in 1851 and the growth of the new contemporary school. *Ennui* (*c.* 1913), in the Tate Gallery, and *Portrait of Victor Lecour* (1924), in the Manchester City Art Gallery, are among his finest work.

**SIGNAC** Paul (1863–1935). Born and died in Paris. Signac loved life and was a man of passionate enthusiasms: for painting, science, literature, politics. Jovial and heavily built, he looked more like a Breton sailor than a painter. Vehement and impulsive in his talk, he delighted in probing problems to their depth; his every comment, in which words of kindness mingled with expressions unfit for print, revealed his intelligence, exuberance, conviction and combative nature, but even his most impetuous outbursts were never tinged by the slightest pettiness or malice. His position was not an easy one, for he was fired with a determination to face all the issues. Yet however violent his opposition might be, it always revealed a generous mind searching for truth, ready to admit different ways of arriving at truth and accepting the validity of research diametrically opposed to his own; but both in art and in life he was the implacable enemy of flattery and pretentiousness, self-seeking and hypocrisy. Signac was in his element when wrestling with problems, whether social or artistic, for they seemed to nourish his vigorous temperament eager for action.

His middle-class family put up no resistance

SICKERT. PREOCCUPATION.

to his early decision to take up painting. At the start he was influenced by Monet – at that time not yet widely appreciated as an artist – and in 1884, at the age of twenty-one, he became one of the founders of the Société des Artistes Indépendants with Georges Seurat and others, and exhibited for the first time in their Salon. Seurat and Signac became intimate friends and were soon to collaborate in formulating the theories of Neo-Impressionism, the most important and revolutionary art movement of the late nineteenth century. They quickly rallied to the cause a small circle of friends of varying degrees of talent, such as Camille Pissarro and his son Lucien, Henri-Edmond Cross, Maximilien Luce, Charles Angrand, Hippolyte Petitjean, Theo van Rysselberghe, Albert Dubois-Pillet and a few others. Signac was the driving force of the group, trying at all costs to attract adherents, untiringly professing his creed in discussions and by letter. After the premature death of Seurat in 1891 he undertook the difficult task of continuing the struggle for their ideals as leader of the group.

Signac had a passion for sailing, which led him

SICKERT. THE BLUE HAT. *Private Collection*

to visit and paint nearly all the French ports. He sailed to Holland and Corsica, travelled to the Alps, Italy and Constantinople. For many years his base was Saint-Tropez, which he 'discovered' as he also 'discovered' Port-en-Bessin, Collioure, etc. From all these ports of call he brought back innumerable water colours, in which line and vibrant colour fuse spontaneously to seize the changing aspects of nature. Afterwards, in the studio, he used these quick sketches for the preparation and execution of large canvases, in which his aim was to balance the different elements of nature in order to achieve what he called 'the most harmonious, luminous and colourful result possible'. Félix Fénéon, a friend of Signac's from the start, described his paintings: 'His colourings spread out in spacious waves, tone down, meet, fuse, and form a polychromatic design similar to a linear arabesque. To express these harmonies and oppositions he uses only pure colours. Arranging these on his palette in the order of the spectrum, the painter mixes only contiguous colours, thus as far as possible obtaining the colours of the prism, adding white to graduate their tone scale. He juxtaposes these dabs of paint on the canvas, their interplay corresponding to local colour, light, and varying shadows. The eye will perceive them mixed optically.

SIGNAC. SAILBOATS.     *Watercolour.* 1924.

The variation of colouring is assured by this juxtaposition of elements, its freshness by their purity and a brilliant lustre by the optical blending, because unlike a mixture of pigments, optical mixing tends to brightness.'

Of insatiable curiosity, Signac threw himself into the study of Chevreul's optical laws and often wrote on behalf of these theories. He wrote *From Eugène Delacroix to Neo-Impressionism* (1899), the vital textbook of the Neo-Impressionist movement, a study on *Jongkind*, a lucid essay on *The Subject in Painting* (*Encyclopédie Française*, vol. XVI, chap. 2), an introduction to the catalogue of an exhibition *Seurat and his Friends* (Paris, 1934),

SIGNAC. THE SAINT-MARTIN CANAL. 1933.     *Private Collection, Paris*

as well as a Diary, of which the entries for the years 1894 to 1899 were later published in the *Gazette des Beaux-Arts* (1949-1953). As though these multiple activities were insufficient to occupy his ebullient temperament, Signac accepted the presidency of the Société des Artistes Indépendants in 1908 and for twenty-six years worked untiringly in the service of his friends, encouraging the younger generation (he was one of the first to buy a picture by Matisse) and advocating the principles of

SISLEY. FLOOD AT PORT-MARLY. 1876.                              *Louvre*

his conception of art. His vigorous personality, which always pushed him into the limelight, may have sometimes caused his contemporaries to overlook the fact that this active, dominating man was also a talented painter of great poetic sensibility.

**SISLEY** Alfred (1839–1899). French painter; born in Paris; died at Moret. Together with Monet, Sisley represents Impressionism *(\*)* in its purest form. He was tempted less than anyone by portraits or still lifes, except at the beginning; he confined himself almost exclusively to landscape, and his work did not undergo any profound change during the course of his life. His first known pictures, notably those he sent to the 1866 Salon, have been compared, in tonality, to the work of Corot and Courbet; this similarity revealed the nature of his preferences. He was lucky enough not to experience materially difficult beginnings like his Impressionist friends, but when he began to fight for the new painting, he was ruined and felt financial hardship even more than they. While in their worst days Pissarro and Cézanne received forty francs for their pictures, Sisley had more than once to

give his away for thirty or even twenty-five. Moreover, he died before he could benefit from the triumph of his ideas and his work. Immediately after his death his talent was recognized, and his paintings soon fetched high prices. Sisley's art consists almost entirely of landscapes, and even for these he confined himself to the valley of the Seine, the Île-de-France, especially the Fontainebleau region, of which he remains one of the most authentic interpreters. He succeeded admirably, and with as much sensibility as Monet, in transcribing the movement of foliage or the scintillation of light on water; but at the same time he succeeded better than Monet in preserving the structure of the landscape by not reducing it to luminous effects with unstable colours. Form remained firm in his work, not dissolved in the atmosphere; a tree is a tree, a house a house. There is nothing systematic in his art. He did not adopt the low horizons of Boudin, and while he gave an important place to the sky in certain pictures, this was because, in its movement and colour, it was part of the subject he was representing. In each of his canvases he gives the impression of having achieved as much as was possible. One could not imagine thicker undergrowth than that he painted in the forest of Fontainebleau, scenes of floods more desperate than those he transcribed at Port-Marly, snow scenes more sadly luminous than those of Louveciennes, springtimes clearer than those at Saint-Mammès, although he avoided dramatizing his subjects. His delicate and tender art enabled him to evoke with infinite poetry and grace the peaceful and picturesque life of the town of Moret, where he lived permanently after 1879. Although he experienced a fate similar to that of the other Impressionists, although he had also attended courses at the Atelier Gleyre (*) in his youth, like Bazille, Monet and Renoir, and had fallen back upon the modest generosity of the baker and collector Murer, little has been written about his work and life. This is not because he lacked talent, but rather because his life was neither adventurous nor picturesque, because his art was entirely ruled by sensibility, did not strive to illustrate a rigorously established system and thus does not lend itself to commentary. Neither a few sojourns in England, his wish to be received at the Salon nor poverty shook Sisley's conviction or altered his art. As modest in his ambitions as he was tenacious in his convictions, he remained true to himself and to his freinds.

**SLADE SCHOOL** Of the three schools which have dominated the teaching of painting and sculpture in England during the past century – the Royal Academy Schools, the Royal College of Art and the Slade – the latter has maintained the most consistently liberal reputation. The history of the recovery of British art from its nadir in the nineteenth century is, in some measure, the history of the students of the Slade. Among those who have passed through the School are D. S. MacColl, Sickert (*), William Rothenstein, Augustus John (*), Gwen John, Ethel Walker, Wyndham Lewis (*), Harold Gilman, Spencer Gore, Mark Gertler, Stanley Spencer, and Paul Nash (*). Felix Slade, who died in 1868, in addition to leaving his own collections to the nation, founded three chairs of fine art at the Universities of Oxford, Cambridge and London. His further

DE SMET. LA LOGE.  *Kunstmuseum, Basel*

endowment of six scholarships to University College, London, led to the founding of the School of Art which opened in 1871 – one of the first in the world to be established within a university.

Sir Edward Poynter, the first Slade Professor, friend of Courbet and Manet, sounded the note of reform at the outset by introducing students to the living model without delay and deploring the meretricious finish demanded by the academic conventions of the day. He was succeeded five years later by Alphonse Legros, who had settled in England some years earlier at the suggestion of Whistler (*). Through his contacts with the leading impressionists, Legros brought to the Slade a knowledge of contemporary French painting which was to affect a whole generation of students. The Professorship passed, in 1892, to Frederick Brown, who appointed Henry Tonks and Wilson Steer (*) among the teachers; in 1919 to Tonks himself; in 1930 to Randolph Schwabe; in 1949 to William Coldstream.

Today the School has some two hundred whole-time students and thirty part-time. Admission is by competitive examination, and most students follow the three-year course leading to the University of London Diploma in Fine Art. Painting, sculpture, graphic and stage design are taught, and emphasis is given, as it always has been, to the history of art. D. S. MacColl, Roger Fry, Tancred Borenius and R. Wittkower have held lectureships or professorships in the history of art, and the school has close ties with the Courtauld Institute of Art.

**SMET** Gustav de (1877–1943). Belgian painter; born in Ghent; died at Deurle. With his younger brother Léon, also a painter, he took part in the business of his father, Jules de Smet, a contractor in interior decoration. However, he attended courses at the Academy of Fine Arts, whose discipline delayed the blossoming of his talent for a long time. No sooner had he emerged from adolescence than he established himself in the country, in the region of the Lys, to which he remained faithful until his death. From 1901 on, he could be seen at Laethem-Saint-Martin *(*)* with Permeke *(*)*, Van den Berghe, Servaes and his brother Léon. In 1914 he took refuge in Holland. After the war he did not hasten to return to his country, although he visited there frequently. He exhibited several times in Brussels, founded 'Selection', a studio of artistic renewal, with André de Ridder, and became one of the most determined advocates of modern painting. In 1922, he established himself in a small village near Ghent, and then, in 1927, at Deurle, where he died after a long illness. His youth had been rather uncertain. It was only in his maturity that his expressionism developed a personal note, and only after 1922 that he found his idiom and painted images in which simplification of design and colour, geometrical construction of forms, reddish

earth tones, and a disjointed composition combine to give the spectator an impression, not devoid of charm, of some scene of childhood. He painted landscapes, acrobats, life in the fields, peasants and their animals, doleful young women and adorable little girls. In these paintings, the baroque artist disappears behind the compassionate and affectionate man. Much less vigorous, more delicate, less gifted, but more sensitive than Permeke, Gustav de Smet represents the other face of Flemish Expressionism, a gracious melancholy rather than sad Expressionism, less taciturn, often even tender. His technique lacked assurance, or at least dexterity. And if he holds an enviable place in the history of Northern Baroque, it is chiefly due to the peacefulness, gentleness and meditativeness that his work contains.

**SMITH** Sir Matthew. Born in 1879 in Halifax, England. After studying at the Manchester School of Art and, later, at the Slade School in London, Smith went to Paris in 1910 and has alternated between France and England ever since. He was a member of the London Group. His father, a well-known collector of academic painting, at first encouraged his son's career, but when he saw that he was being

SMITH. WOMAN WITH ROSE. 1930.                    *Private Collection*

drawn to the work of the Impressionists, he attempted to put a stop to it. It was only in 1908, at the age of twenty-nine, that Smith obtained his father's permission to go to France – and even then he was forbidden to go to Paris! Attracted by the Gauguin legend, he went first to paint at Pont-Aven *(\*)*. When he finally got to Paris, he enrolled at the academy Matisse had founded in the former Convent of the Birds. Unfortunately it closed a month after Smith's arrival. In 1914, he adopted the Fauvist manner, which he retained throughout his career but which he enriched with more and more brilliant arabesques, using rich, oily colour dominated by his sonorous reds. Sir Matthew Smith occupies an important position in the contemporary English school: as the ambassador of French painting he has aroused among his compatriots an interest in 'pure' painting and has restored to the act itself a dignity which it had not known since Turner's day.

In 1950, 26 of Smith's works were shown in the British Pavilion at the Venice Biennale and in 1953, the Tate Gallery held the first complete Matthew Smith retrospective, surveying his career from 1909 on by means of a selection of 81 oils.

**SOIRÉES DE PARIS** After the *Revue Blanche (\*)* suspended publication in 1903, there remained no magazine entirely devoted to contemporary art. Temporarily, *Soirées de Paris*, on the initiative of Guillaume Apollinaire, attempted to fill this gap. However, *Soirées de Paris* was at first an exclusively literary magazine; it was organized as early as 1911, and the first issue appeared in February 1912. Its founders were Apollinaire, Billy, Dalize, Salmon and Tudesq. The novelist and critic André Billy was the editor. Apollinaire's first article, 'On the Subject in Modern Painting', frightened his comrades somewhat. It was a formal defence of the Cubist doctrine, and they feared that such adventures might jeopardize the magazine's success, which was promising. In fact, *Soirées de Paris* remained strictly literary until November 1913, when Apollinaire took over the editorship with Jean Cérusse (pseu-

donym of the painter Serge Jastrebzoff). The magazine set up its offices in the apartment of Baroness Oettingen, Cérusse's sister. Meetings were organized there between men of letters and artists: Picasso, Léger, Kisling, Cendrars, Raynal, Zadkine, Picabia, Archipenko, Dalize, Modigliani, Max Jacob, Severini, Soffici, Chirico, his brother Savinio, who gave memorable piano recitals there, and others, all more or less contributors to the review. From then on *Soirées de Paris* devoted numerous pages to the plastic arts. One issue was entirely devoted to the Douanier Rousseau. Works by Matisse, Picasso, Léger, Vlaminck, Archipenko, Picabia, Marie Laurencin, Gleizes and others were regularly reproduced. Cubism, Futurism, Simultaneism were commented upon. During the two years that the magazine appeared, the general tone of the artistic part was polemical: attacks, retorts, challenging letters followed one another; even duels were provoked but without going farther than an exchange of seconds. With its success, in the spring of 1914 *Soirées de Paris* contemplated publishing art books, which were to be inaugurated by an album of ideograms of Apollinaire, when the order for general mobilization was given, dispersing most of the contributors and thus, abruptly, putting an end to the publication of the magazine. The short life of *Soirées de Paris* did not prevent it from bringing about fruitful exchanges between writers and artists. Full freedom had been granted to the expression of the most diverse tendencies, upon the sole condition of their being disinterested, bold and new. This is why *Soirées de Paris* was soon echoed. Even during the war, those who had not been mobilized gathered together, and new magazines were born, animated by the same spirit: *L' Élan* of Ozenfant (1915), *Nord-Sud* of Reverdy (1917), *SIC* of Pierre Albert-Birot (1917). At the same time a similar effervescence could be witnessed outside France; first in New York, in 1915, in the magazine *291* with Marcel Duchamp and Picabia *(vide* Stieglitz); in Zürich in *Dada (\*)* with Tzara and Arp; in Leyden in *De Stijl*, a review of abstract art founded by Van Doesburg in 1917 *(vide Stijl)*, all publications more or less directly inspired by the example of *Soirées de Paris*.

SOLANA. THE MASKS. 1938.  *Collection of Edgar Neville*

**SOLANA** José Gutiérrez (1885–1945). Spanish painter; born and died in Madrid. The descendant of an old and half-ruined family of Santander, Solana always worked alone, beginning to paint when he was very young, without going through any recognized school. His painting is no more than the illustration of the secret passions of his life, which was spent almost entirely in the slums and suburbs of Madrid, and in the Cantabrian harbours. In very curious literary works, among them the two volumes of *Scenes and Customs of Madrid* (1912 and 1918), written in a direct and bitter style, he drew up a kind of a balance sheet of his interests: he associated his existence closely with the proletarian districts of the Spanish capital or the wretched villages of Castille that he visited tirelessly in stagecoaches, in ramshackle vehicles of another age, or in dirty third-class railway carriages. In rustic feasts and their coarse masquerades he discovered rites of ancient grandeur. At the Madrid 'flea-market', the *Rastro*, he picked up odd debris of the past and filled his studio with exotic or bizarre objects, which became for him an inexhaustible source of inspiration. He was particularly fond of dolls and wax figures, whose coloured effigies come mysteriously to life behind shop windows. A visit to the Musée Grévin in Paris inspired him to a reconstruction of strange revolutionary scenes (*Charlotte Corday, Madame Roland*). He also excelled at painting groups of friends and representatives of the same trade or the same class; he gave living beings something like the plenitude and indifference of objects; individual qualities were obliterated in favour of collective evocations of unusual power; *The Choristers, The Return of the Indian, The Bishop's Visit, Outcasts of Fortune*. Solana painted with thick pigments, charged with greenish glitters, under a dark light, with sometimes blood-red flashes of lightning that recall the black paintings of Goya. It is an essentially physical painting that reflects the author's fondness for terrible smells and strong flavours. But in his extensive graphic work, scenes reduced to their mere structure retain the same quality of presence. In spite of the fear he inspired, Solana was recognized by his countrymen. He was awarded the chief official distinctions of his country, and large exhibitions abroad confirmed his renown. However, until his death he led a gloomy, retired life in Madrid. Isolated and savage, he expressed the anguish and tragic despair of a great, torn nation. While Spanish writers of the preceding generation – Unamuno, Ganivet, Ortega – analyzed the causes of Spanish decadence to find remedies in them, Solana did not want to give up any part of the legacy with whose miseries he was as well acquainted as anyone, but whose haunting qualities and obsessions he loved because he sensed their hidden meanings.

**SOUTINE** Chaim (1894–1943). Russian painter; born at Smilovich, near Minsk; died in Paris. Although hailed as a master while still very young, Soutine remained all his life isolated and almost ignored, most of his work buried in collections. In 1923, for example, Doctor Barnes bought one hundred of his Céret canvases in a lot. Soutine steadily refused to exhibit, not out of false modesty but because of an insuperable restlessness that made him take up again, and often destroy, all the old works within his reach. Except for his participation in the large exhibition of Independent Art in Paris in 1937, one had to wait virtually until the last few years to see important shows devoted to him. And in the meantime he had died. So it is only now possible – thanks also to the accounts published by those who knew him well – to appraise the secret and sensitive personality of this painter. Chaim Soutine was the tenth in a family of eleven children. His father was a poor tailor. To escape the poverty of the ghetto, Soutine went as a boy to Minsk and then to Vilno, where he enrolled in the School of Fine Arts while working as a photographer's assistant. A doctor impressed by

SOUTINE. CHOIRBOY. 1925.
*Collection of M. and Mme Castaing, Lèves*

his gifts gave him the chance to go to France. Arriving in Paris in 1911 to enrol at the École Nationale des Beaux-Arts, Soutine was still almost a child. Besides, he kept for a long time the closed face, with eyes that seemed turned inward, that his friend Modigliani rendered in an unforgettable portrait (1917). He carried awkwardly in front of him the beautiful small, pale hands mentioned by Élie Faure, who also described his frightened ingenuousness and the way he seemed to be fleeing under a shower of rain. He was all gentleness, his friend Henri Serouya adds, recalling his candid child's smile, which showed his big white teeth. He lived in *La Ruche*, the famous phalanstery of the Rue de Dantzig near the Vaugirard slaughterhouses, where Chagall, Lipchitz, Cendrars and Kremégne were already installed. He went through these trying years with the same certainty that had made him thrust his incomprehensible urge to paint upon his family and his scandalized village. His formation was entirely inner, tenacious and obstinate, consisting as much in desultory reading of novelists, poets and philosophers, as in contemplating the works of masters, from Rembrandt to Courbet and Cézanne. He so distrusted his first attempts, which were always secret, that hardly anything is left of them. They constituted much less a technical apprenticeship than the attainment of a state of grace, a moral preparation, a novitiate of which he remained always proud. He needed a chance: he liked the word and believed in what it meant, as do all those who have been miserable. The collector and patron of arts Zborowski, whom he met through Modigliani, gave him this chance in 1919 by sending him to paint in Céret, in the Pyrénées-Orientales. He stayed there for almost three years. During this first respite, at the contact of the dazzling light of the South, the long-awaited transformation was achieved almost at once. Soutine's colours livened little by little, lost their opacity and their resistance as inert material. He succeeded in amalgamating them into his emotions and passions. It seemed that he wanted to charge them with animal or vegetable substances. To discover these, he raked furiously through living tissue; he broke the lines and reliefs of landscapes as if to extract their essence.

SOUTINE. LANDSCAPE. 1939.
*Collection of M. and Mme Castaing, Lèves*

lence in which he no doubt collected his forces. He frequently experienced periods of complete sterility, and then suddenly he threw himself into action, literally killed himself on the canvas, and could accomplish an enormous amount of work. From his stay in Céret he brought back two hundred canvases. This manner of working explains why he considered all preparation not only useless but even harmful, because it involved the risk of dispersing and shattering his inspiration. He never drew, in the traditional sense of the word; he simply roughed in his elements swiftly with charcoal, making the framework and not the delineation of the work to come. These preparatory notes had meaning only for him. This was what he had already done on the walls of his native village, to the horror of his playmates. He could fill in a form, inflect a contour, give it warmth and life only with paint itself. He ground his colours furiously, mixing pastes that he poured out by whole tubes. However, Anne Collié, who knew him well, assures us that he never lost sight of his aim, never put

The secret of Soutine was probably that of immense love. He could not bear the incommunicability of beings, which made him suffer cruelly, or the immobility and vacuity of death. When he interrogated inert faces, he did not hesitate to breathe his own life into them. If he examined rotten flesh, a skinned ox, dead poultry, it was to discover the germs of new growth and resurrection in them. Awareness of his imperfection and his own misery created in him the perpetual dissatisfaction that made him resume the same theme unceasingly and destroy pitilessly all that was not up to his standards. But, in the search for the impossible fusion, never achieved in painting, of the life of the world and the inertia of the materials employed, Soutine perhaps came closer to a solution than anyone else. His painting was charged with substances, fermentations, and movements. He worked under a terrible nervous strain: to begin, to prepare to receive the shock and respond to it, he had first to wake up from a sort of somno-

MODIGLIANI. PORTRAIT OF SOUTINE.

277

a stroke on canvas without having considered it in relation to the preceding one, in a tension of his whole being that exhausted him. After Céret, he stayed in 1925 at Cagnes, where his intense probing of his figures reached a state of paroxysm.

STEER. THE BEACH AT WALBERSWICK. *Tate Gallery, London*

He did numerous portraits and painted the series of *Choirboys* in 1927. In 1929, at Chatel-Guyon, he met M. and Mme Castaing and at last found a home at their Château of Lèves, near Chartres. He made long stays there, frequenting Montparnasse less and less and refusing to take part in any public shows. In 1940 the German occupation brought him‧ painful trials. He took refuge in a small village in Touraine, Champigny-sur-Veude, where he continued to paint admirable landscapes, despite the threats that weighed upon him. At the beginning of August 1943 an intestinal perforation made it urgently necessary that he be moved to Paris. Operated upon too late, he died on the morning of August 9th.

**STEER** Philip Wilson (1860–1942). English painter born in Birkenhead. After studying at the Gloucester School of Art.and then, in Paris, at the Académie Julian and the École des Beaux-Arts, Steer was one of the founders of the New English Art Club. Between 1893 and 1930 he taught painting at the Slade School of Art (*) in London. As a landscapist and, occasionally, a portraitist, Steer was a leading figure, along with Sickert, in the English Impressionist movement. Although he was strongly influenced by Whistler, Manet, and Monet, his first 'manner' has an authentically poetic quality and a sufficiently individual style so that one of his canvases of the period stands out at once from the work of his predecessors or contemporaries. That style is characterized by a sharp emphasis on line and a nervous construction which might seem, at first glance, to be the result of naïve or facile simplification. Those qualities were, on the contrary, achieved through an accomplished mastery of draughtsmanship and a carefully worked out synthesis. His style developed slowly and became fuller, freer and more sensuous, particularly so in his nudes, where the paint has a heavy, unctuous quality. In his landscapes can be seen the influence of Constable and Gainsborough, and in his figure compositions one sometimes notes motifs drawn from Fragonard and Boucher. Toward the end of his career he worked at a series of paintings thinner in texture and whose lyrical quality recalls Turner. By then he was into his seventies and his sight was failing. Up until then, however, he played a leading role in the London art world. He was awarded the Order of Merit, the highest distinction available to a British artist. The Tate Gallery has a wide selection of his works from all periods.

**STEIN** Leo (1872–1947) and Gertrude (1874–1946). American writers, brother and sister, born in Pittsburgh, Pennsylvania. After completing their university studies, Leo and Gertrude Stein arrived in Paris about 1900 and settled themselves in a *pavillon* at 27 Rue de

Fleurus, which shortly became the gathering place for an endless stream of poets, critics and other writers, as well as the leading *avant-garde* artists. The Steins early indicated a preference for the work of Matisse and Picasso, who were still relatively unknown. Over the years, Leo winnowed out his reflections on art in three volumes, *ABC of Esthetics*, *Appreciation: Painting, Poetry and Prose* and *Journey into the Self*. What he had to say about art can be distilled into a single proposition – that an aesthetic accomplishment can be fully seized only if one has first learned to behold nature with the eyes of a painter. This contention, which he sustained with reasons of a highly personal character, enabled him to illuminate the basic impulse of an artist even when he did not altogether sympathize with it, and he did not, in fact, invariably cherish the most advanced men. His sister, on the other hand, never altered in her fidelity to Cubism and its exponents – especially to Picasso and Juan Gris. Her most imposing work is a complex and

warmth and sharpness her account of her many contacts with artists and writers (some of whom subsequently had their complaints to make on her interpretation of history – as did brother Leo). Her name will always be intimately associated with the Cubist adventure and the formation of *avant-garde* taste in America. As a writer, of course, she has long been accredited as a liberating agent, not only in the United States but also in France, which she did not desert – except for brief visits – even during two world wars.

**STEINLEN** Théophile-Alexandre (1859–1923). Swiss painter; born in Lausanne; died in Paris. Among the professional humorists who, like Willette and Forain, influenced him slightly at the time of the *Chat Noir* cabaret, Steinlen, arriving in Paris in 1883 from his Vaudois country, cut a serious figure. He was the friend of all outcasts of fortune and all vagabonds of cities and villages who creep on, thin and bent, under wind and rain, tramps who inspire fear, couples who embrace interminably, nervous dogs and adventurous cats. He took pleasure in illustrating the dreams of a generous generation that believed, with Anatole France, in the coming of 'better times'. His drawing, as enveloping as that of Carrière, seemed to defend and protect. Even in violence and revolt, he preserved a kind of humility and tenderness. In his generosity, he was, like Daumier, the exact opposite of Forain. From

STEINLEN. THE RUE CAULAINCOURT. *Lithograph*

original novel, *The Making of Americans*, and her impish libretto did much to ensure the fame of Virgil Thomson's *Four Saints in Three Acts*. She particularly relished the work of Juan Gris, devoting to him several critiques, notably the one in *Transition*, in 1927. In 1933, in her *Autobiography of Alice B. Toklas* she set forth with

even his most cursory works, from his posters and sketches for *Gil Blas* or *L'Assiette au Beurre*, from his illustrations for the *Dans la Rue* of Aristide Bruant, *Les Soliloques du Pauvre* of Jehan Rictus and *La Chanson des Gueux* of Jean Riche pin, there rises a continuous and comforting warmth. This great craftsman of drawing saw his work as a journalist less as a livelihood than as a means of defending truth and helping his neighbour. While his painting, which is excessively dark, has not always aged well, and while his colour is sometimes uncertain, his etchings and lithographs – his work in black and white, dominated by chiaroscuro – evoke the life of the streets, the factories, and the mines and suggest hunger,

ICI, C'EST ICI STIEGLITZ
FOI ET AMOUR

291

PICABIA

PICABIA. DRAWING FOR THE REVIEW '291'. 1915

accidents, war and love, with a pathetic quality that transcends anecdote and sentimentality. Although he always treats familiar things, his feeling for the epic, which most of his contemporaries lacked, makes us forget his unevenness – the price of his great abundance – to admire only his active goodness and the soaring of his line.

**STIEGLITZ** Alfred (1864–1946). Born in Hoboken, New Jersey. Intending to become an engineer, Stieglitz had enrolled at the Berlin Polytechnic in 1881, but there discovered photography to be his vocation. He was awarded a first prize at an international exhibition in 1887. He returned to the U.S. in 1891 and soon after began working for the recognition

of his medium as an art. He insisted that photography, no less than painting, must be exacting as to design, composition and values, even though these should be kept pertinent to its own purposes. In collaboration with various associates (chiefly Edward Steichen), he founded, in 1902, 'Photo-Secession', in an attic loft at 291 Fifth Avenue, New York City. The next year (and until 1917) he issued his quarterly *Camera Work*, filling it with discussions on art by such writers as Bernard Shaw, Maeterlinck, H. G. Wells, Galsworthy and Gertrude Stein. Starting in 1907 Stieglitz flung himself with still greater vehemence into another cause, adding to the exhibition of photography examples of modern graphic and plastic art. Drawings by Rodin, which he presented in 1908, produced a shudder among the New York public, and a Matisse show (the artist's American première), which followed, prompted charges of imbecility. Thereafter, despite its name, *Camera Work* increasingly devoted its pages to plastic art as well as photographic. And, as a further sign of this change, the gallery was called '291', after its address on Fifth Avenue. Despite the splutters of the conventional, Stieglitz inaugurated the following American 'firsts': Toulouse-Lautrec lithographs (1909), Matisse drawings (1910) and sculpture (1912), Henri Rousseau (1910), Cézanne watercolours (1911), Picasso (1911). Following the 1913 Armory Show in New York, he also presented Picabia (1913), Brancusi (1914), Braque (1914), African Negro Sculpture (1914), Manolo, and others. Aided by Agnes Ernst Meyer he founded in 1916 another periodical, *291*, enlisting as colleagues Marius de Zayas, Picabia, and Marcel Duchamp, and discharging through its pages a series of blasts on 'anti-painting', which almost simultaneously had a counterpart in the Dada movement in Zurich. Stieglitz did not neglect the American moderns then emerging. His shows included John Marin, Alfred Maurer, Hartley, Max Weber, MacDonald-Wright, Walkowitz, and later, from 1925 to 1929, Dove, Strand, Bluemner, Peggy Bacon, Demuth, his own wife Georgia O'Keeffe and the sculptor Lachaise. Finally, installed from 1930 to 1946 at An American Place, 509 Madison Avenue, he continued his efforts there. Regularly he showed his artists, notably Marin, whose name he fully established by thirty-seven years of almost uninterrupted exhibiting. This roll call, both European and American, demonstrates the nature of Stieglitz's fight for modern art, but it hardly indicates the intelligence, pugnacity and alertness required to subdue a public and press consistently hostile. The issue long remained unsettled. His resources were slight, his proceeds were often barely sufficient to support his artists and meet minimal expenses. Stieglitz could often manage only because of disinterested and voluntary outside support. Yet his intention never wavered. He might well be termed the first campaigner for modern art in the United States.

**STIJL** (De) (Style). A Dutch periodical created by Van Doesburg *(\*)* in 1917 for the defence of the Neo-Plastic principle, and whose central figure during the first three years was Piet Mondrian. The other contributors were, besides Van Doesburg himself, the Belgian painter and sculptor Vantongerloo, the painter Vilmos Huszar, the Futurist painter Gino Severini, the Dutch poet Antonie Kok, the architects Wils, van't Hoff and Oud, and, fleetingly, the painter Bart van der Leck. In the second year, the architect Rietveld joined the group and later, in 1921, the film director Hans Richter. In 1923, Van Doesburg, celebrating the fifth anniversary of the review, paid tribute to Mondrian in an editorial: 'Although several artists, in various countries, have worked consciously and unconsciously to evolve a new plastic expression, it was the painter Piet Mondrian who, about 1913, was first to arrive at a realization of the new plastic conception in painting as a logical continuation of Cubism. This accomplishment, which won the approval of the younger generation of artists in Holland, awakened the confidence of the most advanced painters in the possibilities of a new medium. *De Stijl* hails in Mondrian the father of Neo-Plasticism.' However, in the following year Van Doesburg himself forsook the severe principles of Neo-Plasticism and published the manifesto of Elementarism *(\*)*. Meanwhile *De Stijl* had opened its columns to Dadaism by publishing a supplement called

*Mecano*. New names appeared: Van Eesteren, Kiesler, Arp *(\*)*, Antheil, Graeff, Schwitters *(\*)*, Ribemont-Dessaignes, Man Ray, Roehl, Lissitzky *(\*)*, Domela, Vordemberge-Gildewart, Pansaers, Kupka *(\*)*, Parnak; but Mondrian had stopped contributing (his last article appeared in 1924). *De Stijl* ceased to appear in 1928. However, in 1932, Mme Petro Van Doesburg published a last issue, devoted to the memory of her husband, who had died in 1931. Among the number of *avantgarde* magazines, frequently short-lived, that appeared throughout Europe between 1920 and 1930, *De Stijl* exercised an unmistakable influence upon art between the two wars (cf. articles on Mondrian and Van Doesburg).

**SUPREMATISM** The name given by Malevitch *(\*)* to the geometrical abstractionism he derived from Cubism in 1913. The elements of Suprematism were the rectangle, the circle, the triangle and the cross. Although the first public appearance of Suprematism took place in 1913, when Malevitch exhibited his perfect square, black on a white background, the manifesto of the movement was not published until 1915. It was drawn up with the assistance of the Russian poet Maiakovski and other *avantgarde* writers. Almost simultaneously Tatlin originated the Constructivist movement and Rodchenko Non-Objectivism, both closely related to Suprematism. Later (about 1920) Constructivism was revived when Gabo and Pevsner published the *Realist Manifesto* in Moscow. When modern movements were banished by the Russian authorities, Gabo left Moscow for Berlin, and Pevsner for Paris. However, it was chiefly through the activity of the painter and draughtsman El Lissitzky *(\*)* that Constructivist and Suprematist ideas were introduced (starting in 1922) into Germany, where, in Bauhaus *(\*)* circles, they encountered the Neo-Plastic current brought from Holland by Van Doesburg *(\*)* during the same period. The Neo-Plasticism *(\*)* of Mondrian was plastically more reasoned and consequently more dogmatic than Suprematism. While Neo-Plasticism has more deeply affected the art of our time, it is Malevitch that must be given credit for having gone the farthest in the shortest time, by leaping from Cubism to Suprematism in the space of a few months, starting anew on an entirely different and quite simple basis: the black square on a white background.

All painting that takes as its groundwork exact geometrical forms, without any attempt at representation, necessarily descends, therefore, from Malevitch and the Suprematism of 1913. The movement may have appeared futile at that time, but from it has emerged a whole new sphere of art that is far from being exhausted today.

**SURREALISM** The systematic dismantling of established values at which Dadaism had worked could lead to constructive results only by bringing into play and organizing – and this was the role of Surrealism – the host of obscure impulses which, springing from unexplored realms of the mind; called up concepts hitherto considered so many baseless fancies; although in the past, masters like Leonardo da Vinci, Botticelli, Bosch, Breughel, Arcimboldo, Blake, Grandville or Goya had not been unaware of them and had used them for limited and specific purposes. It was a question of themes supplied by the unconscious, chance, madness, dream, hallucination, delirium or humour, psychic states capable of creating in the artist's

imagination zones of 'systematic estrangement' that he would then have to identify and populate. Dada had exhausted itself chiefly by making tracery out of the rubble of its demolitions when Surrealism undertook to experiment scientifically with the mysterious materials furnished by the unconscious and at the same time to liberate sensibility from the grip of the conventions that had governed artists of all times. Therefore, when André Breton published his *Manifesto of Surrealism* in 1924, an absolute directive was given to make a clean sweep of rational vision and to substitute for it an irrational and, so to speak, primal knowledge of things. Accordingly, Max Ernst, in his *Treatise on Surrealist Painting* contended that 'any conscious, mental control of reason, taste, will, is out of place in a work that deserves to be described as absolutely Surrealist'. While traditional aesthetic principles were based upon the 'reflective' discovery of relations to be observed between the various aspects of things, the role of Surrealism consisted in discovering new relations between objects unreflectively, this being possible only through the irruption into life of the irrational, the unconscious, the spontaneous, the fortuitous and an automatism outside all systematization and codification. Moreover, the painter could no longer allow himself to be thwarted by traditional plastic means. Aragon 'defied' painting in a very aggressive manner. Surrealists even went so far as to poke fun at the 'old barnstormer Cézanne' with his 'three apples on a plate'. Every artist was to work alone at his own vision of the world, unconcerned with that of the others, even if they were themselves followers of Surrealism. In answer to a test given to them, which consisted in indicating what painter the sight of a piece of pink velvet suggested to them, Surrealists named in turn Manet, Böcklin, Utrillo, Renoir, Watteau, Monet, Jean-Paul Laurens, Gustave Moreau, Delacroix and El Greco. They were no longer striving toward a single truth capable of stirring sensibility before a given object. Surrealism transcended the ocular perception

ERNST. MY LITTLE MONT BLANC. 1922

on whose value and legitimacy Cubism had already cast doubts. It joined, but more profoundly, and within a freedom of interpretation sometimes carried as far as anarchy, the religious, mythological, fabulous or magic representations that, from remotest antiquity, have heightened man's awareness by upsetting his sensibility. Surrealism refused to see in art an object of enjoyment, but rather discovered in it a way of deepening that knowledge whose progress it associated with that of science.

Surrealism revolted against traditional plastic means, but not in the manner of the Dadaists, who denied the very idea of them. For these means Surrealism substituted others that were boldly new. Whether in the technique of *collage* or in the composition of 'Surrealist objects', its intention was always to bring to the point of paroxysm the association of unlike elements of objects, depriving them of their conventional purpose in order to give them a new one, born of most unexpected and surprising juxtapositions. The most revolutionary ambition of the Surrealists seems to have been revealed by André Breton when he wrote: 'I shall not conceal that for me the strongest Surrealist image is the one that presents the highest degree of the arbitrary, the one that takes the longest to translate into practical language, whether it contains an enormous amount of apparent contradiction, whether one of its terms is curiously concealed, whether, promising to be sensational, it seems to come to a weak conclusion; whether it draws from itself a derisory *formal* justification, whether it is of an hallucinatory nature, whether it lends very naturally the mask of the concrete to the abstract or vice versa, whether it implies the negation of some elementary physical quality, or whether it provokes laughter'. One can wonder now what the Surrealist work of art brought to the general position of the movement. Whether painting, *collage* or Surrealist object, it appears that the chief contribution of the plastic work is to have opposed the precious immobility of an image fixed in space to the undulating, varying and dynamic quality of Surrealist writing proper and its development in time. By the unexpected, even arbitrary nature of the cut of the object, by its sudden coagulation on the

DALI. GIRAFFE ON FIRE. 1935.
*Kunstmuseum, Basel*

canvas, and by the unreal atmosphere that emanates from the whole, the works of Surrealist painters have indeed imposed the anguishing mystery of their upsetting fixity. Feelings of unending expectation, anxiety before enigmas, or the strangeness of certain meetings in an unknown past enabled the artists to uncover mysterious impressions charged with the most secret, sometimes the most baffling, but always a deeply human poetry. Their untiring quest for the marvellous took on various aspects, according to each painter's imagination or gift for premonition. Chirico, in his first 'manner', discovered the secret motives of metaphysical anguish, as it could be born in the unexpected encounter of known objects. Hans Arp caused a strange life to spring up in the very heart of objects supposedly inert. Max Ernst, both in his *frottages* and in his paintings, endowed with real existence, elements suggested to him only by hallucination. As for Joan Miro, he created a universe inhabited by signs that his will for metamorphosis charged with symbolic values.

And while André Masson enquired into the perpetual struggle between life and death in us and in things, it was beyond the infinity of the sky or in the very depths of the ocean that Yves Tanguy sought to capture the essential mysteries. Dali, behind a front of delirious interpretations, deliberately undertook the disquieting organization of a metaphysical universe. Man Ray, who made use of photography for his rayographs, drew particularly moving poetical suggestions from the fixity of objects. Finally, Magritte discovered 'lyrical facts' hitherto unsuspected in the juxtaposition of familiar objects. In short, the intentions of the Surrealists stemmed for painters as well as for poets from a desire to escape the absurdity of events and the stupidity of the official literary and artistic formulae that weighed heavily upon the future of the intelligence. If, then, the young people of 1924–1930 attempted to destroy adulterated values, imagining that they were starting again from scratch, from the very beginnings of sensibility, there was nothing illegitimate in their action. The influence of Surrealist thought is as yet at only an early stage and time will develop its intentions, with certain indispensable amendments. An inevitable necessity has made Surrealism, at last freed of the aggressive challenges that every revolution involves, a discovery that cannot be passed over, and one that will influence decisively the future development of art.

**SURVAGE** Leopold. Russian painter; born in 1879 in Moscow. Having discovered Matisse in the Shchukin collection, Survage went to Paris in 1908 to attend courses at the Academy that Matisse had just opened in the former Couvent des Oiseaux. But he soon discovered Cézanne's work, and later he made the acquaintance of the Cubists, with whom he exhibited at the Salon des Indépendants in 1912. Although he was not one of the creators of Cubism, he joined the movement when it was still growing and the struggle waged by its followers left the door open to any development. In 1917 he came to the austere initial Cubism that bore the mark of Picasso and the Frenchmen who were its originators, among whom Braque

and Léger have remained the most original. There was an element of freshness in his work that recalled his Russian origin, an inclination for imagery and light colours. What he brought to the movement was not *naïveté* but rather a spontaneity that did not exclude reasoning.

SUTHERLAND. HEAD OF THORNS. 1946.
*Private Collection, New York*

Survage was not really a Cubist. His art, in spite of his desire for construction, was dominated above all by a very personal concept of space. While French Cubism, also concerned with construction, applied itself chiefly to the analysis and recomposition of objects and their volumes, Survage was more drawn to spatial problems. Thus he was less attracted by still life than by landscape. In his work city streets broke into large planes that folded and unfolded like the panels of a screen. He was also concerned with the presence of man, a mysterious presence that he more often suggested by the shadow of a figure than by the figure itself. The result was a strange solitude, haunted by tranquil phantoms, and created by a close contact between nature, its atmosphere and the order that man imposes upon it.

Later, like the other Cubists, he escaped the too rigorous system to which he had originally adhered, but in all his work the same themes can be found. By temperament he was particularly suited for large decorations. Diaghilev understood this and commissioned settings for the ballet *Mavra* from him. In addition Survage had the opportunity to execute, for the Paris International Exhibition of 1937, large murals in which he was able to give his imagination free rein. On the largest surfaces he succeeds in preserving his qualities of freshness and gaiety, and even in his more recent production, in which he appears to have drifted away from the picturesqueness of his early work, the continuity of his thought can be followed, always directed toward a synthesis of space and movement.

**SUTHERLAND** Graham. English painter; born in London in 1903. After studying at the Goldsmiths' School of Art, he concentrated on etching and produced landscapes and illustrations of a hallucinatory character. His art then underwent the influence of William Blake and of his disciple Samuel Palmer (1805–1881) and of the Surrealists as well. Following a stay he made in the County of Pembroke in 1936, Sutherland's style showed a marked change: Nature had apparently acted as a catalytic agent in bringing about a new and magical concept of art. From that time on, his vision expanded and his work acquired greater expressiveness. He discovered new forms of life, tinted with hitherto unknown colours. Strange vegetable and mineral forms, insects metamorphosed into totems look out from his canvases on to a mental universe teeming with hidden forces. Anxious eyes, endowed with beneficent or malevolent powers, recall masks from Polynesia and the New Hebrides. They take possession of the spectator as their strange message slowly filters into his consciousness. In Sutherland's work, art reaches back to its primal nature: it inspires in man a mixture of fear, joy, and ecstasy. At once sign and symbol, the work of art becomes, in the hands of this sorcerer, a vehicle for cosmic forces.

Sutherland is, without doubt, the leader of the contemporary English school of painting. In 1944, asked to decorate a church at Northampton, he created a Christ on the Cross which makes one think of certain Spanish primitives, of totems, and, again, of the works of such an

SURVAGE. LANDSCAPE. 1932

artist as Grünewald. Following this, Sutherland devoted considerable time to portraits but he refused to allow himself to be carried away by the tradition of superficial brilliance which has characterized the evolution of portrait painting in English art. The head of a man calls forth from him the same qualities of analysis and synthesis as the phenomena of nature. Thus a portrait dominated by a pair of shrewd, cruel eyes, even though painted in accordance with all laws of realism, seems, at times, not very far from belonging to the plant world, the insect world or the reptile kingdom. In 1951 Sutherland was commissioned to paint a large panel for the Festival of Britain on the theme, 'The Origins of the Earth'. In 1952 he represented England at the Biennale in Venice, where he was awarded the acquisition prize of the Museum of Modern

Art, São Paulo. His work is well represented in the collections of the Tate Gallery; also, in the Museums of Modern Art of New York and of Paris.

**SWEDISH BALLET**  (*see* Ballets Suédois).

**SYMBOLISM** There are two fundamental modes of artistic experience: image and symbol, direct perception and ideal interpretation. Following the progress of science, the effort of the nineteenth century was directed toward realism. The result was Naturalism in literature and Impressionism in painting. From 1885 on, Symbolism, an idealistic reaction, developed in letters and the plastic arts simultaneously. Painters and poets no longer aimed at a faithful representation of the outside world, but at an imaginative suggestion of their dreams through symbolic allusion and the luxuriant apparel of decorative form. The year 1886, with the appearance of Rimbaud's *Illuminations*, the arrival of Van Gogh in Paris and Gauguin's first stay in Brittany, was a turning point that confirmed the break with Impressionism and marked the official birth on the one hand of Neo-Impressionism, a scientific development of Impressionism, and on the other, and at the opposite pole, of Symbolism, which was first expressed in literature. In the Manifesto he published in the *Figaro* of September 18th that year, the poet Jean Moréas put forth the name Symbolism 'as the only word capable of adequately describing the current tendency of the creative spirit in art'. His principal formula was one that would be valid in all the arts: 'To clothe the idea in a sensitive form'. Soon after, there appeared a number of magazines, which propagated the new aesthetic doctrine and showed, by the space they allotted to painting and illustration, the increasing interaction between the plastic arts and literature that was characteristic of the period: as early as 1886 *La Pléiade*, *Le Décadent*, *La Vogue*, *Le Symboliste*; in 1889 *La Plume*, in 1890 *Le Mercure de France*, and in 1891 *La Revue Blanche*. The *Poésies* of Mallarmé appeared in 1887; in 1889, *Parallèlement* of Verlaine, the *Essai sur les Données Immédiates de la Conscience* of

Bergson and the famous work of Edouard Schuré, *Les Grands Initiés*, which advanced the mystical and theosophical current of Symbolism. The same year witnessed the appearance of pictorial Symbolism on the occasion of the exhibition at the Café Volpini of the 'Impressionist and Synthesist Group', that is to say, Gauguin and the School of Pont-Aven (Bernard, Laval, Anquetin, and others). The designation 'Impressionist' had been maintained for publicity's sake, but the aesthetic doctrine of the movement, based on Cloisonnism and Synthesism, was opposed to that of the Impressionists (and Neo-Impressionists), 'who searched', as Gauguin said, 'round the eye and not in the mysterious centre of thought, and so lapsed into scientific reasoning'. Bernard and Gauguin – here in complete contradiction to Cézanne, who was fanatically faithful to nature, and even to Van Gogh, who never separated symbol from reality – maintained the necessity of painting no longer from life but from memory, not 'before the thing' but 'entertaining it in the imagination' that had taken it in, and, after simplification, had retained its 'synthesis', that is to say, 'idea'.

The young critic Albert Aurier, an enthusiastic admirer of Gauguin, whom he introduced into the famous literary circle of the Café Voltaire, dominated by Moréas and Verlaine, defined Symbolism in painting in an article in the *Mercure de France* for March 1891 that caused wide comment: 'The work of art', he proclaimed 'must be: 1. *Ideist*, since its only goal will be expression of the idea; 2. *Symbolist*, since it will express the idea in forms; 3. *Synthetic*, since it will transcribe the forms in a mode of general comprehension; 4. *Subjective*, since the object will never be considered in it as an object, but as the sign of the idea perceived by the subject; 5. (As a consequence) *Decorative*, for decorative painting properly so called, as the Egyptians and very likely the Greeks and the Primitives conceived it, is nothing but a manifestation of an art at once subjective, synthetic, symbolist and ideist'. These characteristics, which put emphasis upon Ideist Symbolism and the tendency toward decorative abstraction, applied in particular to Gauguin and the School of Pont-Aven, as well as to the *Nabi* group – Bonnard, Vuillard,

Roussel, Maurice Denis, Ranson, Vallotton –
connected with Pont-Aven through Sérusier (*vide*
Pont-Aven and *Nabis*); but they were already
evident, in an intuitive and rather literary form,
in three isolated artists with whom the Symbolist
generation claimed kinship: Gustave Moreau,
Puvis de Chavannes, and Odilon Redon.

Gustave Moreau (1826–1898) is in France the
exact equivalent of the English Pre-Raphaelites
that were discovered at the Universal Exhibition
of 1855. Before his fake pictorial jewellery and
the immense miscarriage of his mythical imagery,
one cannot help thinking of the savage *mot* of
Degas: 'He wants to make us believe that the
gods wore watch-chains'. But because of the
mysteriousness of his life, the prestige of his
personality and his idealist intentions, Moreau's
influence was widely felt; not only by decadent
writers like Huysmans and Jean Lorrain, who
maintained a real cult for him, but also by the
*Nabi* painters. 'He, the master sorcerer,' said
Jean Lorrain, 'has cast a spell upon his time,
bewitched his contemporaries and contaminated
with the ideal this sceptical and practical end of a
century.'

While the work of Puvis de Chavannes (1824–
1898), in spite of its nobility and undeniable
harmony, now appears more closely related to an
academic allegorism than to authentic Symbolism, its influence also was considerable, and all
contemporary artists, from Gauguin to the Nabis,
claimed him as a precursor. Albert Aurier and
Maurice Denis, in their doctrinal articles, re-
peatedly cited the fruitful example of his art,
whose three characteristic innovations the
critic Mellerio summed up as follows: 'amend-
ment of direct sensation, simplification of drawing, an ornamental tendency'. Gauguin, while
stressing the differences that separated him from
Puvis de Chavannes, always acknowledged a
debt to him, and his dream was to do 'coloured
Puvis de Chavannes'. The unanimous recognition
accorded at the end of the century to Puvis was
such that a banquet, presided over by Rodin,
was given in his honour in January 1895,
gathering together 550 artists and writers of the
most opposed schools, from Carolus-Duran to
Renoir and Gauguin, and from Brunetière to
Verlaine and Mallarmé.

REDON. ARMOUR. *Circa* 1885.
*Metropolitan Museum, New York*

Odilon Redon (1840–1916), a contemporary
of Impressionism, which he thought 'too low-
ceilinged', made friends with Mallarmé and the
young Symbolist writers, Gide, Valéry and
Francis Jammes, and following the example of
Gustave Moreau and Puvis de Chavannes, whom
he greatly admired, sought in his work 'human
beauty with the prestige of thought'. But whereas
the intentions of those two painters were ham-
strung by academic formulae, Redon succeeded
in creating the plastic idiom of his dreams. He
is the Symbolist painter *par excellence*. This is why
the *Nabis*, Bonnard, Vuillard, Roussel, Sérusier,
Maurice Denis, of whom he executed admirable
lithographic portraits in black, bistre and san-
guine, turned to him with fervour and paid
homage to him in a collective exhibition at
Durand-Ruel's in 1899. In the same category,
and on the same level, though in a different
spirit, can be placed the Belgian painter James
Ensor (1860–1949), who began in the Impressionist manner, but from 1890 on discovered in
masks the expression of his fantastic universe
and the climate of his irony.

All the painters who were more or less influenced by Symbolism, which constituted less a school than the atmosphere of an era, showed their work at twice-yearly exhibitions at the Le Barc de Boutteville Gallery, from 1891 to 1897.

**SYNCHROMISM** (*see* Abstract Art).

# T

**TAEUBER-ARP** Sophie (1889–1943). Swiss painter; born in Davos; died in Zürich. After studying applied art in Munich and Hamburg, Sophie Taeuber was a teacher at the School of Arts and Crafts in Zürich for thirteen years. She belonged to the Dadaist movement together with Arp, whom she met in 1915 and married in 1921. She executed mural paintings and stained glass in Strasbourg, and in particular decorated several rooms of the restaurant *L'Aubette* (which has since been destroyed). From 1928 to 1940, she lived with Arp in Meudon, near Paris, and participated in exhibitions such as *Cercle et Carré* (1930) and *Abstraction-Création* (1933), always showing abstract works with geometrical forms. She founded the review *Plastique*, four issues of which appeared between 1937 and 1939. During the Second World War she took refuge in Grasse and executed coloured lithographs in collaboration with Arp, Sonia Delaunay and Alberto Magnelli. During a trip to Switzerland, she died of asphyxiation from the fumes of a stove. She has left a great number of gouaches, drawings, water-colours and oil paintings, whose importance resides in their simplicity and at the same time in their richness of invention. She was beyond doubt one of the central figures in Abstract Art *(*)* between the two wars. Her art is occasionally related to Neo-Plasticism (cut-outs of 1916 and the decorations of the 'Aubette'); at other times to a Constructivism, optimistic and light in spirit. Her work is an almost inexhaustible catalogue of abstract forms and techniques. The style is sober and of crystalline purity. Her innovations were always directed toward greater simplification, but also toward greater freedom, like exercises on a well-tempered clavichord.

TAEUBER. GOUACHE. 1932.
*Private Collection, Paris*

**TAMAYO** Rufino. Mexican painter born in 1899 in Oaxaca of a Zapotecan family. As a young man Tamayo went to Mexico City and in 1918 studied at the San Carlos Academy. He found the instruction sterile and he left. He interested himself in the archaeology of his country and, through books and magazines, in modern French art. After a stay in New York in the middle nineteen-twenties he returned to Mexico City and was honored with government appointments. In 1933 he was commissioned to execute a mural for the National Conservatory of Music.

RUFINO TAMAYO. SMOKER. PAINTING.

He returned to New York in 1938 and became widely popular. In 1943 he painted frescoes for the library of Smith College. The world of Tamayo's painting is a borderland between the animal and the human, haunted and haunting, a world of harsh, broken lines sometimes relieved by color that occasionally verges on the pretty. It is filled with obsessive symbols which are as much a reflection of modern European preoccupations as of the milieu from which he sprang. *The Cry* (1947), for example, is the expressionist theme of Munch (see p. 96) translated in terms of the artist's own ethnic background. Throughout his work there are references to surrealism. As a result of his affinities to European culture he has been denounced by other, more stridently nationalistic, Mexican painters.

**TANGUY** Julien (1825-1894). Père Tanguy started his career in art as a dealer in artists materials in the rue Clauzel, in Montmartre. In 1870 he decided to add the sale of the works of his painter friends to that of his regular stock. He bought Van Goghs but never sold a single one of them. He was not disheartened, though, and moved by an unyielding faith, continued to pile up canvases by Monet, Sisley, Cézanne, Gauguin and Seurat. Tanguy visited the painters in their studios at Moret and Pontoise, bringing them paints (payment for which was generally long deferred), and he haunted the Salons. It was at his place that Vollard discovered Cézanne, and it is interesting to note that, from 1877 to 1893, his shop was the only place in Paris where Cézanne's canvases could be seen. He unfailingly backed the efforts of his friends, in spite of the fact that his means were always modest, and it was to him that many painters owed, at certain critical moments, their ability to continue working.

**TANGUY** Yves (1900–1955). French painter; born in Paris; died in Connecticut. Of Breton parentage, Tanguy entered the merchant marine. He made several trips, to England, Portugal, Spain, Africa and South America. He came to painting unexpectedly, after having seen a picture by Chirico in the window of the Paul Guillaume Gallery. Although he had never

TANGUY. COMPOSITION.

*Collection of J. Snégaroff, Paris*

touched a brush before or thought of doing so, he discovered that this was his calling; he emerged suddenly into an inner universe independent of the real world. His is a near-unique case of completely autonomous creation. In 1925 he met the Surrealists and joined their group, participating in all their exhibitions in France and abroad. His work espoused the profound aims of the movement in advance and ran the gamut of possible impacts of the psychic upon the physical. Nothing impaired the purity of the messages it transmitted from a mental world, in which the artist lived isolated and whose mystery he succeeded in expressing, if not in explaining. His work has been compared to undersea or extraplanetary scenes. But in reality his vision was purely subjective, populated by forms with no equivalents. If these forms sometimes seem to emerge from the mist of dream or to grow out of the very irregularities of the materials employed (1927–1929 and 1930–1931 periods), they possess, however, a precise structure; they obey an inner logic, and rigorous relations are established between them. This is confirmed by the remarkable drawings which constitute an important part of Tanguy's work. Each of his pictures is like a balcony opening upon the unknown, and André Breton has spoken rightly of 'far expeditions'. Having left for the United States in 1939 and having sojourned in California and Canada, he settled in Woodbury, Connecticut, in 1942. He lived on a farm, where he continued to work. In 1948 he became an American citizen. His work developed in the direction of greater precision, and his increasingly complex structures preserved their inventive integrity, although a certain dryness sometimes weakened their pure poetry.

**TORRES-GARCIA** Joaquin (1874–1949). Uruguayan painter; born and died in Montevideo. The son of a Catalan father and a Uruguayan mother, he went to Barcelona when he was seventeen, studied mural painting there, and executed frescoes at the Palacio de la Deputación. After visiting Paris and Brussels (1910), he returned to Montevideo. In 1920–1922 he stayed in New York and then in

TORRES-GARCIA. COMPOSITION.
*Collection of J. Ulmann, Paris*

Italy. In 1924 he established himself in Paris, where he lived until 1932. During this period, with Michel Seuphor, he founded the review and the group of *Cercle et Carré* and took an active part in the organization of the international exhibition of the same name, which took place in April 1930 and had the participation of the principal abstract painters then alive, notably Kandinsky, Mondrian, Schwitters, Arp, Sophie Taeuber, Pevsner, Prampolini, Vantongerloo, Baumeister, as well as Léger, Ozenfant and Le Corbusier. Then returning to Montevideo for good, he opened an art school that met with great success and exercised a profound influence upon the new generation. At the same time he continued by himself the review *The Circle and The Square* (*Círculo y Cuadrado*), which became the organ of a school rather than a review of abstract art. He published several works, among them a history of his life (*Historia de Mi Vida*, Montevideo, 1939), and executed numerous decorations in Montevideo as well as an important monument (*Monumento Cósmico*) in the Parque Rodo of the same city. Except for a few works of the Paris *Cercle et Carré* period (1930), the work of Torres-García remained figurative, although it showed a tendency towards a free improvisation that was peculiar to him. He seems to have learned his deepest lesson from pre-Columbian art, which he contrasted to and combined with modern European art. His work contains Cubist and Neo-Plastic elements as well as certain aspects of the Klee idiom, all integrated with perfect ease into an ideographic concept of angular style that makes of Torres-García a great Indian artist of our time.

**TOULOUSE-LAUTREC** Henri de (1864–1901). French painter, born in Albi; died at the Château de Malromé at Céleyran, one of his childhood haunts. Lautrec was the descendant of a family that traced its origin back to the Counts of Toulouse, defenders of the Albigensian Cathari, and the Viscounts of Lautrec. Count Alphonse, his father, was an original personality, passionately fond of falcon hunting, exotic weapons, horses and carriages. His disguises and games, carried out with the unalterable seriousness of a totally assured man, foreshadowed the wry humour of the painter, his absolute straightforwardness to the point of violence, his stubbornness of will, his wholehearted participation in every act of life. Lautrec's childhood was quite normal. Except for a short period of schooling at the Lycée Condorcet in Paris, it was spent in his family's country house. His studies were directed by his mother. He began drawing very early, filling the margins of his copybooks with caricatures of his parents, his teachers, his cousins, the animals he observed; he showed a special predilection for horses and applied himself to drawing whole sequences of the same subject, to study its variations and different aspects. Two falls, at Albi in 1878, and at Barèges in 1879, in which he broke both legs, left him after

months of immobility, completely deformed, his torso supported by two weak and shortened legs. From his convalescences came letters and travel notebooks addressed to cousins or friends, whose gaiety reveals a moving self-control. Not only did he not complain, he even stressed his disability, as if to discourage all compassion in advance. He made every effort to behave like a normal man. In his drawings, based upon remarkable observation, he showed great interest in the vitality and movement of people. Acting upon the advice of the animal painter René Princeteau, a friend of his father, he began painting and discovered a new medium in colour. The influence of this first teacher lasted for two or three years, and in many respects was decisive. Being affected himself by a physical handicap – he was a deaf mute – René Princeteau presumably brought a special comprehension and attention to the formation of the young cripple. In his first works, *Artillerymen and Cuirassiers on Horseback*, reminiscences of manœuvres that had taken place near his family's estate, Lautrec made use of an abbreviated and flexible technique of small

TOULOUSE-LAUTREC. SEATED GIRL, BACK VIEW. 1896. *Louvre*

divergent brush strokes, borrowed from his teacher, which was far from the systematic disintegration of tones of Impressionism, but which lent itself to improvisation. In 1882, having received his family's permission to devote himself entirely to painting, he came to Paris to complete his training. He worked at first in the studio of Princeteau and underwent the influence of John Lewis Brown and Forain. In 1883 he entered the École Nationale des Beaux-Arts in the studio of Cormon, a mediocre painter who did prehistoric reconstructions, but was of a tolerant mind, and with whom he worked intermittently until 1885. It was in this studio that he met Emile Bernard, Anquetin and Van Gogh, who impressed him deeply. In 1887, having already lived two years in Montmartre, he set up his studio in the Rue Caulaincourt, on the corner of the Rue Tourlaque. He was next door to the Goupil *(\*)* print shop, where he encountered Maurice Joyant, his former schoolmate at the Lycée Condorcet, who became the chief defender of his work. Lautrec frequented the ballrooms and cabarets of Montmartre, in particular the 'Mirliton', where Bruant sang his social ballads and greeted his clients with offensive remarks. Lautrec illustrated Bruant's most famous songs: *At Batignolles*, *At Belleville*, *At Saint-Lazare*; on the walls of the cabaret he painted dancing scenes, in which La Goulue appeared for the first time; finally, under the influence of Bruant and Raffaelli, he executed realistic works: *Gueule de Bois*, posed by Suzanne Valadon, and *À la Mie*.

Nevertheless, he did not give in to the sentimentality of the slums. He was so intensely interested in the character of his models, whoever they were, that he gave them a remarkable dignity. In the garden of Père Forest, neighbouring his studio, he painted a series of portraits of women out of doors, from Montmartre models and prostitutes whose names or nicknames are barely known: Hélène V., Augusta, Gabrielle, the policeman's daughter, Berthe the Deaf, Casque d'Or, Honorine P., the woman with the gloves. These portraits, rich in psychological and human insight, enabled Lautrec to perfect his pictorial technique. Observing his model in the crude light of day, he accustomed himself to

TOULOUSE-LAUTREC. WOMAN PULLING UP HER STOCKING. 1894. *Albi Museum*

considering it as a whole, without any shadow whatever. He did not think, like the Impressionists, of studying the variations that the time of the day brings to things; he never resorted to chiaroscuro. For him, whose curiosity was concerned with human beings alone, light had only one rôle: to illuminate, not to alter vision or to make changing what is fixed and full. This is why he was led to create the cold and ideal light of which Pierre MacOrlan speaks, and which enabled him to search the face of man and to strip it of its secrets. Thus he presented the model in a sort of moral and psychological nakedness. He did not paint the representative of a profession or a class, but a being whose destiny appears unique in his attitudes and his face. He rejected everything inessential, sometimes setting the scene precisely, but without ever allowing the setting to capture attention and play more than the environmental rôle assigned to it. All the persons whose individuality he fixed can be found in the large compositions of dancing at the Moulin de la Galette and the Moulin Rouge. Here he tried to bring out the generic features of

TOULOUSE-LAUTREC. YVETTE GUILBERT.
*Museum of Western Art, Moscow*

star, an exceptional being, a superior animal who attracts all the interest in a show. He brought out her definitive features by emphasizing them; and one can see, for example, a great actress like Yvette Guilbert become the incarnation of Lautrec's representation of her, which deeply shocked her at first.

Even more personal were the solutions Lautrec brought to other spheres of plastic expression. The appeal that theatres had for him caused him to execute, simultaneously with some theatrical settings that have not come down to us, programme covers, and more particularly posters. In these productions he was not less concerned with making a work of art than he was before a canvas. Advertising, which at the beginning resorted only to a rather crude form of art, thus passed to a higher level. Bonnard was the first to have achieved delicate harmonies of shades and subtle design, suggested to him by his taste for Persian fabrics. Chéret created illusion and obsession with lightness and verve. Lautrec's admiration for Japanese prints and

his models and to give a collective representation of a milieu. These works obey a rhythm that transfigures them, that of the dance, and the dance itself is personified by La Goulue or Jane Avril. These faces, which haunted him or were familiar to him, took on a special intensity as they touched common life. La Goulue, with her partner Valentin le Désossé, is one of Lautrec's most powerful creations and she inspired him to do a host of drawings and pictures. For Lautrec she represented the perfect identity between the human being and his function. But outside the temple where her cult was celebrated she was no longer anything and went from degradation to degradation. On the other hand the personalities of Jane Avril, Yvette Guilbert, May Belfort, May Milton, and later of the actresses Jeanne Granier, Marcelle Lender, Berthe Bady and many others, unfolded as their art evolved. Thus Lautrec attached himself to beings whom he found exceptional and applied himself to discovering their unique features. He was the first to follow the idolatrous cult of the

TOULOUSE-LAUTREC. LA GOULUE AND VALENTIN
LE DÉSOSSÉ. *Lithograph*

the recollection of certain compositions of Degas enabled him to adjust even more completely to mural requirements. He broadened and deepened his pitiless drawing and made it more effective through the arabesque of his foregrounds. His few colours were clear, and applied boldly, and at once established the composition as a whole. Thus in an extreme simplification he gave the silhouette and the movements of his subject the greatest power. The pictures of La Goulue, Bruant, Jane Avril, and Caudieux resulted in a creation of types. The presence that commands attention on the wall with explosive force, Lautrec preserved even in his works of smaller dimensions, almost interior posters, like the pictures of May Belfort and May Milton, the Confetti poster, 'based upon Jeanne Granier's smile', and most of the lithographs in colour. In his black-and-white lithographs, on the contrary, he broke the line and produced a crumbling of form.

Lautrec's interest was not confined to the theatre, music hall, circus, ballroom and bar. With his cousin Gabriel Tapié de Céleyran, who was then a medical student, he frequented the hospital where the famous surgeon Péan operated, capturing his movements with a reporter's curiosity. A few years later, he developed a passion for sporting circles; he followed the training of champions at the Buffalo cycle-racing track, operated by his friend the humorist Tristan Bernard, making sketches of this still unexplored world which he re-created in lithographs and posters. He attended the hearings of great trials. He was extremely fond of travelling and organized his tours with a personal and amusing touch, always dragging along some friend. To go to Bordeaux he embarked every year at Havre and took freighters going to Africa. Once, through admiration for a lady passenger, he went on as far as Lisbon, whence he returned via Toledo, discovering in El Greco the painter who impressed him most, with Cranach and the Japanese. During one of his numerous trips to England, he fell into the midst of the tragedy of Oscar Wilde, whose prodigious swollen night owl's face he drew with a few strokes. In the clearness of his vision, the courage of his analysis, Lautrec renewed all the themes he

TOULOUSE-LAUTREC. JANE AVRIL. 1893
*Lithograph*

treated. Thus the world of prostitution, which had already inspired Constantin Guys and Degas, furnished him with a completely new repertoire of forms. Besides, he attached the greatest importance to this subject. But he was careful not to create a useless scandal and kept all canvases related to it secret. At his exhibition at the Manzi-Joyant Gallery in 1896, he assembled these pictures in a first-floor room to which he alone had the key, and he showed them only to visitors who asked to see them. Almost all of these works, which remained in his studio, are in the Albi Museum. In them Lautrec depicted the atmosphere of the houses with details of exact truthfulness, but as an almost normal and natural life. He was interested in prostitutes and their way of life, without ever alluding to the profession they exercised; he suggested nothing and dramatized nothing. He who hated professional models and their conventional poses found here an ideal subject of observation: the sight of nudes at liberty, unconstrained. He was interested in the types, the customs, the rules of this world situated outside common morality.

TOULOUSE-LAUTREC. LA PARTIE DE CAMPAGNE. 1897
*Lithograph*

ground of cardboard or planes of highly diluted colours, in his last works he came to paint with thick pastes and construct large planes in conflict with each other.

Toulouse-Lautrec was above all an independent. He had friends but never tried to form pupils or disciples. He hated all artistic theories and participated in no movement; nevertheless, he was completely of his time and succeeded in seizing its fundamental problems by instinct. An implacable enemy of old techniques and traditional recipes, he gave a new vision of reality, in all freedom, unconcerned with influencing anyone, and he always considered young painters like Bonnard, Vuillard or Vallotton as his equals. While he admired Renoir and Monet, he felt infinitely closer to Degas and to Manet, who was more involved in the life of his time. For Lautrec, only the human figure counted, and he deplored Monet's early abandonment of the portrait. Later Gustave Moreau would urge his pupils to see a figure by Lautrec, 'all painted in absinthe'. This advice was followed,

He enjoyed the company of this relaxed humanity offered to his analysis. He felt at home in these houses, readily established himself there for several days, receiving friends and working assiduously, living in fraternal sympathy with these beings degraded like himself and alive like himself. This part of his work, alien to all passion or spectator's emotion, is a faithful transcription, accurate beyond all picturesqueness. These personages transcend their condition and partake of the universal.

Beginning in 1898, Lautrec's health deteriorated. Over-indulgence in alcohol extinguished his prodigious vitality; his mood became irritable, the prey of horrible obsessions; he hardly worked at all. Once, after an especially serious crisis, he was taken to a nursing home in Neuilly for a cure. He could not bear the loss of freedom, and to prove that he was still himself, he executed from memory, by a tremendous effort of will, the series of coloured-pencil *Circus* drawings, a synthesis of his most precious recollection of the rings he had frequented passionately since his youth. Restored to normal life, he applied himself to perfecting his past work. In a final effort he undertook to renew his technique. Having started from analysis to develop a linear construction so expressive that it needed only a coloured drawing, taking advantage of the natural

TOULOUSE-LAUTREC CARICATURED BY HIMSELF

TOULOUSE-LAUTREC. LA CLOWNESSE. 1895.
*Louvre*

not only by the *Fauves*, who, after Lautrec's example, remembered that line is both drawing and colour, but also by a young Spaniard, Pablo Picasso, newly arrived from Barcelona, who would draw from the work of his illustrious predecessor examples to reinforce the melancholy and disenchanted vision he had then formed of the universe. While Lautrec is, then, in his whole work, inseparable from his time, in his last works he had a presentiment of the requirements of the new century, at the dawn of which he died, on September 9th, 1901, at the age of thirty-seven.

**TZARA** Tristan. French writer, born in 1896 in Rumania. Tristan Tzara used the word 'Dada' for the first time on February 8th, 1916, at the Maieray café in Zürich, as he would later use the term 'Abstract Art' in one of his lectures at the Kunsthaus in the same city. Coming to Switzerland from Rumania to study mathematics, Tzara met, in 1916, the German poet Hugo Ball, his countryman the painter Marcel

Janco, and Hans Arp. With other writers he frequented Maieray's, which later became the Cabaret Voltaire *(*)*. The establishment was situated in the Spiegelgasse, where, at number 17, lived Lenin, who became Tzara's friend. They were soon exchanging both ideas and chessmen. The first event of the group at the Cabaret Voltaire was a concert of Negro music. Poems were recited by Janco, Hülsenbeck and Tzara, who had organized the meeting. In 1917, works of Picasso, Janco, Arp, Delaunay, Kandinsky, Modigliani, Macke, Prampolini, Chirico and others were exhibited there. The review *Dada* appeared in the same year. The first two issues printed compositions by these artists as well as poems, but the general tendency of the magazine did not yet reflect Dadaism properly so called. It was not until the third issue (1918) that the first Dadaist manifesto appeared, signed by Tzara. Needless to say, these events created a scandal in Zürich, but after certain modifications official circles in the city were soon co-operating with the Dadaist trend. However, the war that was going on did not fail to upset the generous feelings of Tzara and his friends. A certain despair invaded their minds and provoked the 'Dadaist disgust', for which there was no remedy other than an anarchistic revolt, destructive of all social, moral, religious, philosophical, literary and artistic entities. Accordingly, in the Dadaist manifesto of 1918 Tzara attacked the plastic arts, opposing them in all their forms, whether traditional or contemporary like Cubism, Futurism or Expressionism. With a vigour coloured by flashes of his imagination and poetic gift, he wrote: 'We have had enough of Cubist and Futurist academies, the laboratories of formal ideas. Is art made to earn money or to soothe the nice bourgeois? . . . Cubism was born of a simple way of looking at the object: Cézanne painted a cup twenty centimetres below his eyes; the Cubists look at it from above; others complicate appearance by making a perpendicular section and arranging the cup beside it. The Futurist sees the same cup in motion, a succession of objects one next to another, and maliciously adds a few lines of force. This does not prevent the canvas from being a good or a bad painting calculated for the investment of intellectual capital. The new painter protests: he no longer paints (symbolist and illusionist reproduction), but creates directly in stone, wood, iron, tin, and rocks, mobile organisms that can be turned in all directions by the limpid wind of momentary sensation. Every pictorial or plastic work is useless . . . Art has not the importance that we, troopers of the spirit, have been singing for centuries.' He concluded, 'There is a great destructive, negative work to be done: to sweep, to clean'. At the call of this manifesto, the works of the supporters of Dadaism developed in the direction suggested – toward the radical destruction of all conformity, all conventions and routines that generally inspire art, whose very name Tzara wanted to suppress: 'art, a parrot word replaced by Dada, plesiosaurus or handkerchief'. Soon the group gained the support of Marcel Duchamp and Picabia, who came to Zürich from New York (1918). The vigorous campaign that they had conducted in America consisted fundamentally in transgression of the innumerable rules of art by destroying the barriers which, in their opinion, led it to every decadence. At Tzara's side they added to their artistic preoccupations the moral disquiet of Dadaism. In 1919, they accompanied him to Paris, where he was enthusiastically welcomed. The *Littérature* group was then founded by Aragon, Breton and Soupault, whom he joined.

Violent and challenging manifestations were organized, notably at the Palais des Fêtes in 1920; in the fever of revolutionary action, agreement within the group was unanimous. However, in 1921, the wholesale destruction advocated by Tzara disturbed some of the Dadaists. Dissension appeared, and during the Congress of Paris (1922) an open cleavage occurred between Breton, its organizer, and Tzara, supported by Eluard, Arp, Man Ray, Ribemont-Dessaignes and others. The *Littérature* group, with which Tzara broke, violently attacked Dada, whose intent was to preserve the spirit of freedom that animated it and which opposed the first efforts of Surrealism *(\*)*: for Dada, Surrealism was merely a new school coming after the others, based upon scientific reasons that were valueless in its eyes. It was not until much later that Tzara collaborated on *La Révolution Surréaliste* and then *Le Surréalisme au Service de la Révolution*. His contribution to what must be in spite of everything called art – and at heart the poet he is has always been sensitive to all forms of plastic expression of value, and has shown a very enlightened interest in them – this contribution has consisted in radically opposing the outdated and often ridiculous notions that so dangerously imperilled literature and painting, but in attacking them at their very sources, that is to say their intellectual, moral and political foundations.

# U

**UHDE** Wilhelm (1874–1947). Uhde was the type of collector who not only is never concerned with the commercial value of a picture but also is prepared to sacrifice everything to acquire the object of his desire. Of German origin, he established himself permanently in Paris in 1904, after having studied in Munich and Florence. When Picasso and Braque were still unknown to most, he bought their canvases: in 1905 his first Picasso, a picture of the Blue Period, for ten francs, and two years later five Fauvist pictures of Braque, also at a very modest price. He was one of the first to discover – as early as 1906 – the genius of the Douanier Rousseau, many of whose canvases he bought. In 1908 he organized a large exhibition of Impressionists in Basel and Zürich, and in the following years several shows of contemporary French painters in Berlin and New York. In 1912, shortly after having published a work on Rousseau, he organized the first great retrospective exhibition of the Douanier. During a stay in Senlis, in 1913, he discovered the astonishing Séraphine *(\*)* and became her generous supporter. The author of numerous works, notably on Picasso and Van Gogh, his name remains linked to those whom he called 'primitive masters' – Rousseau, Vivin, Séraphine, Bauchant and Bombois, artists whom he backed and defended, devoting all his energies to making their names known to collectors and public alike. In homage to the memory of this German who contributed so much to the renown of contemporary French painting, relatives and friends have given a collection of 'Primitives of the Twentieth Century' to the Museum of Modern Art in Paris, and the room in which the works are exhibited bears Uhde's name. Thanks to the disinterested help of such people as Uhde, Dr Gachet, and a few dealers, French painting has been able to develop so fruitfully over the last hundred years.

**UTRILLO** Maurice (born in 1883 in Montmartre). Utrillo is the illegitimate son of Suzanne Valadon, the travelling acrobat who became the favourite model of Degas and later a painter herself. His father, probably a man named Boissy, disappeared leaving his son no other legacy than a strong penchant for alcohol. In 1891, a Spanish artist, Miguel Utrillo, consented to make the child legitimate. A mediocre and lazy pupil, undisciplined and left to his own devices, the boy thought only of drinking in secret. Expelled from school, he entered a bank but was soon dismissed. Then he was entrusted to the care of his grandmother, at Montmagny. Far from watching him, the old woman let him rove about and get drunk. From this time date the now legendary episodes of Utrillo's life that Francis Carco has recorded in his book, the long drinking bouts followed by

VALADON. MY SON AT THE AGE OF SEVEN. 1891. *Private Collection, Paris*

nervous crises, the wild nights, the days of stupor, internment at Sainte-Anne hospital, the vain admonitions of his mother, the baneful idleness, the first drawings and the first paintings executed under constraint, submitted to as a remedy; and then the establishment in Mont-

UTRILLO. THE MOULIN DE LA GALETTE.
*Private Collection, Paris*

martre, the relapse, the return of an ill-repressed passion. Utrillo had now finally resigned himself to the brush that his mother had put into his hand. Forced to paint, and to paint both without a master and without conviction, Utrillo produced works of surprising originality from the outset. At Montmagny, in Montmartre, in the suburbs of Paris, he executed, from 1902 to 1904, some hundred and fifty pictures, which had nothing in common with anything else that could be seen at the time. After a few months of groping, his palette, formerly thick, rough and rather dark, was transformed – under what mysterious influence no one knows. A painter in spite of himself, he began to paint masterpieces. The boozer, the bad lot, the irresponsible man staggering from café to prison, from prison to

asylum, from asylum to his desolate mother's; the wretch hooted at by crowds, hunted down by urchins, mauled by prowlers, beaten up by policemen, exploited by amateur art dealers and shopkeepers of Montmartre who hoarded his work; the poor defenceless devil who painted to quench his thirst for alcohol painted like one inspired, like a master. Ingenuously realistic, he used an amalgam of plaster, sand and glue to render the white of walls. With the minute thoroughness of a mason and the mysticism of a builder of cathedrals he lovingly shaped the dirty, naked façades of tumble-down Montmartre houses and expressed the desperate monotony of rectilinear suburban streets, the melancholy of courtyards and lanes, the rustic peace of small country squares. Gloomy suburbs, empty avenues, small peasant churches, everything in the world that is poor and banal, he transfigured instinctively, seeing it all through the eyes of a child. The humblest chapel became as majestic as a basilica. He needed only a few clouds strewn about a pale sky to convey a feeling of indescribable lightness. The least stone, soiled and cracked, became fascinating under his brush. During the six years of his 'White Period' (1908–1914) he sold for ridiculously low prices pictures that are treasured today in most museums of the world, masterpieces in which objects are invested with a magic splendour that they seem to lack entirely in the eyes of others.

Utrillo's nights of debauchery and drunkenness did not, apparently, prevent him from working regularly in the daytime, with lucidity and fervour. His production was not diminished by the frequency of his fits or by his various sojourns in hospitals and asylums. After numerous internments, notably at Sannois in 1912 and 1914, then again in 1919 and 1921, he finally underwent a very long seclusion in a nursing home at Ivry. Obsessed by alcohol, he was still able to develop coherent logical, carefully executed work, by no means morbid or unwholesome and, as a result of his evangelical sincerity, full of gentleness and freshness. With no masters other than nature and intuition, Utrillo painted with a knowledge of the craft that, although innate, was nevertheless subtle and profound. It is of little consequence, then, if he painted in his Montmartre studio almost exclusively from illustrated post cards as early as 1909. No theory, no academic discipline having blurred his vision, nature freely gave him his means. Utrillo is a constructor: his buildings are firmly set in the ground; his cathedrals rise boldly in the sky. He is an architect: his quays, streets, boulevards stretch out toward the horizon obeying an infallible perspective. He is a colourist: he has an exact notion of the relations between tones, values, atmosphere. His milky whites, singing greys, pale blues, tender greens, glowing reds, velvety blacks defy analysis. For the charming awkwardness of his first canvases he substituted by dint of work a faultless technique and an ease that did not stifle his blissful *naïveté*. Far from darkening and unbalancing his style, his successive internments seem on the contrary to have strengthened it and enlivened it. It was at the Sannois asylum, in 1912, that his 'white manner' became less gloomy, more sprightly and more sober (*The Moulin de la Galette, The Church of Saint-Aignan, The Water Tower of Sannois*). It was after his seclusion in 1916 that his forms became separated, his colour burst into flame, his realism was accentuated. But this was already the decline. Utrillo had nothing more to say. From then on he would survive himself to witness his own fame, to collect honours and enjoy the benefits of success. He had participated in the Salon d'Automne in 1909. His first one-man exhibition had taken place in 1913, and at that time he was already known and appreciated. He had admirers – writers like Octave Mirbeau, Élie Faure,

Francis Carco. Art dealers sold his works; collectors bought them. Diaghilev commissioned the settings and costumes of the ballet *Barabau* from him. In the same year he established himself with Suzanne Valadon and André Utter in a villa that they had built in the Avenue Junot in Montmartre. In 1928 he was made a Chevalier of the Legion of Honour. In 1935 he married

UTRILLO. BERLIOZ'S HOUSE IN MONTMARTRE. *Private Collection, Paris*

Mme Pauwels (Lucie Valore). His exhibitions became more frequent. The price of his pictures went up, as did the number of his imitators. And he who had been strong in his weakness, who had possessed as his sole wealth his poverty and his innocence, he who had never been so great an artist as in the midst of debauchery, destitution and opprobrium, became the frail old man, clean and of regular habits, the good husband and good citizen, the timorous petit bourgeois, submissive, bigoted, the famous painter, valued, decorated, working no longer to create but to produce. As he settled into his ease, his work dried up. Nevertheless the work he accomplished in a mere ten years will forever remain an oasis of peace for men, but an undecipherable enigma also. Utrillo can be situated among those so-called naïve painters or popular painters of reality, right after Henri Rousseau and before all the others, those who have appeared in our century to keep alive a protest of the heart and instinct (*vide* Primitives of Today).

UTRILLO. THE QUAYS.                    *Lithograph.*

# V

**VALADON** Suzanne (1865–1938). Born at Bessines; died in Paris. As a young girl Suzanne Valadon reigned for a while over the balls and studios of Montmartre. Beautiful, impudent and lively, she attracted attention among the artists – Renoir admired her lustrous skin, Puvis de Chavannes her slenderness, Lautrec her looks, detecting a hint of sadness and depravity beneath her radiant youth. When she was eighteen, her son Maurice (*vide* Utrillo) was born and she settled down to a calmer life and took to drawing herself instead of sitting as model to other artists. She started immediately, as she herself said, 'to work like mad, not to produce beautiful drawings designed to be framed, but good drawings which capture a moment of life in movement – all intensity'. Lautrec, her neighbour, saw these drawings and encouraged her, and later Degas was unstinting in his praise and bought some of her work. Suzanne Valadon's aim was to observe rather than to invent, and to express human form within rigid, almost cruel, outlines.

Acknowledging no debt to other painters – for she had nothing in common with those for whom she had sat as model – she admitted only to having been influenced by the technique of Gauguin and his Pont-Aven friends (*see Nabis*) whose decorative style she had studied at the *Exposition Universelle* in 1889, and gratitude to Degas for the advice he had given her when she

started engraving. In 1909 she gave up drawing and engraving, and took to painting. Apart from a few portraits, mainly of her son (*see page 299*), her drawings had been almost entirely of nude

VALADON. BLUE BEDROOM. 1923.          *Musée d'Art Moderne, Paris*

figures, for which she chose her charwoman or a servant girl rather than more attractive models. She painted landscapes and still lifes, though not entirely abandoning nudes and portraits of her friends. In her pictures we find the same power of expression and sharpness of observation as in her drawings, but the colour does not always accord with the emphasis of her line, with the result that often her canvases give the impression of coloured drawings. But there is no doubt that now and then, when she managed to control her love of crude colours and too obvious contrasts, Suzanne Valadon produced a number of superb oil paintings. She was an unusual artist, who in the feverish hive of

VALADON. NUDE DRYING HERSELF.
*Circa* 1895. *Collection of J. Rewald, New York*

Montmartre worked the miracle of developing a style of her own – a vigorous style in which will is the predominating factor.

**VALLOTTON** Félix (1865–1925). Swiss painter; born in Lausanne; died in Paris. He came to Paris at the age of seventeen to study drawing. Enrolled in the Académie Julian (*), he admired Courbet and Manet, and lunched for thirteen *sous* in a modest restaurant of the Faubourg Saint-Denis. The young Vaudois began by exhibiting the *Portrait of M. Ursenbach* at the Salon of 1885. He made copies in the Louvre and executed etchings. He travelled in Austria and Italy. In 1891 he was struck by the works of Lautrec, Van Gogh and the Douanier Rousseau at the Salon des Indépendants. He painted his first important canvases, for which his sitter was Hélène Chatenay, a model with whom he lived. He tried his hand at the Pointillist manner of Seurat, exhibited at the Salon des Indépendants, worked for the *Revue Blanche* (*), *Le Rire, Le Courrier Français*. A specialist in the black and white of the woodcut, he illustrated the *Livre des Masques* of Rémy

de Gourmont with symbolist portraits (1896). He painted intimate scenes and portraits. 'I dream', he wrote, 'of a great painting stripped of every literal aspect of nature.'

Vallotton has his place among the *Nabis* (*). But while he was also an intimist, he was a fierce one, a .realist after the manner of the novelist Octave Mirbeau, of whom he has left a portrait. Frank, even cynical, his painting oscillated between bitter 'slices of life' lit by the gleam of lamps, and meticulous portraits and still lifes. His painting sometimes has a dimness, an opaqueness without light that makes the artist the opposite of Seurat: a painter without vibration. Vallotton created an art that reveals both a somewhat dry pungency and a certain taste for invention. A disenchanted realism, which frequently does not shrink from an excessively imitative technique, alternates in his work with rather strange distortions in his nudes. In deliberately naïve and stylized landscapes his work sometimes reveals a taste for simplicity, and even a somewhat summary simplification. All this lacks fervour. Often it is nothing more than a report. It would, however, be a mistake to neglect or even underestimate Vallotton as an artist and as a person. Some of his canvases are of an acid and terrible pessimism. One feels that

VALLOTTON. SELF-PORTRAIT. *Woodcut*

he had a horror of the pretty, the chalky and the insipid. Having an acute eye and an honest and courageous mind, Vallotton perhaps alone in his generation dared set up his easel before

VALLOTTON. NUDE HOLDING HER NIGHTGOWN.
1904. *Galerie P. Vallotton, Lausanne*

subjects that were then judged too trite for a serious artist – like a sunset over the sea, for example.

Vallotton may have lacked self-confidence and was not always able to maintain a balance between his temptation to reproduce what he saw and his wish to give a transformed and personal vision of things; hence the schematic appearance of some of his landscapes. But he painted portraits and admirable evocations of woods of the Paris region, alive with lovers and Sunday strollers. In these works the hypersensitive person he was arrived at a very personal style, composed of observation, evocation and sad humour. His art is chiefly introspection, and in his successful works he reveals an implacable discipline that is rare in the painting of the last half-century.

**VAN DOESBURG** Theo (1883–1931). Dutch painter; born in Utrecht, Holland; died in Davos, Switzerland. Van Doesburg at first planned a theatrical career. He wrote fables, plays and articles. In 1913 he published a collection of poems and began his research on the unification of painting and architecture. When still very young, he had begun painting and had exhibited for the first time at The Hague in 1908. In 1915 he published a laudatory article on Mondrian, whose acquaintance he made later. From then on his painting veered towards abstraction. The transformation that Mondrian had undergone slowly from 1911 to 1914 (successive abstractions on the themes of the tree, scaffolding, etc.), Van Doesburg accomplished much more quickly from 1916 to 1917 (themes of a cow grazing, still life, and cardplayers). In 1917, with Mondrian, Huszar, Vantongerloo and several *avant-garde* Dutch architects, he founded the review *De Stijl (\*)*, which, in the years following, exerted great influence upon the evolution of arts, particularly in Germany. In 1921 he left Holland for a crowded lecture tour through Central Europe. He made much commotion, especially at the Bauhaus *(\*)* in Weimar, where in 1924 he published *Fundamentals of the New Art*. After an exhibition of the *De Stijl* group in Paris in 1923 at Léonce Rosenberg's Galerie de l'Effort Moderne, Van Doesburg abandoned the rigorous principles formulated by Mondrian and set out in a new direction, which he would later (1926) call Elementarism *(\*)*. In 1927 he executed the decoration of several rooms of the 'Aubette' dance hall in Strasbourg, where Arp and Sophie Taeuber were also at work. This was his greatest work, unfortunately since destroyed. His last years were, like the others, full of feverish activity. In 1930, with the assistance of the painters Hélion, Carlsund and Tutundjan, he published the only issue of the magazine *Art Concret(\*)*. He died suddenly at Davos, in March 1931, during a treatment for hay fever.

More keen than profound, Van Doesburg was first of all an agitator and then a creator. He divined everything, understood at once, assaulted the obstacle with no concern for prudence. In this he was the exact opposite of

Mondrian, who proceeded slowly, always in search of a deeper understanding of what he had already explored for a long time. Van Doesburg's nature was more aggressive than constructive. In his review he sometimes insulted those whom he had praised the day before (Lissitzky, Malevitch). But this did not prevent his mind from being fertile and sometimes clairvoyant. In Holland, as early as 1916, he published pamphlets on art. But he was above all a brilliant showman, the fiery propagandist of Neo-Plasticism at the side of Mondrian. His chief claim to fame rests in his having divined Mondrian's value. Without the wholehearted support of Van Doesburg, who put *De Stijl* at his full disposal, Mondrian would probably never have codified Neo-Plasticism *(\*)* in the memorable articles he produced from 1917 to 1920.

**VAN DONGEN** Cornelius. Dutch painter, born 1877 at Delshaven, Van Dongen astonished his family by his precocious gifts. When still an adolescent, he drew and painted realistic works, and was soon influenced by the French Impressionists. In 1897, seven years after the death of his countryman Vincent Van Gogh, he settled in Paris. To make a living, he practised all professions – housepainter, porter at the *Halles* – and did sketches on café terraces. Like Steinlen, Jacques Villon and Vallotton, he contributed to satirical papers. He mingled in Montmartre life and acquired a simpler, more nervous, more concise line. In 1906 he rallied enthusiastically to Fauvism *(\*)*, predisposed by a latent expressionism and gifts as a colourist. He was faithful to Fauvism for a long time, through temperament and taste. He attracted attention by his long and flexible arabesques, his clear and intense colour, his rich and oily *matière*. He juxtaposed tones in wide parallel strips, without much concern for depth. At this time he was already making brilliant use of a manner so cursory and elliptical that it would not have escaped unbearable dryness but for his vigorous sensualism. None of the other *Fauves* attained such richness, such fantasy, with means so direct, so concentrated, so simple. Before canvases like *In The Wood* or *The Fellahin* (Museum of Modern Art, Paris) one marvels at the effects he obtained by placing pure white and an ultramarine blue side by side, a vermilion in the light and an acid green in the shadows, by opposing a golden yellow to a bright red background. He was too devoid of intellectualism, too eager to experience sensations to care about drawing and composition. But what dexterity, what a sharp savour, what insolent ease in the works he executed from 1905 to 1913! What sureness of the eye, what life in every form, in every stroke, every passage painted for its own sake! At the end of the First World War, he had already become the fashionable portraitist, the painter in demand, taken up by an aristocratic and dubious society, in which the Maharajah rubbed elbows with the hired dancer, the banker threatened with bankruptcy, the *nouveau riche*, the authentic Marquise, the parvenu actress. All the leading figures of this troubled period wanted their portrait signed by the former porter at the *Halles* whom they had consecrated as the painter of society. And each of them wanted his own portrait done exactly like Van Dongen's others.

Yet while he made some concessions to them, he did not humour them. He did not flatter them with his brush, did not even conceal the contempt he felt for them, did not hide their physical and moral flaws. However, to comply with their wish, he had to practise his art according to an invariable formula. It is thus that he created a sort of feminine type, the Theodora of the drawing-room, the Messalina of the boudoir, the princess of the inter-

VAN DONGEN. RECLINING NUDE. 1904–1905

national set, with an exaggeratedly thin body, her pallor broken only by a gash of lipstick, half-clad in transparent tulle and adorned with glittering jewels. His vision remained nevertheless that of a painter, of an incomparable colourist. If he attenuated the virulence, of his tones in time, sought more to please by using greys, modulations, shading, and to reassure by accentuating naturalistic illusion, he was none the less capable, when working only for himself, through pride and conviction, of producing works of fascinating freedom and mastery. Even as a portraitist he sometimes gave up all constraint. He has left pitiless interpretations of Anatole France, the politician Rappaport and Boni de Castellane, for example, which condemn a period and a class. It is nevertheless in landscape that Van Dongen has best fulfilled himself, no doubt because before nature he was himself again and painted for pleasure, without calculation Then he quite naturally gave up artifice and the display of virtuosity. He showed tact, discretion, vigour, sacrificing the accessory, reducing form to the essential, employing a few tones, but the most direct and telling. However, these fortunate moments of independence and sincerity have become more and more rare. In spite of a vigorous old age, Van Dongen no longer avoids facility, flabbiness, insipidity. Submitted too long to the vanities of the world, his will for expression has given way to a will to

please. His sensuality, his pessimism, his dexterity, his impertinent boldness, his improviser's verve, all seem to have disappeared from his later work.

**VAN GOGH** Vincent (1853–1890). Dutch painter; born at Groot-Zundert, in North Brabant; died at Auvers-sur-Oise. If, in December 1885, Van Gogh had not experienced a near-blinding revelation as a result of which he produced the masterpieces of the five last years of his life, he would no doubt be hailed today as a great painter of labour and poverty, of workmen and peasants overwhelmed by weariness, the first of the Dutch Expressionists. He became a painter in order to solve an inner conflict by which he was torn, to take his revenge in the domain of art for the failures he had experienced in his life. He was of a Protestant family, a family of clergymen. But two of his uncles were art dealers, a fact that allowed him to start out in The Hague as a salesman in a gallery recently sold by one of them to Goupil (*) of Paris. Vincent was sixteen when he entered Goupil's. Soon he was sent by his firm to London, to work in the English branch. In London he fell in love with his landlady's daughter. He asked her hand. He was turned down.

Unstable by temperament, acutely nervous,

VAN DONGEN. THE ENCLOSURE.
*Doctor Roudinesco Collection, Paris*

soon there was conflict. From January 21st to April 30th, 1877, he was a clerk in a bookshop in Dordrecht. But he was unable to adjust himself to a practical and regular existence. Therefore, increasingly tormented by his religious calling, he enrolled at a seminary in Brussels, giving up his studies three months later to be an evangelist in the poorest part of Belgium, the Borinage. He undertook to bring the miners of this forsaken region back to Christ. He adopted their own poverty, slept on a board in a wooden hut, shared their sufferings, attended the sick, showed the exalted zeal of an apostle, but without success. He was then an ill-clothed, gawky, red-haired fellow, with abrupt gestures and too-bright eyes. His spirit of sacrifice seemed astonishing, his excessive asceticism alarming. Men pursued him with sarcasm, children feared him, and as for women – who could love this terrible man? His superiors got rid of him in July 1879. Then began one of the darkest periods of his life, months of poverty, moral distress, anguish, roving on the roads. To his brother Theo, who was about to enter Goupil's in Paris, he wrote a poignant letter, in which he announced his decision to devote himself to painting. He studied drawing in Brussels and made copies from Millet. From April to December 1881, he stayed at Etten with his parents. He experienced another sentimental disappointment there. Turned down by his cousin 'K', he went away

too sincere, he was deeply dejected by this first failure. He left London and went to work at Goupil's head office in Paris, in 1875. He was immediately borne away upon the current of ideas of which Paris was then the centre. He read all the books within his reach, visited museums, underwent the influence of humanitarian writers and of painters concerned with the sufferings of the humble. The Bible became the chief stimulus of this self-taught son of a clergyman. He was dismissed by Goupil in 1876, and went back to England. He worked at a small school at Ramsgate, and then at another, where he did some preaching. He applied for a job as an evangelist among the miners. 'I feel drawn to religion. I want to comfort the humble.' His application was rejected. At Christmas of the same year he returned to Etten, to his parents, but

VAN GOGH. INTERIOR OF CAFÉ

teaching had finally become unbearable to him. Then, in 1883, he returned to his father's house, this time at Nuenen, and courageously gave himself up to painting. He did studies of the heath, cottages, weavers, peasants, executed in the rough, black, dismal manner of *The Boots* and *The Potato-Eaters* (V. W. Van Gogh Collection, Laren), his first large picture. His native tendency, the influence of his environment, the contagion of example – all incited him to persevere in this gloomy realism. How, then, can the radiant masterpieces that were to follow be explained?

In November 1885, he was in Antwerp. His father had just died. His brother Theo, with whom he had been in correspondence for five years, had sent him some money. He had discovered Rubens and the joy of life, and also Japanese fabrics, whose colours delighted him. He bought some, decorated his room with them, spent hours contemplating and studying them. He glimpsed an outlet for his still obscure desires, a new world of light, consolation, balance. He decided all of a sudden to leave for Paris. Theo received and sheltered him affectionately. He was dazzled by Impressionist pictures. He met Pissarro, Degas, Gauguin, Seurat. In June 1886, he enrolled at the École Nationale des Beaux-Arts in the Cormon studio, where he

and settled in The Hague. The painter Mauve, another cousin of his, took him in cordially and gave him useful advice. In January 1882, he met in the street a prostitute named Christine, who was ugly, drunk and pregnant. He took her with him. To this woman he gave all the love of which he was capable. The episode lasted twenty months, until he realized definitely that he was no better at individual love than at the love of humanity and the love of God. From then on his humiliated pride took refuge in art. With his artistic apostolate his misfortunes grew. He quarrelled with his father, who disapproved of his artistic career. He fell out with Mauve and Israels, the teachers of The Hague School, whose

VAN GOGH. SHOES.  *Collection of V. W. Van Gogh*

VAN GOGH. MOORED BOATS. AUGUST 1888.
*Kunstmuseum, Essen*

eagerness for work. Upon the advice of Toulouse-Lautrec, he went to Arles, on February 20th, 1888. In Provence everything delighted him, the orchards in bloom, the beautiful women of Arles, the Zouaves of the garrison, the drinkers of absinthe. He exclaimed with rapture, 'This is the Orient!' He was thirty-five and felt happy. With ease and enthusiasm he drew with a reed, painted well-balanced canvases, firmly arranged, almost serene. At last he had found clear-cut contours, light without shadow, pure colour, dazzling, crackling vermilion red, Prussian blue, emerald green, sacred yellow, the emblem of the Sun. He forsook the finery of Impressionism, gave up the divided stroke, fragmented design, subtle modulations. Vigorous, precise, incisive, his line captured the inner structure of

made friends with Toulouse-Lautrec. He worked desperately. He painted streets of Paris, portraits, flowers. He exhibited a few canvases at Père Tanguy's *(\*)* among others by Monet, Guillaumin and Signac. His brother, who was then the manager of the Goupil Gallery, encouraged and backed him. Obsessed by Japanese prints, he copied the *Bridge under Rain* and *The Tree* of Hiroshige. His palette lightened; he even borrowed the Impressionist pointillist technique, as in the *Portrait of Père Tanguy* (Musée Rodin). In the pictures of Pissarro, Monet, Guillaumin, he rediscovered the light handling and the fresh tones of the Japanese. But French Impressionism had caused a decisive shock to his thinking mind. He felt such a need to emulate the Impressionists that he did more than two hundred pictures during the twenty months of his stay in Paris. But the autumn and winter of 1887 were hard for him. The grey sky, the gloomy streets, the sadness of the capital became unbearable to him. The Parisian painters could not give him more than he had taken from them. The rejuvenation he had received from their contact was already exhausted. He needed light, heat, to warm his frozen soul and awaken his

VAN GOGH. SCHOOLBOY. 1888–1889.
*São Paulo Museum*

objects. He painted over two hundred pictures in fifteen months, executing three, four and sometimes up to five versions of some of them: *Two Barges on the Rhône*, *Mme Ginoux* (*L'Arlésienne*), *Sunflowers*, *The Bridge of l'Anglois*, *The Postman Roulin, his Wife and Children*, *The Café at Night*. From a short stay at Saintes-Maries-de-la-Mer he brought back drawings and canvases, notably his *Barges on the Beach* (Laren) and a *Seascape* (Moscow). He left an admirable representation of his *Bedroom in Arles* (October 1888), of which he later made, at Saint-Rémy, two replicas from memory.

However, his material existence was most precarious. He did not have enough to eat. He sold nothing. He suffered from hallucinations and crises, from which he emerged dazed. The idea of death haunted him. As if he had a presentiment of his approaching end, he hurried, worked furiously, in a state of exaltation that saved him from despair. His mind was on fire. His pictures dripped with golden light. He was 'in the centre of the universal fusion' that transmuted his colours and consumed his brain. Crises grew more numerous. He played with

LETTER FROM VAN GOGH ADDRESSED TO ÉMILE BERNARD FROM ARLES. 1888

a project for an artists' colony that he would have called 'The Studio of the South', where groups of men would work at projects in common. Late in October 1888, Gauguin responded to his appeal. Vincent was quite cheered up. But in stormy discussions the relationship between these two opposed natures soon deteriorated. On Christmas night, during a futile quarrel, Van Gogh threw his glass in Gauguin's face. The next day, Gauguin, walking in the street, heard hurried steps behind him. He turned and saw Van Gogh with a razor in his hand. Under Gauguin's steady gaze Van Gogh stopped, then

fled to his room, cut off his right ear with a stroke of the razor, wrapped it in a handkerchief and went to offer it as a present to a girl in a brothel. After two weeks in a hospital he came back to paint the extraordinary *Man with an Ear Cut Off* (January 1889). Meanwhile his hallucinations returned. Neighbours raised a petition for his internment. His unattractive appearance, his touchy character, his whims had alienated people. He had never analyzed his illness more clearly, endured men's hostility with so much resignation, or spoken of his art with more common sense and lucidity, but now he was considered mad. He was sent back to the hospital. In Paris, Theo, who was going to be married, became alarmed and sent the painter Signac to see him. Signac spent the day of March 20th with Vincent, who kept on painting, reading, writing, in spite of his crises. When he felt too ill, he asked to be interned at the asylum of Saint-Rémy-de-Provence, on May 9th, 1889.

VAN GOGH. HOUSE IN PROVENCE. *Pen Drawing*

The Arles period was over, the most fruitful if not the most original of his career. During the year he remained at the asylum he produced another hundred and fifty pictures, and hundreds of drawings, working as one possessed, interrupted in his labour by three long crises, followed by painful prostrations. He painted *The Asylum in Autumn, Cornfield with Cypress,* delirious landscapes, surging mountains, whirling suns, cypresses and olive trees twisted by heat. His colour no longer had the sonority of the preceding period; the yellows had become coppered; the blues darkened, the vermilions browned. In compensation, rhythm became more intense: whirling arabesques, dismantled forms, perspective fleeing toward the horizon in a desperate riot of lines and colours. What he represented then on his canvases he seems to have seen through a vertigo of the imagination. The fire lit by his hand was communicated to his brain. A feeling of failure overwhelmed him. Could his works be inferior to those of the masters whom he admired? This thought frightened him. In January 1890, he learned of the birth of Theo's son, called Vincent after himself. The generous Theo, so indulgent a brother, at whose expense he, the failure as an artist, the painter incapable of selling a single canvas, had been living so long! Yet, in the *Mercure de France* the critic Aurier had just published the first article devoted to his work. This tribute brought him little comfort. He felt ill, exhausted. Vigilant as ever, Theo asked Doctor Gachet *(\*)* to take Vincent under his care at Auvers-sur-Oise. It was thus that Van Gogh came to Paris, on May 16th, 1890, and settled soon at Auvers. Doctor Gachet attended him, showed him an affectionate friendship, served as a model for him. For Vincent had resumed painting. He did his last self-portrait, now in the Louvre, *The Church of*

VAN GOGH. PORTRAIT OF ARMAND ROULIN.
NOVEMBER 1888. *Folkwangmuseum, Essen*

*Auvers*, also in the Louvre, *The Town Hall of Auvers*, the *Portrait of Mlle Ravoux*, that of *Doctor Gachet* (Louvre), and other works, for which he had at his disposal only a technique which had already begun to disintegrate. He feared a new attack of his illness. An unspeakable sadness invaded him. Work? His hand failed him, the enemy within him was now the stronger. Why persevere? On the last Sunday in July, he went into the ripe cornfields, where he had painted *The Field with Crows* a few days before, and there, facing the sky, he fired a bullet into his chest. He died two days later, in his thirty-seventh year.

Unbalanced, painful, tragic, such was certainly his life. That he suffered from neurosis and epilepsy is equally true. Like Rousseau, like Baudelaire, Van Gogh felt very vividly that his life was a failure and suffered deeply from it. He was perpetually anguished, and against his anguish he tried various means of defence: religion, humanitarianism, art. He gave himself to painting with all the more passion as he saw himself threatened by an implacable disease. Lifted out of himself by art, he was able to overcome his physical failings, or at least not to think of them too much. This unstable, high-strung, obsessed man, in unceasing conflict with society and himself, created a body of work outstanding in its concerted perfection of ends and means. However impetuously inspired and executed it may be, this art is certainly not that of a madman. Although he put all of himself into his painting, Vincent never abandoned his very obvious concern for balance, order and reason. His shortcomings are more than offset by an activity which drew from his very failures enough vigour to fight against his weakness and live in his work. He might have sunk into mental chaos; instead, he triumphed through discipline, work and meditation. In the midst of his greatest

discouragements, he retained his love of simplicity and harmony, sought a reconciliation of form and colour, an abstract, coherent transposition of the world. He gave himself an infallible system of principles and rules to reach the artistic ideal that he had glimpsed in his moments of acute insight. Each of his works was the fruit of a thought, a decision, a wish for serenity rather than for strangeness. What did he want? 'Something peaceful and pleasant, realistic and yet painted with emotion; some-

VAN GOGH. YELLOW WHEAT. 1889. *Tate Gallery, London*

thing brief, synthetic, simplified and concentrated, full of calm and of pure harmony, comforting like music.' He tamed his exaltations and his impulses by the laws he had established for himself. Far, then, from being the painting of a madman, Van Gogh's is that of a thoroughly conscious artist and at the same time of a robust man, a dedicated creator. If anything, he saw too clearly. He sought always elements of a beauty of which he could find only an insufficient amount. 'There is an art in the future, and it will be so beautiful, so young! . . .' What bitterness in this cry of hope! He hoped for, prepared, made possible a golden age of painting, knowing nevertheless that he would not see it. More

VAN GOGH. THE PLAIN AT AUVERS-SUR-OISE. 1890.          *XIXth Century Gallery, Vienna*

assured of his victories than of profits, it was reserved to him, the discoverer and the pioneer, only to bequeath the means of success to those who came after him. In a way he triumphed over his illness, for his suicide prevented his madness. But he did not create the new art of which he had a presentiment and which he announced with moving certainty in his letters, because the moment for it had perhaps not yet come.

The sureness of his hand equalled that of his inspiration. There is no groping, no working over, not the slightest alteration in his landscapes or his portraits, which were almost always undertaken directly on canvas, in the manner of the Japanese. 'It is not only by yielding to one's impulses', he wrote, 'that one achieves greatness, but also by patiently filing away the steel wall that separates what one feels from what one is capable of doing.' So Van Gogh expressed the inner duel that eventually exhausted his strength. But if the man was carried off early, the work remains, and contemporary painting was, in great measure, born of it. Van Gogh appeared when the Naturalist fiction was casting its last glow with Impressionism, at a time when academic conventions were collapsing, when tradition was dying of old age. With Cézanne and Gauguin, he questioned the technique of painting and in doing so prepared for the art of the twentieth century. He used the picture not to imitate appearances or humour the tastes of a cultivated society, but to re-create the world according to his own intelligence and sensibility. While Cézanne was concerned with a new conception of space and Gauguin with composition, Van Gogh emancipated colour, carrying it to its maximum intensity and expressiveness. In his canvases colour reinforces drawing, accentuates form, creates rhythm, defines proportions and depth. It even acquires the value of a sign, addressing itself to the soul as well as to the eye: 'colour not locally true,' he said, 'from the realistic point of view of *trompe-l'œil*, but suggestive of some emotion'. He used it raw, dry, aggressive, in abrupt harmonies, now strident, now muted, without shades, without semitones, with cruel frankness. 'I have tried to express with red and green the terrible human passions', he also wrote. But he always refrained from sacrificing colour to form. And it is right that today his drawings should be admired as much as his pictures. He has left a great number of them, and all of them are surprising in their simplicity and acuteness of expression, their assurance and swiftness of line, the variety of the graphic means which the artist used to transcribe on paper the quivering elements of his vision. And this vision was thoroughly his own, of undeniable depth and originality. He has had no direct descendants, although his influence has been felt by all modern painting: *Fauves* like Vlaminck, Derain, Dufy, Friesz; the Expressionists, in

VAN GOGH. WHEAT FIELD WITH CROWS. 1890.          *Collection of V. W. Van Gogh*

particular Soutine and Utrillo, But Van Gogh was also a poet, a mystic, a thinker. No artist today raises more passionate an interest than he: his painting, his drawings, his correspondence. For Van Gogh lived in advance the drama of our time, a time that 'now liberates and now enslaves'. Nowhere in the history of modern painting is the study of the artist's correspondence more vital than in the case of Van Gogh. Van Gogh's letters to his brother Theo, in addition to the intrinsic interest they have as deeply moving human documents, are indispensable to a thorough understanding of his concepts and intentions. (" The Letters of Vincent van Gogh to his Brother, 1872-1886 ", two volumes, and " Further Letters of Vincent van Gogh to his Brother, 1886-1889. ") The three volumes were published in American by Houghton Mifflin Co., Boston, and in England by Constable & Co. Ltd., London.

**VILLON** Jacques (Gaston Duchamp). French painter, born in 1875 at Damville in the Eure. The son of a notary and the grandson of Émile Nicolle, a painter and engraver of Rouen, he always saw drawing, painting and engraving practised around him. After his secondary studies he entered a notary's office in Rouen as a clerk. But he attended the courses of the School of Fine Arts more assiduously than

he worked at his job. In 1894 he dropped the law and came to Paris. It was then that he took the name of his favourite poet as a pseudonym. Following the example of Forain, Steinlen and especially Lautrec, whom he met every night at the Moulin Rouge, he published satirical and humorous drawings in the papers, notably *Le Chat Noir*, *Gil Blas*, *L'Assiette au Beurre* and *Le Courrier Français*. He devoted the first fifteen years of his career to this minor form of art, unable to liberate himself from it. He also did posters for Parisian cabarets and practised engraving, which he has never given up. He exhibited at the Salon d'Automne from the time of its foundation (1903). Toward 1906 he was able to give himself to painting more exclusively. At first influenced by Degas and Toulouse-Lautrec, he seemed at this time to be seized by the contagion of Fauvism. He carried colour to its highest intensity. In 1911 he took up Analytic Cubism, which met his need for order and discipline. Even then his canvases revealed tendencies and tastes to which he has remained faithful ever since. He organized his compositions carefully and arranged their elements rhythmically around a 'line of intention'. He constructed his forms according to the principle of 'pyramidal vision' formulated by Leonardo da Vinci: an object and its various parts come toward us in pyramids, whose apex is in our eye and whose base is in the object or in a section of the object.

VILLON. RACE HORSE. 1922.                    *Louis Carré Gallery, Paris*

He used this procedure with conviction (*The Set Table*, 1912; *Soldiers Marching*, 1913). Finally, under his sponsorship and in his studio at Puteaux the *Section d'Or (\*)* group was constituted: Gleizes, Léger, Metzinger, Kupka, La Fresnaye, Delaunay, Villon's sister, Suzanne Duchamp, and his two brothers, the sculptor Raymond Duchamp-Villon and the painter Marcel Duchamp. If coloured pyramids permit the breakdown of the object or the figure, it has also to be reorganized in a solid and convincing manner. This was why Villon wished to shore up the Cubist methods with strict rules born of active reflection. The words *Section d'Or* reflected this intellectual requirement, but not the real passion with which he intended to meet it. This method, reinforced and made more flexible, he used for a purpose quite alien to the Cubists' preoccupations. For him the question was less one of transcribing the real in its totality, of accentuating the plastic values of the object, than of taking it apart analytically, giving it more poetry and lyricism, technical skill intervening only to make dream or recollection explicit. Mobilized on August 2nd, 1914, and assigned to the camouflage service, he was discharged in 1919 and eagerly returned to work. From 1919 to 1922, his first abstract period (*The Flight, The Racehorse*), he tried to render the diversity of values by overlapping planes and sought equivalents capable of expressing the essence of things rather than their exterior attributes. His pictures were painted in a scale of very restricted tones — greys and browns. From 1922 to 1930 he was obliged, in order to live, to devote himself almost entirely to engraving. Capable of creating original and powerful works, he humbly executed a series of coloured reproductions of paintings signed by modern masters – Bonnard, Braque, Picasso, Matisse, Dufy, Utrillo. It was an arid period, painful and depressing. Fortunately, he had several successful exhibitions in New York and Chicago. The American public extended a better welcome to him than his own countrymen. In 1930 he was at last able to go back to his easel. Now very attentive to light, he divided his canvas methodically, superimposing coloured planes according to the laws of the chromatic scale. After another period of abstractionism (*The Leap*, 1932; *The Theatre*, 1933), he reverted to direct study and also to pure colours, which served to define space and sustain rhythm (*The Draughtsman*, 1935; *The Wrestlers*, 1939). In 1940 he took refuge in the Tarn, and although he had never before shown curiosity for anything but the human figure, he did numerous studies of the surrounding countryside. After that, he preferred to paint landscape. Since 1944 he has been concentrating all his past experience within the limits of the picture, which comes to us as a complete universe, a paradoxical synthesis of natural phenomena with all the varied, if not contradictory ideas and feelings of which man can avail himself.

How does he work? He tells us himself: 'I begin with studies done from nature. From these, I bring out a construction, a play of arabesques and rhythms; in short, I reflect upon nature, which remains my starting point, and I transform it according to a very carefully studied construction of the canvas to be painted. I try to express a space, to find a space in which I can achieve my work. I am also greatly concerned with research in colour and colour values.' His colours are the rarest, the most exquisite: almond greens, pinks, lilacs, oranges, bluish greys. He spreads them with the tip of the brush according to a minutely controlled hierarchy of planes, while preserving the fineness and purity of the line, its dynamic function, and a coherence without heaviness of composition, a unity upon which skill and imagination confer rigour and an inimitable poetry. Villon has always remained faithful to the French tradition. When he accentuates his non-figurative tendency, he does not betray nature. If he exalts colour, he watches over his drawing even more carefully. In his moments of relaxation or abandon, his delicate architectures remain subject to an unyielding will. Not to sacrifice space to light, solidity to movement, the heart to the intelligence, to express everything and neglect nothing, to remain always open and leave nothing to chance, to be in the vanguard of the struggle and yet revere the masters, paint anecdotal works and yet use only forms and colours, marry Cubism to Impressionism, Abstract Art to Figurative Art – this is an attitude that involves certain risks. Usually by wanting to reconcile everything one finally arrives at compromises.

Villon, however, can take pride in incontestable successes. All conquests, all innovations, all presentiments are paradoxically united – and with what ease – in his work. Unlike non-figurative painters, he has practised discredited genres such as the landscape and the portrait; unlike figurative ones he has executed resolutely abstract works. All the tendencies of this century have found their echo in him. He has subscribed to all discoveries, assimilated them and fused them in the melting pot of his own originality. Intelligence and sensibility, reflection and intuition, audacity and humility, his work is a harmonious synthesis of these contrasts. His long career has been made of advances and retreats, of thrusts and resumptions. Yet there has been no hesitation or disquiet: rather precautions, prudent steps, circumspect explorations, subtle allusions. He has developed a conscious and distinguished art, bold but courteous, balanced, shaded, deliciously ambiguous, limpid in spite of its complexity. The art of a free but shy man, of an innovator, agile but careful not to be disconcerting. Less passion than fervour, more implication than assertion, a great nobility in the pleasure given, and thoughtfulness in the effort, so the work appears

VILLON. ENTRANCE TO THE PARK. 1948.   *Louis Carré Gallery, Paris*

to us. It is less striking than others more tyrannical or more noisy, but there is no doubt that it goes deeper.

**VIVIN** Louis (1861–1936). French painter; born at Hadol in the Vosges; died in Paris. His is an art of urban character, as though it were made from the tracery of the Eiffel Tower. Held in the net of its tenuous lines, Vivin's painting is one of the valid manifestations of naïve art. There is in general nothing so monotonous as folk art: a transfer of a series of identical ideas given the name of a country or a region to differentiate them. From this background, consisting of repeated images of the collective unconscious, there occasionally emerges some more acute art in which a personality is expressed. This is the case with the Douanier Rousseau and Bauchant; it is also the case with Vivin. Drawn stone after stone, block after block, his art is that of a builder. A natural combination of the linear and the pictorial, what he spreads out before our eyes is the most charming world that could be. His sensitive hand wove, as the spider its web, a world of intersecting silk ladders to which, in its best moments, large flat areas, freshly coloured blue,

red, brown and green, serve as backgrounds: leaden skies, hulls of barges, shop signs. The painter gives us a portrait of the curiosities of Paris and its suburbs with occasional excursions to harbours and imaginary Venices dreamed from postcards.

Where there are no buildings, no stones to juxtapose, he relapses into the meek and invertebrate style of the usual folk art: bouquets, still lifes, little scenes of carnage.

When still no more than a child, Vivin covered the doors of his house with drawings. Given a paint box by the village priest, he painted a series of landscapes of his native region. But one has to live, and the boy's father, a teacher, was opposed to a career as a painter for his son. In 1881 Vivin entered the Postal and Telegraph Service, where he later became an inspector. In 1889 he exhibited for the first time in public, showing *The Pink Flamingo* at the postal employees' salon. From then on he lived in a small dusty apartment in Montmartre. From time to time he exhibited out-of-doors at the 'Foire aux Croûtes' near Sacré-Cœur. He was sixty-one when he retired. His days of getting up at five to paint by kerosene lamp before going to his office were over. In 1925 Wilhelm Uhde *(\*)* discovered him and gave him encouragement. Paralyzed, the artist had to give up painting during his last years. With his head framed by tousled white hair, a bushy beard, his forehead lined by wrinkles, a rather thick nose, he had the look of a weary observer, a tramp philosopher. A kind of repressed smile, marked with sad humour, radiated from all his features. He was an uneven painter. Some of his canvases have a monotonous quality in the drawing, or a flabby heaviness of stroke. In this respect he was truly a 'Sunday painter'. He did not have the regularity of inspiration that establishes the value of the Douanier Rousseau. In his best works, however, there is a clearness

VIVIN. THE LOUVRE. 1930.  *Private Collection, Paris*

of colour, a vividness, and a limpidity that fully justify his reputation.

**VLAMINCK** Maurice. French painter; born 1876 in Paris. Vlaminck's father was of Flemish stock and his mother from Lorraine. He spent his childhood in Paris, in the *Halles* district, and later chiefly at Chatou. His parents, both musicians and rather bohemian, seem to have neglected their son's formal education. Vlaminck developed a marked taste for all arts of folk inspiration: sentimental songs, naïve images, small pictures in spun glass,

VLAMINCK. TUG AT CHATOU. 1906.

*Private Collection, U.S.A.*

Negro sculpture. His tastes were frankly plebeian: he liked Sunday amusements, picnics, sporting events, walks and bicycle rides. He was happy among the things of the earth. A painter, a writer, a violinist, he was also a farmer. He boasted of never having set foot in the Louvre; he rebelled against the École des Beaux-Arts, the Academy, aesthetes, 'decadent' art forms, precious and refined works. All constraint, all discipline exasperated him: the teacher, the priest, the sergeant, the policeman. He loathed all that limits the personality. He took pride in being a libertarian. Thus he was happy out of doors. As a bicycle racer and later a motoring enthusiast, he craved speed and wide open spaces. Derain, who was born in Chatou, often saw him either participating in a bicycle race, carrying his violin under his arm or lugging his canvases and paintbox. The two young men became friends. They met almost every day, having endless discussions, going to paint on the slopes of Carrières-Saint-Denis or along the banks of the Seine, while tug-boats were passing followed by a line of barges: 'The colour of all this delighted us . . . this was Chatou!' They shared the same studio, not far from the place that the Impressionists had made famous. Renoir had painted the

*Canoeists* there, and Courbet, in 1856, *Les Demoiselles*. Degas had gone there in search of subjects. It was there that Vlaminck and Derain founded the School of Chatou, one of the sources of Fauvism (*). Recalling this period and their friendship, Derain writes: 'We were always intoxicated with colour, with words that speak of colour, and with the sun that makes colour live!' One can imagine, then, the joy with which Vlaminck came into contact with the *Fauves* of the Académie Carrière (*), and the influence Van Gogh was to exercise upon his work once he had visited the exhibition devoted to the great Dutchman in 1901, and with which he was so enraptured that he exclaimed upon leaving it: 'Van Gogh means more to me than my own father!' A Fauvist: undoubtedly no one has deserved this name more than Vlaminck. No one else had his muscularity, his punch, his vitality. One felt a physical joy in seeing this bragging and jovial giant throw out his chest, flex his calves and lift weights. With his common sense, his noisy enthusiasm, his taste for uproarious practical jokes, his intoxication with colour, his lyrical interpretation of reality, Vlaminck boldly trod the earth ploughed by Vincent. The wild gale, that had shaken the cypresses at Saint-Rémy fifteen years before,

VLAMINCK. HOUSE WITH LEAN-TO. 1920.
*Musée d'Art Moderne, Paris*

that the frail regatta of Argenteuil was put to flight by the howling tugboats of Chatou, even if they dragged acrid smells of fried fish in their wake. This *Fauve* at liberty was a comforting sight, quenching his thirst at the sources of rhythm and browsing on colour in its primal rawness. He painted, discoursed, fulminated, blasphemed, exercised his muscles. Between two pictures he wrote a novel or got on his bicycle, dashed off a newpaper article or hurtled down the roads in his car. Then he returned to his palette and his pipe. In 1907 he painted his last Fauvist canvas, drifted away from Van Gogh and planted his boots in Cézanne's tracks. As he himself has confessed, 'I suffered from not being able to hit harder, from having arrived at the maximum intensity'. It was from 1908 to 1914 that, following the example of Cézanne, Vlaminck sought well-balanced and constructed compositions. He accentuated depth, gave great solidity to volumes, enclosed masses in geometrical contours. Cubism should have attracted him. On the contrary, he turned away from it with rage and was soon denouncing its narrow intellectualism. Around 1915 he broke with Cézannism and settled down comfortably in an expressionism that has, with time, drifted toward an inveterate realism. The Fauvist who let exultant joy burst out in a delirium of crude

developed in his pictures into a storm too violent not to have been consciously expressed. From his thick hands came topsy-turvy forms and frenzied colours, canvases teeming with kinks, thrusts, twistings, freshly squeezed from tubes. The yellow dear to Van Gogh, vermilion, ultramarine, Veronese green, pure white – his favourite tones – he opposed them all and joyfully made them clash. His palette was as exaggerated as his style. Robust, noisy, he shouted and hit hard. But he often hit the mark and persuaded quickly. One swallowed his spiced dishes at a gulp, tired of Impressionist sweets. Monet's evanescent forms and flickering tones were obliterated by the brutal parallels and explosive tones of a picture like *The Red Trees* (reproduced on page 102). No one thought of complaining

VLAMINCK. THE OISE AT SERGY. *Etching*

colours now paints sinister landscapes and faded flowers. Leaden backgrounds, primitive forms, skies slashed with Prussian blue, spinach-green vegetation, dirty-ochre roads, chalky-white walls, trees bent under some unlikely gust of wind – everything in his recent work speaks of his having forgotten his early enthusiasms and his very earthy vision of things. As a landscape painter, he draws on nature very little. As a modern painter, he rejects modern painting and to express himself finds only means borrowed from the old masters of museums: hence the sadness that emanates from the works of his maturity.

**VOLLARD** Ambroise (1865–1939). Coming as a young man to Paris from his native island of Réunion, Ambroise Vollard began as a clerk in a small art gallery. When he became a dealer himself (1893), he prudently began to take interest in 'recognized' painters like Roybet; he told of this later himself with the sly, childish smile that sometimes lit up the usually gruff face made familiar to us by several great painters. To a natural inclination for humour he added penetrating observation. His taste for satire and his horror for routine took on a more concrete significance when, suddenly abandoning Roybet, without transition or half-measure, he adopted Cézanne and in December 1895 organized in his gallery the first great Cézanne exhibition, with a hundred and fifty of his most characteristic canvases. The show created a scandal; the public closed their ranks. Members of the Institut de France who came to the exhibition protested vehemently. Vollard was forced to remove from his window the canvases that provoked the hilarity or hostility of passers-by, but he was beaming; his smile was that of a boy who has played a good trick. Meanwhile real admirers appeared: Auguste Pellerin, Count Camondo, the former King Milan of Serbia, for example. Vollard's shop, his 'cellar', as it was called, became the most brilliant artistic centre in Paris during the first forty years of the century. A drawing by Bonnard, dated 1895, represents him in the midst of the well-known disorder of his shop, surrounded by Rodin, Pissarro, Renoir, Degas and

Bonnard himself. No biography of Vollard can omit a rather impressive iconography: Bonnard painted him in 1905, and then in 1915. Cézanne made, in 1889, the famous portrait of him which is now in the Petit Palais, and which took no fewer than a hundred and fifteen sittings. At about the same time Vollard figured in Maurice Denis's *Hommage à Cézanne* (1901). He sat for four canvases by Renoir, in 1905, 1906, 1915 and 1917, the last time dressed as a toreador. Picasso painted him in the Cubist manner in 1906 and then in 1915 and 1937; Rouault in 1926, Dufy on a ceramic in 1934. But illustrated books came to be his chief concern. In 1905 he published a collection of lithographs by Lautrec, Bonnard and Vallotton. From then on publishing was an activity that never abated until his death. There appeared successively the *Parallèlement* of Verlaine (1900), *Daphnis and Chloë* (1902) illustrated by Bonnard; *The Imitation of Christ* (1903), the *Sagesse* of Verlaine (1911) by Maurice Denis; a Ronsard (1915), a Villon (1918), the *Fleurs du Mal* (1916), the *Little Flowers of St. Francis* (1928), the *Odyssey* (1930) by Émile Bernard; the *Jardin des Supplices* of Mirbeau, by Rodin; the *Chef-d'Œuvre Inconnu* of Balzac (1931), the *Histoire Naturelle* of Buffon (1947) by Picasso; *La Maison Tellier* of Maupassant (1933) and the *Mimes des Courtisanes*, translated by Pierre

VUILLARD. MONTMARTRE, VINTIMILLE SQUARE.

addition he brought out bronzes by Rodin, Renoir, Maillol and Picasso. His tremendous activity won him many friendships and enabled people to forgive the redoubtable business man that he was. He had a very original personality and his conversation was extremely lively. A respectful but vigilant observer, he executed portraits himself – literary ones – depicting Cézanne, Renoir and Degas in vivid and colourful books. In 1937 he published his *Souvenirs d'un Marchand de Tableaux* (published first in English, in 1936, as *Recollections of a Picture Dealer*), which will remain an important source for the art history of our time.

**VUILLARD** Edouard (1886–1940). French painter; born at Cuiseaux, in Saône-et-Loire; died at La Baule. The ways of Vuillard were those of a Parisian petit bourgeois rather than of a provincial. His mother managed a dressmaker's shop. A quiet, orderly, stay-at-home, he spent almost all his life within a small perimeter in Montmartre, in the vicinity of the tiny Square Vintimille, which he has immortalized,

Louÿs (1935) with illustrations by Degas; *La Tentation de Saint-Antoine of Flaubert* by Odilon Redon (1938); the *Réincarnations du Père Ubu* (1932) by Rouault; finally works by Vollard himself with engravings or drawings by Renoir, Puy, Bonnard (*Sainte Monique*) and Rouault, and other books such as the *Dead Souls* of Gogol and the *Fables* of La Fontaine by Chagall that the publisher's death left unfinished.

In 1898 Vollard organized a second retrospective of Cézanne and, in 1899, an important exhibition of the *Nabis*. The year 1901 witnessed the first showing of Picasso, from whom he bought some thirty canvases for two thousand francs in 1905. The first exhibition of Matisse also took place at Vollard's gallery, in 1904. Vollard had an opportunity to show his fondness for Fauvism by acquiring the whole of Vlaminck's studio in 1906. Having met Rouault in 1907, he directed him toward ceramics and later, in 1916, toward the illustration of books, eventually installing a studio for him in his own house, where he invited all the artistic and literary élite of Paris for his famous dinners. In

VUILLARD. THE COOK. 1899
*Lithograph*

and which ought to bear his name. His beginnings at Le Barc de Boutteville's gallery (1890–1895), his presence at Mallarmé's 'Tuesdays' and the meetings in the editorial offices of the *Revue Blanche* *(*)*, his work as designer at the Théâtre de l'Œuvre – where he learned the technique of tempera – everything brought him near the comrades of his youth: Sérusier, a link with Gauguin; Bonnard, whose studio he shared; K.-X. Roussel, who became his brother-in-law; Vallotton, Maillol and Maurice Denis (*vide Nabis*). Vuillard, who called himself derisively the 'intimist',

VUILLARD. IN BED. 1891.                    *Musée d'Art Moderne, Paris*

in his first works skirted realism with extreme caution, as if afraid of frightening it away. A vision of rare subtlety, an innate sense of harmony and layout, made him an heir of Degas and Claude Monet. About 1888 he was painting still lifes and small portraits that related him to Corot and Chardin; then, toward 1890, influenced like Bonnard, by Gauguin and the Japanese, he gave himself up to a kind of 'Pre-Fauvism'. But he soon abandoned exotic composition and all turbulence of the palette, and reasserted his predilection for minor chords and uncontrasting values. The more modest the setting, the more moving is Vuillard's interpretation. For a long time he painted thinly on grey cardboard, whose uncovered parts played through the touches of colour and contributed to the melancholy charm of the composition. Between 1893 and 1914, he did a number of small decorations which might be called 'apartment frescoes': from the *Gardens of Paris* executed for Alexandre Natanson or *Interiors* (ordered by Dr. Vaquez and today in the Petit Palais) to decorations for the Comédie des Champs-Elysées and the Théâtre de Chaillot.

Portraits, together with the small interior scenes and decorations, constitute the essential part of his work. When he was alone with his intimates – his mother, who shared his life, and whom we see in so many compositions, reading, sewing, preparing meals, attending to household duties; his friends, who called themselves 'Prophets' or *Nabis*; Thadée Natanson and Missia, Tristan Bernard, Romain Coolus, Mme Hessel – Vuillard was at his best. He appears less at ease in commissioned portraits, mostly executed in tempera, in which his sympathy, his amusement go chiefly to the play of light, to exchanges between objects. His comparative failure in painting society people and an atmosphere of wealth was due to an incompatibility of ideals and temperament that he did not always confess to himself, faithful as he was to the sweetness of the simple life and to all that reminded him of his early childhood. In reaction against the vanities and confusion that the twentieth century has seen growing, and even against certain oddities that were part of the charm of the small canvases of the *Revue Blanche* and Symbolist periods, where everything is allusion and whispering, this magician applied, toward the end of his life, his seriousness, his scruples about going beyond these amenities to 'finishing' his canvases, even if he was to move us less. He liked to rely upon the known, an inner and so to speak anterior reality. The role

of 'visual memory' is considerable both in his
portraits, almost always executed away from
the model, and in his still lifes and decorations.
So much rigour in the exquisite, so much precision in enchantment recall the greatest poets
of the nuance. The most modest tones are
exalted and become precious solely by virtue of
their nearness one to another, or of differences
that are never discords.

VUILLARD. PORTRAIT OF HIS MOTHER. *Circa* 1914.
*Private Collection, Paris*

**WHISTLER** James (1834–1903). American painter; born in Lowell, Massachusetts; died in Paris. Once, when Vollard showed him a woman's portrait done by Cézanne, Whistler remarked, 'If a ten-year-old child had scrawled that on a slate, his mother – if she was a good mother – would have whipped him'. While the importance of such a quip should not be exaggerated, it does throw some light upon the behaviour of a man who, even though he participated in the revolutionary forays of the Impressionists, generally held back whenever the issue became too disturbing. He was a strange, clever, but timid artist, despite the appearance of liberty he revealed in his more characteristic works. His family traced back to Scotch-Irish ancestors, and his father, a railway construction engineer, was internationally respected. Emulating his father, an Army Major and a West Point graduate, Whistler also enrolled at the military academy, but studies proved too irksome and he was dismissed. At the call of Art he proceeded to Paris, where he soon discovered the Café Guerbois and exchanged ideas with Baudelaire, Manet, Fantin-Latour and Braquemond. His oil *At the Piano*, exhibited at the Salon in 1860, won him the encouragement of Courbet. In 1863, informed that his *Little White Girl* would not be acceptable for hanging in the Paris Salon, he aligned himself with the other famous rebels in the Salon des Refusés. Determined to oust all influences, whether a traditional classicism or a more recent romanticism – and having been spurred to that end by Courbet – he joined this artist during the summers of 1864 and 1865 at Trouville. Shortly afterwards Whistler embarked for Chile, where he affiliated himself with a band of revolutionary exiles. Later he lived in London with his brother-in-law Seymour Haden, the etcher, and still later was attacked by Ruskin,

whom he sued in a celebrated (and successful) court action. Eventually, after much travelling in Italy, Belgium and Holland, he settled in 1890 in Paris, installing himself in a studio at 86 Rue Notre-Dame-des-Champs, where he later conducted classes. Although his works never possessed the force to make of him a major influence (even admitting those followers who had taken note of his flair for the penumbral envelope) he did have his gifts as an improviser who could wed the elegance of his arabesque to a chromatic refinement rightly described as exquisite. Again, whatever the branch of his work, he did commit himself, like the Impressionists, to an unremitting examination of tones, as even his titles emphasize: *Harmony in Grey and Green, Arrangement in Grey and Black, Nocturne in Blue and Green, Symphony in White.* And yet the general trend of his accomplishment did not escape the impersonal. In spite of the sparkle he could impart to his compositions, the underlying substance shows none of that profound humanity invariably present among the other masters of his time. His technical method, while it could be appealing, unsettles and even perplexes because of a propensity for the decadent which leaves the suspicion – however involuntary – that he had overlooked the plastic imperatives in painting, and, even more serious, that he simply could not experience that attachment to nature characteristic of his associates among the Impressionists. He is not to be denied his audacity as a technician of the palette and he did concentrate himself upon certain problems – at least those pertaining to 'cuisine' – but even here he fell upon dangerous recipes, and he so diluted his colours in turpentine that eventually they lost their initial intensity. Yet the cause of his quest was his zeal to eliminate all the brightness his sensibility could not accept. He expounded his principles in a witty lecture,

'Ten O'clock', translated into French by Mallarmé. Here he impaled his enemies among the leading contemporary academicians, demonstrating both by aphorism and example that he was the supreme exponent of an atmospheric vision that few of such contemporaries could even understand.

**WOOD** Christopher (1901–1930). Born at Knowsley, near Liverpool; died at Salisbury by his own hand. By the charm of his character, the tragedy of his early death, and the extraordinary promise of his painting which burst like a golden rocket in the none-too-bright sky of that post-war decade, 'Kit' Wood has become one of the few legends in British art. At fourteen he contracted an illness which rendered him helpless for three years and left him with a permanent limp. On leaving school in 1920 he decided to become a painter. For the next ten years he was hardly ever in one place for more than a month or two at a time; between 1920 and 1924 his wanderings took him from Inverness to Constantinople, and to the greater part of Europe. Notwithstanding this apparently rootless existence, he formed a wide circle of friends – among them Picasso and Cocteau in France, Ben and Winifred Nicholson in England. It was Picasso who persuaded Diaghilev to commission from him the décor and costumes for a *Romeo and Juliet* ballet, which was, however, later abandoned. His first exhibition was at the Beaux Arts Gallery in 1926; his second at Tooth's in 1929. In 1930 he worked in Paris upon another ballet for C. B. Cochran and his third exhibition at Bernheim's. After two months of furious activity at Tréboul, in Brittany, during the summer, he returned to see his mother at Salisbury on August 21st; later that day he was killed by a train in Salisbury station.

It was during this last summer of his life that Christopher Wood found himself completely as an artist. Through all his apprenticeship he had always known exactly where he stood; he had accepted influences eagerly, grasped quickly the kernel of truth which they held for him and discarded the husk. From Van Gogh and Modigliani and Picasso and the old Cornish primitive, Alfred

WHISTLER. MISS CICELY ALEXANDER. HARMONY IN GREY AND GREEN. 1872–1874. *Tate Gallery, London*

Wallis, he learned, in his last painting, how to express a vision that was entirely personal, of an extraordinary freshness and poetry, and characterized by a remarkable sweetness of colour. By contrasting transparent glazes with the most delicate of opaque tints, he contrived to make the darkest tones 'sing' with an effect of pure wonder: though most of his paintings are touched with naïvety, his drawings show the firm construction of which he was capable. His paintings of the Cornish and Breton coasts, with their ink-blue seas, their grey-green jetties and cliffs and cottages, their boats and their fishing nets remain among the most delectable of their time.

# Z

**ZOLA** Émile (1840–1902). French novelist and art critic; born and died in Paris. The powerful personality of Zola deserves to be mentioned in connection with the generous help he gave, at least at the beginning, to the great painters of his time, Manet and Cézanne in particular. His help was so wholehearted and unreserved that one can hardly understand how later he could have so brutally broken the bonds of friendship and esteem that had linked him with most of the Impressionists and denied them any genius. There was a misunderstanding in this, and the deeper reasons are perhaps to be sought elsewhere than in the personality and character of the individuals concerned. In 1857 Zola had known Cézanne at the Collège Bourbon, the future Lycée of Aix-en-Provence. The two schoolboys were of the same age and they took to each other at once. They composed verses and music. Cézanne played the cornet, Zola the clarinet in the college band. When, in 1861, Cézanne obtained leave from his father to go to Paris he hastened to join Zola in his lodgings in the rue des Feuillantines, where afterwards they both lived. At this time Cézanne worked on a portrait of Zola, which they both found bad and which was destroyed. However, relations between the two schoolmates soon became less intimate, although they remained cordial. As a matter of fact, Zola did not have much confidence in Cézanne's painting, particularly after he met Manet, who impressed him more and whose art seemed to correspond in every way to the ordered Naturalism he was dreaming of. At the Café Guerbois *(\*)*, which he had been frequenting since 1866, he made the acquaintance of *avant-garde* critics and the painters who would become the Impressionists. Villemessant, the editor of the newspaper *L'Évènement*, having asked him to write a series of articles on the Salon that had just opened, Zola launched, under the pseudonym of 'Claude', a virulent criticism of the selection committee that had rejected the works sent by his new friends, notably *The Fifer* of Manet. The tone of the articles was admirable; it resounded both as a challenge to conformity and a cry of triumph: 'I calmly admit that I am going to admire M. Manet', Zola wrote '. . . I come today to extend a sympathetic hand to the artists whom a group of his colleagues has thrown out of the Salon . . . and who was found unworthy of figuring among the fifteen hundred or two thousand impotents who were received with open arms . . . M. Manet's place is marked in the Louvre like that of M. Courbet . . . It is impossible – impossible, do you hear? – that M. Manet should not have his day of triumph and not crush the timid mediocrities who surround him.' Such words raised protests from a number of the paper's subscribers and the editor did not hesitate to sacrifice Zola, who did not admit that he was beaten as he published, in the following year, a biographical and critical study on Manet in the *Revue du XIXe Siècle* ('A New Manner in Painting: M. Edouard Manet'). Zola's enthusiasm eventually triumphed: at the Salon of 1868, despite the clamours of the public and the sarcasm of the Press, Manet's famous portrait of him was received. Continuing his campaign for the Impressionists, he wrote another series of articles in *L'Évènement Illustré*, the successor to Villemessant's *L'Évènement*. He called them 'Naturalists' or 'Actualists'. He praised Pissarro, 'one of the three or four painters of our day . . . never have pictures seemed to me of more masterful breadth'. He was of the opinion, speaking of Manet, that he would 'tame the crowd whenever he should choose to do so', and of Renoir, whom he called Henri, he unreservedly admired *Lise*, 'one of our women, rather one of our mistresses, painted with great truthfulness and a well-rewarded research in the modern idiom'. No doubt Zola was little interested in the Impressionist technique and aesthetic doctrine, but the growing authority of his name and the violence of his colourful style did much to create a favourable attitude toward the new school. Yet his personal opinions were by no means objective. In the same year he already permitted a concern, a doubt to appear about the future of the painting whose apostle he had made himself. He wrote: 'I look into the future and wonder what personality is going to emerge, large enough, human enough to understand our civilization and make it artistic by studying it with the masterly breadth of genius'. These reservations and doubts took on a more serious turn when, in 1880, in *Le Voltaire*, he reproached the Impressionists with neglecting the Salon that he had covered with opprobrium, to adopt the system of private exhibitions. This reproach seems to be a pretext, for with the same violence he had used to defend the Impressionists he now disowned and attacked them for their aesthetic intentions, which he seemed finally to have discovered. It was indeed the very dogmas of Impressionism that he reproved: 'What an amazement for the people,' he wrote, 'when they are put before some canvases painted out-of-doors, at certain times of day: they are agape before blue grass, purple earth, red trees, water bearing all the colours of the spectrum . . . The great misfortune is that not a single artist of this group has realized powerfully and definitely the new formula that all of them have scattered in their works . . . The formula . . . one finds nowhere applied by a master . . . They all are precursors. The man of genius has not been born.' After having previously written of Monet, 'Here is a man, here is a temperament', he now reproached him with having been 'fidgeting in a vacuum for ten years' and with being, like Renoir, nothing but a 'renegade'. This article appalled the artists, who retorted by a banquet of protest, at which Pissarro, Duret, Burty, George Moore, Mallarmé, Monet, and others were present. However, Zola once more showed his ill temper toward the painters by publishing in 1886 his novel *L'Œuvre*, in which he represented his former schoolfellow and friend Paul Cézanne as Claude Lantier, a restless painter and a failure.

One can easily discern the reasons behind Zola's behaviour. It was due only to his attachment to realism, which had made him like first Cézanne and then Manet, in so far as their tendencies were in line with his own. Fundamentally what he had liked in Monet, Renoir and Pissarro were the first works, quite evidently inspired by those of Courbet. The only personal basis for his partisan enthusiasm was defence of his Naturalist theories, a fact for which he cannot be completely reproached, since by remaining obstinately true to his temperament and his ideas, he was showing perfect intellectual honesty. Be this as it may, it cannot be forgotten that his action, in 1866 and 1868, was courageous and beneficial, and that it contributed powerfully to causing at least the name of Manet to be respected, and thus opened the way to the future.